In addition to a full bibliography the book is a fascinating commentary on the development of the literary and artistic appreciation of wild and mountainous scenery, tracing the journeys and the reactions of Lake District tourists, from the earliest travellers in search of the picturesque to the Victorian holiday-makers brought there by the railway.

Peter Bicknell's own fine collection of books, prints and maps relating to the Lake District is now in the library of King's College, Cambridge. The Chronological List embodies a detailed catalogue of these, arranged by date of original publication. Over a hundred title-pages are illustrated.

An essay by Peter Bicknell discusses books and prints in relation to the development of the appreciation of Nature and the 'discovery' of the Lakes as a source of 'Picturesque Beauty'.

The Picturesque Scenery of the Lake District 1752-1855

The Picturesque Scenery of the Lake District 1752-1855

A Bibliographical Study

PETER BICKNELL

St Paul's Bibliographies Winchester
Omnigraphics • Penobscot Building • Detroit
1990

First published in Great Britain in 1990
by St Paul's Bibliographies, 1 Step Terrace, Winchester, Hampshire
and in the United States by
Omnigraphics, Penobscot Building, Detroit

The publishers wish to express their appreciation to the Provost and Scholars of King's College, Cambridge, for their assistance with this publication.

British Library Cataloguing in Publication Data
Bicknell, Peter
The picturesque scenery of the Lake District, 1752-1855
1. Cumbria. Lake District. Guidebooks. Bibliographies.
I. Title
016.91427'8
ISBN 0-906795-60-5

Library of Congress Catalog No. 89-43508

∞ *Printed on long-life paper*
Typesetting by Land & Unwin, Bugbrooke, Northants
Printed in Great Britain by Henry Ling Ltd, The Dorset Press, Dorchester,
and bound at Green Street Bindery, Oxford

Contents

'Observations' was first published in
The Book Collector

Illustrations

Between pages 70 and 71

Acknowledgements

One of the greatest pleasures that I have derived from working on this bibliography has been the generous and enthusiastic help I have received from countless people whose friendship now enriches my life. Here I can only acknowledge a few of those to whom I owe a special debt of gratitude.

I could not possibly have compiled this book without the assistance and advice of the librarians and staff of the libraries in which I have worked, in particular that of J.R. Wilkinson of Carlisle, Ron Smith of Barrow-in-Furness, Christine Strickland of Kendal, and Sydney Chapman of the Armitt Library. Sidney Barnes, formerly librarian at Barrow, gave me a wonderful start by magnanimously putting at my disposal the manuscript of his unfinished bibliography of the history and topography of Cumberland and Westmorland. The Yale Center for British Art, by offering me a visiting fellowship, enabled me to make a detailed study of its splendid collection of illustrated books. Don Eddy, a former Munby Fellow at Cambridge and librarian of the Rare Books Library at Cornell University, which includes a remarkable collection of Lake District books, has given me constant encouragement and wise advice. His friendly, patient and expert help and that of his staff made a visit to his library a most rewarding and enjoyable experience.

The original inspiration for this work came from Tim Munby's successor as the librarian of King's College, Cambridge, Peter Croft, whose enthusiastic help gave me much encouragement. After his untimely death his successor, Peter Jones, became deeply involved and has given me unstinted support, as also has his colleague Michael Halls. The checklist which is the basis of the present work was prepared and circulated with the expert cooperation of Frank Collieson who acting as editor devoted endless time and energy to the project.

My association with Dove Cottage and the Wordsworth Library has been a particularly happy one. Terry McCormick first, Peter Laver whose help was tragically cut short, and then Jeff Cowton, have been towers of strength. Above all, Robert Woof has been a continuous source of inspiration, a provider of invaluable correction, and a spur to more conscientious research. But these are only four of all those at Grasmere who show an enthusiasm and sense of commitment which makes it a pleasure to work with them.

David Thomason has with great generosity fed me with the fruits of his unrivalled research. My notes owe much to information which he has given me; and if I have in any case misinterpreted it the blame is not his. Paul Joyner helped me greatly, checking information in the British Library and elsewhere. Diana Handley in answering questions about books in the Armitt Collection carried out much valuable research on my behalf. Nicolas Barker and David McKitterick have both helped in special ways, Fiona Wilson has performed miracles in getting the complicated manuscript through the word processor, and Nigel Luckhurst has dealt with the photography in an outstandingly efficient and friendly way.

To all these whom I have mentioned and to all the other countless lovers of books who have given me their unsparing help, I am deeply grateful.

Peter Bicknell

Introduction

This bibliography is an annotated chronological list of books about the scenery of the English Lake District, first published not later than 1855. It is limited to works which are devoted to scenery and not to other subjects such as agriculture, archaeology, history, dialect, folklore, geology, local industries and sport. Novels set in the Lake District, like directories which include descriptions of scenery, unpublished manuscripts and articles published only in periodicals, are not included; nor are the works of the Lake Poets, apart from a few items, such as Wordsworth's *Guide* and Southey's *Letters from England by Don Manuel Alvarez*, both of which describe scenery and can be regarded as topographical books. The Lake Poets have in any case been covered by many bibliographies and critical works.

Some prints and some maps which are related to the books are included in the list. It is difficult to differentiate between prints which were published as illustrations to books and those which were only published separately. Often, as is the case with 'Warwick' Smith's aquatint views (31) which were advertised as of a suitable size to bind with West's *Guide*, they were sold as loose prints which could be used as illustrations for a book. Alternatively, plates published in books were often sold separately. Only prints which were issued in wrappers, or as illustrations in books, or were frequently bound in sets after issue, are included in the list. The few maps included are those bound into the books, or those specifically intended for the use of tourists, like Smith's map advertised in West's *Guide*. Many of the maps included in the books – those of Otley, for instance – were also sold separately, frequently folded and cased for the pocket, and accompanied by useful tabulated information.

The first item in the list is a print, William Bellers' view of Derwentwater, published in 1752, the first to present the scenery as a prospect of beauty suitable for a picture – the quality which William Gilpin was to call 'picturesque beauty' and to define as 'that which would look well in a picture'. The first book in the list is John Dalton's *Descriptive Poem*, the earliest work in poetry or prose to describe the scenery in picturesque terms.

It has been suggested that I should have made George Smith my starting-point. He was a Cumbrian natural philosopher who has in recent years been the subject of intensive research. He made an expedition from Wigton to the black lead or 'wadd' mines at Seathwaite in Borrowdale in 1749. His 'An Account of a Journey to the Black Lead Mines and the Neighbouring Mountains', with a fascinating semi-pictorial map, was published in the *Gentleman's Magazine* (vol.xxi) of 1751. This account was referred to in the catalogue of the Derwentwater exhibition at Grasmere in 1986 as 'the first published description of the lake at Keswick, and also the scenery which confronts the traveller'. As such it pre-dates Dalton and Brown. However, it does not find a place in this bibliography (which in any case does not include articles in periodicals), for, although Smith refers to 'beautiful islands', which he compares with those described by Homer in *The Odyssey*, and associates the scenery with 'fables of antiquity', his descriptions are highly romantic but are not picturesque in the limited sense in which I have interpreted the term: that is to say, they do not describe the scene as though it were a picture. George Smith's relevance to this bibliography is that he probably played an important part in directing others to the 'picturesque' beauties of the Lakes.

The concluding date for the bibliography, 1855, is somewhat arbitrary. The early 1850s mark the end of an era. Wordsworth and Turner, two great romantics, died in 1850 and 1851. Harriet Martineau's *Complete Guide to the English Lakes*, first published in 1855, is chronologically the last item. It links the romantic and picturesque guides of the first half of the century with the more utilitarian guides of the second half – aimed not so much at gentlemen in search of the picturesque as at middle-class tourists of the railway age.

This book started life as a catalogue of the Lake District collection now in the library of King's College, Cambridge. When I was compiling it I realised that, as the gaps were not too many, by including the titles of works not in the collection it would be a comparatively simple matter to convert it into a complete bibliographical list. So it now appears as both a detailed catalogue of a collection and a checklist of works devoted to a particular subject. Those items which are in the collection are described in detail, including photographs of most of the title-pages of first editions and notes on each particular copy. Items which are not in the collection are described more briefly.

The 'Observations' which introduce this volume were originally written in 1983, and were published in the *Book Collector* in 1986 (vol.36, 1 & 2). They were written at a time when recent exhibitions at Cambridge, Kendal and Grasmere had stimulated an interest in the 'discovery' of the Lakes. Since then two more exhibitions, 'The Discovery of the Lake District' at the Victoria and Albert Museum in 1984, and 'Derwentwater, The Vale of Elysium' at Grasmere in 1986, each with an ample and scholarly catalogue (see 'Bibliographies and catalogues referred to in compiling the list', p.19), have brought to light much previously unpublished research. Both Robert Woof and David Thomason who were responsible for the Derwentwater exhibition have been making discoveries which have altered views expressed by me in the 'Observations'. However these Observations remain essentially as they were originally written, and should be treated as definitely dated 1983.

I will give two examples of these changes of view. Robert Woof, for instance, has suggested that 'Claude Glass' is the wrong name for the reflecting landscape glass so generally used by earlier travellers. I am satisfied that he is right and have added a note on the subject as Appendix 2 of this volume. David Thomason has established that John Brown's seminal *Description of the Lake at Keswick* which has for more than half a century been referred to as the letter to Lord Lyttelton was in fact written to someone else. It is to be hoped that the identity of the recipient of the letter will soon be revealed.

My deep involvement in the Lake District was originally engendered by a miraculous series of holidays at Lower Gatesgarth, the enchanting house which Professor A.C. Pigou built at the head of Buttermere. He was a mountaineering friend of my father, and generously put the house at my parents' disposal for family holidays. My addiction to book-collecting was stimulated by the friendship of that inspired lover of books, A.N.L. ('Tim') Munby. When some years ago I decided that it was time I found a permanent home for my Lake District collection, it occurred to me that there could be no better place for it than the library of King's. The 'Prof' and Tim had been Fellows of King's, and both were devoted to the College. So King's is now the home of the collection, transferred there as a gesture of thanks to these two Kingsmen. There my books will be well cared for and accessible to anyone who shares my enthusiasm for the Lakes.

Observations

Titles of books in the Chronological List are indicated by List numbers in brackets; books mentioned below but not included in the Chronological List are indicated by letters in brackets. Details of these books are given at the end of 'Observations'.

It was in the early 1750s that the first visitors came to the district of the lakes specifically to enjoy the scenery. The first in the field was the topographical artist, William Bellers, who was at Keswick in or before 1752, for on October 10th of that year he published a splendid print entitled 'A View of Derwent-Water towards Borrowdale. A Lake near Keswick'. The plate was etched and engraved by the French artists Chatelin and Ravenet, two of John Boydell's team of fashionable engravers, and the modish figures in the foreground were added, in the manner of Gravelot, by Louis-Philippe Boitard. Similar prints of Windermere, Haweswater, Ullswater and another view of Derwentwater, followed in 1753, and in 1754 a second view of Ullswater. The views are arranged in the manner of the idealised landscapes of the artists working in Italy in the seventeenth century – framing trees and classically grouped figures in the foreground, lakes and islands in the middle distance, and mountains closing the distant view.

Thomas Smith was at Keswick in the 1750s, but it was not until 1761 that his print of Derwentwater appeared, together with two others of Thirlmere and Windermere. The three were republished in 1767, with a fourth of Ennerdale, one of the remoter lakes. Although Smith's views are similar to those of Bellers, they are very different in mood. Arcadian tranquillity has been blown away by a strong gust of the sublime. Salvator Rosa and the Dutch painters are more in evidence than Claude Lorrain. The trees are dead; the rocks are jagged; the skies are storm-wracked. The foreground figures have a robust native look, very different from Boitard's elegant ladies and gentlemen from the court of Versailles. Smith, like Bellers, was associated with John Boydell's successful London publishing house, which had opened in about 1751 and which republished both sets of prints. In this way the beauties of the Lakes were first brought to sophisticated circles in the metropolis.

The artists were soon followed by the writers. The Revd Dr John Dalton of Queen's College, Oxford, and the Revd Dr John Brown of St John's College, Cambridge, both Cumbrians, were the first of a long line of dons and divines who were to record the Lakes. Dalton's poem and Brown's letter are the foundation stones of picturesque writing about the lakes.

After John Dalton had visited Keswick in 1753 he published *A Descriptive Poem addressed to Two Young Ladies at their return from viewing the mines near Whitehaven*, 1755 (2). The two young ladies were the Misses Lowther. After contrasting the satanic charms of the mines where much of the family fortune had been made, with the sylvan beauties of their native Lowther, Dalton suggests that

> If, grown familiar to the sight,
> Lowther itself should less delight,
> Then change the scene: To nature's pride,
> Sweet Keswick's vale, the muse will guide.

There follows a description of Keswick, Borrowdale and Skiddaw in the iambic couplets of Dyer and the landscape poets. Though much of it is made up of picturesque clichés, like 'down the rough rocks of dread Lowdore' and 'the beautious brook of Borrowdale', Dalton shows himself sensitive to the idea of agreeable horror:

> Horrors like these at first alarm,
> But soon with savage grandeur charm,
> And raise to noblest thoughts the mind:
> . . .

I view with wonder and delight,
A pleasing, tho' an awful sight:
. . .

Lines like these exploit the qualities to be defined as 'sublime' by Edmund Burke in *A philosophical enquiry* (a). And lines like

There the brown fells ascend the sky,
Below the green enclosures lye;
Along their sloping sides supine
The peaceful villages recline:
On azure roofs bright sunbeams play
And make the meanest dwellings gay.

show a lively appreciation of colour and the sparkle of sunshine on Honister-slate roofs. Notes to the poem were written by the distinguished physician and chemist Dr William Brownrigg, living near Keswick at Ormathwaite under Skiddaw.

John Brown was familiar with the Lake District from childhood. He spent the first seventeen years of his life in Wigton, within sight of the fells. From 1743 to 1756 he was vicar of Morland, near Penrith and Lowther, whence he made 'an annual voyage to Keswick, not only as an innocent amusement, but a religious act':

> I walk forth in this stupendous scene, as into the grandest earthly temple of the Creator; and as I make my progress thro' its several parts, often break forth with the divine Psalmist in that graceful exclamation "O Lord how manifold are thy works; in wisdom hast thou made them all." (Dr Brown's *Letter*, see 4, note)

After a visit to Lord Lyttelton at Hagley, probably in 1751, Brown made one of these 'annual voyages' and wrote a letter describing Keswick to 'a friend in London'. This was read with interest by the Lyttelton-Gray-Walpole group; and eventually part of it – omitting the poetic rhapsody, 'Now sunk the sun...' – appeared in the *London Chronicle* of 24-26 April 1766, four months after Brown's death. This prose section of the letter was published separately as a pamphlet, *A description of the lake at Keswick* (4.1), five times between 1767 and 1772. Then in 1780 it was included as an Addendum in the second edition of West's *Guide* (13.2), bringing it into general circulation. The poetic rhapsody, first included in Cumberland's *Odes* (11.1) (1776) was also included as a footnote in the 1780 edition of West; and was quoted by Wordsworth in his *Guide*, 'as the Writer was one of the first who led the way to a worthy admiration of this country'.

Brown saw and described the Lake of Keswick as Bellers and Smith had depicted it. Comparing it with Dovedale he writes:

> Were I to analyse the two places into their constituent principles, I should tell you, that the full perfection of KESWICK consists of three circumstances, *Beauty*, *Horror*, and *Immensity* united . . .
>
> But to give you a complete idea of these three perfections, as they are joined in KESWICK, would require the united powers of *Claude*, *Salvator*, and *Poussin*. The first should throw his delicate sunshine over the cultivated dales, the scattered cots, the groves, the lake and the wooded islands. The second should dash out the horror of the rugged cliffs, the steeps, the hanging woods, and foaming waterfalls; while the grand pencil of Poussin should crown the whole with the majesty of the impending mountains.

In his reference to Claude, Salvator and Poussin (in the eighteenth century, when an Englishman referred to 'Poussin' it was normally to Gaspard Dughet, known as 'Poussin', rather than to his now better known brother-in-law, Nicolas Poussin) Brown epitomises the relationship of the picturesque in England to the pictures of the seventeenth-century landscape painters – a relationship already celebrated by the landscape poets. Brown was no doubt familiar with Thomson's couplet in *The castle of indolence* (b): 'Whate'er *Lorrain* light, touched with softening Hue,/Or savage *Rosa* dashed or learned *Poussin* drew.'

Other artists – Vernet, Zucarelli, and the Dutch landscape painters for instance – were also influential; yet for a century after Thomson almost without exception it is to Claude, Salvator and Gaspard that writers, poets, tourists, diarists and novelists refer.

The prints of Bellers and Smith, Dalton's poem and Brown's letter, were manifestations of the vogue for the Picturesque. As David Watkin has succinctly put it, 'the Picturesque became the universal vision of the educated classes' (c). Touring in search of the Picturesque in England, Scotland and Wales became one of the central activities of the movement. The tourist, whether his record was made in picture, poetry or prose, was recording a journey made, in the words of Horace Walpole, 'through a succession of pictures' (d); and for the second half of the eighteenth century the Lake District became the Holy Grail for the picturesque traveller. In the last twenty-five years of the eighteenth century at least fifteen accounts of Lake District tours were published as books, quite apart from many circulated in manuscript and appearing in periodicals. West's *Guide to the Lakes* went through seven editions. Almost without exception these books conformed to the picturesque fashion; they described the lakes and the more accessible valleys rather than the mountains, and they freely plagiarised and quoted from each other; in particular they were influenced by Brown, Gray, West and Gilpin.

The poet Thomas Gray, probably inspired by Dalton and Brown, made his tour of the Lakes in 1769, keeping a journal which he sent to his friend Dr Wharton, who would have been with him had it not been for an attack of asthma. The journal was edited and published by Gray's friend William Mason in 1775 in *The Poems of Mr. Gray* (10) and was widely read when in 1780 it was included as an Addendum to the second edition of West's *Guide*. Gray, at the age of fifty-three, was already experienced in picturesque travel. With Horace Walpole he had visited the Grande Chartreuse in 1739, where he found the scenery 'pregnant with religion and poetry'. In Scotland, in 1765, he had found the mountains 'ecstatic'.

It is not surprising that, like his contemporaries, Gray saw and described the scenery of the Lakes pictorially; indeed he carried a landscape glass in order to reduce nature to a picture. According to Mason, this was a 'plano-convex mirror of about four inches diameter on a black foil, and bound up like a pocket-book'. At the head of Derwentwater 'the glass played its part divinely'; and at Crosthwaite Parsonage he records; 'a little before sun-set, I saw in my glass a picture that if I could transmit to you, and fix it in all the softness of its living colours, would fairly sell for a thousand pounds'. Although occasionally he dramatises his descriptions to the point of absurdity, his writing is distinguished, as Wordsworth said, for its 'distinctness and unaffected simplicity'. Like Wordsworth's *Guide* (95.3), which was to follow forty-two years later, Gray's journal stands out from the rest of the literature of the Lakes as the work of a poet. He shows us Ullswater, 'majestic in its calmness, clear and smooth as a blue mirror, with winding shores and low points of land covered with green inclosures, white farm houses looking out among the trees, and cattle feeding'; and 'Saddleback whose furrowed sides were gilt by the noon-day sun, whilst its brow appeared of a sad purple from the shadow of the clouds as they sailed slowly by it'; and the Derwent at Grange, 'clear as glass, and showing under its bridge every trout that passes'. Passages like the following foreshadow the sparkling prose of Dorothy Wordsworth: 'Oct. 3. A heavenly day; rose at seven, walked out under the conduct of my landlord to Borrowdale; the grass was covered with a hoare-frost, which soon melted and exhaled in a thin bluish smoke; crossed the meadows obliquely catching a diversity of views among the hills, over the lake and islands, and changing prospects at every ten paces.' Gray's discovery of Grasmere as 'one of the sweetest landscapes that art ever attempted to imitate' is strangely prophetic, for he described it as the Wordsworths were to find it: 'not a single red tile, no gentleman's flaring [Gray had written 'flaming' and Mason altered it] house, or garden walls, break in upon the repose of this little unsuspected paradise; but all is peace, rusticity, and happy poverty, in its neatest, most becoming attire.'

However, far from the 'unaffected simplicity' of most of Gray's writing, is his much quoted, much ridiculed, description of the Jaws of Borrowdale:

> . . . the crags named Lowdore-Banks begin now to impend terribly over the way, and more terribly when you hear that three years since an immense mass of rock tumbled at once from the brow, barred all access to the dale (for this is the only road) till they could work their way through it. Luckily no one was passing by at the time of this fall; but down the side of the mountain, and far into the lake, lie dispersed the huge fragments of this ruin, in all shapes and in all directions . . . . Soon after we came under Gowdar-Crag, a hill more formidable to the eye, and to the apprehension, than that of Lowdore; the rocks at top deep-cloven perpendicularly by the rains, hanging loose and nodding forwards, seem just starting from their base in shivers. The whole way down, and the road on both sides, is strewed with piles of fragments, strangely thrown across each other, and of a dreadful bulk; the place reminds me of those passes in the Alps, where the guides tell you to move with speed, and say nothing, lest the agitation of the

> air should loosen the snow above, and bring down a mass that would overwhelm a caravan. I took their counsel here, and hastened on in silence.
>
> "Non ragionam di lor, ma guarda, e passa."

It is an excursion into a world of fantasy, or at any rate the world of Dante and *The Inferno*. It is the same delight in an assumed air of danger and mystery that inspired him to say of the head of Borrowdale:

> . . . all further access is here barred to prying mortals, only there is a little path winding over the fells and for some weeks in the year passable to the dalesmen; but the mountains know well that these innocent people will not reveal the mysteries of their ancient kingdom, "the reign of *Chaos and Old Night*". (10)

He must have known perfectly well that the track over the Sty Head pass was a highroad for the dalesmen and their pack horses at all times of the year.

Gray's visit to the Lakes, like those of John Brown, was a pilgrimage to a particular shrine. Other notable travellers included the Lakes in extensive tours made primarily for reasons other than the enjoyment of the scenery. Pennant and Young included accounts of their passage through the Lake District in their published Tours, and in reacting to the beauties of nature they reflect the fashion of the time. Daniel Defoe, journalist and novelist, writing before 1727, found Westmorland, 'a country eminent only for being the wildest, most barren and frightful of any that I have passed over in England, or even in Wales itself' (e), but Pennant and Young nearly fifty years later felt an obligation to include fulsome descriptions of the scenery.

Thomas Pennant, a Flintshire squire of wide interests, botanist, zoologist, antiquarian, historian, correspondent of Gilbert White and West, friend of Linnaeus, and admirer of Richard Wilson, was described by Dr Johnson as 'a Whig, Sir, a sad dog. But . . . the best traveller I have ever read.' On his return from Scotland in 1769, a country 'as little known to its Southern Brethren as Kamschatca', Pennant travelled rapidly down the main road from Carlisle to Lancaster without actually visiting the Lakes. But in 1772, starting on a tour which was to take him to the Isle of Skye and Loch Assynt in remote Sutherland, he made a detour by Ambleside, Dunmail Raise, Keswick and Cockermouth. When he reached 'the Elysium of the north, the vale of Keswick', and the 'Boasted Lake of Derwentwater' where 'all the possible variety of alpine scenery is exhibited with all the horror of precipice, broken crag, or over-hanging rock' (8.1), he described the scene in a passage which was quoted again and again by his successors. As Pennant did not include draughtsmanship among his many talents, he was accompanied by his retainer, Moses Griffith, who supplied landscape drawings for plates in Pennant's books.

Although the tours of Arthur Young were undertaken as enquiries into the state of agriculture, and *A six months tour through the North of England* (1770) (5) is essentially an agricultural report, it is full of highly picturesque comment on scenery, which he described in terms of the pictures which he had recently seen in some country house. He was drawn to Keswick which had 'too long been an object of desire . . . to neglect the opportunity of seeing it', but he kept his priorities clear by adding, 'but before I attempt anything of a description, let me mention matters of husbandry'. Unlike Pennant, he was his own draughtsman, and the book contains three views of Lake District waterfalls engraved from his drawings.

William Hutchinson, in *An excursion to the Lakes in Westmoreland and Cumberland . . . in the years 1773 and 1774* (7), wrote with a verve and imagination rare in the Lake District prose of the period. An attorney from Barnard Castle, Hutchinson was, as West had originally been, primarily interested in topographical history and archaeology and wrote voluminous histories of the counties of Durham and Cumberland; but in the Lakes he was ready to make the very best of the picturesque and romantic possibilities of the landscape and to allow his ideas to wander 'in the fields of imagination'. He delighted in dramatic incidents, such as a sudden thunderstorm on Skiddaw, where

> the air was remarkably sharp and thin, compared with that in the valley; and respiration seemed to be performed with a kind of asthmatic oppression . . . dense and dark vapours began to arise . . .
>
> Our guide was very earnest with us to quit the mountain as he prognosticated the hazard of being wet, and of losing our way in the heavy vapour, from a storm then collecting, which he assured us would soon cover Skiddaw; the circumstance was too singular to be left by people curious in their observations on natural events; we desired

> our guide would take care of himself, and leave us to our pleasure, but the good attendant had a due sense of our impropriety in wishing to be there, and determined to abide by us. The clouds advanced with accelerated speed; a hollow blast sounded among the hills and dells which lay below, and seemed to fly from the approaching darkness; . . .
>
> We were rejoicing in this grand spectacle of nature, and thinking ourselves fortunate in having beheld so extraordinary an event, when to our astonishment and confusion, a violent burst of thunder, engendered in the vapour below, stunned our sense, being repeated from every rock, and down every dell, in horrid uproar; . . . the mountain seemed to tremble . . . Our guide lay upon the earth terrified and amazed, in his ejaculations, accusing us of presumption and impiety; danger made us solemn, we had no where to fly for safety, no place to cover our heads; to descend, was to rush into inflammable vapour from whence our perils proceeded, to stay was equally hazardous . . . (7)

Eventually they regained the inn at Keswick which they 'now esteemed a paradise'. Adam Walker and his party, on the summit of Skiddaw in 1791, probably having read Hutchinson, prayed for a storm of thunder and lightning; but their prayer was not answered and they had to be content with the discharge of a gun which one of them had happily brought with him. 'The reverberation from the different mountains continued twenty seconds, and was thunder in all its horrors!' (24)

The romantic and sublime effects of Echo were widely cultivated, at first by the established landowners, and soon as a tourist attraction. At Ullswater for instance, Hutchinson was 'accommodated with one of the Duke of Portland's barges . . . sent there by his Grace for pleasuring':

> The vessel was provided with six brass cannon, mounted on swivels; on discharging one of these pieces, the report was echoed from the opposite rocks, where by reverberation it seemed to roll from cliff to cliff, and return through every cave and valley; till the decreasing tumult gradually died away upon the ear . . . At intervals we were relieved from this entertainment, which consisted of a kind of wond'rous tumult and grandeur of confusion, by the music of two French horns, whose harmony was repeated from every recess which echo haunted on the borders of the lake; here the breathings of the organ were imitated, there the bassoon with clarinets; in this place from the harsher sounding cliffs, the cornet; in that from the wooded creek, amongst the caverns and the trilling water-falls, we heard the soft-toned lute accompanied with the languishing strains of enamoured nymphs; whilst in the copse and grove was still retained the music of the horns. All this vast theatre was possessed by innumerable aerial beings, who breathed celestial harmony. (6)

Again following in Hutchinson's footsteps, Adam Walker's party rowing on Derwentwater by moonlight, rested on their oars to listen to the strains of two French horns, playing by intervals on the shore, translated into a full concert by Echo. 'Is it a Choir of Angels ascending and descending? Is it a fairy-ground realized? or an Arabian Night's Entertainment? – Reason gives the reins to Imagination, and visions play before the fascinated senses.' The cult of Echo and of musical effects continued well into the nineteenth century (24). In his *Tourist's New Guide* (1819) (69) William Green sets out the qualifications for Mountain Guides who 'from their infancy ought to be taught the clarionet, the bassoon and perhaps the flute and even the horn, in order to gratify the refined in musical feeling, with elegant and pathetic solos, duets and trios.'

In his descriptions of the scenery itself, Hutchinson is completely pictorial. Like everyone else he quotes Dalton and Brown, and he also borrows from Brown in stating that 'The paintings of Poussin describe the nobleness of Uls-water; the works of Salvator Rosa express the romantic and rocky scenes of Keswick; and the tender and elegant touches of Claude Lorrain, and Smith, pencil forth the rich variety of Windermere.' There seems to be an element of chauvinism in equating Smith with Claude Lorrain. Of the view of Derwentwater which had first attracted Smith and Bellers, Hutchinson avers, 'Claude in his happiest hour never struck out a finer landskip; it . . . is perhaps the only view in England which can vie with the sublime scenes from which that painter formed his taste' (6). Hutchinson's reference to Smith is a rare example of one of these writers referring to a contemporary painter. Gray was familiar with Smith's view of Derwentwater from Crow Park, for on 4 October 1769 he recorded 'Smith judged right when he took his print of the lake from hence' (10).

Hutchinson's *History of the county of Cumberland* (28), published eighteen years after his *Excursion*, intersperses history, archaeology, genealogy and general topography with generous dollops of picturesque description of landscape. It is interesting to compare this interest in landscape with Nicolson and Burn's *History and antiquities of the counties of Westmorland and Cumberland* (1777) (12) where the only concession to the prevailing vogue was the inclusion in the section on Keswick of the universally quoted passages from Dalton and Brown. Like Clarke in his *Survey* (1787) (19), Hutchinson relies for descriptions of scenery almost entirely on quotations. In both the text and copious and lengthy footnotes he plunders a rich variety of sources. In describing Keswick alone he uses, *inter alia*, Dalton, Brown, Pennant, West, Gray, Mason, Cumberland, Young, Gilpin, Payne Knight, Thomson, Bede, Camden, Pliny, Ovid, Virgil and his own *Excursion*. Hutchinson's *History of the County of Cumberland*, which has recently been published in facsimile, constitutes far and away the largest collection of eighteenth-century Lake District writing – a splendid source book.

By the end of the 1770s a comprehensive guidebook for the tourists was clearly needed; in 1778 the need was met by Thomas West's *A Guide to the Lakes: dedicated to the lovers of landscape studies and to all who have visited, or intend to visit the Lakes in Cumberland, Westmorland and Lancashire* (13). Father West was a Jesuit priest who came to Titeup Hall, near Dalton in Furness, in the 1750s, as a member of the English Mission. He spent the rest of his life in the neighbourhood, dying at Sizergh, near Kendal, in 1779. His *Antiquities of Furness* (1774) (9), primarily concerned with historical and antiquarian topography, included 'Descriptive Accounts of High Furness, the Lakes of Coniston, Esthwaite and Windermere' which were devoid of description of the picturesque beauties of the landscape. However these beauties were the subject to which his *Guide*, published four years later, was devoted. It adopts the already conventional attitude that the scenery of the Lakes is to be treated by 'Lovers of Landscape Studies' as a series of pictures:

> The design . . . is to encourage the taste of visiting the lakes, by furnishing the traveller with a Guide; and for that purpose, the writer has here collected and laid before him all the select stations and points of view noticed by those authors who have made the tour of the lakes.

These stations are enumerated and described in the text (they were marked on Crosthwaite's maps (17), and were sometimes marked on the ground). West, the historian and antiquary, has become the apostle of the picturesque. The guided tour is planned so that,

> The change of scenes is from what is pleasing, to what is surprising; from the delicate touches of *Claude*, verified on *Coniston* lake, to the noble scenes of *Poussin*, exhibited on *Windermere-water*, and from these, to the stupendous romantic ideas of *Salvator Rosa*, realised in the lake of *Derwent*.

'To render the tour more agreeable', he recommends that 'the company should be provided with a telescope, for viewing the fronts and summits of inaccessible rocks, and the distant country, from the tops of the high mountains Skiddaw and Helvellyn.'

> The landscape mirror will also furnish much amusement on this tour. Where the objects are great and near, it removes them to a due distance, and shows them in the soft colours of nature, and in the most regular perspective the eye can perceive or science demonstrate. (13)

Two glasses of different convexity are recommended: 'the dark glass answers well in sunshine; but on cloudy or gloomy days the silver foil is better'. The dictum that 'the person using [the mirror] ought always to turn his back to the object that he views', in order to see it as a framed and tinted little picture in a looking-glass, beautifully epitomises the Picturesque.

West's *Guide* was immediately popular, and he began working on a revised edition. However he died before it was completed and the second edition, published in 1780, was edited, revised and greatly enlarged by William Cockin of Burton in Kendal, a friend of George Romney. Cockin added a series of Addenda, among which were Brown's *Description*, Dalton's *Descriptive Poem*, Gray's *Journal* and Cumberland's *Ode to the Sun*, all extolling Keswick and its lake, the established

Elysium of the North. In later editions Mrs Radcliffe's 'Description of the Scenery in a Ride over Skiddaw' was also added. The addenda made a handy anthology of pre-1780 Lake District literature. The revised *Guide* became a vade-mecum for Lake District visitors, and remained so for half a century.

In 1779, the year after the publication of West's *Guide*, William Wilberforce, a twenty-year-old undergraduate at St John's College, Cambridge, made a long-vacation tour of the Lakes. It was his third visit to the Lake District and his account shows that he had completely assimilated the conventions of the picturesque tour. He carried West's *Guide* with him, to which he made frequent reference. He was familiar with Gray, whose Journal he said was 'the best thing of the kind he ever read'. He sought out West's stations, and like Gray he employed the Glass, in which, near Lowdore, he caught the finest picture his eyes ever beheld. Gowdar-Crag, which had overawed Gray, Wilberforce found finer than Salvator could have depicted. Among the group of friends he joined at Keswick were a fellow Johnian, Wordsworth's uncle William Cookson, and the landscape artist and diarist Joseph Farington, who together were to produce the first book of views of the Lake District. With them Wilberforce went on Derwentwater where 'the echoes were vastly fine & repeated like Thunder after one had imagined them lost', and the reflections were so perfect that 'in the Glass (which answered delightfully) it was difficult to say which was the Shadow and which was the Reality' (164).

The guidebook for those in search of the picturesque was provided by West, the manual by Gilpin, the most dedicated picturesque traveller of them all. William Gilpin was born at Scaleby Castle, six miles north-east of Carlisle. His father, John Bernard Gilpin, was an amateur artist of some distinction who delighted in portraying scenes of mountain, lake, cataract and precipice, several of which were actual Lake District views. He had a 'regular painting room in Carlisle', and taught his sons William and Sawrey to draw. Dr John Brown, only nine years older than William, was a friend of the Gilpin family and for a time acted as William's tutor at Scaleby. When William returned to Oxford to complete his interrupted work for a degree it was John Brown who made it possible with a loan. From an early age William Gilpin was familiar with the Lake District and with the intellectual circle that was 'discovering' it.

From 1752 to 1777 Gilpin was headmaster of a school at Cheam in Surrey, which he ran on progressive principles.

> During the summer vacation, every year, at least after his circumstances became easy, Mr. G. used to take a journey into some part of England. His great amusement from his childhood was drawing; a love for which he inherited from his father and grandfather. And his pleasure on these journeys was to make remarks on the face of the country in a picturesque light; and to take sketches of such scenes as most pleased him. A number of these remarks, and sketches he brought home from each journey in well filled memorandum books.(f)

In 1772 Gilpin made a tour of the Lakes; and from memorandum books he compiled in manuscript 'A Tour through England; more particularly the Mountainous parts of Cumberland and Westmorland', bound in eight volumes, containing 208 drawings and 41 sketch maps and panoramas. He sent this to, among others, his friend William Mason, who was so delighted with it that he held up publication of his edition of Gray's works to add a long footnote to Gray's *Journal*, in which he said:

> . . . I have seen one piece of verbal description which completely satisfies me because it is throughout assisted by masterly delineation . . . This Gentleman [Gilpin], possessing the conjoined talent of a writer and designer, has employed them in his manuscript to every purpose of picturesque beauty in the description of which a correct eye, a practised pencil, and an eloquent pen could assist him. He has, consequently, produced a work Unique in its kind at once. (10)

This note excited the interest of people of influence in London who encouraged Gilpin to publish his tours. Among those who read the manuscript were the Duchess of Portland, Mrs Delaney, Lord Warwick, Horace Walpole, the Prince of Wales, Queen Charlotte and George III. Publication began in 1782 with the shorter Wye Tour, *Observations on the river Wye* (g). This was an immediate success, so Gilpin went ahead with the more ambitious work on the Lakes. He reduced the eight volumes of manuscript to two, and selected a number of drawings for plates. So in 1786, fourteen years after Gilpin had made the tour, his account originally written with 'no idea but of mere amusement', and enlivened with sketches which 'were little better than mere outlines' – appeared as the two octavo volumes of *Observations, relative chiefly to picturesque beauty, made in the year 1772, on several parts of England, particularly the mountains and lakes of Cumberland, and Westmoreland*, illustrated with sepia plates engraved in the new aquatint process (18).

The book is neither a guide for visitors nor a straightforward account of a tour, but a treatise of instruction on how the scenery should be viewed, according to the true principles of Picturesque Beauty. Of the thirty-two chapters only ten are actually devoted to the Lake District, seventeen to the journey to and from the Lakes, and six and a long introduction deal with general picturesque theory. The tour of the Lakes in fact only lasted five days. As Gilpin said in his introduction to the *River Wye*: 'The following little work proposes a new object of pursuit; that of not barely examining the face of the country; but of examining it by the rules of picturesque beauty.'

Gilpin returned from the Highlands of Scotland in 1776 by way of Cockermouth, Keswick and Ambleside, and two chapters of *Observations on the Highlands of Scotland* (1792) are devoted to the Lake District. Again he is concerned with theory rather than topography. In relation to Skiddaw, he discusses at length '*false shadows*; which are occasioned by small floating clouds intercepting the light, and throwing their light promiscuously . . . Scarce anything gives higher offence to the picturesque eye'. At Keswick, that 'inexhaustible fund of beauty', he was able to ride round the lake which he had never done before. But for all its beauties, he still had to suggest how it might be improved, 'it might be rendered *more accessible* – it might be *cleared of deformities* – it might be *planted* – and it might be *decorated*' (23).

Gilpin was the first to concern himself with the theory of the Picturesque; indeed, in *A dialogue upon the gardens . . . at Stowe* (1748) (h) he was probably the first to use and apply to landscape the word 'picturesque', which he defined in his *Essay upon prints* (1768) (i) as 'a term expressive of that peculiar kind of beauty which is agreeable in a picture'. Later he coined his own term, 'picturesque beauty' for those aspects of nature which were not covered by Burke's sublime and beautiful. Gilpin saw that what was beautiful in nature is not necessarily beautiful in a picture. In fact he stated that 'Painting is the *art of deceiving*'. He confessed that if nature got it wrong, he could not help putting her right. This he did in the illustrations in his books. These he constantly explained were in no sense topographical portraits. 'Indeed Mr. Farington's prints render any other *portraits* unnecessary. They are by far, in the author's opinion, the most beautiful views of that romantic country which he hath seen' (18). Gilpin's drawings are of two kinds: those that 'illustrate and explain picturesque ideas, which may often be explained better by a few strokes of the pencil, than by a volume of the most laboured description'; and those imaginary views which give a general idea of a country, and can be carried in the reader's imagination, while he reads the whole description. One of the plates is a diagram of 'the shapes and lines of mountains', which 'rising in regular, mathematical lines, or in whimsical grotesque shapes, are displeasing . . . All form disagreeable lines.' Only the easy line pleases.

In general, Gilpin's descriptions of the natural scene are reasonably restrained; but occasionally, as in his account of the ascent from Borrowdale to Watendlath, fantasy takes over:

> "Which way to Watendlath?" said one of our company to a peasant, as we left the vale of Borrowdale. "That way," said he, pointing up a lofty mountain, steeper than the tiling of a house.

and then,

> to see our companions below *clinging*, as it appeared, to the mountain's side; and the rising breasts and bellies of their horses, straining up a path so steep, that it seemed, as if the least false step would have carried them rolling many hundred yards to the bottom.

would seem fantastic to a modern tourist walking up the fell track behind Rosthwaite. On his way up Dunmail Raise from Grasmere, Gilpin evokes Salvator Rosa, in another flight of fancy:

> The whole view is entirely of the horrid kind. Not a tree appeared to add the least chearfulness to it. With regard to the adorning of such a scene with figures, nothing could suit it better than a group of banditti. Of all the scenes I ever saw, this was the most adapted to the perpetration of some dreadful deed. The imagination can hardly avoid conceiving a band of robbers lurking under the shelter of some projecting rock. (18)

This might well be from a novel by Mrs Radcliffe.

Gilpin did not neglect the romantic effects of Echo. On Ullswater instead of cannon he recommends the introduction of a few French-horns and clarionets, the music of which would transform the whole lake 'into a kind of magical scene; in which every promontory seems peopled by aerial beings, answering each other in celestial music'.

Although Gilpin's contribution to aesthetics was imprecise, contradictory and amateurish, it launched the battle of words in the last decade of the century when the Picturesque became a matter for detailed analysis and ponderous argument. The works of the two chief protagonists, Richard Payne Knight with *The landscape, a didactic poem*, (1794) (j) and *An analytical inquiry into the principles of taste* (1805) (k), and Uvedale Price, with *An Essay on the picturesque* (1794) (l), are only relevant to the Lakes in so far as they influenced the way people reacted to the natural scene. Neither Knight nor Price visited the Lakes or showed any particular interest in them. Knight, in *The Landscape*, makes an attack on the Elysium of the North:

> . . . Keswick's favour'd pool
> Is made the theme of every wondering fool;
> With bogs and barrenness here compass'd round,
> With square inclosures there, and fallow'd ground;
> No lofty trees, high over-arched, imbower;
> No winding creek or solitary bay,
> 'Midst pendant rocks or woods is seen to stray;
> But small prim islands, with blue fir-trees crown'd,
> Spread their cold shadows regularly round;
> Whilst over all vast crumbling mountains rise,
> Mean in their forms, though of gigantic size.

disparaging the features of the landscape which had been so generally eulogised. In his *Essay* Price established the Picturesque as a third aesthetic category to supplement the Sublime and the Beautiful, as defined by Edmund Burke thirty-eight years earlier. Price's Picturesque was essentially rough, asymmetrical, irregular and endowed with variation – more precise and very different from Gilpin's vague kind of beauty which is agreeable in a picture.

A refreshing counterblast to picturesque writing was provided by James Clarke, land-surveyor of Penrith, who fancied himself as a down-to-earth practical sort of man. In 1787 he published *A survey of the Lakes of Cumberland, Westmorland and Lancashire* (19). This was a handsome folio volume containing eleven large folding maps, varying in scale (some as large as six inches to the mile), covering the routes from Penrith to Ullswater and to Keswick, and from Keswick to Ambleside, together with the lakes of Ullswater, Derwentwater, Bassenthwaite, Thirlmere, Grasmere, Rydal and Windermere. 'The business' of these plans, Clarke explains in his introduction, 'is to conduct the stranger to those places which furnish the views and landscapes of different kinds in the neighbourhood of the Lakes, and which the taste of the times has been so pleased with.' The extensive text is to inform rather than to guide. It describes the history, customs, dialect, antiquities, the soil and the climate of the district, and the Border Wars, interspersed with abundant anecdotes, historical and contemporary. Clarke quotes, for instance, the curious and singular account of a journey made by a gentleman who went from Penrith to the summit of Helvellyn, in order to dine in a snow-drift on Midsummer-day. For descriptions of the views and landscapes Clarke relies almost entirely on quotations from his predecessors. While making extensive use of Brown, Gray, West and others, he misses no opportunity of disparaging them. For example, he precedes a long extract from West's *Guide* by saying, 'Mr. West speaks much of a station near this place for the artist; I shall give his words, for I do not admire it myself.' And on the shores of Derwentwater he says, 'When I visited this place, I had with me Dr. Brown's elegant description of it; and it would be only exposing my own weakness were I to attempt to describe it after him; I shall therefore give it in his own words.' The much-quoted passage from Brown's *Description of the Lake of Keswick* which follows ends: 'Let me now . . . conclude with one circumstance more, which is, that a walk by still moon-light . . . among these inchanting dales, opens a scene of such delicate beauty and solemnity, as exceeds all description.' Clarke adds: 'I am as pleased with an evening walk as well as Dr. Brown or Mr. Gray; yet I had rather be up at four o'clock in a calm morning, and walk about half way up Skiddaw, if there is a fog or mist in the valley; for when the mist lyes in the valleys very thick in a morning, the tops of the mountains are quite clear.'

Clarke constantly reprimands Gray and others for missing the beauties of places which are his own particular favourites. He also makes fun of Gray for his timidity, and fabricates incidents, such as the poet drawing down the blinds of his chaise to avoid seeing the horrors of Skiddaw, or blindfolding himself in case he should witness the repetition of a boat disaster which had occurred on Windermere in the previous century. But above all Clarke attacked the 'pompous phraseology' of the 'magnified bombastic' accounts of the country by the picturesque writers. In commenting on recent landscaping developments on Belle Isle his attack is directed at the picturesque school in general:

> The whole of this outcry against regularity seems to me to have arisen from the cant style of painting which Gilpin and some others have introduced into writing. Not a tree, a shrub, or an old wall, but these gentlemen take measure of the painter's scale: A poor harmless cow can hardly go to drink, but they find fault with a want of grace in her attitude; or an horse drive away the flies with his tail, but these critics immediately find fault with the too-great quickness of his motions. Whoever examines these 'abortive nothings', which Mr. Gilpin calls Landscapes, will hardly he able to trace one view, how well soever he may be acquainted with it; for my own part, they put me in mind of nothing so much as those landscapes and figures which boys fancy they see in the sky at sunset, or in the fire on a frosty evening. (19)

For all Clarke's desire to appear an iconoclast, he was sensitive to painting. 'Where painting goes, there generally goes poetry; their walks are the same; their beloved schemes are similar, and have always been so from the Grecian Tempe, to the green glens of Britain.' He had a painter's eye for the subtle effects of changing light and atmosphere, and there is a hint of poetry in such remarks as, 'clouds and vapours intersperse varieties of aerial scenery, which change as if it were by magic'.

Clarke was really only interested in the more accessible lakes and highroads, ignoring the fells, which are not even shown on the plans. All that indicates Helvellyn and its neighbours on the map of Thirlmere are the words 'From here a ridge of very high mountains to Ambleside'. For him the mountains and the remoter valleys were still the Wilderness. Of the route to Buttermere over Newlands, 'which some of the curious who visit the country wish to see', he observes, 'I do not admire this journey through roads where a carriage can hardly travel amidst deserts'. And the 'rocks and mountains about Buttermere', he says, 'are truly awful and romantic; but the same kind of views may be seen where roads are better, and the villages more inhabited.'

Another visitor, in 1792, at the height of the Lake District boom, who prided himself on avoiding picturesque description was Captain Joseph Budworth. The early tourists did very little walking; even the top of Skiddaw could be reached on a pony. But Budworth was the exception. In *A fortnight's ramble to the Lakes* he recounts how he walked 'upwards of two hundred and forty miles, besides boat and chaise conveyance'. It is the first recorded walking tour. Budworth clearly enjoyed fell-walking. He made ascents of Skiddaw and Coniston Old Man – possibly the first tourist to climb Helm Crag and the Langdale Pikes – and traversed Helvellyn over Rydal Fell and probably Fairfield: covering a distance of thirty miles in one morning. For the more adventurous expeditions he took a local guide, and he carried a spiked stick, such as the dalesmen used. But for all his energy and enthusiasm he had difficulty in steep places – not surprising, as he had lost an arm and no doubt his sense of balance, in the siege of Gibraltar. Coming down from the Langdale Pikes he recounts:

> and when we had got a good way down, we came to a part where we had to pass over a large bulging part of the mountain, across a sward nearly perpendicular, and of an immoderate height. . . and knowing that taking time to resolve when danger is near ever increases it, I tied up my right eye, which could not have borne the vast precipice almost perpendicular under me, I laid hold of one end of his [young guide, Paul's] pole, cautioned him as to his pace, and with my left eye on the sheep-walk, not more than three inches broad, my head almost close to the mountain, and thus piloted, we were in about eight minutes safe moored; and when I looked back I had reason to be thankful. (26)

Revisiting Scale Force in January 1798, hoping to find the fall 'bound up in icicles', he made many efforts to overcome the glassy hill. But after tumbling twice and sliding bodily down the hill again, he abandoned the attempt and 'determined to bear a great disappointment with due meekness'.

Budworth indulges in no picturesque descriptions of scenery. He dismisses the Vale of Keswick as 'rich, but too broad and extensive for landscape'. Though he does quote some of Dalton's poem when speaking of Lowdore, he has no words himself for the beauties of Derwentwater; he is more interested in the phenomenon of the floating island, the clarity of the water and the largest wild strawberries he ever ate. From mountain tops it is such matters as the number of lakes which can be seen that concerns him. He had no time for the insincerity of tourists like the gentleman on Windermere who was heard to say, 'Good God! how delightful! – how charming! – I could live here for ever! Row on, row on, row on: and then ordered his horses into his phaeton, and flew off to take an equally flying view of Derwentwater'. Budworth enjoyed his food and describes meals with great gusto. The dinner which he had at Robert Newton's in Grasmere before his ascent of Helm Crag has passed into Lake District history. It consisted of

Roast Pike, stuffed,
A boiled fowl,
Veal-cutlets and ham,
Beans and bacon,
Cabbage,
Pease and potatoes,
Anchovy sauce,
Parsley and butter,
Plain butter,
Butter and cheese,
Wheat bread and oat cake,
Three cups of preserved gooseberries, with a bowl of rich cream in the centre;

For two people at ten-pence a head.

No wonder Helm Crag 'looked formidable; and not the less so, to speak in plain English, from having a complete belly-full'. On Helvellyn on 2 August 1792 he was moved to verse, not by the beauties of the prospect but when parched with thirst by the discovery of a spring.

A SPRING! the clearest Heav'n e'er sent. . .
  I kissed the moisten'd ground.

Eager I drew the cooling stream,
And all fatigue was gone. . . a dream!
  Helvellyn's praise to sing;
Thy carpet was the liveliest green,
Thy sheep the swiftest I have seen,
  All owing to thy spring. (26)

After his second visit to the Lakes 'in the gloomy month of November' 1797, which he covered in the third edition (1810) of *A Ramble*, Budworth did write a long poem entitled *Windermere* (27) describing the physical appearance of the landscape, the flocks, the crops, the flora and the fauna, but as free of picturesque epithets as *A Ramble*. He was sympathetically interested in people and was fascinated by local characters. The uninhibited way in which he portrayed some of the people he encountered led him into trouble. A chapter which contained a scurrilous account of the 'Queen of Patterdale' had to be omitted from the third edition of the *Ramble*, 'as some respectable people were hurt at it'. Budworth also had to revise what he had said about the Beauty of Buttermere. When he stayed at the Fish Inn in 1792 he was enchanted by Mary Robinson, the landlord's fifteen-year-old daughter. He described this very Lavinia of his imagination as such an angel of beauty that when his book was published she rapidly became a tourist attraction. Budworth evidently had a conscience over the trouble he might have caused, for in January 1798 he returned to Buttermere in order to tell her, 'You are not so handsome as you promised to be; and I have long wished by conversation like this, to do away what mischief the flattering character I gave of you may expose you to.' His account of the 'Revisit to Buttermere' was published in the *Gentleman's Magazine* for January 1800, and was included as an Appendix in the third edition of *A Ramble*. But Budworth's warning did not prevent a sad sequel. In July 1802 Mary married a notorious impostor, who called himself the Hon. Alexander Hope, but was actually John Hatfield, a bigamist, who was hanged for forgery at Carlisle on 3 September 1803, before Budworth's Appendix had been published. This rather pathetic tragedy received immense publicity. It was retold in countless Lake District guides and journals, was the subject of several books such as *James Hatfield and the Beauty of Buttermere, a story of modern times*, with illustrations by Robert Cruikshank (1841) (m), and a novel entitled *Augustus and Mary* or *The Maid of Buttermere, a domestic tale*, by William Mudford (n); it was also recounted on broadsheets, and performed in London as a melodrama.

Budworth's *A Ramble* differs from other Lake District books of the period in its hearty delight in the physical pleasures of a walking holiday, its keen interest in people, who are not treated as figures in a picture, and its lack of any pretensions to fine writing. It is also significant that when Budworth returned to the Lakes at the end of 1797 he found that since his previous visit the larger lakes were becoming 'adorned by fine houses, and studied cottages. . . with their contaminating train of luxury and town servants'. The period of discovery was over. The centre of gravity was moving from Keswick's favoured pool to Windermere, Ambleside and Grasmere, which were beginning to be colonised by 'offcomers' from the south.

By the end of the century the tour to the Lakes had become a subject for satire. In the tradition of the literary dons, James Plumptre, a Fellow of Clare Hall, Cambridge, paid visits to the Lake District in 1796, 1797 and 1799, on which he kept detailed 'Memorandums'. Those for 1799 he expanded into a book of great interest. It remains unpublished, elegantly bound in three volumes of manuscript (in Cambridge University Library), entitled 'A narrative of a pedestrian journey. . . ' (o). Plumptre was a true pedestrian, for on this tour he covered a distance of 2,236 miles, of which 1,774¼ were on foot. He knew the distance to the nearest quarter of a mile as among the travelling impedimenta which he called his 'Knick-Knacks' he carried a pedometer, along with drawing and memorandum books, a compass, a magnifier for botany, a telescope, a barometer, a Gray's Glass and a Claude Glass, and two volumes of Cowper's poems. He was a keen botanist, and an ardent amateur of the theatre and opera, advocating the claims of the stage as a moral educator. After his second visit he wrote *The Lakers: a comic opera in three acts*. The author fixed the scene of his drama at Keswick:

Where Cumbria's mountains in the north arise,
Where cloud-capp'd SKIDDAW seeks the azure skies
Nature hath shower'd from forth her lavish hand
Her choicest beauties o'er the favoured land.

Thither, attracted from their peaceful home,
The Poet and the Painter love to roam.

There CUMBERLAND enrich'd his moral muse
And FARINGTON produced his matchless Views.
There, too, the botanist, with prying eyes,
Culls the fair flowers in all their thousand dyes;

Each season there delighted myriads throng
To pass their time these charming scenes among;

And these same visitors, e'en one and all,
The Natives by the name of LAKERS call. (37)

The wording of the Dedication: 'To Tourists in General, but more particularly to those who have taken, or intend to take, the Tour of the Lakes', follows the title of West's *Guide*; and the familiar lines from the Dalton which include 'sweet Keswick's Vale' and 'the beautious brook of Borrowdale' appear on the title-page. In the Preface Plumptre gives a Key for anyone who is neither acquainted with *the Lakes*, nor *a picturesque Traveller*, nor *a Botanist*, recommending him to peruse: West's *Guide to the Lakes*; Mrs Radcliffe's *Observations during a Tour to the Lakes; The Botanic Garden: a Poem in Two Parts*; Some of the Tours and Novels of the present day, &c.&c. . . . For these are the principal objects of his ridicule.

The third scene of the opera is set in Crow Park, which as Sir Charles Portinscale points out to Miss Beccabunga Veronica, is West's second station. In a later scene when Sir Charles informs the party that this is 'the delightful village of Grange, celebrated for its hospitality to Mr Gray; and this the gorge of Borrowdale, whose terrible appearance intimidated him from exploring farther these finest of scenes', Miss Veronica exclaims, 'don't speak, lest the agitation of the air should loosen the rocks above, and bring down a mass that would overwhelm us'. She is the character most deeply committed to the affectations of the Picturesque. She is a writer of Gothic romances, in which she is careful always 'to introduce a great deal of scenery' which, like Mrs Radcliffe, she has never actually seen. However she is planning to lay the scene of her next romance, 'The Horrors of the Hermitage', upon Derwentwater. She invariably carries a sketch-book, and shows herself a devoted follower of Gilpin when she declares, 'If it is not like what it *is*, it is what it *ought* to be. I have only made it picturesque.' She is a dedicated botanist and makes great play with Latin names. When a flute is heard at a distance she cries, 'what a picturesque sound!', and breaks into her own little *ariette*. She is equipped with a variety of glasses. 'Give me my glasses. Where's my Gray? Oh! Claude and Poussin are nothing. By the bye, where's my Claude-Lorrain? I must throw a Gilpin tint over these magic scenes of beauty. How gorgeously glowing! Now for the darker. How gloomily glaring! Now the blue. How frigidly frozen!' Finally when she has nearly run her prospective husband to earth, she quizzes him in her glass, saying, 'I'll throw a Gilpin tint over him. Yes, he's gorgeously glowing. I must not view him with the other lights, for a husband should not be either glaringly gloomy or frigidly frozen.'

It is not surprising that there has never been a public performance of Plumptre's opera, which is in fact only the script for a comedy with occasional airs and duets (like *The Beggar's Opera*), for which no music had been written. But it has certainly fulfilled the hope of Sir Charles Portinscale whose last words were 'I trust that the adventure of the LAKERS at Keswick will afford an innocent amusement to those who become acquainted with them.' Plumptre evidently felt that he owed Gilpin an explanation for having made fun of his theories, for two years later he wrote to him to apologise for having written 'in somewhat an unhandsome manner against' his principles of the picturesque. He explained that 'the object was to ridicule . . . not the picturesque but only the affectation of it'. He also raised the vexed question of the liberties which Gilpin took with nature in his views. Gilpin in a courteous reply vigorously defended himself, suggesting that dramatists took still greater liberties with nature than did artists.

As a satire *The Lakers* was somewhat esoteric; since it could only be appreciated by those familiar with the affectations of the Picturesque. Doctor Syntax had a much more universal appeal. Rowlandson's burlesque coloured plates and Combe's boisterous stanzas had an immediate attraction and were immensely popular. *The tour of Doctor Syntax in search of the Picturesque*, published as a book in 1812, had begun to appear in the *Poetical Magazine* in 1809; it was a direct satire of the tours of the late Doctor Gilpin and his theories. The alternative title is 'Doctor Syntax's Tour of the Lakes', and the climax of the tour is when Syntax 'the town of Keswick reached at last'. Here Rowlandson depicts him sketching the lake, seated on his picturesque pony, unaware of impending events:

> . . . Grizzle, in her haste to pass,
> Lur'd by a tempting tuft of grass,
> A luckless step now chanc'd to take,
> And sous'd the Doctor in the lake.

On another occasion the Doctor clearly enunciates one of Gilpin's principles when he declares,

> He ne'er will, as an artist shine,
> Who copies nature line by line;
> Who'er from nature takes a view,
> Must copy and improve it too;
> To heighten every work of art,
> Fancy should take an active part. (76)

Little reference was made in eighteenth-century tours to maps. West's *Guide* did not include one until the third edition in 1784, and then it was only small in scale (¼ inch = 1 mile) and little more than a diagram, only covering the limited areas described in the *Guide*. It only recorded main roads, lakes and the principal towns and villages. Helvellyn, Skiddaw, and one or two other hills are indicated: but the areas between the roads, 'as directed in the Guide', are practically blank. The whole of upper Dunnerdale, Eskdale, Wastwater and Ennerdale are free of any detail; in this area no roads are shown, even Scawfell and Stye Head are not indicated. The map was only a key to the routes covered by the *Guide*. If a tourist strayed from the beaten track, he had to rely on being accompanied by a guide in human form.

In 1779 Wilberforce did carry a map of some sort, which occasionally led him badly astray. For his more adventurous expeditions he relied on the services of a local guide. The earliest pocket map for tourists was Smith's *New and accurate map of the Lakes* (1800) (42). This came mounted on linen and folded in a neat slip-case, but it gave the tourist little more information than the one in West's *Guide*. The Ordnance Survey for the Lake Counties was not published until the 1860s, Cumberland being the last county in England to be completed. Before 1800 there were a few attractive maps, intended for tourists, with decorative landscape vignettes, Jeffrey's *Westmorland* (1770), and Martin's *A New and Exact Map of the Beautiful Vale of Keswick in Cumberland* (1784), for instance, which did recognise the picturesque appreciation of landscape. Crosthwaite's maps, or Plans of the Lakes as he described them, are unique.

Peter Crosthwaite was the son of a farmer of Dale Head in the parish of Crosthwaite near Keswick. At the age of 43, after several years at sea in the Far East and twelve as an excise officer, he returned to Keswick in 1779. There he threw all his energies into exploiting the tourists. His activities are summarised by the inscription on 'An Accurate Map of the matchless Lake of Derwent', on which he describes himself as 'Admiral at Keswick Regatta, who keeps the Museum at Keswick, & is Pilot, Geographer, & Hydrographer to the Nobility and Gentry who make the Tour of the Lakes'. His maps show, with reasonable accuracy, the outlines of the lakes, nautical details such as depths and directions of currents, West's stations supplemented by some of his own, properties and their owners. They are decorated with little vignettes of notable sights like gentlemen's residences, Pocklington's conceits, the Bowder Stone, and so on. The maps were revised five times between 1783 and 1819, which makes them an interesting record of changes in the owners of property. Pocklington's Island got a map of its own, drawn by Joseph Pocklington himself. He had purchased Vicar's Island on Derwentwater in 1778, where he built a house and a series of eccentricities which came in for general ridicule from both residents and visitors. These included a church, built as Budworth laconically says 'as an object'; a fort and a battery, fitted with cannon for echoes; a boat-house looking like a Primitive Methodist chapel; and, most endearing of all, a Druid Circle fifty-six feet in diameter, which Pocklington honestly but misleadingly described as 'supposed to be the most compleat and last built temple in Europe'. These were not Pocklington's only follies. He built and adorned two other houses in the Vale of Keswick, and at the Bowder Stone, according to 'Don Espriella', he 'erected an ugly house for an old woman to live in who is to show the rock . . . [and he] dug a hole underneath through which the curious may gratify themselves by shaking hands with the old woman'.(62)

Crosthwaite and Pocklington co-operated in organising the Keswick Regatta, the central event of which was an elaborate naval battle, The Storming of Pocklington's Island. The only easily accessible published account of the Regatta is in the *Cumberland Pacquet* (a weekly paper published in Whitehaven), (1782), which was reprinted in many of the Lake District books. However, in the King's College Collection there is a copy of the 1780 edition of West's *Guide* which was lavishly annotated by an unidentified tourist in 1782. In a long marginal note he records that on '15th August 1782, I viewed the Lake of Keswick & hired Admiral Crosthwaite to accompany Me, who gave me the following Acct, of the Expedition agt. Pocklington's Island performed in Augt. 1781'. There follows the detailed battle order for the whole engagement, made up of instructions such as 'the Gallies will return the fire keeping it up pretty constant . . . and taking special Care of their Powder (that no Person be injured by blowing up)'. Half-way through the battle there was a break:

> By this time the Tars will be pestered with Hunger and Thirst. The Governor, sensible of this lays an Ambuscade of Roast Beef and Brown Ale in the Block house. A Tar will put off his jacket and spread itagainst the S.W. Wall of the Block house as a Signal to the Governor that Bellies are full and all hands well again. On this the Governor will bear to Arms and make a heavy fire upon the Tars with great Guns and Small Arms.

To complete the operation 'the Garrison will down Dutch Colours and up English at the Battery and Block house with 3 chears, carry off the wounded and finally make a General Salute for Victory'. Quite recently (1983) David Thomason has unearthed in the British Library a splendid coloured etching of a drawing by Robert Smirke which shows in detail the storming of Pocklington's Island. It depicts the affray as set out in 'Admiral' Crosthwaite's description – even to the ambuscade of roast beef and brown ale (the marginal note is quoted in full in Appendix 1).

Crosthwaite's principal enterprise was his museum in Keswick, which was visited by all the tourists, and described by most of those who wrote about their visits to Keswick. It housed a remarkable collection of miscellaneous objects. In 1792 a handbill advertised 'Natural and Artificial Curiosities, from every Quarter of the World; the *Fossils*, Spontaneous *Plants*, and *Antiquities Of Cumberland; Coins, Medals, Arms, Quadrupeds, Birds, Insects, Shells, Landscapes, Pictures, Grottos*, and his much admired *Organ*. And among the items for sale were 'Mr. *Farington's* Twenty

Landscapes of the Lakes; . . . *West's* and *Shaw's* GUIDES; *Gray's* Landscape Glasses; Claude Lorrain's Do. Pocket Compasses, Music, Spar, &c.' Crosthwaite was passionately jealous of competititon, making acrimonious attacks on Clarke for his maps of the Lakes, and on Thomas Hutton who had opened a rival museum in Keswick in 1782. Crosthwaite's museum survived until 1870, and the musical stones and several other exhibits are still to be seen in the Fitz Park Museum, Keswick. The popularity of the museum shows that visitors, apparently dedicated to the picturesque, were happy to devote time to curiosities, just as they were fascinated by natural phenomena, such as the Bottom Wind and the Floating Island, and continued to be interested in mining and quarrying activities like the famous graphite or wad mines which had drawn visitors to Borrowdale before picturesque scenery had been 'discovered'.

The popularity of a tour of the Lakes soon created a demand for prints and for illustrations for books. Bellers and Smith had led the way, and indeed had drawn tourists to the Lakes. We have already seen that Gray was familiar with Smith's view of Derwentwater from Crow Park, but the earliest published accounts of tours were only sparsely illustrated with plates of landscape. Hutchinson in 1774 included no views of Lake District scenery in nineteen plates of archaeological interest. Pennant, accompanied by his draughtsman, Moses Griffith, could only spare one for the Lakes. And in the first edition of West's *Guide* in 1778 there were no plates at all.

The first publication which can be looked upon as a book of Lake District pictures, the first of the drawing-room-table books, was *Views of the lakes* (1789)(22) by Joseph Farington. This was an oblong folio volume of twenty engravings, with a page of descriptive letterpress, in French and English, opposite each plate, almost certainly written by Farington's friend and companion William Cookson of Penrith, who was Wordsworth's maternal uncle. Farington's views, as was pointed out by William Gilpin, are accurate topographical portraits, and make few concessions to picturesque arrangement. They were advertised in the year of their publication in West's *Guide*. According to Upcott, in his *English Topography* (1818) they were occasionally bound with Clarke's *Survey*. At the Yale Center for British Art there is an album of Lake District drawings by Farington which were intended to be used as illustrations for Gray's 'Journal'. What a splendid book this would make! Another artist who was active in recording the Lakes with illustrations in mind was a Cumbrian, John 'Warwick' Smith. His twenty *Views of the Lakes*(32), published in parts, 1791, 1792, 1795, are large engravings, comparable with Farington's. They were not accompanied by any letterpress.

These sets of prints from the drawings of Farington and Smith were made from copper plates etched and engraved in the traditional way, but *Sixteen views of the Lakes* from drawings by John Smith and John Emes, 1794, 1795 (31), are aquatints. They were advertised as 'of a proper size to bind with' West's *Guide*. Copies incorporating these plates are frequently found, and there is evidence that the book was sometimes sold bound with the extra illustrations.

The process of aquatint engraving was used for the first time in English book production by Paul Sandby in his *Views in . . . South Wales* (1775) (p). William Gilpin was anxious to get from Sandby the secrets of the new process, recently introduced from France. Sandby was not co-operative; but with the help of 'Warwick' Smith Gilpin was able to use it for the plates in his *Observations relative chiefly to . . . the mountains, and lakes . . .* (1786) (18.1), the first Lake District book to be illustrated with aquatints. In the 1790s aquatints were being generally used for picture books. Peter Holland's *Select views* (1792) (25) exploit crude engravings by C. Rosenberg in a somewhat distorted and fantastic view of nature. It includes, however, a delightful plate showing the title of the book engraved on the Bowder Stone. John Rathbone's *Select views* (1794, 1795) (30) beautifully aquatinted by John Hassel contrast strikingly with Holland's; they are prints of considerable elegance.

One most unusual book of this decade is James Bourne's *Interesting views of the lakes* (36). This is a splendid folio volume, consisting of a fine engraved title-page with an aquatint vignette, a printed page of dedication, 67 pages describing a tour, printed and offered for sale in London, with twelve original watercolours as illustrations. Only four copies of this book are known to exist, each illustrated with watercolours, though only two have the full complement of twelve. The views in different copies appear to be by different hands, but it is not established which, if any, are by Bourne himself. No copy of the book with engraved illustrations exists. It is a mystery why so few copies of a book so lavishly produced and offered for sale should have been issued and why it was only illustrated with original drawings.

The period from about 1810 to 1830 was the golden age of the coloured aquatint. The process of etched line, followed by aquatint tones and transparent coloured washes, resembles the watercolour artist's traditional technique of line, monochrome wash and colour. In this way watercolour drawings were faithfully reproduced. The process, though requiring considerable virtuosity from the engraver, was less time-consuming than copper-plate engraving. It appealed, therefore, to publishers as a method which produced coloured plates of great beauty at less cost than the previously popular engraving. French emigrés and children provided cheap labour for colouring the plates.

Three Lake District colour-plate books illustrated with aquatints are outstanding. William Westall, an artist who portrayed the scenery of the Lakes with loving fidelity, was a highly skilled engraver. The twelve aquatints which he used for *Views of the Lake and of the Vale of Keswick* (1820) (92), are of the highest quality, particularly two which were commented on by Sara Hutchinson in a letter to John Monkhouse (15 October 1820). Of 'Keswick Lake from Barrow Common', which shows a storm gathering dramatically at the head of the lake, she says, 'Westall tells me [it] has gained him great credit amon[g] the Artists for its execution'; and of 'Keswick Lake from the east side' which she describes as a 'Twilight scene', she says she 'could not have believed that an Engraving could have given the quiet and solemn feeling inspired by such a scene'. She also says that Southey furnished Westall with the letterpress for the book 'gratis'. Westall was a close friend of the Southeys, and provided a series of six engravings of views near Keswick for *Colloquies* (107). He was also on good terms with the Wordsworths and prepared a series of engravings, including views of Rydal Mount, for an illustrated edition of Wordsworth's works which was never published. However several of the prints were published as separate volumes. The other two of these attractive books were produced by T.H.A. Fielding who like Westall did his own engraving. *A picturesque tour of the English Lakes* (1821) (100) was published by Ackermann, the impresario of aquatint publications, with forty-eight coloured plates by Fielding, thirty-five from drawings by himself, twelve by J. Walton and one by William Westall. *Cumberland, Westmoreland and Lancashire illustrated* (1822) (101) is a collection of views, all drawn and engraved by Fielding. Each plate is accompanied by a page of description. The author of neither of these two books is known, though it is probably Fielding himself.

In about 1830 engraving on steel instead of copper became general. The almost indestructible nature of steel plates meant that unlike copper plates they could be used over and over again, a quality which made steel engravings an attractive proposition for publishers of illustrated books. Engravings on steel became a popular form of illustration for topographical picture books, such as Thomas Rose's *Westmorland, Cumberland, Durham and Northumberland, illustrated* (1832), (112). This came out in 26 parts, as a section of *Fisher's Picturesque Illustrations of Great Britain and Ireland*. It consisted of 213 views (more than half are of the Lake District) engraved on steel from the works of the topographical artists Allom, Pickering and Gastineau, by no less than twenty-six highly skilled engravers. These artists showed a remarkable facility for producing delightful picturesque compositions which were reasonably accurate records of the scenes. The engravers showed considerable virtuosity in handling the delicate line possible on a steel plate to achieve splendid tonal effects. The supply of prints from these plates seems to have been almost inexhaustible. They were reissued in three annuals, entitled *Gage d'Amitiée;* The Lake District views were grouped in two volumes as *The British Switzerland* or *Picturesque Rambles in the English Lake District*. The plates were passed from publisher to publisher, and until late in the century prints were sold in separate little albums, used as illustrations in various books and as letter-headings. Pictorial notepaper was in use in the Wordsworth circle before William's death. Steel engraving was economical and suitable for comparatively small plates for books, but not for large ones, as the amount of labour involved in engraving was excessive. These steel engravings are still in abundant supply, incorrectly coloured and framed, or mounted on table mats.

It had been a 'coffee-table book', with large plates, that first introduced Wordsworth's *Guide* to the public when it was included as an anonymous introduction to the Revd Joseph Wilkinson's *Select Views in Cumberland, Westmoreland, and Lancashire* (1810) (73). Wilkinson was born in Carlisle, and at Ormathwaite under Skiddaw was a neighbour of the Coleridges until he moved to a living in Norfolk in 1804. His book consisted of 48 soft-ground etchings of his own somewhat amateurish pencil drawings, by the reputable artist and engraver W.T. Wells. Embarrassed by the quality of Wilkinson's work, Wordsworth only agreed to contribute provided his name did not appear in the book. The gradual development of Wordsworth's *Guide* and its complicated bibliography have been discussed in some detail by Ernest de Selincourt in the introduction to his scholarly edition of the *Guide*, and analysed with meticulous care by W.J.B. Owen and J.W. Smyser in *The prose works of William Wordsworth* (1974) (q). Wordsworth himself was responsible for five editions, and before his death three more were edited and published by John Hudson of Kendal. So for the last forty years of Wordsworth's life the work which became *A guide through the District of the Lakes* was never far from his mind. When it was annexed to *The River Duddon . . . Sonnets* in 1820, he explained in a prefatory note that it was written 'in the same spirit which dictated several of the poems, and from a belief that it will tend naturally to illustrate them'. In 1822 it was published separately as a pocket guide with a map, as *A description of the scenery of the Lakes* (95.3). In its fifth and final form in 1835 it was actually called a 'Guide', but only twenty of its 137 pages were devoted to 'Directions and information for the tourist'. The publisher, with the permission of the author, added a Tabulated Itinerary. The rest of the book, apart from an edited version of Dorothy Wordsworth's account of 'Excursions to the Top of Scawfell and on the Banks of Ullswater', consists of general description of, and comment on, the scenery of the Lakes. Wordsworth's book differed from other writing on the Lake District in two fundamental ways. It was written by a resident with intimate knowledge of the country and the people that he wrote about (according to Thomas de Quincey Wordsworth must have walked 'a distance of 175,000 to 180,000 English miles'(r)); and it introduced to the reader the completely new view of nature which inspired his poetry. After 1835 the Guide was taken over by John Hudson and incorporated, with Wordsworth's co-operation, in *A complete guide to the Lakes* (122), which with its interest in botany and geology and a wealth of practical information for the tourist, had moved a long way from the guide books which preceded Wordsworth's original contribution to Wilkinson's *Select Views*.

Jonathan Otley clearly summed up the situation in 1823 when he said in his introduction to *A concise description of the English Lakes* (102), 'before this little manual made its appearance, the public had been supplied with Guides to the Lakes in various forms; but wholly devoted to the picturesque appearance of the country, to the exclusion of other important considerations'. His own guide is purely factual, with clearly arranged information for tourists and little picturesque description. In later editions he included notes on mineralogy, geology, meteorology, the floating island on Derwentwater and the black lead-mines, as well as 'sketches of the outline of the most remarkable ranges of the mountains' – topics which were to become normal features of later Guides. Jonathan Otley, the son of a dalesman who made wooden sieves and baskets, was born at Scroggs by Loughrigg Tarn, near Grasmere, and settled at Keswick about 1797, where he combined the callings of watchmaker, surveyor and guide. He showed a remarkable interest in what might now be called 'popular science', and in guiding Dalton of the Atomic Theory and the geologist, Professor Adam Sedgwick, he proved himself an informed companion.

From the time of Otley's *Description* in 1823 there was a steady flow of Guides and Companions to meet the demand from tourists for the detailed information they needed to plan and enjoy their tours. These little books showed a developing interest in the topographical details of mountains, large-scale maps of limited areas, tabulated information about routes, expeditions, means of transport and accommodation – and towards the end of the period information about trains and steamers. The influence of Wordsworth and quotations from his poetry began to appear in the 1830s. *Black's guide to the Lakes* (1841) (123), one of the Edinburgh publisher's successful series of 'Picturesque Guides', boasts of 'numerous quotations from the works of the Lake Poets'. By the end of the century *Black's Guide* was in its 22nd edition.

Very different from the small pocket guides was William Green's *The Tourist's New Guide* (1819) (69a), 'being the result of observations made during a residence of eighteen years in Ambleside and Keswick'. This was a two-volume book, written round sixty prints which were published separately, and illustrated with either twenty-four or twelve aquatints, and occasionally also twelve etchings – clearly intended for the library rather than the pocket. It was described by Wordsworth as 'a complete Magazine of minute and accurate information'. It covered the whole of the Lakes more completely than any previous work.

Five years after Wordsworth's death, when Hudson's *Complete Guide* was in its fourth edition, Harriet Martineau's *Complete guide to the English Lakes* (1855) (155) was published. It is a strange mixture of sound advice and prejudice. Miss Martineau had come to live at Ambleside in 1844, and devoted herself energetically to collecting the information for her book. She accepted that the Lakes had finally become a 'playground' where secure middle-class visitors, brought by the railway, could enjoy holidays in lodgings and hotels. It was no longer a remote Elysium where travellers in search of the picturesque, moving from inn to inn, could enjoy the adventure of discovery. She acknowledged the status of the resident gentry by including a Directory of their names and addresses, but she was anxious to improve the social and physical conditions of those less fortunate, rather than to romanticise them as figures in a landscape.

In 1853 the most splendid of all Lake District drawing-room-table books was published in Manchester. In about 1848 Thomas Agnew of Manchester commissioned James Baker Pyne to paint a series of pictures of the Lake District, twenty-five of which were issued by Agnew in *The English Lake District* (154a), accompanied by descriptive notes by the poet Charles Swain. It is certainly the biggest Lake District book (28 x 21 in.), and the plates are examples of the acme of the art of coloured lithography. They show the unsuspected paradise taken over by the tourists; the new steam locomotives puff in and out of Windermere station, family parties picnic on the fells and enjoy the delights of the regatta.

The photographic camera had arrived; in 1849 John Ruskin had taken the first 'sun picture' of the Matterhorn; and in 1864 *Our English Lakes, Mountains and Waterfalls, as seen by William Wordsworth* (s) was illustrated with actual photographs – events which completely altered the nature of Lake District illustrated books.

Cambridge 1983 Peter Bicknell

Books referred to in 'Observations'

(a) Edmund Burke, *A philosophical enquiry into the origin of our ideas of the sublime and the beautiful* (1757)

(b) James Thomson, *The castle of indolence: an allegorical poem* (1748)

(c) David Watkin, *The English vision. The picturesque in architecture, landscape and garden design* (1982)

(d) Horace Walpole, *Anecdotes of painting in England* (1762-71)

(e) Daniel Defoe, *A tour through England and Wales* (1724-6)

(f) William Gilpin, *Memoirs of Dr. Richard Gilpin . . . together with an account of the author by himself* . . . , ed. William Jackson (London and Carlisle, 1879)

(g) ——— *Observations on the river Wye, and several parts of South Wales, &c. relative chiefly to picturesque beauty; made in the summer of the year 1770* (1782)

(h) ——— *A dialogue upon the gardens . . . at Stowe* (Buckingham, 1748)

(i) ——— *An essay upon prints; containing remarks upon the principles of picturesque beauty* (1768)

(j) Richard Payne Knight, *The landscape, a didactic poem* (1794)

(k) ——— *An analytical inquiry into the principles of taste* (1805)

(l) Uvedale Price, *An essay on the picturesque* (1794)

(m) Anonymous, *James Hatfield and the Beauty of Buttermere, a story of modern times* (1841)

(n) William Mudford, *Augustus and Mary, or the Maid of Buttermere, a domestic tale* (1803)

(o) James Plumptre, 'A narrative of a pedestrian journey . . . to the Highlands of Scotland and home by the Lakes . . . in the summer of 1799', Cambridge University Library, Add. MSS. 5814-16

(p) Paul Sandby, *XII views in aquatinta from drawings taken on the spot in South-Wales . . .* (1775)

(q) *The prose works of William Wordsworth*, eds. W.J.B. Owen and J.W. Smyser (Oxford, 1974)

(r) *The collected writings of Thomas de Quincey*, 'The Lake poets: William Wordsworth', ed. David Masson (1896)

(s) *Our English lakes, mountains and waterfalls, as seen by William Wordsworth* (1864)

Bibliographies and catalogues referred to in compiling the Chronological List

Abbey	*Scenery of Great Britain and Ireland in aquatint and lithography, 1770-1860*, from the library of J.R. Abbey. A bibliographical catalogue (London: 1952).
Abbey, *Life*	*Life in England in aquatint and lithography, 1770-1860* . . . from the library of J.R. Abbey. A bibliographical catalogue (London: 1953).
Anderson	*The book of British topography*. A classified catalogue of the topographical works in the library of the British Museum relating to Great Britain and Ireland, John P. Anderson (London: 1881).
Barnes	Manuscript bibliography of the history and topography of Cumberland and Westmorland, compiled by Sidney Barnes (incomplete).
Healey	*The Cornell Wordsworth Collection*, G.H. Healey (Ithaca, New York: 1957).
Hodgson	*A bibliography of the history and topography of Cumberland and Westmorland*, compiled by Henry W. Hodgson (Carlisle: 1968).
Jackson	*City of Carlisle. Bibliotheca Jacksoniana*, Catalogue by James Pitcairn Hinds (Kendal: 1909).
Moir	*The Discovery of Britain: The English tourists 1540-1840*, Esther Moir (London: 1964). Bibliography includes manuscripts as well as books.
Nicholson	*The Lakers: The adventures of the first tourists*, Norman Nicholson (London: 1955). Includes a 'Picturesque bibliography' and a list of 'Some prints and illustrated books of the period'.
Sanderson	'Bibliographical history of Westmorland and Cumberland'. Album, 2 vols. Collection of manuscript and printed extracts (Carlisle Public Library).
Upcott	*A bibliographical account of the principal works relating to English topography*, William Upcott (London: 1818).
Burkett	*The Viewfinders*, Abbot Hall Art Gallery, Kendal, 1980.
Bicknell	*Beauty, horror and immensity. Picturesque landscape in Britain, 1750-1850*, Fitzwilliam Museum, Cambridge, 1981.
Bicknell and Woof	*The discovery of the Lake District 1750-1810. A context for Wordsworth*, Wordsworth Museum, Grasmere, 1982.
Bicknell and Woof	*The Lake District discovered. The artists, the tourists, and Wordsworth*, Wordsworth Museum, Grasmere, 1983.
(Murdoch)	*The discovery of the Lake District. A northern arcadia and its uses*, Victoria and Albert Museum, London, 1984.
Thomason and Woof	*Derwentwater: the Vale of Elysium*, Wordsworth Museum, Grasmere, 1986.

Notes

Items are arranged in chronological order of first publication, followed by later editions or issues. The revised title is given when this has changed. Editions published after 1855 but before 1900 are included.

List numbering:

100.1, 100.2, 100.3	first, second or third edition
100a, 100b, 100c	variants which are not numbered editions
100F, 100G	text in French, German
100A	American edition

Items in the King's Collection are described in detail. A brief note on the binding when it is of contemporary or particular interest is included. 'Gilt' indicates gilt decoration on the boards, edges, spine or label.

Titles in six libraries which possess outstanding collections on the Lake District have been scrutinised. These are shown as:

Copies:	Armitt	Armitt Library, Ambleside
	BL	British Library
	Cornell	Cornell University Library, Ithaca, NY
	Jackson	Jackson Collection, Carlisle County Library
	Kendal	Kendal Public Library
	Wordsworth	Wordsworth Library, Dove Cottage, Grasmere
	K	King's College, Cambridge, Bicknell Collection

Where there is no copy in the King's Collection, or in one of the six libraries, the source of the information or the name of the library is given. All recorded locations are shown of a particularly rare book.

Locations of prints and maps are not recorded unless they form part of a book.

Books which are listed in the Abbey catalogues (ref. Abbey and Abbey *Life*, with catalogue and not page number) are now in the Library of the Yale Center for British Art, New Haven, Connecticut.

'Advert.' is used to describe an advertisement which offers something for sale. 'Advertisement' is not abbreviated when it is the heading of a section in a book.

All illustrations are from photographs of books or plates in the King's Collection. Trimmed page sizes are given in millimetres.

† indicates that the title-page or cover is illustrated in the Chronological List; § in the plates section.

1752

WILLIAM BELLERS (artist) fl. 1750-1770

William Bellers, the son of an artist, was active in the second half of the eighteenth century, painting landscapes in the Lake District, Wales, Derbyshire, Hampshire and Sussex.

1 *Six select views in the North of England*

Set of six uniform engravings. Plate size approx. 395 × 530 mm.

1 A View of Derwent-Water towards Borrodale. A Lake near Keswick in Cumberland

'To Edward Stephenson Esqr. of Cumberland This Plate is inscribed by his most Obliged humble Servant Willm. Bellers. Published according to Act of Parliament October 10th. 1752.'

Signed: Painted after nature by William Bellers. Engraved by Messrs. Chatelin & Ravenet.

Imprint: Printed and sold by William Bellers in Poppins Court, Fleet Street, London. 'No.1'.

2 A View of Derwent-Water from Vicar's Island towards Skiddaw

As (1) except: *Engraved by Messrs. Chatelin & Grignion*
Dedicated to the Marquis of Rockingham
Published 1753

3 A View of Bywell Bay in Northumberland
Engraved by Mason & Canot
Dedicated to William Fenwick Esq. of Bywell
Published 1754

4 A View of Winander-Meer near Ambleside, A Lake between Lancashire & Westmoreland
Engraved by Mason & Müller
Dedicated to Sir William Fleming Baronet of Rydale
Published 1753

5 A View of Haws-Water, a Lake near Banton in Westmoreland
Engraved by Chatelin & Müller
Dedicated to Sir James Lowther Baronet of Lowther
Published 1753

6 A View of Uls-Water towards Poola Bridge, A Lake between Cumberland and Westmoreland
Engraved by Chatelin & Canot
Dedicated to Charles Howard Esq. of Greystock
Published 1753

Proposals for these six prints were published in the *London Evening Post,* 13-15 Dec. 1753: 'Five of the prints are finished and to be seen at his House in Poppins Court, Fleet Street, where subscriptions are taken in, at One Guinea each sett'.

London Evening Post, 13-16 April and 27-30 April 1754: 'This Day was published at One Guinea the Sett Six Select Views in the North of England . . . Drawn on the Spot with the greatest Accuracy, by Mr. William Bellers, and sold at his House in Poppins Court, Fleet Street.'

The set with three additional prints was republished in 1757. *Daily Advertiser*, 21 May 1757: 'This Day were published, at £1.11s.6d. the Set, Nine Views of the Lakes in the North of

England, &c. from Drawings taken on the Spot with the greatest Accuracy by William Bellers . . . and executed by the best Engravers'.

The six views were published again in 1774 by John Boydell with the addition of A View of the Head of Ulswater towards Patterdale, engraved by Chatelin & Mason dedicated to Charles Howard Esq,§ and South-East View of Netly Abby (sic) Near Southampton, engraved by Toms & Mason, as *Eight Views of the Lakes in Cumberland* . . . by John Boydell in Cheapside and Robert Sayer in Fleet Street (Upcott, Cumberland xviii, pp. 126-7).

The six plates are the same as the original issue, but the imprint has been altered.

Bellers visited the Lakes in or before 1752 and probably again in 1758. The View of Derwent-Water towards Borrodale, published on 10 October 1752, (plate 1), is the earliest Lake District print to adopt the picturesque conventions of the landscape painters working in Italy in the seventeenth century.

Bellers' engravers were members of the fashionable team who worked for Boydell in London. The elegant figures in the prints are by Boitard Jnr. (J. Hodgson, *The Beauties of England and Wales*. XV, *Westmorland* (1814), p.110, no.48)

A smaller engraving, A View of the Town and Vale of Keswick in Cumberland from the Side of Castle Head Cragge, painted after nature by William Bellers, engraved by Peck & Toms, finished by J. Mason, and dedicated to Captain William Crosby of Carlisle, was published in 1758.

1755

JOHN DALTON 1709-1763

John Dalton, D.D., poet, divine and Fellow of Queen's College, Oxford, was born at Dean between Cockermouth and Arlecdon. He should not be confused with John Dalton (1766-1844), the chemist and pioneer of the Atomic Theory, who was born a couple of miles away at Eaglesfield.

2 ***A descriptive poem, addressed to two ladies, at their return from viewing the mines near Whitehaven, to which are added, some thoughts on building and planting, to Sir James Lowther, of Lowther-Hall, Bart.*** London. Printed for J. and J. Rivington in St. Paul's Church-yard, and R. and J. Dodsley in Pall-Mall, 1755. Quarto.†

Text: Title, verso blank; Preface iii-viii; Text (1)-25; Letter 26, 27; blank; Divisional title 'Some thouhgts (sic) on building and plantations, to Sir J. Lowther of Lowther Hall', verso blank; Text (31)-35; Advert. (36)

King's copy: In contemporary flowered Dutch paper wrappers. Inscribed on upper cover 'Dr. Dalton's Mines at Whitehaven' and on free endpaper 'from the Author'.

Notes: The poem is the earliest published description of Lake District scenery in picturesque terms. 'The poem was written almost two years ago' (Preface, p.iii). It therefore appears to have been written, probably at Lowther Hall, in 1753, the year after the publication of Bellers' first print of Derwentwater (1) (see Thomas Cooper, *A poetical prospect of Keswick* (163)). It is addressed to the Misses Lowther, the two sisters of Sir James, whose family fortune had been made from their Cumbrian coal-mines. It compares the picturesque beauties of Derwentwater and the Vale of Keswick with the sylvan charms of their home at Lowther.

The Letter (pp.26, 27), is to the Author from W.B. Brownrigg dated Whitehaven, Nov. 20 1754, who also wrote the notes to the poem. He refers in one of these (p.16) to drawings by Mr Dalton. Dr William Brownrigg, the distinguished physician and chemist, moved from Whitehaven to Ormathwaite under Skiddaw in 1760.

The poem was reprinted by George Pearch in all four editions of his *Collection of poems by several hands* (London, 1768, 1770, 1775, 1783). An extract was included as an Addendum in the second (1780) and subsequent editions of West's *Guide* (13) and many other Lake District books.

Copies: K; Armitt; BL; Cornell; Jackson; Wordsworth

1761

THOMAS SMITH (Smith of Derby) (artist) died *c.* 1767

Thomas Smith was a topographical artist working in Derby from 1743 or earlier, when a group of his views of Derbyshire, engraved by Vivares, were published. He was the father of the artist John Raphael Smith (1752-1812).

3a ***Three views in the North of England***

Set of uniform engravings. Plate size 390 × 550 mm.

1 A View of Darwentwater &c. from Crow-Park
2 A View of Thirlmere
3 A View of Windermere

All painted, engraved and published by Thomas Smith, London, 1761.

3b ***Four views in the North of England***

A view of Ennerdale Broadwater, added to views nos. 1§, 2 and 3, with altered imprints.

All four plates painted and engraved by Thomas Smith and published by John Boydell, 1767.

3c Published with ***A short historical account of four views in the North of England. With some cursorary*** [sic] ***observations on the adjacent country.*** No imprint or date. Pamphlet, 8pp.

Copy: Jackson

Notes: A short historical account was first issued before 1767. Some of the prints dated 1761 and all of those dated 1767 have had numbers added to distinguish the features in the view which are described in the account.

The view point of Derwentwater from Crow Park is West's station 2 (see West's *Guide*, 13). In 1769 Thomas Gray considered that 'Smith judged right when he took his print of the lake from hence' (Gray's *Journal*, 10). It is not known when Smith first visited the Lakes, but it was probably not until after William Bellers' second visit in 1758. It was unusual at that time for tourists to visit Ennerdale, though it was the nearest lake to Whitehaven.

1767

JOHN BROWN 1715-1766

The Revd John Brown, D.D., of St John's College, Cambridge, theologian and author, best known for his *Estimate of the manners and principles of the times* (1757), was brought up in his father's vicarage at Wigton, Cumberland, which remained his home for most of his life. He was closely associated with the Gilpin-Dalton-Brownrigg group in the north (for a time during the 1770s he was tutor to Wiliam Gilpin).

4.1 ***A description of the lake at Keswick, (and the adjacent country) in Cumberland. Communicated in a letter to a friend. By a popular writer.*** Newcastle; Printed in the year 1767. Pamphlet, Octavo.

Published posthumously.

Copies: Jackson; and Trinity College, Cambridge

4.2 ——— [Second separate edition]. By a late popular writer. Kendal: printed by J. Ashburner. 1770. Pamphlet, Octavo.

Copies: Armitt; Wordsworth; and Bodleian, Oxford

4.3 ——— [Third separate edition]. By a late popular writer. Kendal: printed by W. Pennington. Sold by J. Hodgson at the Queen's Head in Keswick, 1771. Pamphlet, Octavo.†

Text: Title, verso blank; Text [3]-8.

King's copy: In original grey paper wrappers

Copies: K; BL; Cornell; Kendal; Wordsworth; and Deighton Bell & Co. Catalogue 221 (1981), no. 155 (now in private collection)

4.4 ——— [Fourth separate edition]. By a popular writer. Whitehaven: Printed by John Dunn. 1772. Pamphlet, Octavo.

Copy: Jackson

4.5 ——— [Fifth separate edition]. London: T. Sherlock. 1772. Quarto.

A dedication was added to this edition: 'To the Gentlemen of Cumberland this animated description of Keswick, the production of their celebrated country man, Dr Brown, is most respectfully addressed to the Editor'.

Copy: BL

The copies of all five editions are the only ones recorded.

Notes: A description reproduces part of a letter (now lost) written after a visit to Keswick, made after visiting Lord Lyttelton at Hagley in 1751. This part of the letter was first published in *The London Chronicle*, 24-26 April 1766, as 'Description of Keswick in Cumberland, in a Letter from a Gentleman to his friend in London'. The original letter contained Brown's *Poetical Rhapsody*, 'Now sunk the sun . . . ' which was first printed in Cumberland's *Odes* (1776) (11). The whole letter is reconstructed by Donald Eddy in 'John Brown: "The Columbus of Keswick"', *Journal of modern philology*, vol. 73, No. 4, Part 2 (May 1976), pp. S80-S82; and was published as a pamphlet with a brief introduction by Andrew F. Wilson, London, 1985.

A description was reprinted by George Pearch as a footnote to Dalton's *Descriptive poem* (2) in all four editions of his *Collections of poems by several hands* (1768, 1770, 1775, 1783); and as an addendum to the second edition (1780) and subsequent editions of West's *Guide* (13). The *Poetical Rhapsody* was also included in West's *Guide* as a footnote (1780, pp. 115, 116); and by Wordsworth in the fourth edition of *A description of the scenery of the Lakes* (1823), (p. 34), 'The Fragment is well known; but it gratifies me to insert it, as the Writer was one of the first who led the way to a worthy admiration of this country'. There is a comprehensive list of references to both *A description* and *Poetical Rhapsody* in books about the Lakes in Donald D. Eddy, *A bibliography of John Brown* (New York, 1971).

Brown's *Description*, with his statement that 'the full perfection of Keswick consists of three circumstances, *Beauty, Horror,* and *Immensity* united . . . but to give a complete idea of these three perfections, as they are joined in Keswick, would require the united powers of *Claude, Salvator,* and *Poussin*', became a pattern for picturesque writing about the Lake District for the next half century.

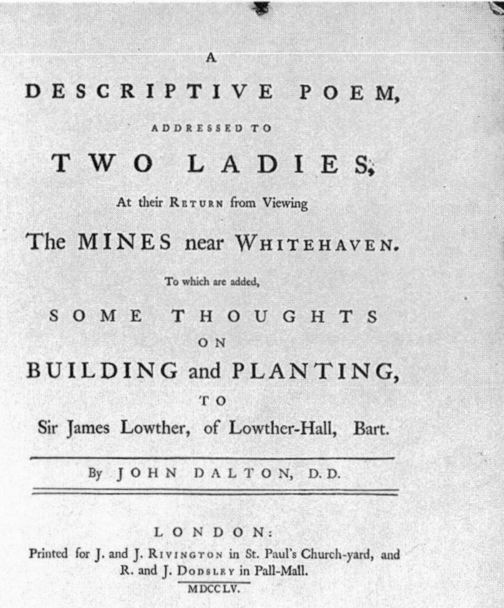

A

DESCRIPTIVE POEM,

ADDRESSED TO

TWO LADIES,

At their RETURN from Viewing

The MINES near WHITEHAVEN.

To which are added,

SOME THOUGHTS

ON

BUILDING and PLANTING,

TO

Sir James Lowther, of Lowther-Hall, Bart.

By JOHN DALTON, D.D.

LONDON:

Printed for J. and J. RIVINGTON in St. Paul's Church-yard, and R. and J. DODSLEY in Pall-Mall.

MDCCLV.

2 290 x 220 mm.

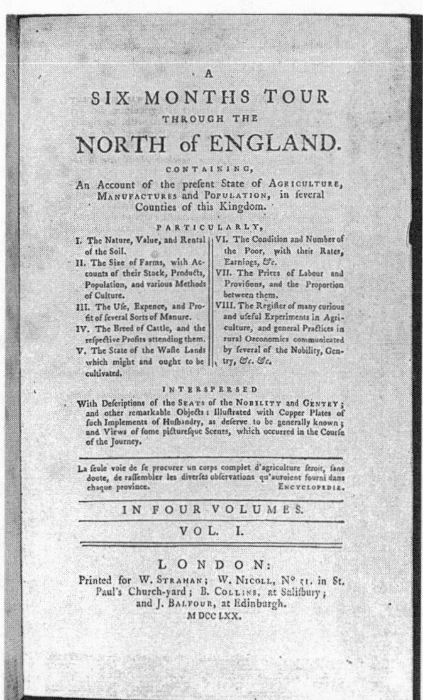

A

SIX MONTHS TOUR

THROUGH THE

NORTH of ENGLAND.

CONTAINING,

An Account of the present State of AGRICULTURE, MANUFACTURES and POPULATION, in several Counties of this Kingdom.

PARTICULARLY,

I. The Nature, Value, and Rental of the Soil.

II. The Size of Farms, with Accounts of their Stock, Products, Population, and various Methods of Culture.

III. The Use, Expence, and Profit of several Sorts of Manure.

IV. The Breed of Cattle, and the respective Profits attending them.

V. The State of the Waste Lands which might and ought to be cultivated.

VI. The Condition and Number of the Poor, with their Rates, Earnings, &c.

VII. The Prices of Labour and Provisions, and the Proportion between them.

VIII. The Register of many curious and useful Experiments in Agriculture, and general Practices in rural Oeconomics communicated by several of the Nobility, Gentry, &c. &c.

INTERSPERSED

With Descriptions of the SEATS of the NOBILITY and GENTRY; and other remarkable Objects: Illustrated with Copper Plates of such Implements of Husbandry, as deserve to be generally known; and Views of some picturesque Scenes, which occurred in the Course of the Journey.

La seule voie de se procurer un corps complet d'agriculture seroit, sans doute, de rassembler les diverses observations qu'auroient fourni dans chaque province. ENCYCLOPEDIE.

IN FOUR VOLUMES.

VOL. I.

LONDON:

Printed for W. STRAHAN; W. NICOLL, N° 51. in St. Paul's Church-yard; B. COLLINS, at Salisbury; and J. BALFOUR, at Edinburgh.

MDCCLXX.

5.1 200 x 120 mm.

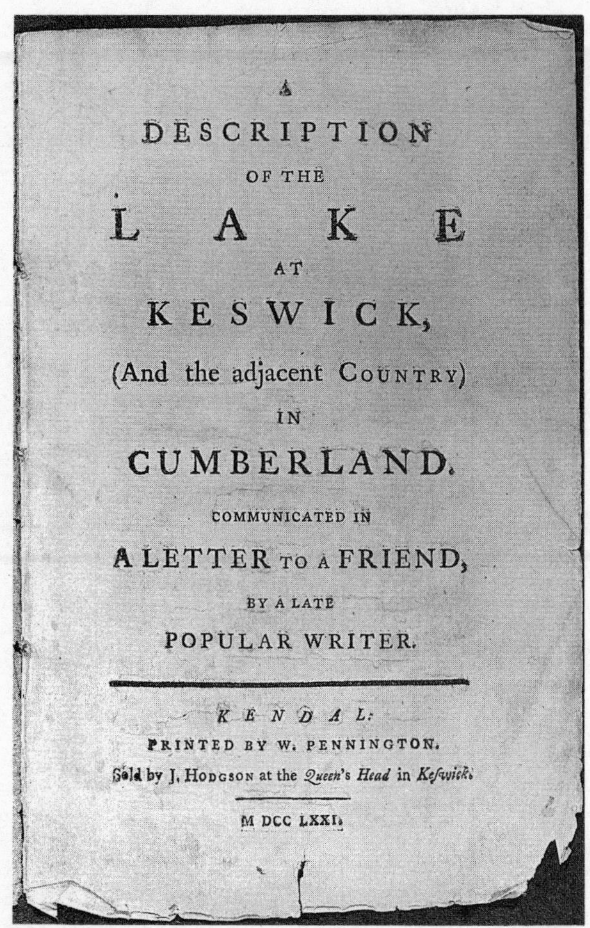

A

DESCRIPTION

OF THE

LAKE

AT

KESWICK,

(And the adjacent COUNTRY)

IN

CUMBERLAND.

COMMUNICATED IN

A LETTER TO A FRIEND,

BY A LATE

POPULAR WRITER.

KENDAL:

PRINTED BY W. PENNINGTON.

Sold by J. HODGSON at the *Queen's Head* in *Keswick*.

M DCC LXXI.

4.3 180 x 140 mm.

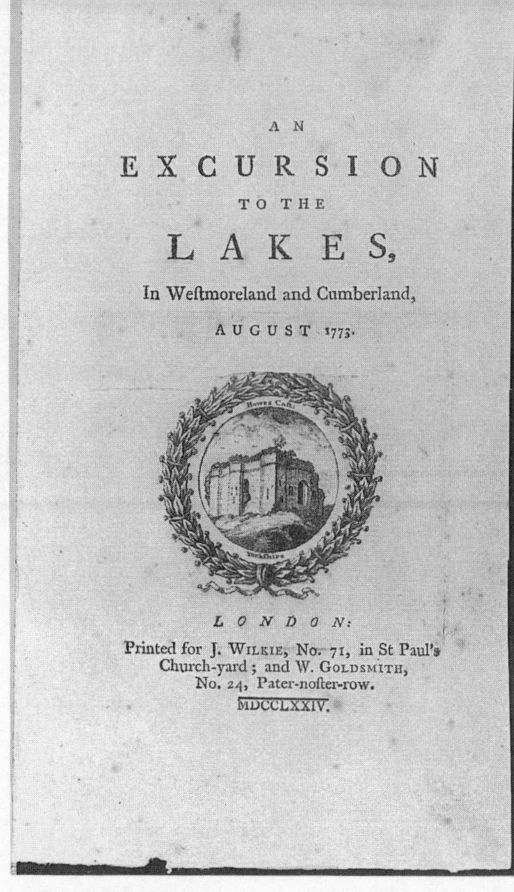

AN

EXCURSION

TO THE

LAKES,

In Westmoreland and Cumberland,

AUGUST 1773.

LONDON:

Printed for J. WILKIE, No. 71, in St Paul's Church-yard; and W. GOLDSMITH, No. 24, Pater-noster-row.

MDCCLXXIV.

6 225 x 130 mm.

1770

ARTHUR YOUNG 1741-1820

Well known agriculturist, author of *Travels in France, during the years 1787, 1788 and 1789* (1792), *Tour in Ireland* (1780), and many works on agricultural and political subjects.

5.1 ***A six months tour through the North of England...*** 4 vols. London: printed for W. Strahan; W. Nicholl, No. 51 in St Paul's Church-yard; B. Collins, at Salisbury; and J. Balfour, at Edinburgh, 1770. Quarto.†

Text: Vol. 1 Title, verso blank; Dedication (Oct. 1 1769), verso blank; Contents [i]-iv; Preface iii-xxv; blank; Text [1]-401; Adverts. 3 pp.

Vol. 2 Title, verso blank; Contents [i]-vii; Text [1]-502

Vol. 3 Title, verso blank; Contents [iii]-vii; blank; Text [1]-440

Vol. 4 Title, verso blank; Contents [iii]-viii; Text [1]-596

Plates: Vol. 1 7 engravings (6 folding)

Vol. 2 8 engravings (6 folding)

Vol. 3 12 engravings (7 folding)

Vol. 4 1 engraving (folding), 6 tables (folding).

There are three views of waterfalls near Keswick (all Lowdore), Vol. 3, pls. 1, 2, 3, from sketches by Young. No signature, title or imprint.

Lakes: Letter XVII, Vol. 3, pp. 117-188.

Itinerary: Penrith, Derwentwater, Thirlmere, Ullswater, Haweswater, Kendal and Windermere.

King's copy: In contemporary calf, rebacked. Inscribed on paste-down endpapers 'Hugh Bethel'.

Note: Although his book was primarily devoted to observations on the state of agriculture, Young included many picturesque descriptions of the beauties of the scenery which were much quoted and pirated in subsequent Lake District books.

Copies: K; Armitt; BL; Cornell; Kendal

5.2 ——— Second edition. Corrected and enlarged. 1771. Octavo. Engravings.

Copies: Armitt; BL; Cornell; Kendal

5a ——— Dublin: printed for P. Wilson, J. Exshaw etc. 1770. Engravings.

Copy: University of Chicago

5G ——— *Sechs monatliche Reise durch die nördliche Provinzen von England.* German translation. Leipzig: Gaspar Fritsch, 1772

Copy: University of Kansas

1774

WILLIAM HUTCHINSON 1732-1801

William Hutchinson, F.S.A., of Barnard Castle, lawyer, topographer, antiquary and historian, wrote county histories of Durham 1785 and Cumberland (see 28). See also Mavor (38).

6 ***An excursion to the Lakes, in Westmoreland and Cumberland, August 1773***. London: printed for J. Wilkie, No. 71, in St Paul's Church-yard; and W. Goldsmith, No. 24, Pater-noster-row. 1774. Octavo.†

Text: Title (vignette), verso blank; Text [1]-193

Itinerary: Ullswater; Vale of St John; Keswick; Skiddaw; Thirlmere; Grasmere; Windermere; Kendal

King's copy: Rebound, binder's label on paste-down endpaper 'Bound by J.W. Jackman, Basinghall St., Leeds'

Notes: The excursion was made with William Hutchinson's brother Richard, who acted as draughtsman.

The book includes a generous amount of rich picturesque description, and lively accounts of unusual incidents. Dalton's *Poem* (2) and Brown's *Description* (4) are quoted.

Copies: K; Armitt; BL; Cornell; Jackson; Kendal

7 ***An excursion to the Lakes in Westmoreland and Cumberland, with a tour through part of the Northern Counties, in the years 1773 and 1774.*** London: for J. Wilkie, No. 71 St. Paul's Church-yard, W. Charnley, in Newcastle, 1776. Octavo.

Text: Title, verso blank; Text [1]-382, Itinerary 2 pp.; Order of Plates 1 p.; Errata 1 p.

Plates: 19 engravings from drawings by (Richard) Hutchinson, except pl. 4 by Lodge. No views of Lake District scenery.

Incorporates *An Excursion* of 1773 (6) with little alteration, which ends on p. 199. To it is added an excursion to other parts of Cumberland, Hexham and parts of Durham and Yorkshire.

King's copy: In contemporary calf, repaired, original leather label on spine

Copies: K; Armitt; BL; Cornell; Jackson; Kendal; Wordsworth

Ref: Upcott, p. 120

THOMAS PENNANT 1726-1798

Thomas Pennant, a Flintshire squire of wide interests, was, *inter alia*, a botanist, zoologist, antiquarian, historian, correspondent of Gilbert White, friend of Linnaeus, admirer of Richard Wilson and an inveterate traveller.

8.1 ***A tour in Scotland, and voyage to the Hebrides; 1772***. Chester: printed by Monk, London: for Benj. White 2 parts, 1774, 1776. Quarto. Engravings.

Copy: BL

8.2 ——— [Second edition] Part 1 [only]. London: Benj. White. 1776. Quarto. Engravings.

Copies: BL; Cornell

8.3 ——— [Part 1 third edition, Part 2 second edition] 2 vols. London: Printed for Benj. White. 1790. Quarto†

Text: Part 1 Engraved title (vignette), verso blank; Dedication i, ii; Advert. iii-v; Plates vi, vii; blank; Text [1]-429; Itinerary 430-434; Index 435-440.

Part 2 Engraved title, *A Tour in Scotland*, (vignette), verso blank; Advert (Downing, Dec. 26, 1790) i, ii; Plates vi, vii; Text [1]-368; Appendices 369-479; Index 480-487.

Plates: Part 1 44 engravings. Plate 2, View of Skiddaw. Signed *Moses Griffith del. P. Mazell sculp.* (only Lake District view).

Part 2 45 engravings (no Lake District views)

Lakes: Vol. 1, pp. 31-51

King's copy: In contemporary mottled calf, gilt, uniform with *A Tour in Scotland, 1769,* fifth edition, 1790, and *A Tour in Wales, 1784,* 2 vols. Set of 5 vols.

Note: On his way to Scotland and the Hebrides Pennant travelled by Furness Abbey, Ulverston, Coniston, Hawkshead, Windermere, Rydal, Thirlmere, Keswick, Bassenthwaite and Cockermouth. He was accompanied by Moses Griffith (1747-1819) as draughtsman. Returning from Scotland in 1769, Pennant had followed the main road from Carlisle to Lancaster by Penrith, Shap and Kendal, but did not penetrate into the Lake District (see *A tour in Scotland, 1769* (London, 1771)).

Copies: K; BL

8G ——— *Reise durch Schotland und die Hebridischen Inseln*. German translation by J.P. Ebeling. Leipzig: Wendgaschen. 2 vols. 1779, 1780. Octavo. Engravings in vol. 1 only.

Copy: BL

THOMAS WEST *c.*1720-1779

Thomas West, born in Scotland and educated in Edinburgh, joined the Society of Jesus in 1751, was trained at the English Jesuit College in Liège, arrived back in England in 1769 and later became chaplain at Titeup Hall, near Dalton in Furness, where he wrote *The Antiquities*. Later he moved to Ulverston, where he prepared his *Guide to the Lakes*. He died in Sizergh, near Kendal, and is buried in Kendal parish church. See (13) and (14)

9.1 ***The Antiquities of Furness*** . . . [Anonymous]. London, printed for the author, by T. Spilsbury, in Cook's Court, Carey-Street, Lincoln's Inn: and sold by J. Johnson, in St. Paul's Church-Yard; J. Ridley, in St. James's Street; and S. Leacroft, at Charing-Cross. 1774. Octavo.†

Text: Title, verso blank; Dedication (Thomas West, Titeup in Furness. 1774) 4 pp.; Preface 2 pp.; List of Subscribers 5 pp.; blank; Contents 3 pp.; Errata 1 p.; Explanation of the ground plan 2 pp.; Descriptive view of Furness [i]-lvi; Sub-title, 'The Antiquities of Furness', verso blank; Text [1]-[288]; Appendices 142 pp. (not numbered); Conclusion 2 pp.

Plates: 3 Engravings. No views of scenery.

Map: A map of the Liberty of Furness in the County of Lancaster. As Surveyed by Wm. Brasier 1745 & copied by T. Richardson 1772. Signed: W. Darling fect., Newport Street, London. Plate size 343 × 425 mm. Scale: 1 in = 2 miles.

A chart of the Atlantic and Southern Oceans (frontispiece)

King's copy: Bound in contemporary calf, gilt, leather label

Note: The book includes 'A descriptive view' (pp. xxxii ff.) which is concerned with Furness Abbey and the antiquities of High Furness, the area in which the lakes of Coniston, Esthwaite and part of Windermere lie. It does little to foreshadow the rich picturesque passages of West's *Guide* (13).

Copies: K; Armitt; BL; Cornell; Jackson; Kendal; Wordsworth

Ref: Upcott, p.477

——— Facsimile. *The Antiquities of Furness by Thomas West of Titeup Hall in Furness 1774*. Republished 1977 by Michael Noon at the Beckermet Bookshop, Beckermet, Cumbria.

9.2 ——— *Illustrated with engravings. A new edition, with additions, by William Close.* Ulverston: Printed and sold by George Ashburner, and may be had of R.S. Kirby, London-House-Yard; Messrs. Lackington; Allen and Co., London; H. Mozley, Gainsborough; Wilson and Spence, York; Troughton, and Gore, Liverpool; Thompson and Sons, Manchester; Ware, Whitehaven. 1805. Octavo.†

Text: Title, verso blank; Dedication 4 pp.; Preface 2 pp.; Advertisement 2 pp.; Contents 5 pp.; Directions and Errata 1 p.; List of subscribers 8 pp.; Text [1]-426; Index 6 pp.; Imprint on last page, *Finis* (in device): *Ulverston, Printed by G Ashburner.*

Plates: 4 tinted aquatints and 2 engravings, signed. *Drawn by W. Close.* Cuts in text, some tinted green. No views of scenery.

Map: A map of Furness. Signed: *W. Close del. R. Hixon Sc. 355 Strand.* Plate size 210 × 133 mm. Scale: 1 in. = 4 miles.

King's copy: Rebound

Note: The second edition, published twenty-six years after West's death, contains extensive alterations and additions which are described in the Advertisement, signed, William Close, Dalton, November 26, 1804. 'The Descriptive View' is similar to the first edition, but significantly enlarged. It includes extracts from West's *Guide* (13) (already in its eighth edition), and from Young's *Tour* (5), which describe scenery in picturesque terms; but the illustrations are limited to antiquities. A Supplement by the editor includes an account (p. 409) of Thomas West, principally by Mrs Strickland of Sizergh.

Copies: K; Armitt; BL; Cornell; Jackson; Kendal; Wordsworth

Ref: Upcott, p. 478

9.3 ——— Ulverston: Ashburner. 1813. Octavo

Copies: BL; Wordsworth; and Barrow-in-Furness Public Library

9.4 ——— Ulverston: Ashburner. 1822. Octavo.

Copy: Armitt

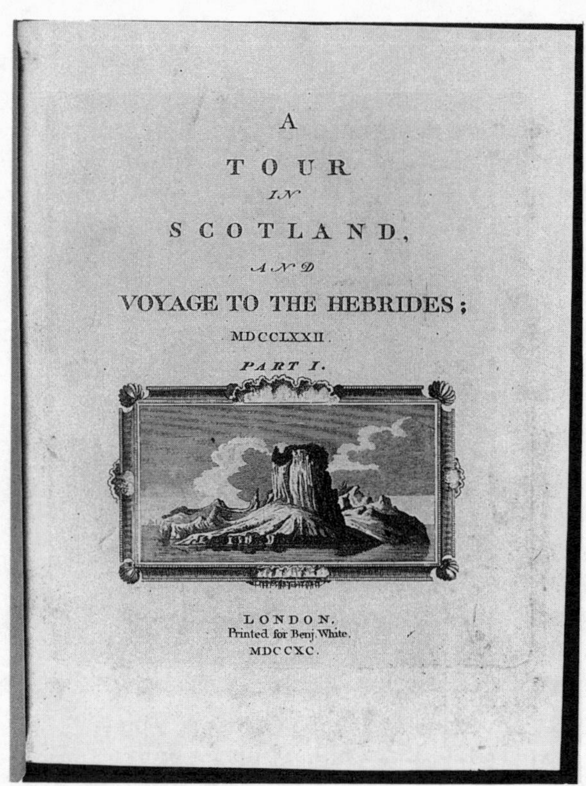
A
TOUR
IN
SCOTLAND,
AND
VOYAGE TO THE HEBRIDES;
MDCCLXXII.
PART I.

LONDON.
Printed for Benj. White.
MDCCXC.

8.3 247 x 190 mm.

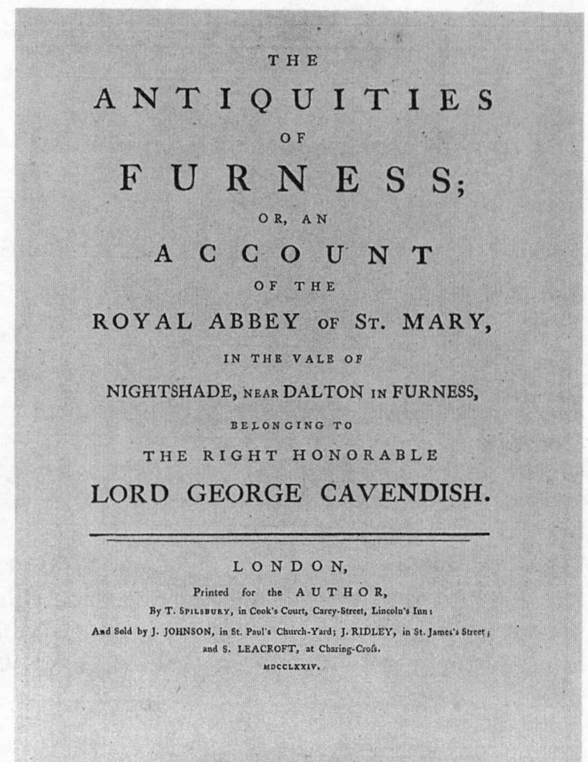
THE
ANTIQUITIES
OF
FURNESS;
OR, AN
ACCOUNT
OF THE
ROYAL ABBEY OF ST. MARY,
IN THE VALE OF
NIGHTSHADE, NEAR DALTON IN FURNESS,
BELONGING TO
THE RIGHT HONORABLE
LORD GEORGE CAVENDISH.

LONDON,
Printed for the AUTHOR,
By T. Spilsbury, in Cook's Court, Carey-Street, Lincoln's Inn:
And Sold by J. JOHNSON, in St. Paul's Church-Yard; J. RIDLEY, in St. James's Street;
and S. LEACROFT, at Charing-Cross.
MDCCLXXIV.

9.1 260 x 210 mm.

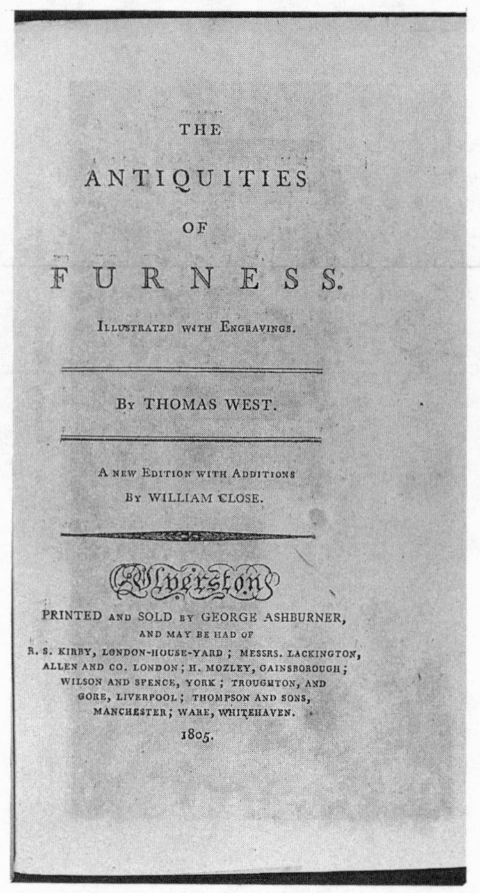
THE
ANTIQUITIES
OF
FURNESS.
Illustrated with Engravings.

By THOMAS WEST.

A new Edition with Additions
By WILLIAM CLOSE.

Ulverston
PRINTED and SOLD by GEORGE ASHBURNER,
AND MAY BE HAD OF
R. S. KIRBY, LONDON-HOUSE-YARD; MESSRS. LACKINGTON,
ALLEN AND CO. LONDON; H. MOZLEY, GAINSBOROUGH;
WILSON AND SPENCE, YORK; TROUGHTON, AND
GORE, LIVERPOOL; THOMPSON AND SONS,
MANCHESTER; WARE, WHITEHAVEN.
1805.

9.2 210 x 130 mm.

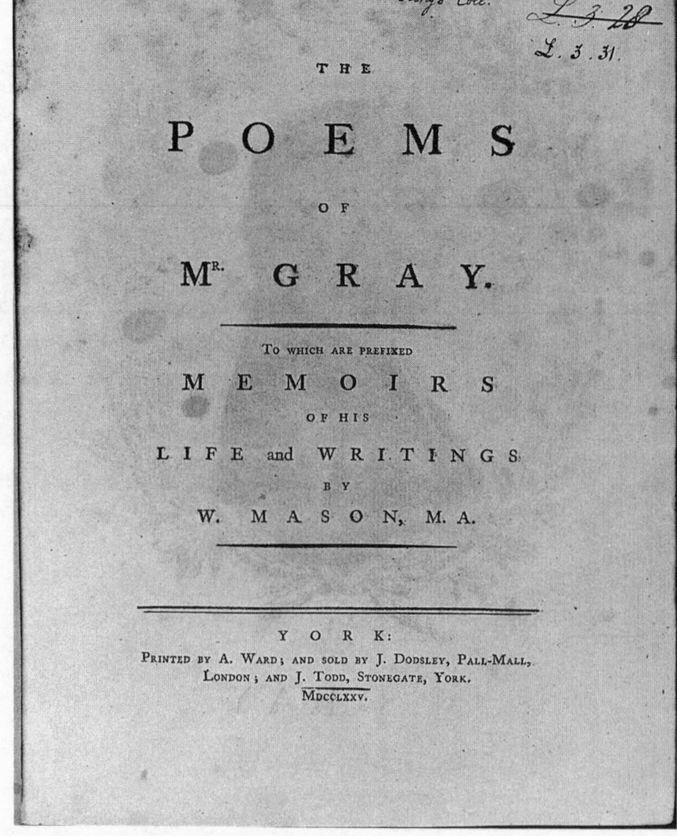
King's Coll.
L. 3. 28
L. 3. 31.
THE
POEMS
OF
MR. GRAY.

To which are prefixed
MEMOIRS
OF HIS
LIFE and WRITINGS
BY
W. MASON, M.A.

YORK:
Printed by A. Ward; and sold by J. Dodsley, Pall-Mall,
London; and J. Todd, Stonegate, York.
MDCCLXXV.

10.1 260 x 210 mm.

1775

THOMAS GRAY 1716-1771

The poet, Thomas Gray, touring France and Italy in 1739 with Horace Walpole, found the 'sublimities of the Grande Chartreuse . . . one of the most poetical scenes imaginable', and on a journey in the Scottish Highlands in 1765 he found the mountains 'ecstatic'.

10.1 ***The poems of Mr. Gray. To which are prefixed memoirs of his life and writings by W. Mason, M.A.*** York: printed by A. Ward; and sold by J. Dodsley, Pall-Mall, London; and J. Todd, Stonegate, York. 1775. Quarto.†

Text: Title, verso blank; Divisional title, 'Memoirs . . .', verso blank; Errata, verso blank; Text [1]-404; Contents of the Memoirs [405]-416; Divisional title, 'The poems', verso blank; Text [3]-71; blank; Divisional title, 'Imitations . . .'; Advert. [74]; Variations and additional notes [75]-111; Contents of the poems [112].

Frontispiece: Engraved portrait of Gray

King's copy: In contemporary calf, rebacked with leather label remounted. This copy has probably been in the library of King's College since the time of publication.

Notes: Letter IV, to Dr. Wharton, Aston Oct. 18, 1769 (pp. 350-79), is the first edition of Gray's *Journal* in the Lakes.

Gray started on a tour to the Lakes in 1767, with Wharton, but Wharton was taken ill at Keswick and the joint tour was abandoned. Again in 1769 Wharton was taken ill, this time at Brough, where Gray left him and continued on his own. He spent two nights in Penrith, 30 September and 1 October, visiting Ullswater; then six at Keswick, visiting Bassenthwaite and the Castlerigg stone circle. He returned by Dunmail Raise, Grasmere, Ambleside. Kendal, Lancaster, Settle and Skipton, visiting Malham and Gordale Scar. The Journal ends with the entry for 14 October.

The Journal was not intended for publication, and was written solely for Wharton's amusement. After his tour Gray transcribed it and sent it in a series of letters to Wharton. Mason printed the letters continuously, omitting, inserting and rewriting passages. It was published, as edited by Mason, as an addendum to the second (1780) and subsequent editions of West's *Guide*; and was included in *Sketch of a tour from Lancaster round the principal lakes in Lancashire, Cumberland and Westmorland,* Carlisle: F. Jollie. 1803 (49).

At the Yale Center for British Art there is an album of drawings by Joseph Farington intended to be illustrations for Gray's *Journal*.

Copies: K; BL; Cornell

10.2 ——— Second edition. London: Hughes for Dodsley; and Todd, York. 1775. Quarto. Engravings.

Copies: BL; Cornell

10.3 ——— [Third edition] 'to which are added' replaces 'to which are prefixed'. In four volumes. York: printed by A. Ward; and sold by J. Dodsley, Pall-Mall; T. Cadell, in the Strand, London; and J. Todd, York. 1778. Octavo.

Text: Vol. 1 Title, verso Advertisement; Divisional title, 'The poems of Mr Gray. Vol. 1', verso blank; Text [3]-168; Contents [169]

Vol. 2 Title, verso blank; Divisional title, 'Memoirs of the life and writings of Mr. Gray, containing the first and second sections', verso blank; Contents [v]-xv; blank;Text [11]-161

Vol. 3 Title, verso blank; Divisional title, 'Memoirs of the life and writings of Mr. Gray, containing the third and first part of the fourth section of the memoirs', verso blank; Contents [v]-xii; Text: [1]-166

Vol. 4 Title, verso blank; Divisional title, 'Containing the second part of the fourth, and the fifth and last section of the memoirs', verso blank; Contents [v]-xiv; Text [1]-239

Frontispiece: Portrait of Mr. Gray, etched by W. Doughty from an original drawing

King's copy: In contemporary mottled calf, gilt; leather labels

Copies: K; BL; Cornell

10.3a ——— Third edition. 2 vols. London: Vernor Hood. 1807. Octavo.

Copy: BL

10.4 ——— Fourth edition. 2 vols. London: Vernor Hood. 1807. Octavo.

Copy: BL

10a ——— 2 vols. Dublin: Chamberlain, Potts n.d. *c.* 1776. Octavo.

Copies: BL; Cornell

1776

RICHARD CUMBERLAND 1732-1811

Richard Cumberland, dramatist, author, poet, politician and Fellow of Trinity College, Cambridge, accompanied the Earl of Warwick on a visit to the Lakes, probably in 1775.

11.1 ***Odes.*** London: for J. Robson, New Bond Street. 1776. Quarto. Dedicated to George Romney.

Copies: BL; Cornell; Wordsworth

11.2 ——— Second edition. Dublin: Printed for S. Price, W. Whitestone, N. Watson, J. Sheppard, J. Potts, S. Watson, J. Williams, W. Collis, J. Armitage, G. Burnet, C. Jenkin, W. Wilson, R. Moncrieffe, T. Walker, and P. Higly. 1776. Octavo.

Copies: BL; Cornell

Notes: Cumberland's ode 'To the Sun' is devoted to the Lakes. It incorporates the opening line of Gray's ode, 'The Bard' – 'Ruin seize thee ruthless king'. In the introduction, addressed to Mr George Romney (1734-1802), Cumberland says that no topographical notes are needed, 'as all the scenes hinted at in the poem are described in Gray's *Journal* [10], a book in everybody's hands'. He includes the first publication of the poetical rhapsody 'Now sunk the sun', from Dr John Brown's letter, omitted from *A description of the Lake at Keswick* (4).

The ode 'To the Sun' was reprinted in West's *Guide,* 2nd-11th editions (13.2-11).

1777

JOSEPH NICOLSON 1706-1777 and RICHARD BURN 1710-1784

12 ***The history and antiquities of the counties of Westmorland and Cumberland.*** 2 vols. London: Strahan & Cadell. 1777. Engravings. Maps. Quarto.

Notes: Each of the joint historians wrote about his own county. Joseph Nicolson, born of a well-established Carlisle family, and a nephew of the distinguished antiquarian, Bishop William Nicolson, dealt with Cumberland. The Revd Richard Burn, L1.D., of humbler origins than Nicolson, who spent his life as schoolmaster and parish priest in and around Kirkby Stephen, dealt with Westmoreland. With one exception, their book makes no concessions to picturesque scenery. Keswick, already established as the centre of the picturesque tourist industry, called for the quotation of Dalton's *Poem* (2) and Brown's *Description* (4). Dr William Brownrigg, who had provided the notes for Dalton, also provided notes on the coal-mines at Whitehaven for Nicolson and Burn.

Copies: Armitt; BL; Cornell; Kendal; Jackson; Wordsworth

——— Facsimile edition. EP Publishing Ltd, East Ardsley, Wakefield (1976).

1778

THOMAS WEST *c.*1720-1779

See 9

13.1 ***A Guide to the Lakes: dedicated to the lovers of landscape studies, and to all who have visited, or intend to visit the Lakes in Cumberland, Westmorland and Lancashire. By the author of the Antiquities of Furness.*** London: for Richardson and Urquhart, under the Royal Exchange, and W. Pennington, Kendal. 1778. Octavo.†

Text: Title, verso blank; Text [1]-196; The Lakes (tables, etc.); [197]-203; Errata [204]. [p.197 is incorrectly numbered 107]. (Some copies include half-title.)

King's copy: In contemporary half-calf marbled boards, red leather label; bookplate, George A. Auden; inscribed on endpapers, 'William Gleadell', 'G A Auden, Westco'.

Note: This book, dedicated in the title to 'lovers of landscape studies and to all who have visited or intend to visit the lakes', is the earliest guide to picturesque mountain scenery. For nearly half a century it was carried by almost every visitor to the Lakes. West treats the landscape as a series of pictures, to be seen from 'stations' which are numbered and described. He recommends the use of the landscape mirror. A definite tour is described which starts from Lancaster, crossing the Lancaster and Ulverston sands to Coniston, Windermere, Rydal, Grasmere, Thirlmere, Derwentwater, Borrowdale, Bassenthwaite, by Newlands to Buttermere, Crummock and Loweswater; then Penrith, Ullswater and over the Kirkstone to Ambleside; or Penrith, Haweswater and down Longsleddale to Kendal. The tour does not include the western lakes, Wastwater and Ennerdale, nor the Duddon. West is almost exclusively concerned with the lakes and pays little attention to the mountains except as a background to the picture.

Copies: K; Armitt; BL; Cornell; Jackson; Kendal; Wordsworth

13.2 ——— Second edition. London and Kendal: 1780. Octavo.

Title: As 1778 except:
'dedicated to lovers of landscape. . . the Lakes' omitted
Extract from *Paradise Lost* replaces 'Quis non malarum . . .'
'The Second Edition revised throughout and greatly enlarged' added

'J Robson, New Bond Street' added to imprint
'1780' replaces '1778'.

Text: Title; Dedication 1 p.; Preface (September 12th 1779) [iii]-vi; Tables and Articles vii, viii; Text [1]-184; Tables 185-190; Divisional title, 'Addenda', verso blank; Addenda [193]-291 (Errata 291); Advertisement [292]

Plate: Engraved frontispiece: 'Grasmere', signed *Feary delin. Engraved by J. Caldwall.*

Addenda:

1 Dr. Brown's description . . .
2 Extract from Dr. Dalton's Descriptive poem
3 Mr. Gray's Journal of his northern tour
4 Mr. Cumberland's Ode to the Sun
5 Description of Dunald-mill-hole
6 Description of natural curiosities in the edge of Yorkshire
7 Tour to the caves in the West-Riding of Yorkshire
8 Further account of Furness fells, &c.
9 Specimens of the Cumberland dialect
10 Some remarks on the provincial words . . .

King's copies:

1 In original grey paper boards, rebacked. Uncut. Inscribed: 'Edw: [?] Curteis Ch. Ch. Oxford I bought this book at Lancaster, 1783', on paste-down endpaper; 'Mary Curteis', on title-page.

2 This copy has been copiously annotated by an unidentified tourist in August 1782, and by another tourist, 'J.P.', in October and September 1807. The notes are reproduced as an Appendix to this volume: The notes were made in the margins of an uncut copy, which has been rebound with leaves cut, and many of the notes neatly folded. 3 extra printed sheets have been tipped in.

Note: After West's death on 10 July 1779, the revision and enlargement of the *Guide,* already well in hand, was taken over by William Cockin (see 15). The text was considerably extended, and ten articles were included as Addenda. These formed an accessible anthology of Lake District writing. The preface includes a 'short memorial of his [Mr West's] exit'. An engraving of Grasmere was added as a frontispiece.

Copies: K; Armitt; BL; Cornell; Jackson

13.3 ——— Third edition. 1784. Octavo.

Title: As 1780 except:
'The third edition' replaces 'The second edition'
'B. Law, Ave Maria Lane' added to imprint
'1784' replaces '1780'

Text: Half-title, verso blank; Title, verso blank; Preface [v]-ix; Adverts. ix, x; Tables and Articles xi, xii; Text [1]-188; Divisional Title, 'Addenda', verso blank; Addenda [191]-306; Adverts. [307]

Plate: Engraved frontispiece as 1780.

Map: A Map of the Lakes (folding). Signed: *Paas sculp. No. 53 Holborn.* Size: 208 × 405mm. Scale: 1 in. = 3½ miles.

Preface as 1780, but a note on the third edition is added

Addenda: As 1780 except:
11 'Address to the Genius of the Caves' added.

Note: Six views of the Lakes engraved by William Byrne &c. from drawings by Mr. Farington are advertised on pp. ix-x (see 22).

King's copy: In contemporary half-calf, marbled boards, leather label, gilt. Inscribed: 'Warren W.R. Peacocke' [?], on title-page.

Copies: K; Armitt; BL; Cornell; Jackson; Kendal; Wordsworth

13.4 ——— Fourth edition. 1789. Octavo.†

Title: As 1784 except:
'Milton' replaces *Paradise Lost*
'The fourth edition' replaces 'The third edition'
'Revised throughout and greatly enlarged' omitted
Device 'W.P.' added
Imprint altered to 'Printed for W. Richardson, under the Royal Exchange; J. Robson, New Bond Street; and W. Pennington, Kendal, 1789'.

Text: Title, verso blank; Preface to the second edition (September 28th 1779) [v]-viii; Advertisement to the Third Edition (May 4th 1784) ix; Advertisement to this Edition (April 10th 1789) x, xi; Tables and Articles xii-xiv; Text [1]-190; Divisional Title, 'Addenda', verso blank; Addenda [193]-311; Adverts. [312].

Plate: Engraved frontispiece as 1780

Map: As 1780

Addenda: As 1780 except:
'Address to the Genius of the Caves' replaced by 'Account of Ennerdale'

Note: Twenty views from drawings of Mr Farington, by Mr Byrne and others, advertised on pp. x-xi (see 22),

King's copy: In original grey paper boards, rebacked

Copies: K; Armitt; BL; Cornell; Kendal; Wordsworth

13.5 ——— Fifth edition. 1793. Octavo.

Title: As 1789 except:
'*Paradise Lost*' replaces '*Milton*'
'The Fifth Edition' replaces 'The Fourth Edition'
'W. Clarke, New Bond Street' added to imprint
'1793' replaces '1789'

Text: Half-title, verso blank; Title, verso blank; Adverts. [iii], [iv]; Preface to the second edition [v]-viii; Advertisement to this edition (May 1 1793) ix, x; Text [1]-192; Divisional Title, 'Addenda', verso blank; Addenda [195]-311; Adverts. [312]-[314]

Plates: 2 engravings:
1 Frontispiece as three previous editions
2 Engraving, Lowdore, signed *Drawn by Josh. Farington R.A. Engraved by William Byrne.* Imprint *Published as the Act directs, 1 Feb. 1793, by W. Pennington, Kendal.*

Map: Same as previous two editions

Addenda: Same as previous edition, 1789

Note: The advertisement, pp. ix-x, draws attention to the added view of Lowdore and to the series of Views of the Lakes, advertised [p.314] as 'a series of Views of the Lakes in Aqua-tinta of a proper size to bind with West's Guide from Drawings by Messrs. Smith & Emes'. These plates are bound into the King's copy (see 31 for details of plates).
Also advertised are:
Plans of the Lakes by James Clarke, in a portable Quarto volume (p.iv) (see 19.3).
An Ode to the Genius of the Lakes by William Cockin [editor of West's *Guide*], p.312 (15)

King's copy: Bound in contemporary mottled calf, gilt, leather labels. 16 additional plates bound in. Water marks on free endpapers 1794. Pencil sketches on free endpapers.

Copies: K; Armitt; BL; Cornell; Wordsworth

13.6 ——— Sixth edition. 1796. Octavo

Title: As 1793 except:
'The Sixth Edition replaces' 'The Fifth Edition'
'1796' replaces '1793'

Text: Title, verso blank; Preface to the second edition [v]-viii; Advertisement to this edition (Kendal, June 21, 1796) ix, x; Tables and Articles xi, xii; Text [1]-192; Divisional title, 'Addenda' verso blank; Addenda [195]-313; Adverts. [314]-[316]

Plates: 2 engravings, as previous edition

Map: As previous editions

Addenda: As 1793 except:
'Some remarks on the Provincial Words' replaced by 'Mrs Radcliffe's description of the scenery in a ride over Skiddaw'

King's copy: Contemporary marbled calf, rebacked, original spine and leather label remounted, gilt, 16 plates bound in, as 1793. Watermarks 1795. Inscribed on free endpaper 'C.J. Francis Harwall The Friarage Penrith 27.7.06.'

Copies: K; Armitt; BL; Cornell; Jackson; Kendal; Wordsworth

13.7 ——— Seventh edition. 1799. Octavo

Title: As 1796 except:
'The Seventh Edition' replaces 'The Sixth Edition'
'1799' replaces '1796';
'W.J. and J. Richardson' replaces 'W. Richardson under the Royal Exchange'.

Text: Title, verso blank; Preface to the second edition iii-vi; Advertisement to this edition (Kendal, July 7th 1799) vii, viii; Tables and Articles ix, x; [1]-190; Divisional title, 'Addenda', [191], verso blank; Addenda 193-311; Adverts. [312]-[314]

Plates: 2 engravings as previous editions

Map: As previous editions

Addenda: As previous edition

Note: Advertisement as previous edition but reset and redated, Kendal, July 7, 1799.
No significant alterations to text.

King's copy: In contemporary half-calf, marbled boards, gilt.

Copies: K; Armitt; BL; Cornell; Jackson; Kendal; Wordsworth

13.8 ——— Eighth edition. 1802. Octavo

Title: As 1799 except:
'The Eighth Edition' replaces 'The Seventh Edition'
Imprint altered to 'Kendal, printed by William Pennington; and sold by W.J. and J. Richardson, Royal Exchange; and W. Clarke, New Bond Street - London. 1802'.

Text: Title, verso blank; Preface to the second edition [iii]-vi; Advertisement (Kendal August 22, 1802) 1 p.; Tables and Articles 1 p.; Text [1]-190; Divisional title, 'Addenda', verso blank; Addenda 193-311; Adverts. (312).

Plates: 2 engravings as previous edition, but bound in different positions in King's copy

Map: As previous edition, but 'improved and neatly coloured'

Addenda: As previous edition except:
'A Night-Piece on the Banks of Windermere, by the Rev. James Plumptre' replaces 'Description of natural curiosities in the edge of Yorkshire'

A

Guide to the Lakes:

DEDICATED TO

THE LOVERS OF LANDSCAPE STUDIES,

AND TO

ALL WHO HAVE VISITED, OR INTEND TO VISIT

THE LAKES IN

CUMBERLAND, WESTMORLAND,

AND

LANCASHIRE.

BY THE AUTHOR OF

THE ANTIQUITIES OF FURNESS.

Quis non malarum, quas amor curas habet,
Haec inter oblivifcitur?

LONDON:
Printed for RICHARDSON and URQUHART,
under the Royal Exchange,
and W. PENNINGTON, KENDAL.
1778.

13.1 188 x 110 mm.

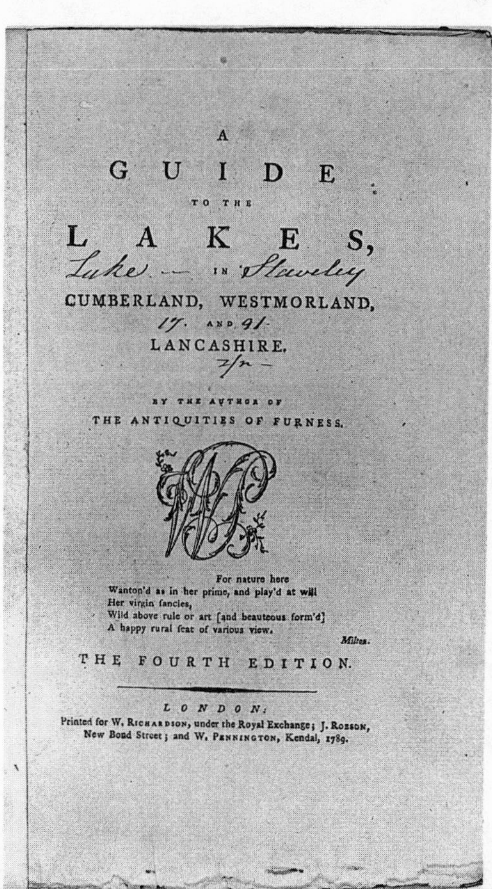

A

GUIDE

TO THE

LAKES,

IN

CUMBERLAND, WESTMORLAND,

AND

LANCASHIRE.

BY THE AUTHOR OF

THE ANTIQUITIES OF FURNESS.

For nature here
Wanton'd as in her prime, and play'd at will
Her virgin fancies,
Wild above rule or art [and beauteous form'd]
A happy rural feat of various view.
Milton.

THE FOURTH EDITION.

LONDON:
Printed for W. RICHARDSON, under the Royal Exchange; J. ROBSON,
New Bond Street; and W. PENNINGTON, Kendal, 1789.

13.4 222 x 134 mm.

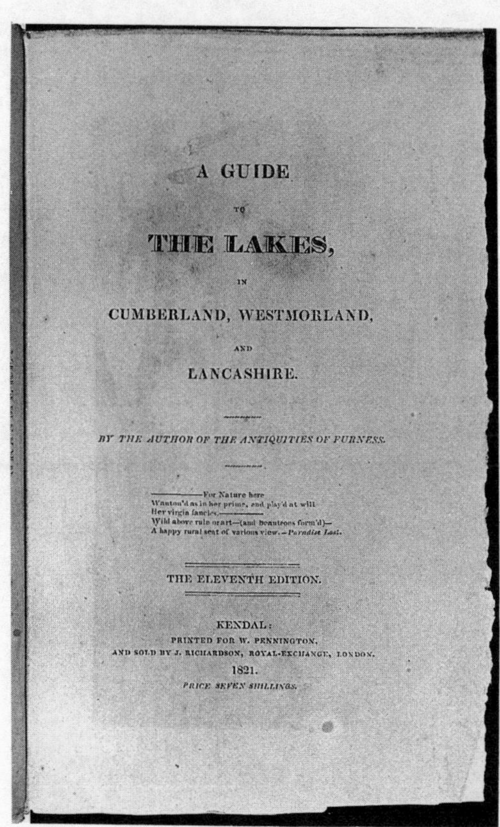

A GUIDE

TO

THE LAKES,

IN

CUMBERLAND, WESTMORLAND,

AND

LANCASHIRE.

BY THE AUTHOR OF THE ANTIQUITIES OF FURNESS.

——For Nature here
Wanton'd as in her prime, and play'd at will
Her virgin fancies,——
Wild above rule or art—(and beauteous form'd)—
A happy rural seat of various view.—*Paradise Lost.*

THE ELEVENTH EDITION.

KENDAL:
PRINTED FOR W. PENNINGTON,
AND SOLD BY J. RICHARDSON, ROYAL-EXCHANGE, LONDON.
1821.
PRICE SEVEN SHILLINGS.

13.11 215 x 135 mm.

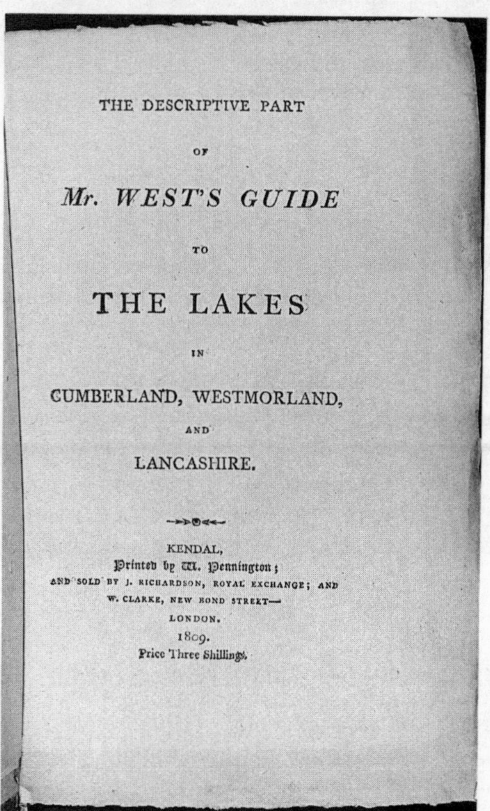

THE DESCRIPTIVE PART

OF

Mr. WEST'S GUIDE

TO

THE LAKES

IN

CUMBERLAND, WESTMORLAND,

AND

LANCASHIRE.

KENDAL,
Printed by W. Pennington;
AND SOLD BY J. RICHARDSON, ROYAL EXCHANGE; AND
W. CLARKE, NEW BOND STREET—
LONDON.
1809.
Price Three Shillings.

14.1 188 x 110 mm.

Note: The Advertisement to this edition, signed 'W.P. [W. Pennington] Kendal, August 22, 1802.' notes that 'the late ingenious Mr W. Cockin of Burton' for the first time 'wrote the Preface to the second edition of this work, and revised the whole after the death of Mr West: he also wrote all the articles marked with the letter X', viz: Preface to the second edition; notes and poems pp. 11, 29, 30, 31, 43, 62, 63, 72, 73, 74, 75, 88, 89, 124, 125, 128, 129, 130, 132, 139, 140, 148, 175, 184; Addenda, Article 8, p. 286. Cockin left the North West for Nottingham in 1784, so he was probably only responsible for editing the 2nd (1780) and 3rd (1784) editions of the *Guide.*

'Some necessary corrections made throughout the whole work.'

The following articles sold by Wm. Pennington, Kendal, and other Booksellers, are advertised p. (312):

Sixteen Views of the Lakes by Messrs. Smith and Emes (see 31)

Twenty Views of the Lakes by Mr. Farington (see 22)

Twenty Select Views of the Lakes by Mr. Holland (see 25)

Four Views of the Lakes by Mr. Walmsley, engraved by Mr. Jukes (two of these aquatints are in the King's College Collection).

Smith's Map of the Lakes (see 44)

A Map of the Lakes (as in *The Guide*)

Crosthwaite's Maps of the Lakes (see 17)

King's copy: In contemporary grey paper boards, rebacked. Uncut. Inscribed: 'Mr Goodford' (address illegible) on upper cover; 'John Goodford 1803' on title page. J.G. and crest stamped on free endpaper. 'John Goodford' on paste-down endpaper. Traces of pencil sketch on free endpaper.

Copies: K; Armitt; BL; Cornell

13.9 ——— Ninth edition. 1807. Octavo.

Title: As 1802 except:
'The Ninth Edition' replaces 'The Eighth Edition'
'1807' replaces '1802'.

Text: Title, verso blank; Preface to second edition [iii]-vi; Advertisement (Kendal 1 July 1807) 1 p.; Tables and Articles 1 p: Text [1]-190; Divisional title, 'Addenda', verso blank; Addenda [193]-311; Adverts. [312]

Plates: None

Map: Coloured as previous edition

Addenda: As previous edition

Notes: 'In this edition, such corrections and improvements are made, as have appeared necessary since the publication of the former, in order to make the whole complete.' Advertisement. Kendal, July 1, 1807.

The text is not entirely reset: to p. 55, as previous edition.

The adverts. for Farington's Twenty Views and Walmsley's Four Views are omitted.

King's copy: In original brown paper boards, rebacked. Uncut. Inscribed: 'Times Octr. 19 / 7 Ullswater Bot [illegible] John Grange' on paste-down endpaper. Label on paste-down endpaper, 'Aspern Bookseller No. 32 Cornhill'.

This uncut copy in publisher's boards contains the sixteen extra aquatints, showing that some copies were issued in this form with the extra plates.

Copies: K; Armitt; BL; Cornell; Kendal; Wordsworth

13.10 ——— Tenth edition. 1812. Octavo.

Title: As 1809 except:
'The Tenth Edition' replaes 'The Ninth Edition'
'1812' replaces '1809

Text: Title, verso blank; Preface to the second edition [iii]-vi; Advertisement (Kendal June 1 1802) 1 p.; Tables and Articles 1 p.; Text [1]-190; Divisional title, 'Addenda', verso blank; Addenda [193]-311; Adverts. [312]

Plates: None

Map: Coloured as previous editions

Addenda: As previous edition

Notes: 'Such corrections and improvements as have appeared necessary'.
The text is not entirely reset: to p. 161, as previous edition
The advertisement for Holland's Twenty Views and Crosthwaite's Maps are omitted.
Advertisement for *The Descriptive Part of West's Guide to the Lakes* is added (see 14).

King's copy: In original grey paper boards, rebacked, uncut.

Copies: K; Armitt; BL; Cornell; Kendal; Wordsworth

Ref: Upcott, p. 123

13.11 ——— Eleventh edition. Kendal: printed for W. Pennington, and sold by J. Richardson, Royal Exchange, London. 1821. Price seven shillings. Octavo.†

Text: Title, verso *Printed by J. Kilner, Market Place, Kendal;* Preface to the second edition [iii]-v; Advertisement (Kendal 1822) [vi]; Tables and Articles 1 p., verso blank; Text [1]-192; Addenda [193]-312; imprint p.312 *Printed by John Kilner, Gazette Office, Market Place, Kendal.*

Plate: Coloured aquatint (frontispiece), Grasmere; Signed: *I. Feary delint. Engraved by Rob. Havell & Son.*
Imprint: *Published as the Act Directs, April 1, 1821 by W. Pennington, Kendal*

Map: As previous edition, coloured

Addenda: As previous edition

Notes: The aquatint is from the same view of Grasmere by I. Feary as the engraved frontispiece of previous editions.
This edition has been updated by the inclusion of the coloured frontispiece and the use of a more modern type-face.

King's copy: Rebound in brown paper boards, original printed paper label mounted on spine, uncut

Copies: K; Armitt; BL; Cornell; Jackson; Wordsworth

Ref: Abbey, 193

14.1 ***The descriptive part of Mr West's Guide to the Lakes in Cumberland, Westmorland, and Lancashire.*** Kendal, Printed by W. Pennington; and sold by J. Richardson, Royal Exchange; and W. Clarke, New Bond Street, London. 1809. Price Three Shillings. Duodecimo.†

Text: Title, verso blank; Advertisement 1 p.; Table of the Lakes 1 p.; text [1]-146; Roads from Lancaster to the Lakes 147-149; Advertisement [150]

Map: As West's *Guide*, 1784 (13.3), uncoloured

Note: 'To accommodate those who wish to have a *Guide to the Lakes* in a small size, this Epitome is published. It contains the descriptive part of Mr. West's larger work, leaving out the antiquarian and historical researches, most of the notes, and the whole of the Addenda.' (Advertisement)
The text is based on the 1807 edition of the *Guide* (13.9), but is considerably abbreviated.

Advert: Lately published and sold by W. Pennington, Kendal . . .

1 The Ninth Edition of *West's Guide to the Lakes*. Price 6 shillings.

2 16 Views of the Lakes, by Messrs. Smith and Emes, engraved by Mr Alken [no. 35], price 1*l*. 1*s*.

3 Also, 20 select Views of the Lakes, by Mr. Holland, engraved by Mr. Rosenberg, price 1*l*. 6*s*. [no. 25].

4 Smith's map of the Lakes, neatly coloured, price 4*s*. Or on canvas, in a case, 6*s*. [no. 44]

5 A Map of the Lakes, neatly coloured (the same as in the Guide). Price 1*s*.

King's copy: In the original blue/grey printed paper boards, rebacked, uncut. Upper cover lettered as title-page but imprint differs. Given by Donald D. Eddy. Inscribed on paste-down endpaper 'Elizabeth Brown, Woodbridge'.

Copies: K; Armitt; BL; Cornell; Jackson; Wordsworth

14.2 ——— [Second edition]. 1813.

Title: As 1809 except:
'1813' replaces '1809'
'and T. Richardson, Kendal' replaces 'and W. Clarke, New Bond Street'.

Text: Title, verso blank; Advertisement 1 p.; Table of the Lakes 1 p.; Text [5]-150; A table of the higher mountains and lakes . . . 151, 152; Roads from Lancaster to the Lakes; Advert. [156]

Map: Folding, as 1809

Note: The adverts. are similar, but the 10th edition (1812) of West's *Guide* and not the 9th is advertised, and adverts. 2 and 3 are omitted. The table of the higher Mountains and Lakes, by Mr John Dalton, is added.

King's copy: In the original grey printed paper boards, uncut. Upper cover lettered as title-page, but imprint differs. 'West's Guide to the Lakes. Price 3*s*.' on spine. On lower cover advert. for the 11th edition of West's *Guide,* with 'a highly coloured View of Grassmere Water; Smith's map, on canvas, now 7*s*. 6*d*.; a map of the Lakes [as 5 above], and Westall's Views of the Lakes'.

As the 1821 edition of West's *Guide* is advertised on the printed cover, this copy must have been bound and issued at least eight years after the publication date, 1813.

Copies: K; Armitt; Wordsworth

1780

WILLIAM COCKIN 1736-1801

William Cockin of Burton in Kendal was a master at Lancaster Grammar School, 1764-84. He wrote poems, school texts and religious pamphlets. He was responsible for the revision and editing of the 2nd and 3rd editions of West's *Guide* (see 13.2). He died at Kendal in the house of his friend, the portrait painter, George Romney.

15.1 ***Ode to the genius of the Lakes. A poem.*** London: for the author. 1780. Octavo.

Copies: Armitt; Kendal; Wordsworth

15.2 ——— Reprinted in *The rural sabbath, a poem in four books and other poems*. London: W. Bulmer and Co., Cleveland-Row, St. James's; For G. and W. Nicol, Booksellers to His Majesty, Pall Mall; and J. Asperne, Cornhill. 1805. Octavo.

Copies: BL; Cornell; Jackson; Kendal

RICHARD JOSEPH SULIVAN died 1806

Sir Richard Sulivan, Bart, was born in Ireland. He spent some of his early life in India, was MP for New Romney, 1790, and for Seaford, 1802. Seee Mavor (38).

16.1 ***Observations made during a tour through parts of England, Scotland, and Wales in a series of letters [in 1778].*** London: Printed for T. Becket, Adelphi, Strand, Bookseller to His Royal Highness the Prince of Wales, Bishop Osnaburgh, Prince William, and Prince Edward. 1780. Quarto.

Lakes: Letters 24, 25

Note: Sulivan only made a brief tour through the Lakes on his return from Scotland. From Penrith he visited Lowther and Ullswater; then Keswick and south to Kendal by the usual route over Dunmail Raise and by Windermere. He indulges in little picturesque description of scenery, but quotes Dalton and Brown.

Copies: BL; and Cambridge University Library

Ref: Upcott, p. xxxvii

16.2 ——— *A tour through parts of England, Scotland and Wales, in 1778.* Second edition, corrected and enlarged. 2 vols. London: Printed for T. Becket, Pall-Mall, Bookseller to His Royal Highness the Prince of Wales and their Royal Highnesses the Princes. 1785. Octavo.

Copies: BL; and Cambridge University Library

Ref: Upcott, p. xxxvii

16.G ——— German translation. Leipzig: Breitkopf. 1781. Octavo.

Copy: BL

1783

PETER CROSTHWAITE 1735-1808

Peter Crosthwaite returned in 1775 to his native Vale of Keswick, after four years active service at sea in the Far East, and several years as a customs officer on the coast of Northumberland. At Keswick he opened a museum and devoted his considerable energies to exploiting the craze for travel to the Lakes in search of the picturesque, thus helping to create what he called 'this tourist business'. He described himself on his maps as 'Admiral at Keswick Regatta: who keeps the Museum at Keswick, & is Guide, Pilot, Geographer & Hydrographer to the Nobility and Gentry, who make the Tour of the Lakes'. He strongly resented competition, attacking Hutton for starting a rival museum in Keswick, and refusing to sell Clarke's maps (see 19) in his own museum, as he considered them inaccurate and misleading. He co-operated with the eccentric Joseph Pocklington in various enterprises, notably the Keswick Regatta (see Appendix 1).

17 ***Seven maps of the Lakes.*** London, published [dates] and sold by Peter Crosthwaite, the Author, at his Museum at Keswick.

1 An Accurate Map of the matchless Lake of Derwent (situate in the most delightful Vale which perhaps ever Human Eye beheld) near Keswick, Cumberland; with West's eight Stations . . . *Engraved by S. Neele* 1783, 1788, 1794, 1800, 1809, 1819.

2 Pocklington's Island. *Joseph Pocklington Invent et delineavit 1783 H. Ashby sculpsit 1783.* 1783, 1788, 1794, 1800, 1809.

3 An Accurate Map of the Grand Lake of Windermere, being the largest in England, situate in Westmorland and Lancashire. *Engraved by H. Ashby* 1783, 1788, 1794, 1800, 1809, 1819.

4 An Accurate Map of the beautiful Lake of Ulls-water, situate in Cumberland and Westmorland. *Engrav'd by H. Ashby.* 1783, 1788, 1794, 1800, 1809, 1819.

5 An Accurate Map of Broadwater or Bassenthwaite Lake near Keswick, Cumberland; with West's Four Stations . . . *Engraved by S. Neele, London* 1785, 1788, 1794, 1800, 1809, 1819.

6 An Accurate Map of Coniston Lake, near Hawkshead, Lancashire; with West's four stations . . . *J. Ellis sculp* 1788, 1794, 1800, 1809, 1819.

7 An Accurate Map of Buttermere, Crummock & Lowes-Water Lakes; Scale Force &c; . . . *Neele Sculpt. 352 Strand* 1794, 1800, 1809, 1819.

Scale: 3 in. = 1 mile, except 3, Windermere, 2 in. = 1 mile, 2, Pocklington's Island (scale not indicated).

Note: The maps show West's stations, supplemented by additional stations, depths and currents in the lakes, properties with the names of owners, and other features of interest to the tourist. The maps are surrounded by vignettes of buildings and objects such as the Bowder Stone and Pocklington's follies. The same plates were re-used for each issue. Information as to owners of property, etc., was altered on, and added to, the plate each time, including additional vignettes; and the new date added to the imprint. In 1809 the figure 1800 was altered to 1809, so there is no record on the 1809 and the 1819 prints of the 1800 issue. An earlier version of the Lake of Derwent, engraved by H. Ashby, was published in 1782 (see Appendix 1). The sets of maps were frequently sold bound without title or text.

King's copies: 1800, 1809 and 1819, each bound in contemporary quarter leather, marbled boards, leather labels. Bookplate (1819 copy): H.W. [Hugh Walpole] Brackenbury. Pencil drawing of Barrow House (?) on paste-down endpaper.
1800 copy includes *Proposals for publishing by subscription.* One loose sheet. June 1, 1783.†

Copies: K; Armitt; BL; Cornell; Jackson; Kendal; Wordsworth

——— Facsimile of 1809 edition, with introduction and notes by William Rollinson. Newcastle upon Tyne. 1968.

17a ——— Reprint of maps with text. Anonymous. *The Lake District sixty years ago.* Kendal: Titus Wilson. 1863.

Copies: Cornell; Jackson; Wordsworth

1786

WILLIAM GILPIN 1724-1804

The Revd William Gilpin, born at Scaleby near Carlisle, was the son of the talented amateur artist, Bernard Gilpin, and elder brother of Sawrey, the animal painter. At home he was associated with Dr John Brown and the group in the north of England that were discovering the picturesque charms of the Lake District, and in the south with Gray and Mason and their intellectual circle. He was a dedicated traveller in search of the picturesque. Between 1769 and 1774 he made a series of tours which he recorded in journals and sketches, subsequently published as *Observations relative chiefly to picturesque beauty.* He was the first to write on the theory of the picturesque. See William D. Templeman, *The life and work of William Gilpin* (Urbana, Illinois, 1939) and Carl Paul Barbier, *William Gilpin* (Oxford, 1963). See (25).

18.1 ***Observations, relative chiefly to picturesque beauty, made in the year 1772, on several parts of England; particularly the mountains, and lakes of Cumberland, and Westmoreland.*** 2 vols. London: Printed for R. Blamire, Strand. 1786. Octavo.†

Text: Vol. 1 Half title, verso blank; Title, verso blank; Dedication [i]-iii; blank; Preface [v]-xxxi; blank; Table of Contents to vol. 1 and vol. 2 [i]-xvi; Explanation of the prints [i]-vii, blank; Text[1]-230.

Vol.2 Half title, verso blank; Title, verso blank; Text [1]-268, last page dated July 3, 1772; Explanation of the prints vol. 1 & vol. 2 ix-xiv; Errata xv, xvi [placing of table of contents, explanation of prints, etc., varies in different copies].

Plates: No titles, signatures or imprints on plates. (Oval sepia-tinted aquatints unless otherwise noted)

Vol. I 15 plates.

1 [Warwick Castle]
2 [Tuscan Vases] (untinted aquatint)
3 [Mountain Shapes] (etching)
4 [Lake]
5 [Lake and Ruin]
6 [Valley]
7 [Effect of light]
8 Windermere (plan, coloured etching)
9 [Windermere]
10 [Furness-abbey]
11 [Wild Country]
12 Keswick Lake (plan, coloured etching)
13 [Rocky Scenery]
14 [Borrodale]
15 [Gatesgarth Dale]

Vol. II 15 plates. From drawings by Sawrey Gilpin:

16 [Vale]
17 Ulleswater (plan, coloured etching)
18 [Ulleswater]
19 [Dacre-Castle]
20 [Scaleby-Castle]
21 [Two Views] (tinted soft-ground etching)
22 [Matlock]
23 [Dovedale]
24 [Landscape in Leicestershire]
25 [Horse and Cow] (tinted aquatint)
26 [Bull and Cow] (tinted aquatint)
27 [Larger Cattle]
28 [Larger Cattle]
29 [Smaller Animals]
30 [Smaller Animals]

King's copy: Bound in contemporary tree calf, leather labels, gilt

Note: Gilpin's tour of the lakes was made in 1772, when he spent less than a week in the district, visiting Windermere, taking the high road to Keswick, where he made expeditions to Borrowdale, Watendlath and Buttermere, and returning by Ullswater and Lowther. The drawings and manuscript were completed by 1774. Bound in eight volumes (in the Bodleian Library), they were widely circulated privately before the publication of the book in 1786. The published work consists largely of picturesque theory, and is neither a journal nor a guide. The illustrations, engraved in the first edition by John 'Warwick' Smith, Sawrey Gilpin and William Sawrey Gilpin, from sketches by William and his brother Sawrey, are mostly oval sepia-tinted aquatints. In later editions the plates were re-engraved by various artists. It is the first Lake District book to be illustrated with aquatints. It was widely read and had an important influence on the way people looked at, portrayed and described the Lake District.

Copies: K; BL; Cornell; Jackson; Kendal; Wordsworth

Ref: Abbey, 183; Upcott, p. 124

——— Facsimile edition. Introduction by Sutherland Lyall. The Richmond Publishing Co. Ltd, (1973). 2 vols. in one.

18.2 ——— Second edition. 2 vols. 1788. Plates re-engraved.

Copies: BL; Cornell; Jackson

Ref: Upcott, p.124

June 1, 1783.

PROPOSALS

For Publiſhing by Subſcription

Four moſt accurate Plans, with Ornaments, Deſcriptions, &c. of the grand Lakes of *Windermere*, *Ulls-water*, *Derwent*, and *Pocklington's Iſland*,

Situate in Lancaſhire, Cumberland, and Weſtmorland.

THOSE three Lakes are the principal which the Nobility and Gentry take in the Northern Tour; they will be engraven by a Capital Hand; were ſurveyed by P. CROSTHWAITE, formerly Naval Commander in the Eaſt Indies; who now keeps the Muſeum at Keſwick, and in that Quarter acts the Part of Guide, Pilot, Geographer, &c. to Touriſts. He takes no Money till the Plans are delivered, which will be in the Courſe of the enſuing Month. The Four Plans, with their Ornaments, Deſcriptions, &c. will amount to no more than 5 s. 6 d. although on four large Half-ſheets. This Work has met with the greateſt Encouragement from a vaſt Number of the Nobility and Gentry, who have already ſeen it, being looked on as Patriotic, &c. And he begs the Noblemen, Ladies, and Gentlemen, who pleaſe to honour him with their Subſcriptions, will ſend their Names and Places of Reſidence as ſoon as poſſible, to Mr. *Hodgſon*, Stationer, No. 425, *Strand*; Mr. *Robinſon*, Bookſeller, *Pater-noſter-row*; Mr. *Flexney*, Bookſeller, No. 319, *Holborn*; Mr. *Stockdale*, Bookſeller, oppoſite *Burlington Houſe*; or Mr. *Faulder*, Bookſeller, No. 42, *New Bond Street*; and their Favours ſhall be moſt thankfully acknowledged, by their very humble and obedient Servant,

PETER CROSTHWAITE.

A well intended Plan,
To draw the noble Touriſts down,
And ſpend their Wealth at Home.

17 228 x 140 mm.

OBSERVATIONS,

RELATIVE CHIEFLY TO

PICTURESQUE BEAUTY,

Made in the YEAR 1772,

On ſeveral PARTS of ENGLAND;

PARTICULARLY THE

MOUNTAINS, AND LAKES

OF

CUMBERLAND, AND WESTMORELAND.

VOL. I.

By WILLIAM GILPIN, M. A.
PREBENDARY OF SALISBURY;
AND
VICAR OF BOLDRE, IN NEW-FOREST, NEAR LYMINGTON.

LONDON;
PRINTED FOR R. BLAMIRE, STRAND.
M.DCC.LXXXVI.

18.1 240 x 145 mm.

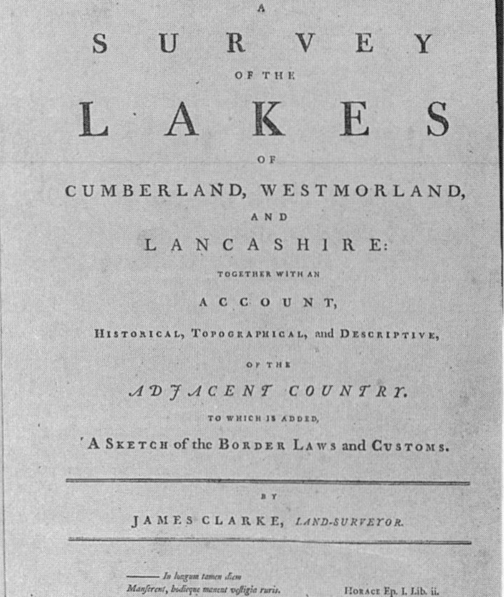

A

SURVEY

OF THE

LAKES

OF

CUMBERLAND, WESTMORLAND,

AND

LANCASHIRE:

TOGETHER WITH AN

ACCOUNT,

HISTORICAL, TOPOGRAPHICAL, and DESCRIPTIVE,

OF THE

ADJACENT COUNTRY.

TO WHICH IS ADDED,

A SKETCH of the BORDER LAWS and CUSTOMS.

BY

JAMES CLARKE, *LAND-SURVEYOR.*

——— *In longum tamen diem*
Manſerent, hodieque manent veſtigia ruris. HORACE Ep. I. Lib. ii.

LONDON:

Printed for the Author, and ſold by him at *Penrith, Cumberland*; alſo by J. ROBSON, and J. FAULDER, New Bond-Street; P. W. FORES, No. 3, Piccadilly; the Engraver, S. J. NEELE, 352, Strand, *London*.—L. BULL and J. MARSHALL, *Bath*; ROSE and DRURY, *Lincoln*; TODD, Stonegate, *York*, WARE and SON, *Whitehaven*; C. ELLIOT, *Edinburgh*; and moſt other Bookſellers in the Kingdom.

M.DCC.LXXXVII.

[*Entered in Stationers-Hall, according to Act of Parliament.*]

19.1 403 x 250 mm.

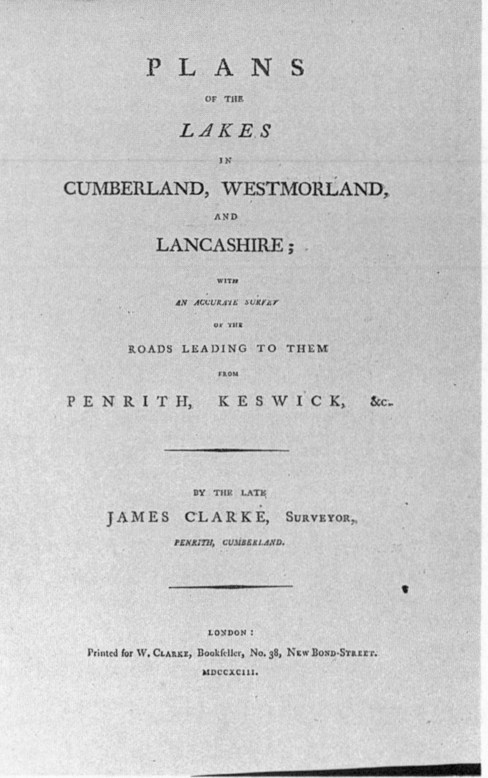

PLANS

OF THE

LAKES

IN

CUMBERLAND, WESTMORLAND,

AND

LANCASHIRE;

WITH

AN ACCURATE SURVEY

OF THE

ROADS LEADING TO THEM

FROM

PENRITH, KESWICK, &c.

BY THE LATE

JAMES CLARKE, SURVEYOR,

PENRITH, CUMBERLAND.

LONDON:

Printed for W. CLARKE, Bookſeller, No. 38, NEW BOND-STREET.

MDCCXCIII.

19.3 285 x 220 mm.

18.3 ——— Third edition. 2 vols. 1792. Plates re-engraved. Octavo.

'Copies of the edition of 1792 were taken off in small quarto.' (Upcott, p.124)

Copies: Armitt (vol.2 only); BL; Cornell; Kendal

Ref: Upcott, p.124

18.4 ——— [Fourth edition], erroneously called 'the third'. 2 vols. London: T. Cadell and W. Davies. 1808. Octavo. Plates revised.

Copies: Armitt; Cornell; Kendal

Ref: Abbey, 187; Upcott, p.124

18F ——— *Voyage en différentes parties de l'Angleterre . . . et particulièrement dans les montagnes et sur les lacs du Cumberland & du Westmoreland . . .*

Translated from the third edition by M. Guédon de Berchere. 2 vols. Paris: Defer de Maisonneuve. Londres: Blamire, 1789. Octavo. Engravings (not aquatints), plans. Prix, 12 liv. les deux Vol. brochés (paper-bound) [actually translated from 2nd not 3rd edition].

Copies: Cornell; and PB

A second edition of this translation was published in Paris in 1797. (Templeman, p.302). Another edition, *Observations pittoresque sur différentes parties*——— Translated by le Baron **** [Beaulieu]. Templeman (p.305) refers to a German translation by G.F. Kunth (Leipzig, preface dated 1798).

1787

JAMES CLARKE

James Clarke, a land surveyor resident in Penrith, was profitably employed by landowners in the Penrith, Derwentwater, Bassenthwaite area in the 1760s and 1770s. In 1783 he acquired the Griffin and White Swan inns in Penrith, which brought him into close contact with tourists. In 1784 and 1786-7 he made excursions to the Lakes to collect material for *A Survey*.

19.1 ***A survey of the Lakes of Cumberland, Westmorland, and Lancashire: together with an account, historical, topographical, and descriptive, of the adjacent country*** . . . London: Printed for the Author, and sold by him at Penrith, Cumberland; also by J. Robson, and J. Faulder, New Bond-Street; P.W. Fores, No 3 Piccadilly; the Engraver, S.J. Neele, 352, Strand, London. L. Bull and J. Marshall, Bath; Rose and Drury, Lincoln; Todd, Stonegate, York, Ware and Son, Whitehaven; C. Elliot, Edinburgh; and most other Booksellers in the Kingdom. 1787. Folio.†

Text: Title, verso blank; Dedication, verso blank; Introduction [i]-xlii; Divisional Title, 'Book first'; Contents, Book 1; Text [3]-42; Divisional Title, 'Book second'; Contents, Book 2; Text [45]-87; Divisional, Title 'Book third'; verso blank, Contents; Book 3; Text [91]-102; Divisional Title, 'Book fourth'; Contents; Book 4; Text [105]-154; The Border History [155]-188; Appendix 189-193; Errata [194]

Plates: 2 engraved plates, not numbered
Diagram of view from Penrith Beacon, folding, plate size 440 × 260 mm.
Silver 'Fibula'. 1787

Maps: 1 A Map of the Town of Penrith and the Country Adjacent. 495 × 685 mm
2 A Map of the Town of Penrith in the County of Cumberland. 495 × 610mm

3 A Map of the roads between Penrith and Ullswater. 495 x 902 mm
4 A Map of the Lake of Ullswater and its Environs (not folded)
5 A Map of the Roads, Waters etc. Between Penrith and Keswick. 482 × 927 mm
6 A Map of Derwentwater and its Environs (not folded)
7 A Map of the Roads etc. between Keswick and Broadwater. 660 × 863 mm
8 A Map of Broadwater and its Environs. 490 × 890 mm
9 A Map of Roads, Lakes etc. between Keswick and Ambleside. 495 × 895 mm
10 A Map of the Northern Part of the Lake of Windermere and its Environs. 495 × 130 mm
11 A Map of the Southern Part of the Lake Windermere and its Environs. 490 × 1042 mm

Engraved, folding (except map 4) maps, with plate number in right upper corner. Scales vary. Each plate has an ornamental title, some of which include views; all vary; all include the words 'Surveyed by James Clarke', and in various forms the information 'Engraved by Samuel John Neele, 352 Strand, London.' Imprint on each plate (except 1 and 9) *Published Feby. 10th. 1781 by James Clarke, Penrith* (exact wording varies).

King's copy: Rebound, original leather label mounted on spine. This is not a true first issue of the first edition, as pp. 127, 180 and 181, misnumbered in the first edition, have been corrected. The Errata have not been corrected.

Note: Clarke's large-scale maps were intended for the guidance of tourists. 'The business of the following plans is to conduct the stranger to those places which furnish the views and landscapes of different kinds in the neighbourhood of the Lakes and with the tastes of the times' (Introduction, p. xxxv). They cover the routes from Penrith to Ullswater and Keswick, and from Keswick to Ambleside, with plans for the lakes of Ullswater, Derwentwater, Bassenthwaite, Thirlmere, Rydal and Windermere. The mountains are hardly indicated. The text is full of lively anecdote, but relies for descriptions of scenery on quotations from Clarke's predecessors, though he is highly critical of Gilpin and the other picturesque writers. Peter Crosthwaite's (see 17) copy of Clarke's *Survey* (Barrow Public Library) is extensively annotated with bitterly critical allegations of lies, inventions, distortions and inaccuracies.

Copies: K; BL; Cornell; Jackson; Kendal

Ref: Upcott, pp. 121-3

19.2 ——— Second edition. London: for the author. 1789. Folio. Text and maps reissued, title reset.

King's copy: In half Russia, patterned paper boards, leather label, is not a true second edition. Pages misnumbered: 2 for 22, 126 for 127, 182, 183, for 180, 181. Errata not corrected. 'Some copies have a reprinted title-page 1789, purporting to be a second edition, but containing no alteration other than page number corrections' (Upcott, note p. 122).

Copies: K; Armitt; BL; Jackson; Kendal; Wordsworth

19.3 ——— ***Plans of the Lakes . . . with an accurate survey of the roads leading to them from Penrith, Keswick, &c.*** by the late James Clarke, Surveyor, Penrith, Cumberland. London: Printed for W. Clarke, Bookseller, No. 38, New Bond Street. 1793. Quarto.†

New Title, with list of plans on verso; 11 folding maps as 19.1; engraved diagram of the Prospect from Penrith Beacon. No text.

King's copy: In contemporary tree calf, gilt rebacked, uncut

Note: This issue of Clarke's plans was advertised in the 5th edition of West's *Guide*, 1789, as 'Plans of the Lakes by James Clarke, in a Portable Quarto Volume. Sold for his widow'; and by W. Clarke in Plumptre's *The Lakers*, 1798, as 'Clarke's *Plans* published as a portable quarto (to be carried around on the tour), 123 . . . and with 16 Views 1*s.* 6*d.*'

According to Upcott (pp. 127-9), 'Warwick' Smith's *Views of the Lakes* (32) were 'usually bound up with' and Farington's *Views of the Lakes* (22) were 'occasionally bound with' Clarke's *Survey*. Upcott gives page references in both cases. As only one copy of the *Survey* bound with Farington's views and none with Smith's have been seen or recorded, and both sets of engravings were published after the book, it appears that Upcott misinterpreted the publicity of the publisher, W. Clarke, who advertised Farington's and Smith's views together with the *Survey*. ('A Survey of the Lakes, etc . . . one vol. fol. price one guinea; the same plus 20 views, 6*l*').

Copies: K; Jackson

1788

THOMAS NEWTE

There is some confusion over the identity of Thomas Newte, as S.A. Allibone in *A critical dictionary of British and American authors* (London and Philadelphia, 1870) quotes a Dr Parr who says, 'Newte's Tour is a work replete with profound research and useful information. It was written by Dr. Wm. Thompson.' It has been suggested that this was William Thomson, the translator of Cunningham's *History of England, 1688-1714*, a book which was extensively quoted in Newte's *Tour*. However there is little doubt that it was written by Thomas Newte of Tiverton, whose name appears on the title-page of the second edition and who signed the dedication.

20.1 ***A tour in England and Scotland, in 1785. By an English Gentleman.*** London: Printed for G.G.J. and J. Robinson, Pater-Noster-Row. 1788. Octavo.†

Text: Half-title, verso blank; Title, verso blank; Itinerary [iii]-x; Text [1]-367

Plates: 6 engravings

1. Ulswater, A Lake in Cumberland, Signed *G. Barret R.A. Pinxit. Heath Sculp.* Imprint: *Published as the Act directs June 2d. 1778 by C. Robson & Partners.* Only Lake District view.

Lakes: pp. 51-69

Itinerary: Kendal, Windermere, Esthwaite, Coniston, Low Wood, Keswick, ride up Skiddaw, Ullswater, Penrith, Carlisle. 9-19 June 1785.

King's copy: In contemporary calf, leather labels, gilt. Book plate: 'Pro Rege et Patria'.

Copies: K; Armitt; BL

20.2 ***Prospects and observations; on a tour in England and Scotland: natural, oeconomical, and literary. By Thomas Newte, Esq.*** [Second edition of *A tour in England and Scotland*, 20.1] London: printed for G.G.J. and J. Robinson, Paternoster Row. 1791. Quarto.†

Text: Title, verso blank; Dedication (T. Newte, Tiverton, Devon. June 1, 1791) [iii], iv; Advert. [v]; Errata and Directions to the Book Binder [vi]; Contents [vii], viii; Text [1]-437; blank 438; Appendix 439, 440.

Plates: 24 engravings. Plate 1. Uls Water as pl. 1 previous edition

Lakes: pp. 37-46, unaltered from previous edition
Reprinted in Mavor's *British Tourists* (1798) and subsequent editions (38).

King's copy: Mottled calf, gilt, rebacked, original leather label mounted on spine

Copies: K; BL; Cornell

Ref: Upcott, p. xxxvii

STEBBING SHAW 1762-1802

The Revd Stebbing Shaw, F.S.A., Fellow of Queens' College, Cambridge, author and topographer, edited and contributed to *The Topographer* 1789-91.

21 ***A tour in 1787 . . . including excursions to the Lakes of Westmorland and Cumberland***. . . . [Anonymous] London: Printed for L. Davis, Holborn; Messrs. Robson and Clarke, New Bond Street; W. Lowndes, Fleet Street; H. Gardner, Strand; and J. Walker, Paternoster-Row. n.d. (1788) Duodecimo.†

Text: Title, verso blank; Preface [i]-ix; blank; Text [1]-303; Errata [304].

Lakes: p. 64 ff.

Itinerary: Across the Sands; Ulverston; Coniston; Esthwaite; Windermere; Ullswater; Rydal; Grasmere; Leatheswater; Derwentwater; Buttermere; Loweswater; Ennerdale; Bassenthwaite

King's copy: In contemporary calf, rebacked. Book plate: Holland House. Inscribed on free endpaper, 'Elizabeth Vernon given to her by the Marquis of Lansdown 1792'

Note: Shaw made his tour while acting as tutor to the 17-year-old (Sir) Francis Burdett. He made extensive use of West's *Guide*, conscientiously visiting West's 'stations' and often commenting critically. He refers *inter alia*, to Young, Hutchinson, Gray, Gilpin, Pocklington, and Crosthwaite.

Copies: K; Armitt; BL; Cornell

1789

JOSEPH FARINGTON (artist) 1747-1821

Joseph Farington, topographical artist and diarist, was born at Leigh in Lancashire where his father was vicar. He spent much time in the Lake District. At the age of sixteen he became a pupil of Richard Wilson (1714-82); he was one of the first students at the Royal Academy; exhibited there 1778-1813, was elected an A.R.A. in 1783 and R.A. in 1785. In 1775 he returned to the North and worked in the Lakes continuously until 1781. In 1777 he was sketching there with his patron and friend, Sir George Beaumont (1753-1827) and the artist, Thomas Hearne (1744-1817). Farington was the first artist systematically to record the scenery of the Lake District with a view to publishing prints. His twenty *Views of the Lakes* (1789) was the earliest of the many drawing-room-table books of Lake District views. In 1790 he compiled an album of drawings as illustrations for Gray's *Journal* (10) (now in the Yale Center for British Art). From 1793 until his death in 1821 he kept the diary which is one of the principal sources of information about the arts and artists during those years. (See (86), (87)).

22 ***Views of the lakes, &c. in Cumberland and Westmorland. Engraved from drawings made by Joseph Farington, R.A.*** Published by William Byrne, London, 1789. Oblong Folio.†

Text: Title, verso blank; text i-xx (one page of letterpress, in English and French, after each plate)

Plates: 20 engravings, plate size 260 × 365mm

1 Derwentwater, and the Vale of Keswick from Ashness; Bassenthwaite Lake in the distance. *1 Decr. 1784*
2 The Grange, in Borrowdale. *1 Decr. 1784*
3 Derwentwater and Skiddaw. *15 April 1785*
4 Lowdore Waterfall, from Brandelow Woods. *15 April 1785*

5 Grasmere. *1 Feb. 1785*
6 Rydal Mere. *1 March 1785*
7 The upper end of Ulswater. *1 Jany. 1787*
8 The lower end of Ulswater. *1 Jany. 1787*
9 North Entrance to Keswick. *2 April 1787*
10 Brathay Bridge near Ambleside. *15 March 1787*
11 The Palace of Patterdale. *1 Jany. 1788*
12 Patterdale from Martindale Fell. *1 Jany. 1788*
13 The Lower Waterfall at Rydal. *15 Jany. 1788*
14 View of Windermere, from Gill-Head. *15 Jany. 1788*
15 View from Rydal, looking towards Windermere. *1st May 1789*
16 View of Ambleside. *1 Jany. 1789*
17 West view across Windermere, looking over the Great Island. From the Hill above the Ferry House. *1 April 1789*
18 View looking down Windermere. Taken above Rarig. *1 Jany. 1789*
19 View looking down Windermere. *1 April 1789*
20 View of the Bridge, and part of the Village of Rydal. *15 May 1789*

Imprints: Published as the Act directs, (date), *by W. Byrne, (or Wm Byrne) No. 79 Titchfield Str. London.*

Signatures: *Drawn by Josh. Farington.* Plates 1-6
Drawn by Josh Farington R.A. Plates 7-20
Engraved by W. Byrne & T. Medland. Plates 1, 2, 4, 7-10, 12, 19
Engraved by B.T. Pouncy. Plates 3, 5, 6, 13, 15
The Figures engraved by J. Heth. The Landscape by W. Byrne & J. Landseer. Plate 11
Engraved by T. Medland. Plates 14, 16
Engraved by W. Byrne & J. Landseer. Plates 17, 18, 20

King's copy: In two volumes in contemporary half black morocco, marbled boards, repaired, original red leather labels on spines, black leather labels on upper covers, lettered 'Hon: Genl. Harcourt' (General William Harcourt 1743-1830, governor of the Military College at High Wycombe, 1802; later Field Marshal and 3rd Earl of Harcourt. Acquaintance of Farington. Married Mary (*neé* Danby), amateur artist, pupil and admirer of Alexander Cozens. Harcourt took a keen interest in the teaching of drawing and the appointment of drawing-masters at the College.)

Watermarks: Title-page 'S. Lay'; Text 'G.R. and Taylor'.

Notes: The plates are those advertised in the fourth edition of West's *Guide* (1789) (13.4), pp. x, xi. See 19.1, note. The plates were also issued as proofs without letters in the etched state before engraving. Such proofs of plates 1, 4 and 9 have been tipped into the King's copy.

Originally published in parts. First 6 plates published separately, 1786. First 14 published separately, 1789. (Copy: Armitt)

Farington asked William Cookson, Wordsworth's maternal uncle, in 1783 to write the letter-press for the plates, and presumably the descriptions are his.

Copies: K; Armitt; BL; Cornell; Jackson; Wordsworth

Ref: Upcott, pp. 128, 129

——— Facsimile edition limited to 200 copies was published by The Reminder Press of Lower Brook Street, Ulverston, Cumbria (December 1977).

VIEWS of the LAKES, &c.

IN

CUMBERLAND AND WESTMORLAND.

ENGRAVED FROM DRAWINGS MADE BY

JOSEPH FARINGTON, *R. A.*

PUBLISHED BY WILLIAM BYRNE, LONDON, MDCCLXXXIX.

22 420 x 545 mm.

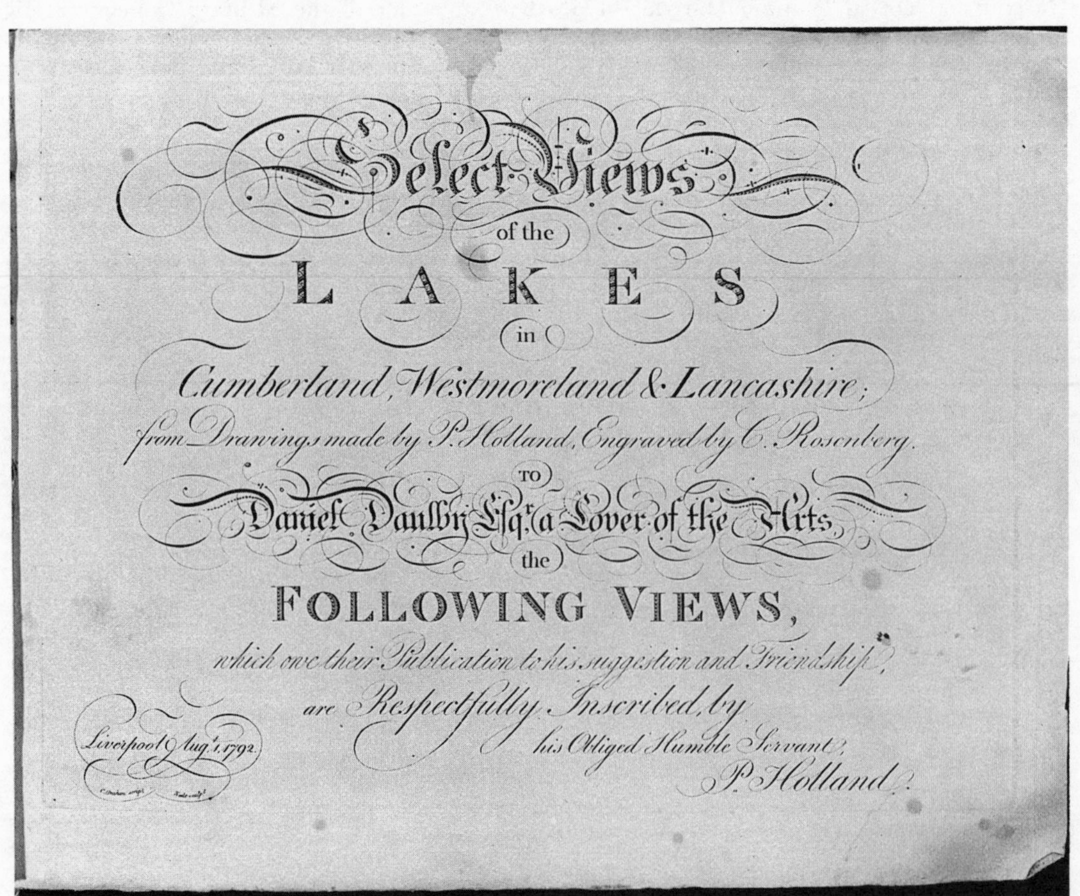

Select Views
of the
LAKES
in
Cumberland, Westmoreland & Lancashire;
from Drawings made by P. Holland, Engraved by C. Rosenberg.
TO
Daniel Daulby Esq.r a Lover of the Arts,
the
FOLLOWING VIEWS,
which owe their Publication to his suggestion and Friendship,
are Respectfully Inscribed, by
his Obliged Humble Servant,
P. Holland.
Liverpool Aug.t 1, 1792.

25 200 x 268 mm.

WILLIAM GILPIN 1724-1804

See 18

23.1 ***Observations, relative chiefly to picturesque beauty, made in the year 1776, on several parts of Great Britain; particularly the High-lands of Scotland.*** 2 vols. London: Printed for R. Blamire, Strand. 1789. Octavo.

Text: Vol. 1 Title, verso, blank; Dedication (Vicar's Hill April 20 1799) [iii]-vii; blank; Contents [i]-xi; blank; Text [1]-221
Vol. 2 Title, verso blank; Text [1]-196; Account of the prints [i]-xii; Translations, Errata, note [xiii]-[xxi]

Plates: 40 (34 sepia aquatints; 5 plans of lakes, etched and coloured; 1 diagram, etched)

Vol. 2, plate 38 [View from the Ray], oval sepia aquatint from a drawing by Gilpin. The only Lake District view: it shows Skiddaw.

Lakes: Vol. 2, pp. 147-72

King's copy: In contemporary half calf, marbled boards, gilt, leather labels

Note: Gilpin returned south from Scotland in 1776 by way of Carlisle, Cockermouth, by Bassenthwaite to Keswick, where for the first time he made a circuit of Derwentwater. His observations are, as before, largely devoted to picturesque theory rather than topographical description.

Copies: K; BL

——— Facsimile edition. Introduction by Sutherland Lyall. Richmond Publishing Co. Ltd (1973). 2 vols in one.

23.2 ——— Second edition. 1792. Plates re-engraved.

Copy: BL

23.3 ——— Third edition. London: Cadell and Davies. 1808. Plates re-engraved.

Copies: Armitt; BL

Ref: Abbey, no. 487

Note: Templeman (see 18F) refers to a French edition, translated by le Baron de B*** (Breslau, 1801) and a German edition, translated by G.F. Kunth, Leipzig (between 1799 and 1801).

1792

ADAM WALKER *c.* 1731-1821

Adam Walker, born in Patterdale, Ullswater, author and inventor, became a travelling lecturer on physics and 'Experimental Philosophy'. He settled in London, and was employed at Eton and Winchester Colleges.

24.1 ***A Tour from London to the Lakes: containing natural, oeconomical, and literary observations, made in the Summer of 1791. By a Gentleman.*** London: Printed and sold by John Abraham, at his Circulating Library, Lombard-Street. 1792. Duodecimo.†

The book consists of 21 letters, dated July 13-Sept. 1, 1791.

Text: Title, verso blank; Text [1]-117; Adverts. 117, 118.

Itinerary: Lancaster, by the Sands to Ulverston, Furness Abbey, Coniston, Bowness, Ambleside, by Kirkston Pass to Ullswater, Keswick, ascent of Skiddaw, Thirlmere, Grasmere, Rydal, Kendal, Lancaster, 8 August-1 September.

King's copy: In contemporary half leather, marbled boards, rebacked, original leather label mounted on spine. Inscribed on title page A.L.

Copies: K; Armitt; BL; Cornell; Jackson

24.2 ————*Remarks made in a Tour from London to the Lakes of Westmoreland and Cumberland, in the Summer of 1791, originally published in the Whitehall Evening Post and now reprinted with additions and corrections. . . By A Walker. . .* London: printed for G. Nicol, bookseller to his Majesty, Pall-Mall; and C. Dilly in the Poultry. 1792. Octavo.† Second edition of previous item, 24.1

Text: Half-title, verso blank; Title, verso blank; Advertisement (H. Walker George Street Hanover Square, June 14, 1792) 3 pp., blank; Text [1]-114; Divisional title, 'Travelling Remarks', verso blank; Text [117]-251.

Notes: The text is the same as the first edition except for minor alterations.

The numbers of the Letters have been corrected, and the titles of the Letters altered. '1791' is omitted from all Letters; Letter 11, 'Bowness' not 'Ulverstone'; Letter 12, 'Ambleside' added: Letter 13, 'Ambleside' not 'Ulverstone': Letter 14, 'Keswick, August 19' not 'Ulverstone August 18, 1791': Letter 19, 'Ambleside' not 'Keswick'; 'Good Night' omitted from end of Letter 19; 'Keswick' not 'Armathwaite' first word of Letter 18.

King's copy: Contemporary marbled boards, rebacked, paper spine, uncut.

Copies K; Armitt; Cornell; Wordsworth

PETER HOLLAND (artist)

Peter Holland was a Liverpool artist about whom little is known. He exhibited 1781-93. He visited Ambleside in 1797, and his *Select Views* are dedicated to Daniel Daulby Esq. of Rydal Mount.

25 ***Select views of the Lakes in Cumberland, Westmoreland & Lancashire: from drawings made by P. Holland, engraved by C. Rosenberg. . .*** Liverpool. 1792. Oblong Quarto.†

Text: Engraved title, *Liverpool Augt. 1, 1792. G. Graham script. Neale sculpt;* 21 pages, rectos blank (one page of text to each plate).

Plates: 21 aquatints. All signed *P. Holland delt. C. Rosenberg fect.* Imprint: *Published as the Act directs by P. Holland. Augst. 1st. 1792*

1 Bowdar Stone in Borodale [title and signature depicted as carved on the stone]
2 The Eagle Crag in Borrowdale
3 The Grange in Borrowdale
4 Keswick Lake from Brow Top
5 Skiddaw
6 Lodoar Waterfall
7 The Vale of Newlands
8 The Village and Upper Lake of Buttermere
9 Cromac Water
10 Ullswater from Gobarrow Park
11 Ullswater from Lyulphs Tower

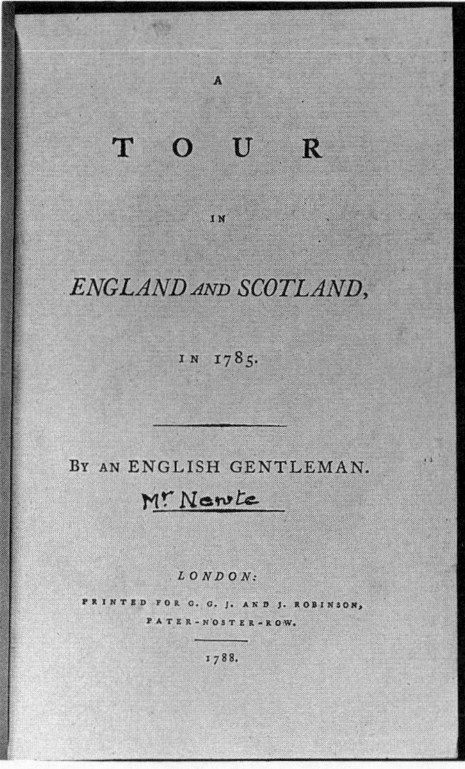

A

TOUR

IN

ENGLAND AND SCOTLAND,

IN 1785.

BY AN ENGLISH GENTLEMAN.

Mr Newte

LONDON:

PRINTED FOR G. G. J. AND J. ROBINSON, PATER-NOSTER-ROW.

1788.

20.1 207 x 130 mm.

PROSPECTS AND OBSERVATIONS;

ON A

TOUR

IN

ENGLAND AND SCOTLAND:

NATURAL, ŒCONOMICAL, AND LITERARY.

BY THOMAS NEWTE, ESQ.

LONDON:

PRINTED FOR G. G. J. AND J. ROBINSON, PATERNOSTER-ROW.

1791.

20.2 265 x 205 mm.

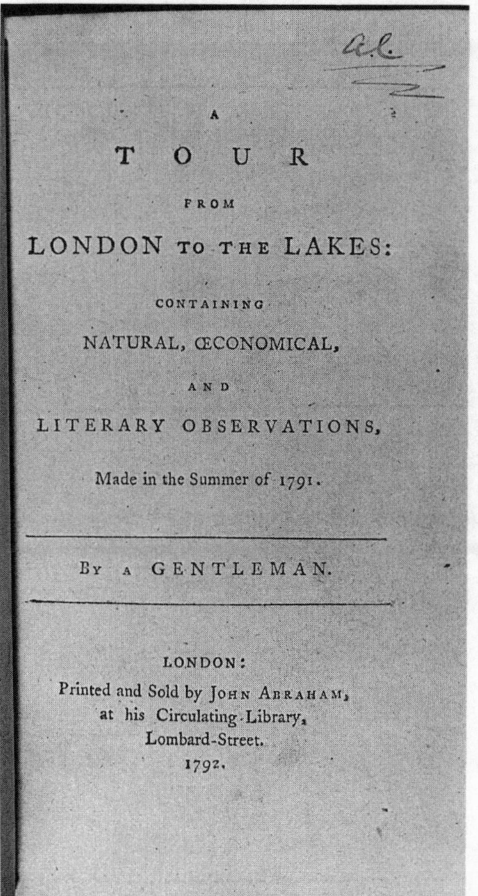

A

TOUR

FROM

LONDON TO THE LAKES:

CONTAINING

NATURAL, ŒCONOMICAL,

AND

LITERARY OBSERVATIONS,

Made in the Summer of 1791.

BY A GENTLEMAN.

LONDON:

Printed and Sold by JOHN ABRAHAM, at his Circulating-Library, Lombard-Street.

1792.

24.1 165 x 94 mm.

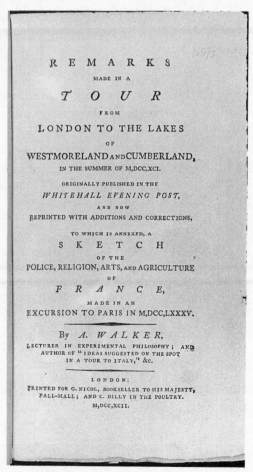

REMARKS

MADE IN A

TOUR

FROM

LONDON TO THE LAKES

OF

WESTMORELAND AND CUMBERLAND,

IN THE SUMMER OF M,DCC,XCI.

ORIGINALLY PUBLISHED IN THE

WHITEHALL EVENING POST,

AND NOW

REPRINTED WITH ADDITIONS AND CORRECTIONS,

TO WHICH IS ANNEXED, A

SKETCH

OF THE

POLICE, RELIGION, ARTS, AND AGRICULTURE

OF

FRANCE,

MADE IN AN

EXCURSION TO PARIS IN M,DCC,LXXXV.

By *A. WALKER,*

LECTURER IN EXPERIMENTAL PHILOSOPHY; AND AUTHOR OF "IDEAS SUGGESTED ON THE SPOT IN A TOUR TO ITALY," &c.

LONDON:

PRINTED FOR G. NICOL, BOOKSELLER TO HIS MAJESTY, PALL-MALL; AND C. DILLY IN THE POULTRY.

M,DCC,XCII.

24.2 226 x 135 mm.

12 Ullswater from Patterdale
13 Wythburn Water
14 Grassmere from near Dunmail Raise
15 Grassmere
16 Rydalmere
17 The Lower Waterfall at Rydal
18 Coniston from Water Head
19 View of the Parsonage House and the Ferry at Windermere
20 View looking up Windermere, Taken near Bowness
21 View looking down Windermere, Taken from an Eminence near Troutbeck

King's copy: In half calf, rebacked, original marbled boards, and leather label on upper cover. Coloured probably after issue. It is doubtful if coloured copies were issued.

Note: This is the first book of Lake District views in aquatint (the aquatints in Gilpin's *Observations* (18), 1786, are illustrations of the text rather than views). Haweswater and Bassenthwaite, and the less frequently visited western lakes, Wastwater and Ennerdale, were not included.

Copies: K; Armitt; Cornell; Jackson; Wordsworth (all uncoloured)

25a ——— Another issue. As previous issue except the engraved title is replaced with a printed title, with the imprint *Liverpool. Printed by James Smith for John Peelin, King Street.* n.d.

Copies: Armitt (2 copies, both uncoloured)

JOSEPH BUDWORTH 1756-1815

Joseph Budworth, Captain in the Royal Manchester Volunteers, wrote extensively for the *Gentleman's Magazine* as 'A Rambler'. In 1811 he changed his name to that of his wife, Palmer. Fellow of the Society of Antiquaries. Visited the Lakes in the summer of 1792 and in the winter of 1797-8.

26.1 ***A fortnight's ramble to the Lakes in Westmoreland, Lancashire and Cumberland. By a rambler.*** London: printed for Hookham and Carpenter, New and Old Bond Street. 1792. Octavo.†

Text: Title, verso blank; Reference 1 p., verso blank; Preface (A Rambler, London, August 20th, 1792); [v]-xvi; Contents xvii-xxvii; blank; Text [1]-267.

King's copy: In contemporary stained mottled calf, gilt, leather label. Inscribed on free endpaper, 'The gift of the Author to C.B. Whitehead'. Bookplate C.B. Whitehead.

Note: This is the first published account of a Lake District walking tour. Joseph Budworth's itinerary was Kendal, Windermere, Rydal, Grasmere, Windermere, Patterdale, Coniston, Ambleside, Hawkshead, Keswick, Derwentwater, Buttermere, Penrith, Ullswater, making ascents with local guides of Helm Crag, Coniston Old Man and Skiddaw. In all he 'walked upward of 240 miles besides boat and chaise conveyance' (Preface). The account of the ascent of Helm Crag, p. 102 ff., was also published in the *Gentleman's Magazine*, 1792, pt. 2, pp. 882-3. The two versions are not identical. He drew attention to Mary Robinson, the Beauty of Buttermere, whose misfortunes became a *cause célèbre*.

Copies: K; Armitt; BL; Cornell; Jackson; Wordsworth

26.2 ——— The second edition. London: printed for J. Nicols, Red-Lion-Passage, Fleet Street. 1795. Octavo. Price 5*s*. in boards.

Text: Title, verso blank; References iii, verso blank; Dedication v-vi (Jos. Budworth, Sloane Street, May 23, 1795); Preface vii-xx; Contents xxi-xxxii; Text [1]-292.

Plate: Frontispiece, engraved portrait of Mr William Noble

King's copy: In contemporary calf, rebacked with original leather labels remounted, in one volume with *Windermere, a poem* (27). Page 186 misnumbered 86. Inscribed on title page 'From the Author Col. H.R. Gale Blyth Camp Septr. 4th 1778 (probably intended to be 1798)'; and on free endpaper 'T. Gale Aug. 1st. 52'.

Notes: The text is completely revised and the Preface rewritten. There are numerous additions, including 'A Village Wedding', pp. 12-15, several poems with an extract from Dalton's *Descriptive Poem* (2) numerous notes; and some omissions.

'1000 copies of the second edition were printed of which more than 500 perished in a fire, necessitating a third edition of which only 250 were printed.' (Preface of 3rd edition)

Copies: Armitt; BL; Cornell: Jackson: Kendal

26.3 ——— The third edition. By Jos. Budworth, Esq., F.S.A. London: Printed for the Author, by John Nicols and Son, Red-Lion-Passage, Fleet-Street; And sold by T. Cadell and W. Davies, Strand; and John Upham, Bath. 1810. Octavo.†

Half-title added. 6 lines of a poem by Thomson transferred from title to half-title.

Text: Half-title, verso blank; Title, verso blank; Dedication (Jos. Budworth, Clifton, Bristol, May 17, 1810) [v]-vi; Preface to the third edition [vii]-x; Preface to the second edition [xi]-xix; blank; Contents [xxi-xxx]; blank; Contents of Appendix xxxi; blank; text [1]-413. Imprint on last page, *Printed for J. Nicols and Son Red Lion Passage.*

Plate: Frontispiece as previous edition, but *The Friend of Man* added at head of plate, and *of Pall Mall* added after *Westmorland.*

King's copy: In half calf renewed, original grey paper boards

Notes: Chapter XII, 'Patterdale', which contains a scurrilous account of the Queen of Patterdale is omitted ('some respectable people were hurt at it'). A new chapter 'Such as it is, it speaks for itself', is substituted. Chapter XXX, 'Sally of Buttermere', becomes ' Mary of Buttermere'. In a note Budworth refers to her misfortunes since 1792. An account of an ascent of the Langdale Pikes in 1797 (the first known ascent by a tourist) is added to Chapter XXXII.

Appendix No. 1, 'Revisit to Buttermere', made in January 1798 again deals with Mary Robinson. First published in the *Gentleman's Magazine* (vol. lxx, p. 18, January 1800), a considerable time before she became the subject of general commiseration (Note, p. 407). Subsequently there were many books about 'the Beauty of Buttermere' and her seducer James Hatfield. See, for instance, *James Hatfield and the Beauty of Buttermere: a story of modern times*, by 'James' with illustrations by Robert Cruikshank. 3 vols. (London: Colburn, 1841); *The Life of John Hatfield commonly called the Keswick Imposter*, Anonymous (Keswick, Ivison, *c.* 1849); and a novel by Melvyn Bragg, *The Maid of Buttermere* (1987).

Only 250 copies of the third edition of the *Ramble* were printed. (Preface)

Copies: K; Armitt; BL; Wordsworth

27 ***Windermere, a poem. By Joseph Budworth, Esq., author of a fortnight's ramble in the Lakes.*** London: printed for T. Cadell Jun. and W. Davies (successors to Mr Cadell) in the Strand. 1798. Octavo.

Text: Half title, verso blank; Title, verso blank; Text [1]-28

Advert. on last page for the second edition of *A fortnight's ramble* (1798), 'lately published. Price 5*s.* in Boards'.

King's copy: Bound with *A fortnight's ramble* (1798) [Price one shilling] on half-title

Notes: There is little description of picturesque scenery in the poem

Copies: K; Armitt (in original grey paper wrappers); Cornell; Jackson; Wordsworth

1794

WILLIAM HUTCHINSON 1732-1801

See 6

28 ***The history of the county of Cumberland*** . . . . 2 vols. Carlisle, printed by F. Jollie; and sold by D. Law and Son, W. Clarke, and T. Taylor, London. 1794. Quarto.†

Text: Vol. 1 Engraved half-title, verso blank; Title, verso blank; Dedication, verso blank; List of subscribers [i]-v, blank; Introduction [1]-42; History of Cumberland [43]-600; Glossary 4 pp.
Vol. 2 Engraved half-title, verso blank; Title, verso blank; History of Cumberland [3]-688; List of Sheriffs i-iv; List of animals, plants, and fossils. [1]-54; Subscribers 1-6; Index [683]-686.

Plates: Vol. 1 24 full-page engravings, including Frontispiece, half-title, folding plan and 3 maps. No Lake District views. Pictorial map of area of Skiddaw and Saddleback opposite p. 47. Cuts in the text.
Vol. 2 25 full-page engravings, including Frontispiece, half-title, folding map of places in Cumberland and tables. Also 20 half-page and one quarter-page engravings in text. Of these 5 are Lake District views:

1 A view from the north of Pocklington's Island, near Keswick in Cumberland. Drawn on the spot by Joseph Pocklington Esqr of Carlton house near Newark, Nottinghamshire, 1787. *Published as the Act directs, March 29, 1787.* Signed: *Joseph Pocklington Esq. del. S. Middiman sculpsit.* Plate size: 100 × 127 mm.
2 Druids Monument at Keswick. *J. Lowes Sc.* 80 × 135mm.
3 Grange. *Jas. Lowes Sc.* 77 × 125mm.
4 Bowder Stone. *J. Lowes Sculpst.* 80 × 125mm.
5 Bassenthwaite Lake. *J. Lowes Sculpt.* 80 × 130mm

Also cuts in text.

Note: Medium Paper, price 3*l.* Fine Demy Paper, 2*l.* 12*s.* 6*d.* (advert. Housman's *Topographical Description,* 41).

King's copy: In contemporary half calf, leather labels, uncut. Vols. 1 and 2: bookplate of Bateman of Middleton Hall (by Youlgrave) in the County of Derby. Vol. 2 only: bookplate of Myles Storr Nigel Kennedy and MS. label 'Ex Libris J.N. Postlethwaite, Hallthwaites, Cumberland'. Lacks folding map.

Note: This differs from previous county histories in the amount of space devoted to descriptions of scenery, which are made up of quotations from the standard works of West, Gray, Young, Gilpin, Pennant, Clarke, Brown, Dalton, Hutchinson's own *Excursion* and others. There are copious notes, which are also largely quotations from these authors. The sections which deal with the Lakes of Cumberland are a rich anthology of eighteenth-century poetry and prose. Many little-known works are quoted, for example, the poems 'Now sinks the sun . . .' from John Brown's letter, and Ritson's 'The winds upon Blenkarthur's head . . .', as well as a description from the *Cumberland Pacquet* of 1781, and a Descriptive Poem of 1786, on the Derwentwater regatta (see Appendix 1).

Copies: K; Armitt; BL; Cornell; Jackson; Kendal; Wordsworth

Ref: Upcott, p. 108

——— Facsimile edition. EP Publishing Ltd, East Ardsley, Wakefield 1974.

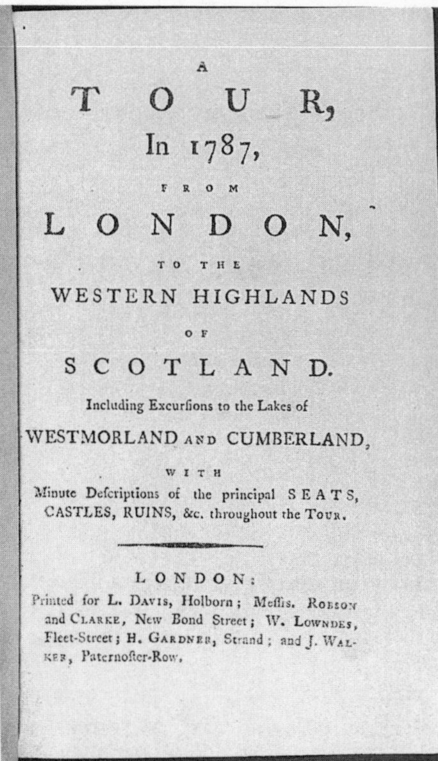

A

TOUR,

In 1787,

FROM

LONDON,

TO THE

WESTERN HIGHLANDS

OF

SCOTLAND.

Including Excurſions to the Lakes of

WESTMORLAND AND CUMBERLAND,

WITH

Minute Deſcriptions of the principal SEATS, CASTLES, RUINS, &c. throughout the TOUR.

LONDON:

Printed for L. DAVIS, Holborn; Meſſis. ROBSON and CLARKE, New Bond Street; W. LOWNDES, Fleet-Street; H. GARDNER, Strand; and J. WALKER, Paternoſter-Row.

21 172 x 105 mm.

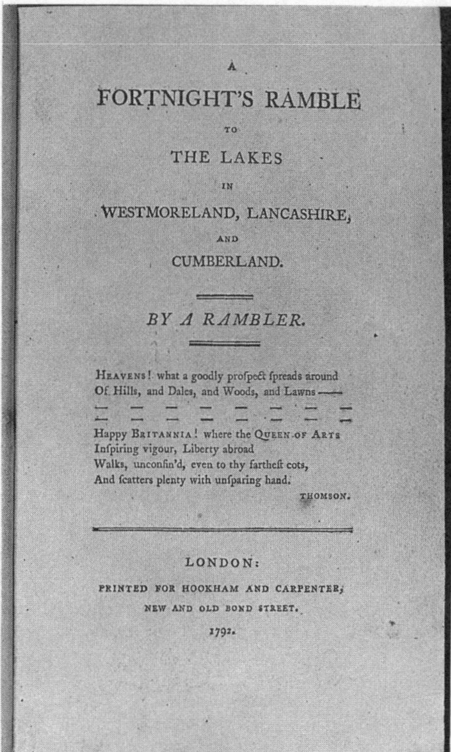

A

FORTNIGHT'S RAMBLE

TO

THE LAKES

IN

WESTMORELAND, LANCASHIRE,

AND

CUMBERLAND.

BY A RAMBLER.

HEAVENS! what a goodly proſpect ſpreads around
Of Hills, and Dales, and Woods, and Lawns——
— — — — — — — —
Happy BRITANNIA! where the QUEEN OF ARTS
Inſpiring vigour, Liberty abroad
Walks, unconfin'd, even to thy fartheſt cots,
And ſcatters plenty with unſparing hand.

THOMSON.

LONDON:

PRINTED FOR HOOKHAM AND CARPENTER,

NEW AND OLD BOND STREET.

1792.

26.1 210 x 128 mm.

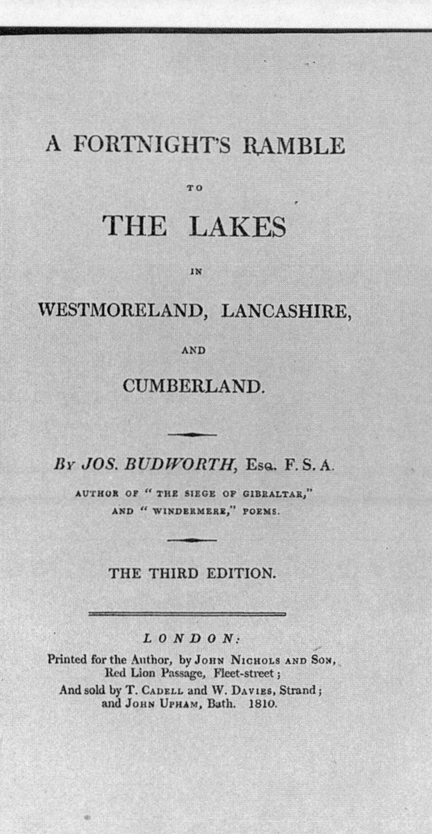

A FORTNIGHT'S RAMBLE

TO

THE LAKES

IN

WESTMORELAND, LANCASHIRE,

AND

CUMBERLAND.

BY *JOS. BUDWORTH*, ESQ. F. S. A.

AUTHOR OF "THE SIEGE OF GIBRALTAR," AND "WINDERMERE," POEMS.

THE THIRD EDITION.

LONDON:

Printed for the Author, by JOHN NICHOLS AND SON, Red Lion Passage, Fleet-street;
And sold by T. CADELL and W. DAVIES, Strand; and JOHN UPHAM, Bath. 1810.

26.3 210 x 130 mm.

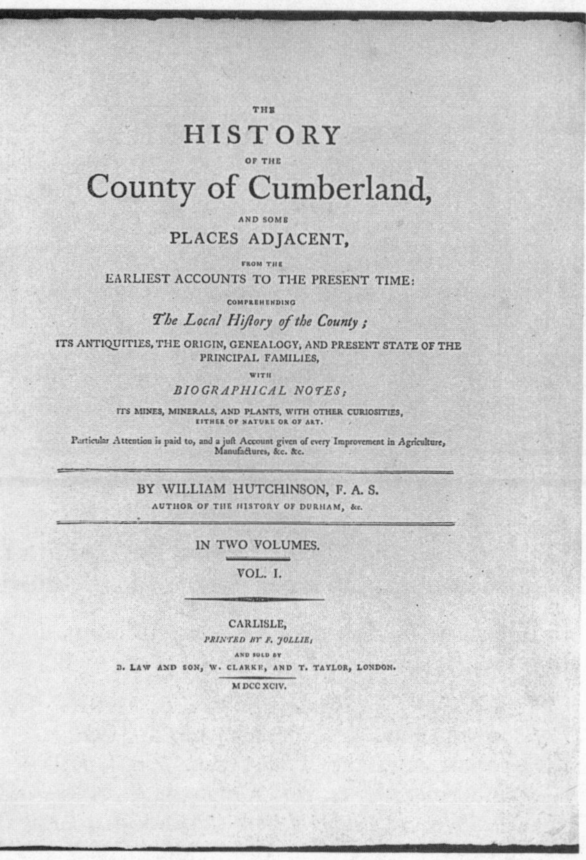

THE

HISTORY

OF THE

County of Cumberland,

AND SOME

PLACES ADJACENT,

FROM THE

EARLIEST ACCOUNTS TO THE PRESENT TIME:

COMPREHENDING

The Local Hiſtory of the County;

ITS ANTIQUITIES, THE ORIGIN, GENEALOGY, AND PRESENT STATE OF THE PRINCIPAL FAMILIES,

WITH

BIOGRAPHICAL NOTES;

ITS MINES, MINERALS, AND PLANTS, WITH OTHER CURIOSITIES, EITHER OF NATURE OR OF ART.

Particular Attention is paid to, and a juſt Account given of every Improvement in Agriculture, Manufactures, &c. &c.

BY WILLIAM HUTCHINSON, F. A. S.

AUTHOR OF THE HISTORY OF DURHAM, &c.

IN TWO VOLUMES.

VOL. I.

CARLISLE,

PRINTED BY F. JOLLIE;

AND SOLD BY

B. LAW AND SON, W. CLARKE, AND T. TAYLOR, LONDON.

MDCCXCIV.

28 280 x 220 mm.

WILLIAM BURGESS (artist) 1713-1812

William Burgess, an accomplished topographical artist, toured South Wales and the Wye valley in 1785.

29 ***View of the Lakes.*** London: Burgess. 8 aquatints by F. Jukes from drawings by Wm. Burgess. Imprints 1792, 1793, 1794. Issued coloured and uncoloured, sometimes bound in printed wrappers. No title, no text. Oblong folio.

Copy: Yale Center for British Art

1795

JOHN RATHBONE (artist) *c.* 1750-1807

John Rathbone, topographical draughtsman of London, Manchester and Preston, was a friend of J.C. Ibbetson (1759-1817) who lived for a time at Ambleside and Troutbeck, and of G.C. Morland (1763-1804).

30 ***Select views of the lakes of Cumberland and Westmoreland, &c. engraved in aquatints by J. Hassel.*** London: Wm. Richardson, Castle Street, Leicester Square, [*c.* 1795]. Oblong folio.

12 coloured aquatints, imprints 1794, 1795, plate size: 150 × 220 mm. One page text to each plate. 'From original pictures, painted on the spot, by J. Rathbone'. Issued in paper wrappers. No text.

Copies: Cornell (includes title-page); and Yale Center for British Art

JOHN 'WARWICK' SMITH (artist) 1749-1831 and JOHN EMES (artist) died *c.* 1809

John Smith who was born at Irthington, Cumberland, spent his early life in the county, where he was for a time gardener to Captain Bernard Gilpin's sister. The Captain and later Sawrey Gilpin taught him drawing. Smith worked for William Gilpin on the plates for his books. He acquired the sobriquet 'Warwick' through the patronage of George Greville, 2nd Earl of Warwick (1746-1816), who sent him to Italy from 1776 to 1781, where he worked with Francis Towne (1740-1816), travelling back through the Alps with him. He made a large number of drawings of the Lake District.

John Emes, etcher, engraver and topographical artist, visited the Lake District in the 1790s.

31 ***Views of the Lakes.*** Drawn by J. Smith and J. Emes. Printed for W. Clarke, New Bond Street, London. No title, no text. Imprints on plates, 1794, 1795.

16 aquatints, issued coloured and uncoloured. Plates signed: *S. Alken fecit* [artist as noted]. Imprint, *Published as the Act directs* [date] *by W. Clarke, New Bond Street, London.*

1 The Vale of Lonsdale *J Emes delt. April 14, 1794*
2 Coniston Lake *J. Smith delt. Jany 1, 1795*
3 Windermere Lake *J. Smith delt. Jany 1, 1795*
4 Windermere Lake from Calgarth *J. Smith delt. May 1, 1795*
5 Elter-Water *J. Emes delt. J. Apostool fecit April 14, 1794*
6 Stock-Gill Force near Ambleside *J. Emes delt. April 1, 1794*
7 Upper Cascade Rydal *J. Emes delt. from a sketch by Laporte April 1, 1795*

8 Rydal Water *J. Smith delt. Jany 1, 1795*
9 Grasmere Lake *J. Smith delt. Jany 1, 1795*
10 Leathes Water *J. Smith delt. Jany 1, 1795*
11 Derwent-water; from Castle-crag *J. Emes delt. April 14, 1794*
12 Derwent-water; from Ormathwaite *J. Emes delt. from a sketch by Laport, Jany 1, 1795*
13 Buttermere Water *J. Smith delt. May 1, 1795*
14 Lowes Water *J. Smith delt. April 1, 1795*
15 The Upper end of Ull *J. Emes delt. April 14, 1794*
16 Ulleswater *J. Smith delt. May 1, 1795*

These are the plates advertised in the fifth edition (1793) and subsequent editions of West's *Guide* as 'of a proper size to bind with the Guide', and are frequently found bound in copies of the *Guide*.

Notes: The plates were issued on sheets, 232 × 305 mm, plate size 215 × 275mm, cut when bound into the *Guide*.

John Laporte (1761-1839), who provided the sketches for plates 7 and 12, was a landscape artist and drawing-master. He worked on a series of soft-ground etchings of subjects by Gainsborough with W.F. Wells, the artist who engraved the plates for Wilkinson's *Select Views* (73). Nicholson (p. 230) records 'La Porte. Drawings engraved by B. Comte.'

Abbey, 184, in pink card wrappers, black paper label on front, gilt lettered within decorative border: *Views of the Lakes of Westmoreland and Cumberland. By Alken. 16 plates 10s.*

Abbey, 186, Blue paper wrappers with white paper label on front cover: *Sixteen Views of the Lakes in Cumberland and Westmorland. Drawn by J. Smith and J. Emes – Engraved by Alken* [sixteen titles]. *Printed for W. Clarke, New Bond Street, London.* Watermarks, Ruse & Turners 1807.

King's copy: Rebound, plates coloured.

Copies: K; Cornell; Wordsworth

Ref: Abbey, 184 and 186; Upcott, pp. 129, 130

——— 'issued in octavo boards, with map, 1812' (Sanderson)

JOHN 'WARWICK' SMITH (artist)

32 ***Views of the Lakes in Cumberland and Westmorland: from original drawings by J. Smith.*** Published by R. Blamire, Strand, London, 1791, 1792, 1795. Oblong folio. Issued in parts in printed paper wrappers. No title, no text. Price to subscribers, One Guinea each Number. Titles on covers. 20 engravings, with some use of aquatint. Plate size 330 × 470 mm.†

Number I

1 Buttermere Lake, taken a little above the Village
2 Wyburn Lake at the Lower end
3 Elter Water in Langdale
4 Belleisle Lodge, on the great Island in Windermere, belonging to John Christian Curwen Esq. to whom these Twenty Views of the Lakes in Cumberland etc. are most humbly inscribed by his most obedient and much obliged Humble Sert. John Smith
Plates 1-4, *March 1791*

Number II

5 Lodore Water-Fall
6 The Ferry on Windermere Lake
7 Coniston Lake, and Village
8 Windermere Lake, at the Upper End
Plates 5, 6, 7, *March 1792;* plate 8, *April 1792*

NUMBER I.
OF
VIEWS of the LAKES
IN
Cumberland and Weſtmorland:
From ORIGINAL DRAWINGS by J. SMITH.
CONTAINING

1. On the great Iſland in WINDERMERE.
2. BUTTERMERE LAKE.
3. WYBURN, or LEATHES WATER.
4. ELTER WATER.

This WORK will be compriſed in FIVE NUMBERS: Price to Subſcribers, ONE GUINEA each Number.

Publiſhed *April* 1791, by R. BLAMIRE, *Strand*, *London*.

32 435 x 600 mm.

A Description
OF
A SERIES OF SIXTY SMALL PRINTS,
ETCHED BY
WILLIAM GREEN, OF AMBLESIDE,
FROM DRAWINGS MADE BY HIMSELF.

LONDON:
PRINTED FOR THE AUTHOR, BY JOHN TYLER, RATHBONE PLACE;
AND PUBLISHED BY
WILLIAM GREEN, AMBLESIDE.
1814.

67 185 x 240 mm.

Number III

9 Paterdale Grange
10 Entrance to Borrodale §
11 Ulls-Water in Paterdale
12 Windermere Lake, taken a little below the Ferry, on the side in Westmoreland
Plates 9, 10, 11, *June 1792*

Number IV & V (issued as one part)

13 Grasmere Lake
14 Rydal Lake
15 Keswick Lake from Castle Rigg
16 Pocklington's Island, Keswick Lake
17 Lows Water
18 Broad Water, at the upper end of Paterdale
19 Near Clappersgate, on the River Bratha
20 Lower Cascade at Rydal

Plates 13, 14, 16, 20, *May 1795;* 15, 17, 18, 19, *June 1794.*

All plates except 12 signed, *Drawn by J. Smith. Engraved by Merigot.* Imprint, *Published as the Act directs* [date] *by R. Blamire, Strand, London.*

The order and titles of the plates given above differ from those printed on the covers.

Upcott (p. 127) records, probably mistakenly, that these plates are 'usually bound up with *Clarke's Survey of the Lakes*' (see note, 19.3), and gives page placings.

King's copy: The four original parts in printed grey paper wrappers.

Notes: The Cornell copy is bound in one volume with a title-page and *Proposals for publishing by subscription* bound in. The conditions of publication are: I. The Work to be published in Numbers, each containing Four Prints: the Size of the Print Fifteen Inches and a Half by Ten Inches. Price to Subscribers, One Guinea [each Number]. II. The Whole to be completed in Twenty Prints, and *Etched in a high-finished Manner,* from original Drawings, made in the Year 1788, by John Smith for John Christian Curwen, Esq; under whose particular Patronage the Work is undertaken. III. *No Subscription Money required* until the Delivery of each Number.

Some of Smith's original watercolours for this work are still in the Curwens' house on Belle Isle, Windermere.

Copies: K; Armitt; Cornell

Ref: Upcott, p. 127

Note: Nicholson (p. 230) records 'John Smith. *Scrapbook Containing Views of the Lakes,* 1798.'

HENRY SKRINE 1755-1803

Henry Skrine, of Warley in Somerset, topographical writer, published *A general account of all the rivers of note in Great Britain,* 1801, which covers the rivers of the Lake District from the Eden to the Kent, very briefly described and shown on a map.

33.1 *Three Successive Tours in the North of England, and a great part of Scotland* . . . . London: Printed by W. Bulmer and Co. and sold by P. Elmsly, Strand. 1795. Quarto.†

Text: Title, verso blank; Preface [1]-7; Errata [8]; Divisional title, 'Travels in Derbyshire, Yorkshire, and Nottinghamshire', verso blank; Text iii-xxvii; blank; Divisional title, 'First Tour on the North of England', verso blank; Text [1]-90; Divisional title, 'Second Tour in the Eastern Counties, and Northern Highlands of Scotland'; verso blank; Text [93]-164.

Lakes: First Tour in the North of England pp. 11-32

Itinerary: Skrine approached the Lakes from the south, making the conventional tour from Kendal to Windermere, visiting Furness Abbey, Coniston and Hawkshead, then to Keswick by Rydal, Grasmere and Leathes Water, the ascent of Skiddaw, Bassenthwaite, Penrith, Ullswater and Penrith, leaving out Buttermere, Crummock, Loweswater, Ennerdale, Wastwater and Haweswater,

Note: The Armitt Library copy includes engravings after P. Sandby

King's copy: In original grey paper boards, rebacked, uncut. Divisonal title erroneously bound as half-title.

Copies: K; Armitt; BL

33.2 ——— Second edition. *Three successive tours in the North of England, to the Lakes and a great part of Scotland,* with maps of the Lakes and of Scotland. London: T. Turner. 1813. Quarto

Copy: BL

ANN RADCLIFFE 1764-1823

Mrs Ann Radcliffe's Gothic novels abound in descriptions of highly picturesque and sublime scenery, frequently in places which she had not visited. Her last novel, *The Italian* (1797), was published three years after she made her tour of the Lakes, after which she devoted much time to travel with her husband.

34.1 ***A journey made in the summer of 1794, through Holland [etc.]: to which are added observations during a tour to the Lakes . . .*** London: Printed for G.G. and J. Robinson, Paternoster-Row. 1795. Quarto.†

Text: Title, verso blank; Note [v], vi (May 20, 1795); Contents [vii]-x; Text [1]-500.

Lakes: pp.368-500

Itinerary: Kendal, Bampton, Haweswater, Ullswater, Brougham, Penrith, Keswick, ascent of Skiddaw, Bassenthwaite, Borrowdale, Thirlmere, Grasmere, Rydal, Windermere, Hawkshead, Coniston, Ulverston, Furness, across the sands to Lancaster. The tour did not include Buttermere, Crummock and Loweswater, nor Ennerdale and Wastwater.

King's copy: In half calf, marbled boards, leather label, gilt, lacks half-title. Inscribed on title page, 'Ann Ward'.

Note: An extract entitled 'Description of the scenery in a ride over Skiddaw' was included as an Addendum to the sixth and subsequent editions of West's *Guide*.

Copies: K; Armitt; BL

34.2 ——— Second edition. 2 vols. 1795. Octavo.

Title: As first edition except:
'In two volumes, - vol. I [or II]' added
'Second edition' added.

Preface and text unaltered.

King's copy: In contemporary half leather, marbled boards, leather labels, gilt. Bookplate of Thomas Hammond, Foxcroft.

Copies: K; Armitt; Jackson

THREE SUCCESSIVE
TOURS
IN THE
NORTH OF ENGLAND,
AND GREAT PART OF
SCOTLAND.
INTERSPERSED WITH
DESCRIPTIONS OF THE SCENES THEY PRESENTED,
AND OCCASIONAL OBSERVATIONS
ON THE STATE OF SOCIETY, AND THE MANNERS AND
CUSTOMS OF THE PEOPLE.

BY HENRY SKRINE, ESQ.
OF WARLEY IN SOMERSETSHIRE.

LONDON:
PRINTED BY W. BULMER AND CO.
AND SOLD BY P. ELMSLY, STRAND.
1795.

33.1 310 x 238 mm.

A
JOURNEY
MADE IN THE SUMMER OF 1794,
THROUGH
HOLLAND
AND THE
WESTERN FRONTIER OF GERMANY,
WITH A
RETURN DOWN THE RHINE:
TO WHICH ARE ADDED
OBSERVATIONS DURING A TOUR TO
THE LAKES
OF
LANCASHIRE, WESTMORELAND, AND CUMBERLAND.

BY ANN RADCLIFFE.

LONDON:
PRINTED FOR G. G. AND J. ROBINSON, PATERNOSTER-ROW.
M DCC XCV.

34.1 263 x 200 mm.

THE
BRITISH TOURISTS;
OR
TRAVELLER'S
POCKET COMPANION,
THROUGH
ENGLAND, WALES, SCOTLAND,
AND IRELAND.
Comprehending the moſt
CELEBRATED TOURS
IN THE
British Islands.

———My genius ſpreads her wing,
And flies where *Britain* courts the weſtern ſpring;
Where lawns extend, that ſcorn *Arcadian* pride,
And brighter ſtreams than fam'd *Hydaſpis* glide.
Goldſmith's Traveller.

BY WILLIAM MAVOR, LL.D.

VOL. I.
SECOND EDITION.

LONDON:
Printed by J. Swan, and Co. Jeruſalem-Court, Gracechurch-Street;
FOR E. NEWBERY, ST. PAUL'S CHURCH-YARD;
AND SOLD BY EVERY BOOKSELLER
IN THE THREE KINGDOMS.
1800.

38.2 140 x 83 mm.

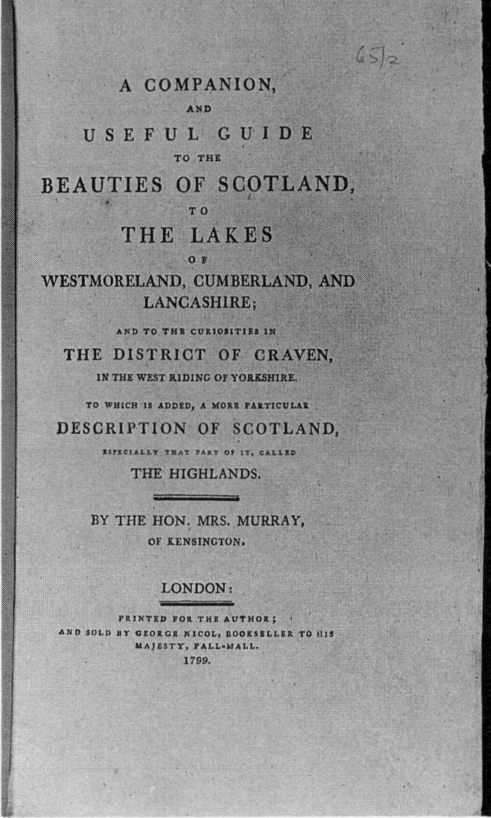
A COMPANION,
AND
USEFUL GUIDE
TO THE
BEAUTIES OF SCOTLAND,
TO
THE LAKES
OF
WESTMORELAND, CUMBERLAND, AND
LANCASHIRE;
AND TO THE CURIOSITIES IN
THE DISTRICT OF CRAVEN,
IN THE WEST RIDING OF YORKSHIRE.
TO WHICH IS ADDED, A MORE PARTICULAR
DESCRIPTION OF SCOTLAND,
ESPECIALLY THAT PART OF IT, CALLED
THE HIGHLANDS.

BY THE HON. MRS. MURRAY,
OF KENSINGTON.

LONDON:
PRINTED FOR THE AUTHOR;
AND SOLD BY GEORGE NICOL, BOOKSELLER TO HIS
MAJESTY, PALL-MALL.
1799.

39.1a 230 x 143 mm.

34a ——— Another edition. Dublin: Porter for Wogan, Byrne . . . 1795. Octavo

Copies: Armitt; BL; Cornell

It is interesting to note that all three editions were published in the same year – 1795.

1796

B. ROGERS (artist)

B. Rogers was a landscape and architectural painter. He exhibited at the Royal Academy 1800-03, and was a drawing-master at Stafford who gave lessons to Peter de Wint (1784-1849).

35 ***Six views in Westmoreland and Cumberland engraved by S. Alken from designs by B. Rogers*** Stafford: Rogers. 1796. Oblong folio, plates only; no title, no text.

Plates: 6 aquatints

Signed: *B. Rogers delt. S. Alken fecit.* Imprint: *May 10th. 1796, Published as the Act directs by B. Rogers, Drawing Master Stafford.* Plate sizes: 300 × 425 mm.

1 The Lake & Vale of Keswick with a distant view of Basinthwaite Lake
2 View of Newlands Vale & part of the Lake of Keswick
3 View of Grasmere Lake from a small hill above the Village
4 View of Rydal Westmoreland
5 View of Windermere Lake taken from Collgarth
6 View of Conistone Lake, taken from the Road near the foot

Issued coloured and uncoloured; probably not issued bound.

King's copies: Unbound, sepia prints

Copies: K; BL (bound)

JAMES BOURNE (artist) 1773-1854

The Revd James Bourne was born at Dalby in Lincolnshire. He worked in Manchester for about five years from *c.* 1791 to *c.* 1796. He was patronised by Lord Spencer, the Duchess of Sutherland and Sir Thomas Gage, through whom he may have met Girtin and Turner; he toured Wales in 1800 with Sir George Beaumont; and was in the Lakes in 1789.

36 ***Interesting views of the lakes of Cumberland, Westmoreland, and Lancashire*** London: printed for the Author, and sold by T. Gardner, Bookseller to Her Royal Highness the Duchess of Cumberland, Princes Street, Cavendish Square. Printed by J. Barfield, Wardour Street. n.d. (*c.* 1796/7). Folio.

Engraved title with aquatint vignette, printed dedication and 67 pp. text. 12 original mounted watercolour views.

Note: Only five copies of this remarkable book are recorded, all of which are illustrated with watercolours. No copies with printed plates are known to exist. The illustrations though of exactly the same views are by different hands. They are referred to in the text, which describes a tour and is probably by Bourne.

Itinerary: Kendal, Windermere, Hawkshead, Coniston, Ambleside, Rydal, Grasmere, Thirlmere, Keswick, Borrowdale and Honnister, Buttermere, Crummock, Bassenthwaite, Keswick, Penrith. As usual the western lakes and Haweswater were not visited.

Note: The text is conventional. The date of the tour has not been established.

The watercolours:

1 [Windermere Lake from Bowness]
2 [Esthwaite Lake]
3 [Coniston Lake]
4 [Windermere Lake from the Ferry]
5 [Rydal Lake]
6 [Wythburn Lake]
7 [Grasmere]
8 [Keswick Lake]
9 [Bridge in Newlands]
10 [Buttermere Lake]
11 [Bassenthwaite Lake]
12 [Ulswater]

Copies: Armitt (watermarks 1794, 1796); Wordsworth (watermarks 1801); British Museum, Print Room (6 views only); Victoria & Albert Museum, Library (9 views only); *Book Auction Records*, 1931

1798

JAMES PLUMPTRE 1770-1832

James Plumptre of Queens' College and Clare Hall, Cambridge, divine, dramatist, author and amateur of opera and the stage, made tours of the Lakes in 1796, 1797 and 1799. These he recorded in detailed 'Memorandums' (Cambridge University Library, Add. MSS 5802, 5809, 5814-16). That of 1799 he expanded into a three-volume book which remains only in manuscript. His correspondence, including an exchange of letters with William Gilpin, is also in the Cambridge University Library. At Grasmere he met William Gell (see 166).

37 ***The Lakers: a comic opera in three acts***. London: Printed for W. Clarke, New Bond Street. 1798. Octavo.

Note: The Lakers satirised the affectations of tourists, like the author himself, in pursuit of the picturesque. It is a comedy with incidental songs. The only recorded performance was given (without music) at the Wordsworth Summer School at Grasmere in 1987.

Copies: Armitt; BL; Cornell; and Cambridge University Library

WILLIAM FORDYCE MAVOR (editor) 1758-1837

The Revd William Mavor was a compiler of educational books, schoolmaster and vicar.

38.1 ***The British Tourists; or traveller's pocket companion, through England, Wales, Scotland, and Ireland. Comprehending the most celebrated tours in the British Islands***. 6 vols. London: E. Newbery. 1798 & 1800. Duodecimo. Maps.

The first edition was published in 5 volumes in 1798, the 6th was added in 1800.

The British Tourists consists of a collection of works on the topography of the British Isles, written in the second half of the eighteenth century. Most of the tours are abridgements of the originals, and are written in the third person.

For a list of articles on the Lake District see next item, second edition.

Copies: Armitt; BL

38.2 ——— Second edition. London: Printed by J. Swan, and Co. Jerusalem-Court, Gracechurch-Street; for E. Newbery, St. Paul's Church-Yard; and sold by every bookseller in the three Kingdoms. 1800 †

Text: Vol. 1 Title, verso blank; Contents 1 p., verso blank; Dedication [iii], [iv]; Preface [v]-xii; Text [1]-302
Vol. 2 Title, verso blank; Contents, verso blank; Text [1]-342, printer's imprint on last page, as title-page
Vol. 3 Title, verso blank; Contents, verso blank; Text [1]-323, imprint on last page
Vol. 4 Title, verso blank; Contents, verso blank; Text [1]-313, imprint on last page
Vol. 5 Title, verso blank; Contents, verso blank; Note 1 p., verso blank; Text [1]-281 blank; Index [283]-[310], imprint on last page; Adverts. 2pp.
Vol. 6 Title verso blank; Contents, verso blank; Adverts. 2 pp.; References to plan, 3 pp. blank; Text [1]-280; List [281]-308; Indices [309]-[316], imprint on last page.

Plate: Engraved frontispiece in vol. 1 only

Maps: Folding coloured map in each volume except vol. 4

Articles on the Lake District are:
Vol. 2 Excursion to the Lakes in 1773 and 1774, by W. Hutchinson (see 7)
Vol. 3 Tour through different parts of England, Scotland and Wales, by Richard Joseph Sulivan Esq. performed in 1778 (see 16)
Vol. 4 Tour in England and Scotland, performed in 1785, by Thomas Newte Esq. (see 20)
Vol. 5 Journal of a Three Week Tour, in 1797, through Derbyshire to the Lakes. By Johnson Grant, Esq. of the University of Oxford (not published elsewhere).

King's copy: In contemporary tree calf, repaired. Heraldic bookplate in each vol.

Copies: K; BL

38.3 ——— Third edition.

Title: As second edition except:
'celebrated, modern, and recent tours in the British Islands; with several originals. In six volumes' replaces 'celebrated tours in the British Islands'.
'Third edition, improved and much enlarged' replaces 'Second edition'.
Imprint altered to 'London: printed for Richard Phillips, Bridge Street,Black Friars; and sold by every bookseller in the Kingdom. 1807'.
'[Price One Guinea and a Half, in boards]' added.

Note: 'A tour to the Lakes of Cumberland & Westmorland in August 1798. By Henry Kett, B.D. &c. &c. &c.' is added to Vol. 5, pp. [117]-157 (not previously published).

King's copy: vol. 5 only, rebound. Inscribed 'W.W. Woodruff' on title-page; 'A.M. Pinnery' on next leaf.

Copies: K; BL

Ref: Upcott, p. xxxix, gives 3rd edn 1814.

1799

SARAH AUST (The Hon. Mrs Murray) 1744-1811

The Hon. Mrs Murray (*née* Maese), wife of William Murray, later married George Aust. She visited the Lakes in 1794 and 1796. See *Gentleman's Magazine,* lxxxi, pt ii, 586.

39.1a ***A companion, and useful guide to the beauties of Scotland, to the Lakes of Westmoreland, Cumberland and Lancashire***; . . . . . ***By the Hon. Mrs. Murray, of Kensington.*** London: Printed for the Author; and sold by George Nicol, bookseller to His Majesty, Pall-Mall. 1799 [vol. 1] Octavo.†

Text: Half-title, verso blank; Title, verso blank; Advertisement (S. Murray, Kensington, March the 30th, 1799) [v], verso blank; Letter [vii], viii; Contents [ix]-xii; Divisional Title, 'A Guide to the Lakes . . .', verso blank; Text [3]-30; blank; Divisional Title, 'A guide to the Beauties of Scotland' verso blank; Text [39]-95; blank, Divisional title, 'A Description of part of Scotland particularly the Highlands'; blank; Text [97]-396.

Notes: 'The Lakes of Westmoreland and Cumberland, having been so often *described*, by very able pens, I shall only offer *directions* for seeing beauties and curiosities, seldom mentioned by, or known to, *general* tourists.' Preface vol. 1, p. iii.

Mrs Murray only covers a limited itinerary: from Kendal to Windermere, Coniston, over the Kirkstone Pass to Ullswater, then by Dunmail Raise to Keswick, Watendlath, Borrowdale, over Honister to Buttermere, the district of Bassenthwaite and Cockermouth.

She showed considerable enterprise, walking from Gatesgarth to the Seathwaite Wad mines over Honister and back. She probably descended to Gatesgarth by the rocky ridge of Fleetwith. It 'is somewhat tremendous; but was descended, in 1796, by a female'. She also walked from Buttermere over the fells to Ennerdale and back.

King's copy: In original grey paper boards, rebacked, printed paper label remounted on spine, uncut. Bookplate of Sir Richard Brooke, Bart., on paste-down endpaper, covering ms. List of borrowers dated August 1900 to Feby. 1802. This presumably was a lending library copy.

Copies K; Armitt; BL; Cornell; Kendal; Wordsworth

39.1b ——— Volume 2. 1803. Published separately.

Note: 'A guide to the Lakes' precedes 'A description of part of Scotland' in vol. 1. There is no reference to the Lake District in vol. 2

Copies: Armitt; BL; Cornell

——— Volume 1. Second edition. No information

39.2bq ——— Volume 2. Second edition. 1805

Copies: K; BL; Cornell

39.3a ——— Volume 1. Third edition. By the Hon. Mrs Murray Aust. London: Printed by W. Bulmer and Co., Cleveland-Row, for the Author; sold by G. and W. Nicol, Booksellers to His Majesty, Pall-Mall; and Bell and Bradfute, Edinburgh. 1810.

Price in boards £1. 5*s*. Two Volumes.

King's copies: 39.3a and 39.2b bound together in contemporary dark blue cloth, leather label, gilt

Copies: K; BL; Cornell; Jackson

1800

DENNIS BROWNWELL MURPHY (artist) *c.* 1755-1842

Dennis Brownwell Murphy, miniaturist and landscape artist, was born in Dublin. He moved to England in 1798, living first in Manchester, then in Newcastle upon Tyne and London. He exhibited at the Royal Academy, 1800-26. He visited the Lakes in 1798 with the amateur artist, John Harden (1772-1847) before Harden occupied Brathay Hall in 1804.

40 ***A tour on the Lakes in Westmoreland.*** London: Published by R. Ackermann, No. 101, Strand, J. Barfield, Printer, No. 91, Wardour Street, Soho.

Oblong folio. 8 aquatints from drawings by Murphy, engraved by Bluck, imprints 1789, 1800. Issued in two parts in paper wrappers. One page of text to each plate. Titles on printed labels on covers. Issued coloured and uncoloured. Price, nine shillings (per part).

Five of the plates are of buildings; only one, of 'Kirkstone Mountain', is of landscape.

Copy: Armitt (part 1 only)

Ref: Abbey, 185

JOHN HOUSMAN 1764-1802

John Housman was the son of Henry Howard's gardener at Corby Castle, Cumwhitton, near Carlisle. The success of the notes he supplied to the Carlisle publisher, Francis Jollie, on soils and agricultural matters, for Hutchinson's *History of . . . Cumberland* (28), led to Housman accompanying a gentleman (possibly Henry Howard) on a tour through England in 1797-8. While making the tour he sent a narrative to the *Monthly Magazine* which published it serially as 'Tour through England' in 1797-8. On his return to Cumwhitton he wrote his *Descriptive Tour*. This was published by Jollie dated 1800 and with the addition of the *Topographical Description* republished in October 1800.

41.1 ***A descriptive tour, and guide to the Lakes, Caves and Mountains . . .*** Carlisle: Printed by F. Jollie; and sold by C. Law, Ave-Maria-Lane, London. 1800. Quarto.

Text: Title; verso blank; Advertisement (Corby, June 1, 1800) [iii], iv; Index 1 p.; References 1 p.; Distances 1 p.; blank; Text [1]-226; imprint, *Printed by F. Jollie, Carlisle, June, 1800.*

Plate: Frontispiece, engraving, North View of Furness Abbey *I.W. delint. R. Scott sculpt.*

Maps: 1 Lancashire, Westmoreland, Cumberland & a Part of Yorkshire, with a Sketch of the Soils Canals &c., folding, coloured.
Size: 420 × 255 mm. Scale: 1 in. = 7 miles.
2 Lakes in Cumberland. *J. Lowes Sc.* 210 × 260mm. Folding [9 lakes collected on one sheet].

Itinerary: Kendal, Longsleddale to Haweswater, Penrith, Ullswater, Keswick, Derwentwater, Borrowdale, Styehead to Wastwater, Watendlath, Bassenthwaite, Buttermere, Crummock, Loweswater, Thirlmere, Grasmere, Rydal, Windermere, Esthwaite Water, Coniston, Ulverston

Note: This is a more extensive tour than usual: few tourists at the time crossed Styehead Pass, nor crossed from Longsleddale to Haweswater

King's copy: In contemporary calf, rebacked, old spine remounted. Inscribed on title-page 'Lieut. Jno. W.Y. Bayfield'

Copies: K; Armitt; Cornell; Kendal

41.2a ***A topographical description of Cumberland, Westmoreland, Lancashire . . .*** Carlisle, Printed by Francis Jollie, and sold by C. Law, Ave-Maria-Lane, and W. Clarke, New Bond Street, London. 1800. Quarto.†

Text: Title, verso blank; Address dedicatory (Corby, October 30, 1800) [iii]-v, blank; Index [vii]-ix; Distances and Directions [x], xi; References [xii]; Text, (Topographical Description) [1]-173; blank; Divisional title, 'A Descriptive Tour . . . forming a guide to tourists, particularly those visiting the Lakes', verso blank; Text [177]-536, imprint on 536, *Carlisle, printed F. Jollie - 1800;* Additions 1 p.; Errata 1 p.; Adverts. 1 p.

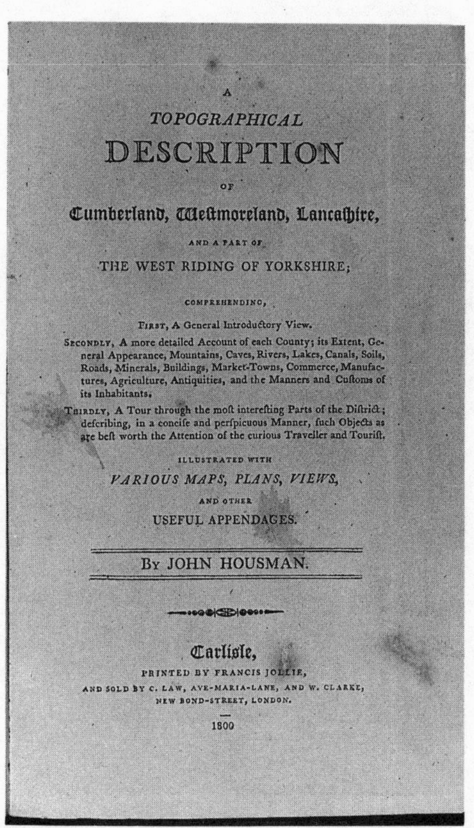

A
TOPOGRAPHICAL
DESCRIPTION
OF
Cumberland, Westmoreland, Lancashire,
AND A PART OF
THE WEST RIDING OF YORKSHIRE;
COMPREHENDING,
FIRST, A General Introductory View.
SECONDLY, A more detailed Account of each County; its Extent, General Appearance, Mountains, Caves, Rivers, Lakes, Canals, Soils, Roads, Minerals, Buildings, Market-Towns, Commerce, Manufactures, Agriculture, Antiquities, and the Manners and Customs of its Inhabitants.
THIRDLY, A Tour through the most interesting Parts of the District; describing, in a concise and perspicuous Manner, such Objects as are best worth the Attention of the curious Traveller and Tourist.
ILLUSTRATED WITH
VARIOUS MAPS, PLANS, VIEWS,
AND OTHER
USEFUL APPENDAGES.

BY JOHN HOUSMAN.

Carlisle,
PRINTED BY FRANCIS JOLLIE,
AND SOLD BY C. LAW, AVE-MARIA-LANE, AND W. CLARKE, NEW BOND-STREET, LONDON.
1800

41.2a 219 x 130 mm.

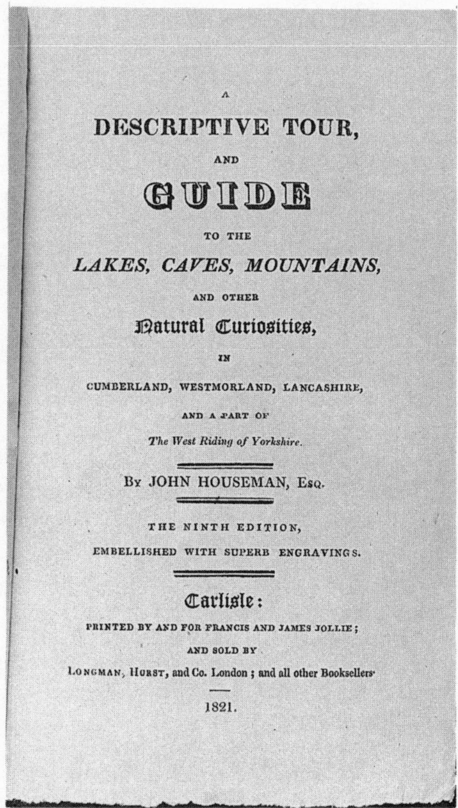

A
DESCRIPTIVE TOUR,
AND
GUIDE
TO THE
LAKES, CAVES, MOUNTAINS,
AND OTHER
Natural Curiosities,
IN
CUMBERLAND, WESTMORLAND, LANCASHIRE,
AND A PART OF
The West Riding of Yorkshire.

BY JOHN HOUSEMAN, ESQ.

THE NINTH EDITION,
EMBELLISHED WITH SUPERB ENGRAVINGS.

Carlisle:
PRINTED BY AND FOR FRANCIS AND JAMES JOLLIE;
AND SOLD BY
LONGMAN, HURST, and Co. London; and all other Booksellers.
1821.

41.9 190 x 110 mm.

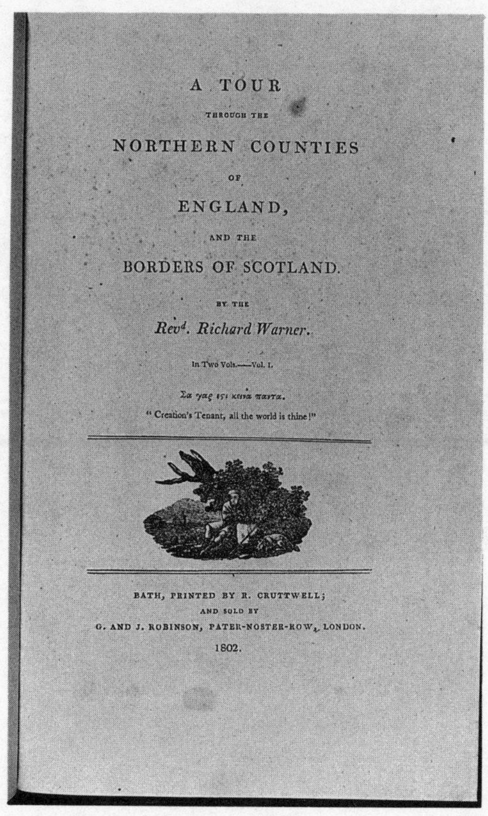

A TOUR
THROUGH THE
NORTHERN COUNTIES
OF
ENGLAND,
AND THE
BORDERS OF SCOTLAND.
BY THE
Revd. Richard Warner.
In Two Vols.——Vol. I.
Σα γαρ εϛι κτισα παντα.
"Creation's Tenant, all the world is thine!"

BATH, PRINTED BY R. CRUTTWELL;
AND SOLD BY
G. AND J. ROBINSON, PATER-NOSTER-ROW, LONDON.
1802.

43 215 x 130 mm.

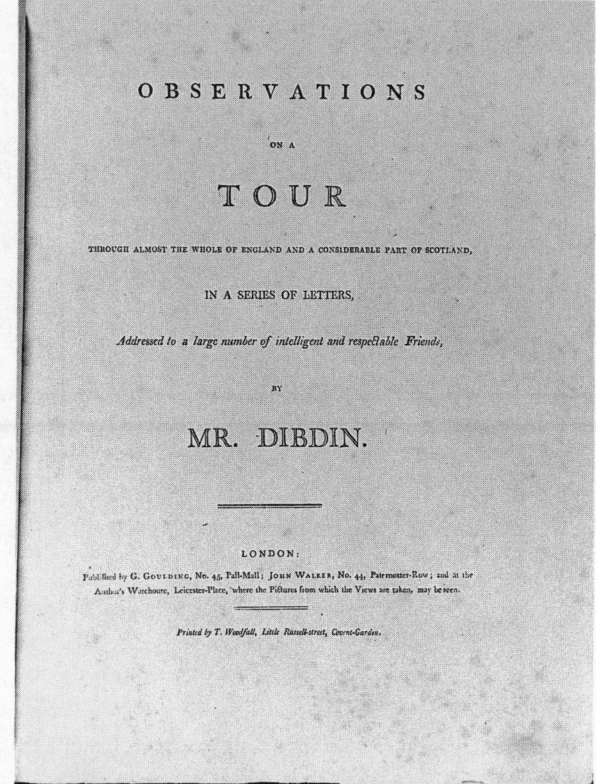

OBSERVATIONS
ON A
TOUR
THROUGH ALMOST THE WHOLE OF ENGLAND AND A CONSIDERABLE PART OF SCOTLAND,
IN A SERIES OF LETTERS,
Addressed to a large number of intelligent and respectable Friends,
BY
MR. DIBDIN.

LONDON:
Published by G. GOULDING, No. 45, Pall-Mall; JOHN WALKER, No. 44, Paternoster-Row; and at the Author's Warehouse, Leicester-Place, where the Pictures from which the Views are taken, may be seen.

Printed by T. Woodfall, Little Russell-street, Covent-Garden.

44 267 x 210 mm.

Plates: 14 engravings of which 6 are of Lake District views
1 Ullswater looking into Patterdale
2 Stonethwaite, & Eagle Crag, Borrowdale
3 The Head of Wastwater
4 Derwent Water or Keswick Lake from Ormathwaite
5 Bassenthwaite Lake, from Armathwaite
6 North View of Furness Abbey [as 41.1]

All signed: *I.W. delint. R. Scott sculpt.*

Maps: 1 Map of the Soils, folding, coloured [as no. 41.1]
2 Plan of Kendal. *J. Lowes Sculp. 1798.* 210 × 260 mm
3 Lakes in Cumberland. *J. Lowes Sc.* Folding. 210 × 118 mm [9 lakes collected on one sheet, as 41.1]
4 Lakes in Lancashire & Westmoreland. *McIntyre Sculps. Edinr.* Folding. [7 lakes collected on one sheet]
5 Plan of Lancaster. *McIntyre Sc.*
6 Plan of Liverpool. *Jas. Lowes Sculpt.* Folding. 210 × 273 mm
7 A Pocket Plan of Manchester and Salford. *The words engraved by Kirkwood & Sons, Edinr.* Folding. 381 × 495 mm

'The Six elegant Views given in this book, may be had separately, at 6*d.* each.' advert. on last page

Note: This includes the true second edition of the *Descriptive Tour* (41.1) which is added to the *Topographical Tour,* with little alteration except for page heads, numerals and signatures. Most of it is not reset.

King's copy: Contemporary tree calf, rebacked, original leather label remounted, gilt

Copies: K; Armitt; BL; Cornell; Jackson; Kendal

41.2b ——— Second edition. [true 3rd edition] Carlisle. 1802. Quarto. Embellished with several additional plates.

Text: As 41.1a, 1800, not reset, except:
Advertisement reset, dated June 15, 1802
Page number 85 corrected
Page heads corrected
'Finis' and imprint, p. 226, omitted
One page, Additions and Corrections added
One page, Directions and Adverts. added.

6 engravings, and 7 maps and plans same as *A topographical description,* 41.2a.

King's copy: In contemporary tree calf; leather label, gilt book plate of James Hatch Esqr.

Copies: K; Armitt; BL; Cornell; Jackson; Kendal; Wordsworth

41.3 ——— Third edition. Embellished with superb engravings. Carlisle: Printed by and for F. Jollie and Sons; and sold by Crosby and Co. and C. Law, London; T. Brown, Edinburgh; Clarke and Co., Lancaster; Branthwaite, Kendal; Soulby and Brown, Penrith; Hetherton, Wigton; Crosthwaite, Keswick; Crosthwaite and Wilson, Whitehaven; Bowness, Borrowdale, and Mordy, Workington; and most other booksellers. 1808. Duodecimo.

Text: All as first and second editions, reset

Note: Advertisement same as previous edition, except, 'Third Edition' replaces 'Second Edition' and is undated

Maps and plates all as previous edition, except folded to fit smaller format

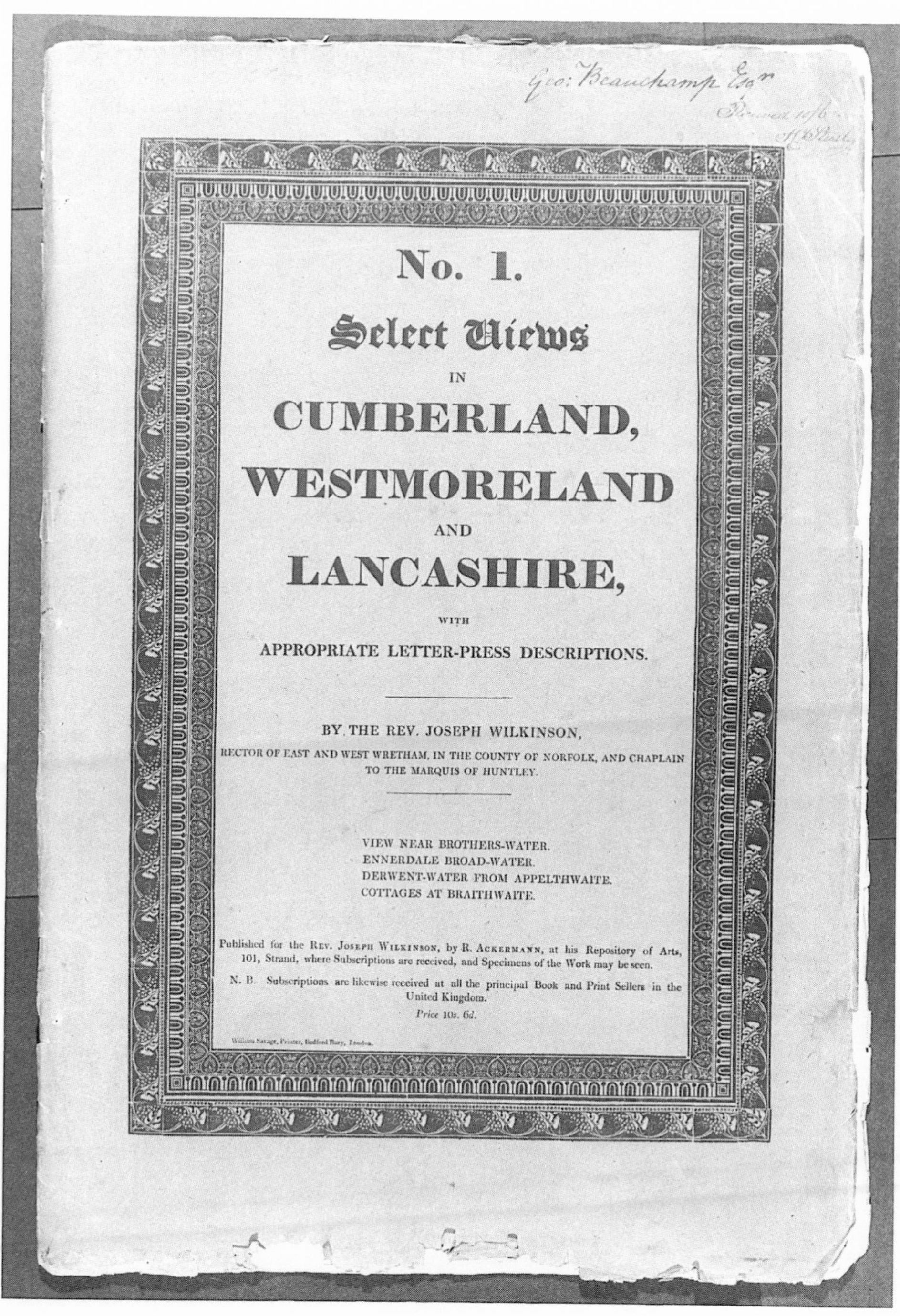

No. 1.

Select Views

IN

CUMBERLAND,

WESTMORELAND

AND

LANCASHIRE,

WITH

APPROPRIATE LETTER-PRESS DESCRIPTIONS.

BY THE REV. JOSEPH WILKINSON,

RECTOR OF EAST AND WEST WRETHAM, IN THE COUNTY OF NORFOLK, AND CHAPLAIN TO THE MARQUIS OF HUNTLEY.

VIEW NEAR BROTHERS-WATER.
ENNERDALE BROAD-WATER.
DERWENT-WATER FROM APPELTHWAITE.
COTTAGES AT BRAITHWAITE.

Published for the Rev. Joseph Wilkinson, by R. Ackermann, at his Repository of Arts, 101, Strand, where Subscriptions are received, and Specimens of the Work may be seen.

N. B. Subscriptions are likewise received at all the principal Book and Print Sellers in the United Kingdom.

Price 10s. 6d.

William Savage, Printer, Bedford Bury, London.

A Printed paper cover (510 × 120 mm.)
Joseph Wilkinson, *Select Views* (73)

THE LAKES OF ENGLAND.

C. Hancock W. Giller

15, APRIL 1836

LONDON.

PUBLISHED BY SHERWOOD & C° PATERNOSTER ROW,

AND HUDSON & NICHOLSON, KENDAL.

B Title-page, engraved by W. Giller from a drawing by C. Hancock (196 × 120 mm.)
George Tattersall, *The lakes of England* (116)

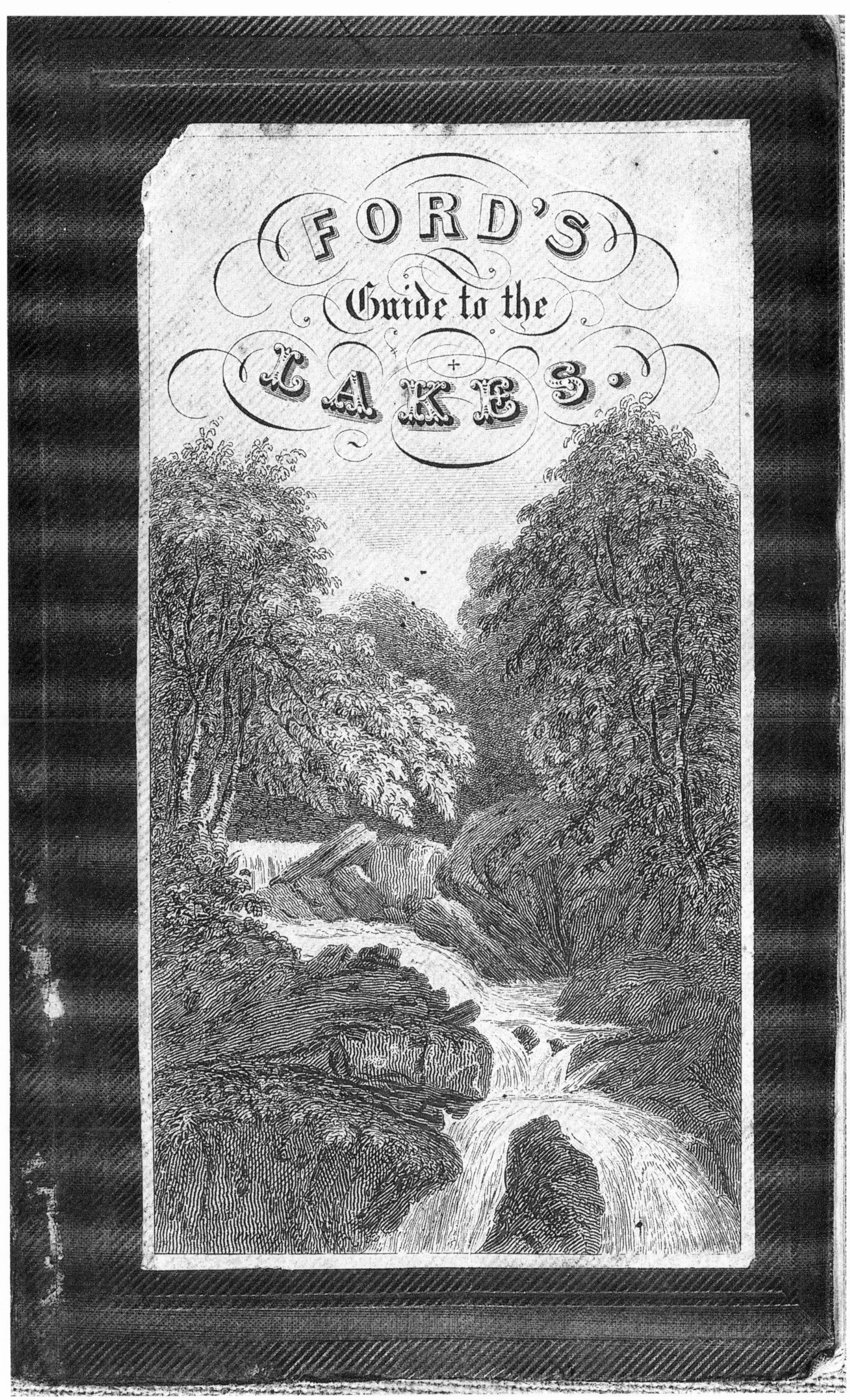

C Engraving mounted on cloth cover of publisher's binding (185 × 115 mm.)
William Ford, *A description of the scenery in the Lake District* (118)

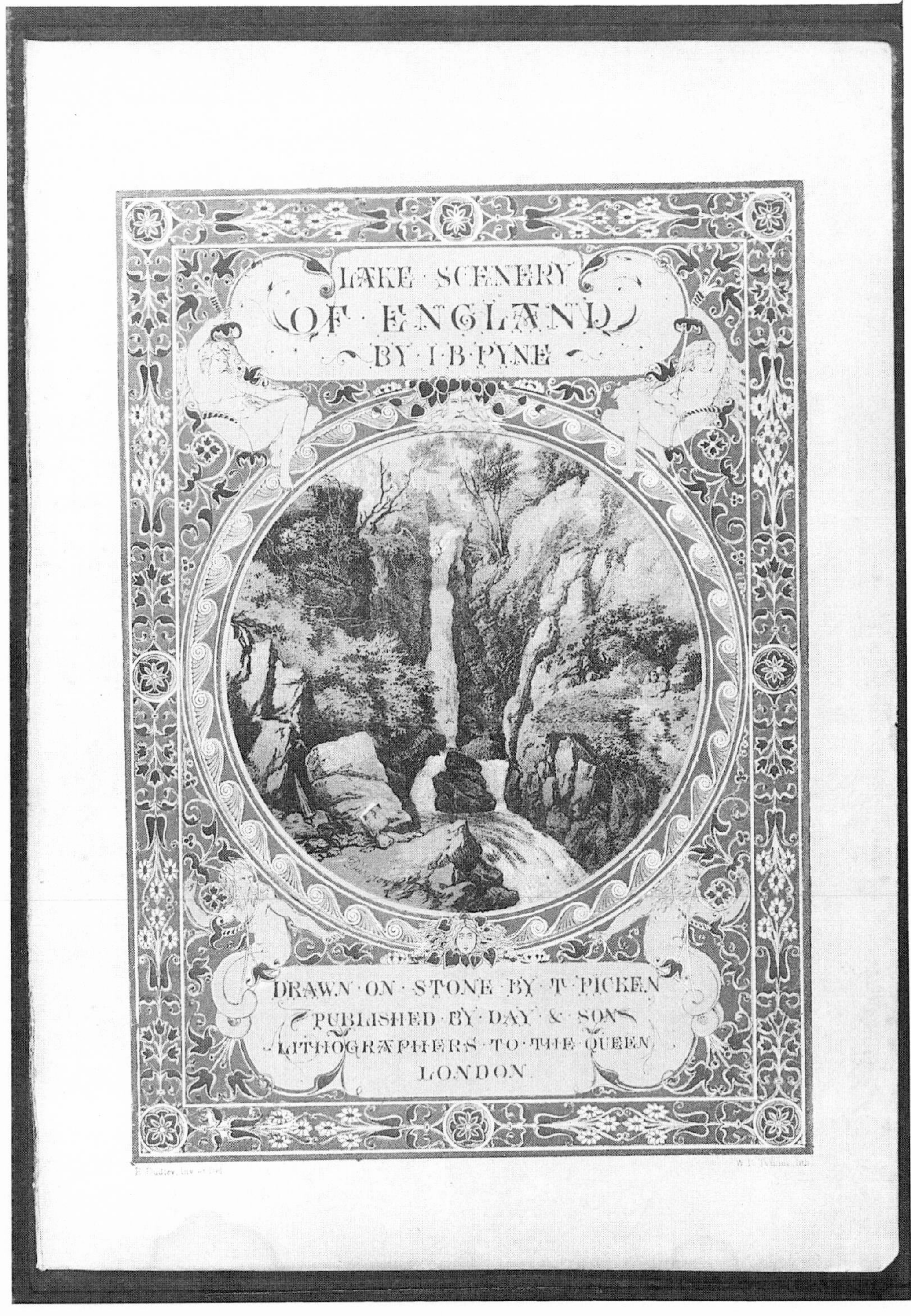

D Title-page, drawn by R. Dudley, chromo lithograph by W.P. Tymms (290 × 200 mm.)
J.B. Pyne, *Lake scenery of England* (154c)

E 1 A View of the Head of Ulswater towards Patterdale, engraved by Chatelin & Mason
William Bellers, *Eight Views of the Lakes in Cumberland* (1)

E 2 A View of Darwentwater & c. from Crow-Park, painted and engraved by Thomas Smith
Four views in the North of England (3b)

F 1 Entrance to Borrodale, by John Smith, engraved by J. Merigot 1792
John 'Warwick' Smith, *Views of the Lakes in Cumberland and Westmorland* (32)

F 2 Stockley Bridge, drawn, etched and tinted by William Green 1814
A description of a series of sixty small prints (67)

G 1 Keswick Lake, from the East side 1820. Aquatint, drawn and engraved by William Westall
A series of views of the Lakes of Cumberland and Westmorland (91)

G 2 Kirkstone Pass, 1821, drawn and engraved by T.H. Fielding
A picturesque tour of the English Lakes (100)

H 1 Honister Crag, by T. Allom, engraved by W. Floyd 1833
Thomas Rose, *Westmorland, Cumberland . . .* (112)

H 2 Brothers' Water, painted by J.B. Pyne, lithographed by W. Gauci 1853
J.B. Pyne, *The English Lake District* (154a)

King's copy: In original grey printed paper boards. Uncut. Upper cover printed as title-page. Lower cover, Reviews of books.

Copies: K; Wordsworth

——— Fourth, fifth editions, no information

41.6 ——— Sixth edition. 1814. Duodecimo.

Copies: BL; and Alpine Club

41.7 ——— Seventh edition. 1816. Octavo.

Copies: K; Armitt; BL

41.8 ——— Eighth edition. 1817. Duodecimo.

Copy: BL;

41.9 ——— Ninth edition. 1821. Octavo.†

Copies: K; Cornell; Jackson

41.G ——— *John Housmans Reise durch die nördliche Gegenden von England, nebst einer Beschreibung von Cumberland, Westmoreland* . . . German translation. Weimar: Verlage des Landes, Industrie Comptoirs. 1811. Duodecimo.
Copy: New York Public Library

CHARLES SMITH (mapseller)

42.1 ***Smith's new and accurate map of the Lakes, in the Counties of Cumberland, Westmorland, and Lancaster.*** London: C. Smith. 1800. Scale: approx. 1 in. = 2 miles. Size: 610 × 485 mm. Coloured.

42.2 ——— (Second edition) As 1800 edition except dated July, 1802.

King's copy: Imprint: *London, Printed for C. Smith, Mapseller, no. 172 corner of Surrey St. Strand. July 1802.* In marbled slip case, with printed paper label, *Map of the Lakes in Cumberland, Westmorland & Lancashire. Sold by W. Pennington, Kendal.* The map is dissected and mounted on linen.

——— Other editions: 1814, 1821 and 1824.

Notes: It is the earliest pocket map of the Lake District intended for tourists (18 years earlier than Otley's Map, no. 88). It includes a list of inns which supply Post Horses and Carriages. The hills are delineated very inaccurately.

Advertised in West's *Guide*, 8th. edn. 1802, p. [332], and 9th. edn. 1807, p. [312]: 'Smith's Map of the Lakes. Neatly coloured. Price, 4*s*., or on Canvas in a Case, 6*s*.'

Prior to the publication of Smith's map in 1800 the tourists had to make the best of the small-scale map first included in West's *Guide* in 1784, those of Crosthwaite and Clarke which did not cover the whole district, and Donald's 1-inch scale maps which derived from Thomas Jeffery's 1-inch maps of Cumberland and Westmorland. These were all on sale at Crosthwaite's museum in Keswick after 1781. In 1783 a reduced version of Donald's maps was advertised as suitable for those making the tour of the Lakes.

1802

RICHARD WARNER 1763-1857

Born in Edinburgh. Divine, antiquary and topographical writer. Author of *A walk through Wales in . . . 1797* (1798) and *A second walk through Wales in . . . 1798* (1799).

43 ***A tour through the Northern Counties of England, and the Borders of Scotland.*** 2 vols. Bath, printed by R. Cruttwell; and sold by G. and J. Robinson, Pater-Noster-Row, London. 1802. Octavo.†

Text: Vol. 1 Title verso blank; Itinerary [iii], iv Text [1]-316.
Vol. 2 Title, verso blank; Itinerary [iii], iv Text [1]-300; Imprint, *Cruttwell Printer, Bath.*

Maps: Diagrammatic map in text at head of each letter

Lakes: vol. 2, pp. [61]-[147] Letter VI, Ambleside, July 13th [1801] Letter VII, Manchester, July 20th [1801]

Itinerary: Penrith, Haweswater, Ullswater, Keswick, Borrowdale, Buttermere, Grasmere, Windermere, Coniston, Ulverston, Lancaster over the sands

King's copy: 2 vols bound in one in contemporary half calf, grey paper boards. Book plate, Thomas Munro.

Copies: K; Armitt; BL; Jackson; Kendal

Ref: Upcott, p. xxxviii

43.G ——— German edition, translated by Carl Gottlob Kultness. 2 vols. Leipzig: Göschen. 1803.

Copies: University of Yale; University of Chicago

CHARLES DIBDIN 1745-1814

Charles Dibdin, singer, song writer (wrote 'Tom Bowling'), composer, impresario and actor, and amateur landscape painter.

44 ***Observations on a tour through almost the whole of England and a considerable part of Scotland, in a series of letters, addressed to a large number of intelligent and respectable friends, by Mr Dibdin.*** 2 vols. London: G. Goulding, No 45, Pall Mall; John Walker, No 44, Paternoster-Row, and at the Author's Warehouse, Leicester-Place, where the Pictures from which the Views are taken, may be seen. Printed by T. Woodfall, Little Russell–street, Covent-Garden. n.d. [*c.* 1802]. Folio.†

Text: Vol. 1 Title, verso blank; sub-title, vol. 1, verso blank; Advertisement (Leicester Place, Nov. 16, 1801); Prefatory Hints 2 pp.; Contents 1 p; Directions 1 p; Text [1]-404
Vol. 2 Sub-title, vol. 2, verso blank; Text [1]-407; 88 letters, signed and dated Nov 5, 1800-April 10, 1802

Plates: 60 oval sepia aquatints. 40 large, numbered, no titles, no signatures. Imprints: *London, Published by Mr. Dibdin, 1801/1802.* 20 vignettes, numbered, no titles, no signatures. Imprints: *London, Published by Mr. Dibdin, 1801/1802*

Lake District views:

20 [Windermere]
21 [Cascade at Rydall]
22 [The Derwent]
23 [Skiddaw]
24 [Lowdore]
25 [Review of the Derwent]

These are the titles in the Directions which do not all appear to be correct. The plates are from sketches by the author.

Lakes: Vol. 1 Letter XXXIV. Westmoreland (description of the County). Aug 12, 1801.
Letter XXXV. Cumberland (description of the County).
Vol. 2 Letter LIX. Describes tour in 1800: Kendal, Ambleside, Grasmere. Jan 12, 1802.
Letter LX. Cumberland. Continuous description of tour. Leathes Water, Keswick.

Note: Dibdin used 'one of Gray's glasses' when sketching

King's copy: Bound in contemporary marbled calf, gilt, leather labels. Title misplaced.

Copies: K; BL

Ref: Upcott, p. xxxviii

JOHN BRITTON 1771-1857 and EDWARD WEDLAKE BRAYLEY 1773-1854

John Britton and Edward Wedlake Brayley, F.S.A., who each contributed prolifically to the publication of topographical and antiquarian works, combined in producing *The Beauties of England and Wales, or delineations, topographical, historical, and descriptive of each county*. This was published, county by county in alphabetical order, in 18 volumes, 1801-15, and published as a complete set in 1818 with an introductory volume by J. Norris Brewer. The three Lake Counties are included in volumes 3, 9 and 15.

45 ***The beauties of England and Wales: or, delineations, topographical, historical, and descriptive, of each county. Embellished with engravings***. Vol. III. [Cumberland, Isle of Man, Derbyshire] London: Printed by Thomas Maiden, Sherbourne-Lane, for Vernor & Hood, Longman & Rees, Cuthell & Martin, J. & A. Arch, W.J. & J. Richardson, and B. Crosby. 1802. Octavo.

Text: Engraved half-title, verso blank; Title, verso blank; Cumberland [3]-247; Isle of Man [248]-290; Derbyshire [291]-552; List of books 10 pp.; Index 11 pp.; Corrections and additions 1 p. Imprint on last p. *Printed by Thomas Maiden, Sherbourne Lane, Lombard Street.*

Plates: 30 engravings: 8 of Cumberland, one of the Isle of Man and 21 of Derbyshire. Only 4 Lake District Views:

1 Ara Force, in Gowbarrow Park, Westmoreland ['Westmoreland' was corrected to 'Cumberland' in later issues], The Seat of his Grace The Duke of Norfolk. Signed: *Engraved by T. Bonnor from a drawing by W.M. Craig.* Imprint: *Published by Vernor & Hood Poultry July 1st, 1805*
2 Derwentwater, Cumberland. *Engraved by B. Compte from a drawing by W.M. Craig.*
3 Borrowdale, From Bowder Stone. *Engraved by Hay from a Drawing by A. Wilson. Oct 1st. 1803*
4 The Bowder Stone. *Engraved by I. Greig from a Painting by G. Arnald. July 1st. 1803.*

Imprints on all plates similar

The other Cumberland plates are of Lanercost Priory, Carlisle Cathedral and Castle, Dacre and Calder Castles

King's copy: In contemporary half-calf, marbled boards, gilt. Bookplate of Sir Richard Birnie. Label mounted on paste-down endpaper, *Bound by Broadbere, Hanover Builgs., Southampton*

Copies: K; Armitt (extra-illustrated); BL; Cornell; Wordsworth

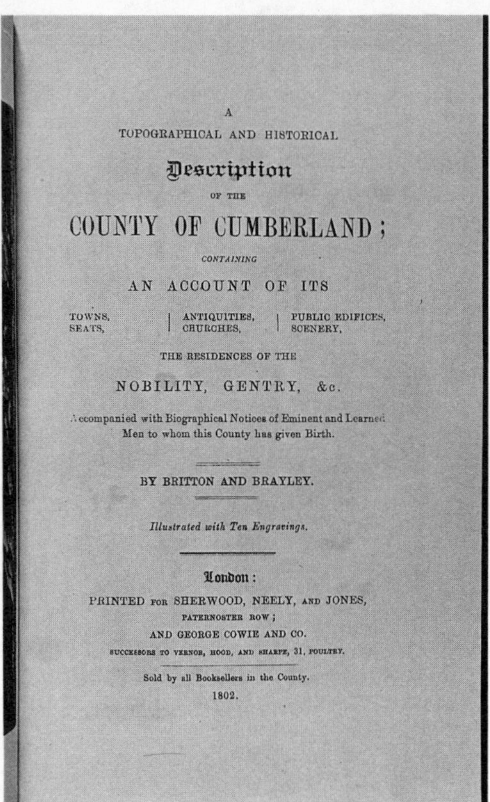

A
TOPOGRAPHICAL AND HISTORICAL
Description
OF THE
COUNTY OF CUMBERLAND;
CONTAINING
AN ACCOUNT OF ITS
TOWNS, SEATS, | ANTIQUITIES, CHURCHES, | PUBLIC EDIFICES, SCENERY,
THE RESIDENCES OF THE
NOBILITY, GENTRY, &c.
Accompanied with Biographical Notices of Eminent and Learned Men to whom this County has given Birth.
BY BRITTON AND BRAYLEY.
Illustrated with Ten Engravings.
London:
PRINTED FOR SHERWOOD, NEELY, AND JONES,
PATERNOSTER ROW;
AND GEORGE COWIE AND CO.
SUCCESSORS TO VERNOR, HOOD, AND SHARPE, 31, POULTRY.
Sold by all Booksellers in the County.
1802.

45a 210 x 130 mm.

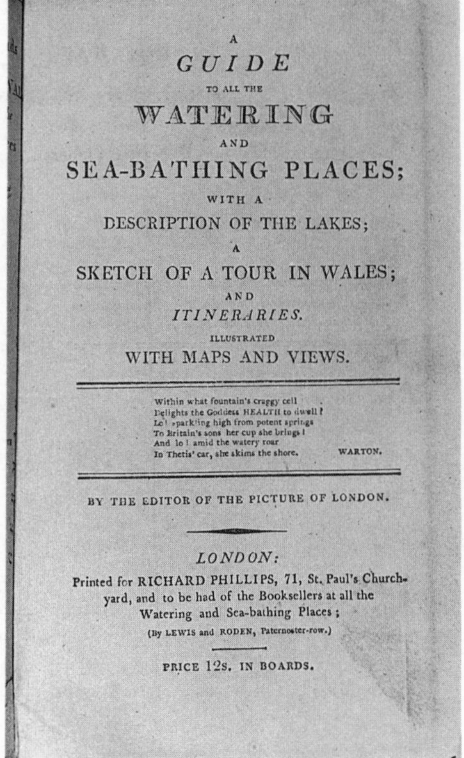

A
GUIDE
TO ALL THE
WATERING
AND
SEA-BATHING PLACES;
WITH A
DESCRIPTION OF THE LAKES;
A
SKETCH OF A TOUR IN WALES;
AND
ITINERARIES.
ILLUSTRATED
WITH MAPS AND VIEWS.

Within what fountain's craggy cell
Delights the Goddess HEALTH to dwell?
Lo! sparkling high from potent springs
To Britain's sons her cup she brings!
And lo! amid the watery roar
In Thetis' car, she skims the shore. WARTON.

BY THE EDITOR OF THE PICTURE OF LONDON.
LONDON:
Printed for RICHARD PHILLIPS, 71, St. Paul's Church-yard, and to be had of the Booksellers at all the Watering and Sea-bathing Places;
(By LEWIS and RODEN, Paternoster-row.)
PRICE 12s. IN BOARDS.

50.2 158 x 96 mm.

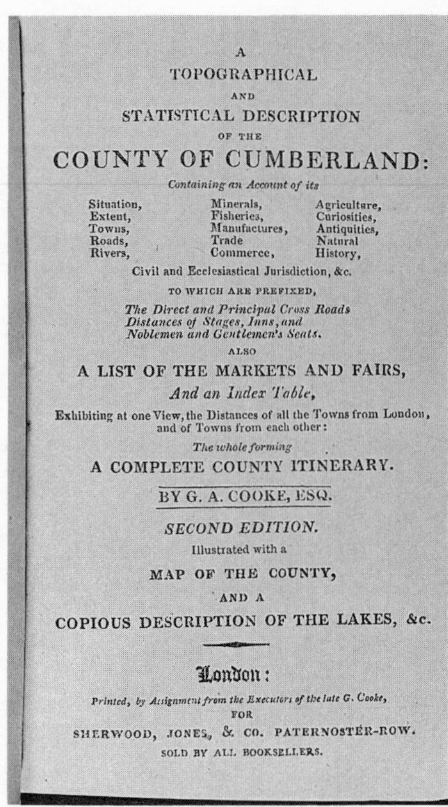

A
TOPOGRAPHICAL
AND
STATISTICAL DESCRIPTION
OF THE
COUNTY OF CUMBERLAND:
Containing an Account of its
Situation, Extent, Towns, Roads, Rivers, Minerals, Fisheries, Manufactures, Trade Commerce, Agriculture, Curiosities, Antiquities, Natural History,
Civil and Ecclesiastical Jurisdiction, &c.
TO WHICH ARE PREFIXED,
The Direct and Principal Cross Roads Distances of Stages, Inns, and Noblemen and Gentlemen's Seats.
ALSO
A LIST OF THE MARKETS AND FAIRS,
And an Index Table,
Exhibiting at one View, the Distances of all the Towns from London, and of Towns from each other:
The whole forming
A COMPLETE COUNTY ITINERARY.
BY G. A. COOKE, ESQ.
SECOND EDITION.
Illustrated with a
MAP OF THE COUNTY,
AND A
COPIOUS DESCRIPTION OF THE LAKES, &c.
London:
Printed, by Assignment from the Executors of the late G. Cooke,
FOR
SHERWOOD, JONES, & CO. PATERNOSTER-ROW.
SOLD BY ALL BOOKSELLERS.

51.2 140 x 84 mm.

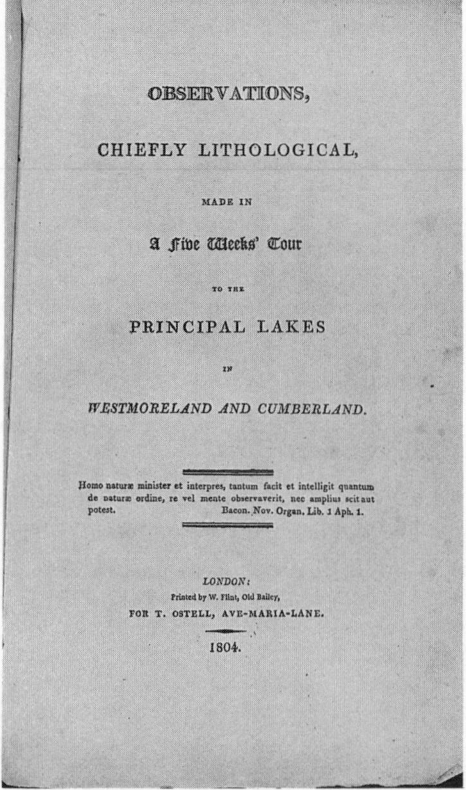

OBSERVATIONS,
CHIEFLY LITHOLOGICAL,
MADE IN
A Five Weeks' Tour
TO THE
PRINCIPAL LAKES
IN
WESTMORELAND AND CUMBERLAND.

Homo naturæ minister et interpres, tantum facit et intelligit quantum de naturæ ordine, re vel mente observaverit, nec amplius scit aut potest. Bacon. Nov. Organ. Lib. 1 Aph. 1.

LONDON:
Printed by W. Flint, Old Bailey,
FOR T. OSTELL, AVE-MARIA-LANE.
1804.

54 225 x 125 mm.

45a ——— *A topographical and historical description of the County of Cumberland . . .* By Britton and Brayley. Illustrated with Ten Engravings. London: printed for Sherwood, Neely, and Jones, Paternoster Row; and George Cowie and Co. successors to Vernor, Hood, and Sharpe, 31, Poultry. Sold by all booksellers in the County. 1802. Octavo.†

King's copy: Large paper. Rebound in two vols extra illustrated with 116 additional plates of views, antiquities, armorial bearings and maps, including prints from drawings by Barret, Farington, Fielding, Gilpin, Dibdin, Green, Griffith, Havell, Heath, Loutherbourg, Middiman, Powell, Rothery, Westall and others.

46 ——— By John Britton F.S.A. Vol. IX [Lancashire, Leicestershire, Lincolnshire] Imprint as Vol. III except 'Vernor & Hood' has become 'Vernor, Hood & Sharpe', 'Longman & Rees' has become 'Longman, Hurst, Rees, & Orme'. 1807.

Text: Engraved title (May 1808), verso blank; Title (1807), verso blank; Dedication (March 1807) 1 p., verso blank; Introductory Observations [iii]-vi; Lancashire [5]-312; Leicestershire [313]-522; Lincolnshire [523]-808; List of books 13 pp.; blank; Index 16 pp.; Corrections 1 p., imprint on verso, *W. Wilson, Printr, St. John's Square.*

Plates: 24 engravings. Only Lake District view, Newby Bridge *Engraved by White.* Imprint: *London. Published by Vernor, Hood & Sharpe, Poultry. Sept. 1, 1811.*

Copies: BL; and PB

47 ——— Vol. XV [Part 1] Worcestershire, Westmoreland and part of Wiltshire [Westmoreland by the Rev. J. Hodgson] London: Printed for J. Harris; Longman and Co.; J. Walker; R. Baldwin; Sherwood and Co.; J. and J. Cundee; B. and R. Crosby and Co.; J. Cuthell; J. and J. Richardson; Cadell and Davies; C. and J. Rivington; and G. Cowie and Co. 1814.

Text: Engraved half-title Sept. 1, 1814, verso blank; Title, verso blank; Preface [iii]-v; blank; Directions to the binder, 2 pp.; Worcestershire [1]-402; List of Books [403]-407; Index 8 pp.; Errata 1p.; Westmoreland [1]-238; List of books 7 pp.; blank; Index 6 pp.; Wiltshire [1]-240.

Plates: 20 engravings. 13 of Worcestershire, one of Wiltshire (in this volume), 6 of Westmoreland. Only 3 views of Lake District scenery:

1 Gellforth Spout, in Long-sle-dale. Signed: *Engraved by J. Storer, from a drawing by W.M. Craig.* Imprint: *London, Published by Vernor & Hood, Poultry. Dec. 1. 1803*
2 View in Scandale, near Ambleside. Signed: *Engraved by Willm. Cooke from a painting by G. Arnald.* Imprint: *London, Published by Vernor, Hood & Sharpe, Poultry Novr. 1st. 1807.*
3 View in the Valley of Langdale, (looking Westward towards Langdale Pikes). Signed: *Engraved by W. Angus from a Painting by G. Arnald.* Imprint: *London; Published by Vernor, Hood & Sharpe, Poultry, Augt. 1. 1807.*

King's copy: In contemporary half-calf, marbled boards, uniform with 45, rebacked. Bookplate of Sir Richard Birnie.

Copies: K; BL; Cornell; Wordsworth (Westmoreland only)

The descriptions of the Lakes in each of the three volumes consist largely of quotations from Housman, Hutchinson, Gilpin, Radcliffe, Warner and others.

The sections on the three Lake Counties were published separately in various editions. Sherwood, Neely & Jones, and George Cowie, successors to Vernor, Hood and Sharpe, purchased the stock and issued it in separate counties with new title-pages (see 45a).

48 ***A topographical and historical description of the County of Westmoreland*** . . . by the Rev. Mr. Hodgson. London: for Sherwood, Neely, and Jones, Paternoster Row, and George Cowie and Co. successors to Vernor, Hood and Sharpe, 31 Poultry. Printed title 1811; engraved title 1820. Octavo. New edition of 47.

Copies: BL; Armitt (1814); Jackson

Copies of *Westmoreland* are to be found with a new title-page and imprint, *London: James Cawthorne, Cockspur Street, n.d.*

1803

FRANCIS JOLLIE (printer and publisher)

See 74

49 ***Sketch of a tour from Lancaster, round the principal lakes in Lancashire, Cumberland and Westmorland. To which is added Mr. Gray's Journal.*** Carlisle: Printed and sold by F. Jollie. 1803. Duodecimo.

Folding map of the Lakes, engraved by J. Lowes.

Note: Gray's *Journal*(see 10) is preceded by Preliminary Remarks and a six-page tabulated sketch of a tour of the lakes, indicating mileages and recommended inns (noted that chaises are kept at ten of the eighteen recommended inns). The tour is devised so that the tourist 'is always conducted towards the head of each lake; a circumstance of no small moment, in a country where the waters originate in grandeur and flow into tranquility'. He is recommended to 'go to Scale Force especially with such a guide to it as I had, Mary Robinson, the Beauty of the Lakes' (see 26.1), and to carry Gray's *Journal* and Smith's map (42).

Copies: Kendal; Jackson

JOHN FELTHAM

50.1 ***A guide to all the watering and sea-bathing places; with a description of the Lakes; a sketch of a tour in Wales; and itineraries. Illustrated with maps and views. By the editor of the Picture of London.*** London: Printed for Richard Phillips, 71, St. Paul's Churchyard, and to be had of the Booksellers at all the Watering and Sea-bathing Places; (By Lewis and Roden, Paternoster-row.) n.d. [1803]. Duodecimo. Engravings, maps, tables. 'Outline of a tour of the Lakes in Cumberland, Westmoreland, and Lancashire' forms a separate Appendix.

Copies: Armitt; BL

50.2 ——— [Second edition] Title as first edition. Price 12*s.* in boards [1804] †

Text: Title, note on verso; Advertisement [iii], iv, dated London, 1804; Text [1]-450; Adverts. 4 pp.

Plates: 33 engravings (3 folding, one extra). One folding table.
Windermere. Signed *F. Chesham sc.*, facing p. 404
Ullswater. Signed: *Neele sc. Strand.* facing p. 406
Derwentwater. Signed: *Neele sc. Strand,* facing p. 408

Maps: 20 maps (4 folding).

Folding map of the Lakes, facing p. 398. Size: 183 × 158 mm Scale: 1 in. = 5 miles.

Appendix: 'Tour of the Lakes in Cumberland, Westmoreland, and Lancashire.' pp. 398-408

King's copy: In contemporary half-russia, marbled boards, leather label, gilt. Bookplate Henry Carrington Bowles.

Copies: K; Cornell

50.3 ——— [Third edition] Title as previous edition except the imprint is altered to 'London: Printed for Richard Phillips, 6 Bridge Street, Blackfriars, and to be had of the Booksellers at all the Watering and Sea-bathing places. W. Lewis, Printer, Paternoster-Row. Price 13s. in boards; or, 14s. Bound in Red' [1806].

Text: Title, note on verso; Advertisement [iv], v, (London, 1806); Text [1]-500.

Plates, table, and maps as previous edition
'Numerous changes since the publication of the first edition' Advertisement

Appendix: 'Outline of a tour of the Lakes in Cumberland, Westmoreland, and Lancashire.' pp. 450-59. The same as previous edition except final paragraph added, 'It will be satisfactory to those who feel an inclination to visit the romantic regions, to learn that the horses are sure footed and easy, and the inns clean, comfortable, and reasonable.'

King's copy: In contemporary calf, gilt, black leather label. Bookplate, Lord Sinclair.

Copies: K; BL

——— Other editions:

1809	1815 BL; Barrow-in-Furness
[1810] BL	[1824] BL
1812 Library of Congress	[1825] BL

Editions, 1809-1812, London: Phillips; 1815-1825, Longman [etc.]

GEORGE ALEXANDER COOKE

The modern British traveller or tourists guide. 47 vols. London: for C. Cooke. n.d. [*c.* 1803-10] Duodecimo. Being an accurate and comprehensive description of all the counties in England, Scotland and Wales.

Each county has a separate title-page, and could be sold separately.

A description of the Lakes is incorporated in the general description of each of the three counties, and does not form a separate section.

The three Lake District volumes are:

51.1 ***A topographical and statistical description of the County of Cumberland*** . . . London: for C. Cooke, Duodecimo. Plates, map, tables.

Copies: BL; Jackson; Wordsworth

51.2 ——— *Cumberland.* Second edition. Illustrated with a map of the county, and a copious description of the Lakes, &c. Printed, by Assignment from the Executors of the late G. Cooke, for Sherwood, Jones, & Co. Paternoster-row. Sold by all Booksellers. n.d. Duodecimo.†

Text: Title, imprint on verso, *D. Sidney and Co. Printers Northumberland Street, Strand;* tables etc. [3]-[5]; Itinerary, etc. [6]-24; General and Topographical Descriptions [25]-169; Provincial Terms 170-174; Index [175]-176; Index to the Lakes [177]-180; Preface [iii]; Introduction [iv]-x; Text [1]-136.

Plates: 8 engravings on four pages by J. & H. Storer

1 Carlisle Cathedral	5 Patterdale Palace
2 Narworth Castle	6 Rydal
3 Dacre Castle	7 North Entrance to Keswick
4 Lanercost Priory	8 Brathay Bridge

Map: Folding map of Cumberland. Size: 140 × 135 mm. Scale: 1 in. = 16 miles

Note: The description of the Lakes in the first edition has been extracted from the general description, and follows the Topographical Description 'A copious description of the Lakes; &c.', (page head 'Excursions to the Lakes of Cumberland, &c.'), with its own preface, introduction, index, and pagination.

King's copy: Half-calf, marbled boards, rebacked, original spine remounted, gilt.

Copies: K; Armitt; BL; Cornell; Jackson

51.3 ——— *Cumberland.* A new edition. London: Sherwood, Jones. n.d. Printed by J. Gillet for Sherwood, Neely & Jones; and B. & R. Crosby & Co.

'Copious description of the lakes' now entitled 'Excursion to the Lakes'

Copies: Armitt; and Barrow-in-Furness

52 ***A topographical and statistical description of the County of Lancaster*** . . . London: for C. Cooke, Duodecimo. Plates, map, tables.

Copy: BL

53 ***A topographical and statistical description of the County of Westmoreland*** . . . for C. Cooke, Duodecimo. Plates, map, tables.

Copies: BL; Armitt; Jackson; Wordsworth

Undated advertisement issued by Sherwood, Neely, and Jones, Paternoster-Row: 'Cooke's Topography of Great Britain, or British Traveller's Pocket Directory, being an accurate and comprehensive topographical, and statistical description of all the counties . . . The Work is *completed,* and any *County* may be had *separately,* at the Price affixed' – Cumberland, 1*s.* 6*d.* 'A Superior Edition is printed on large *Wove Vellum Paper*, hot pressed, with the Maps coloured, Price 2*s.* 6*d.* each Part.' – 'Persons desirous of possessing the Work Complete, may have it neatly done up in extra Boards, in 26 portable Volumes, price £4 11*s.*; or, any Volume may be had separately, viz. Westmoreland and Cumberland 3*s.* 6*d.* N.B. It may be had also *bound*, in any manner agreeable to the purchaser.'

The counties were subsequently published separately by Sherwood, Gilbert and Piper, London, n.d., as *Cooke's topographical library of Great Britain. The British Traveller's guide; or pocket county directory*. Price 4*s.* each county. Whiting, Beaufort House, Strand.

1804

T. OSTELL (publisher)

54 ***Observations, chiefly lithological, made in a five weeks' tour to the principal lakes in Westmoreland and Cumberland***. [Anonymous] London: Printed by W. Flint, Old Bailey, for T. Ostell, Ave-Maria-Lane. 1804. Octavo.†

Text: Title, verso blank; Preface [iii]-vi; Contents and errata [vii], viii; Text [1]-80; Imprint on verso of p. 80, *W. Flint, Printer, Old Bailey*

King's copy: In original blue-grey paper wrappers, uncut

Note: The anonymous author made Keswick his headquarters for nearly three weeks in June and July 1803. His itinerary was: Carlisle; to Keswick by Wigton and Bassenthwaite; Borrowdale: by Newlands to Buttermere and by Honister back to Keswick; Thirlmere, Windermere; back to

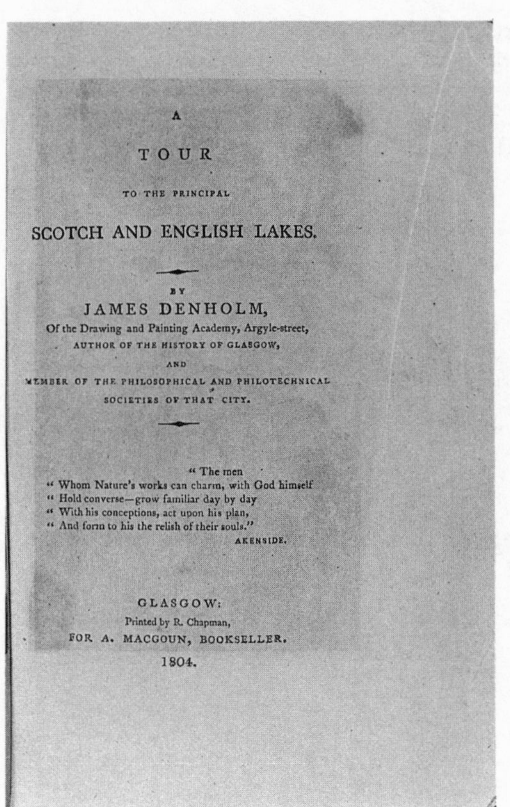

A

TOUR

TO THE PRINCIPAL

SCOTCH AND ENGLISH LAKES.

BY

JAMES DENHOLM,

Of the Drawing and Painting Academy, Argyle-street,

AUTHOR OF THE HISTORY OF GLASGOW,

AND

MEMBER OF THE PHILOSOPHICAL AND PHILOTECHNICAL SOCIETIES OF THAT CITY.

" The men
" Whom Nature's works can charm, with God himself
" Hold converse—grow familiar day by day
" With his conceptions, act upon his plan,
" And form to his the relish of their souls."

AKENSIDE.

GLASGOW:

Printed by R. Chapman,

FOR A. MACGOUN, BOOKSELLER.

1804.

55 218 x 135 mm.

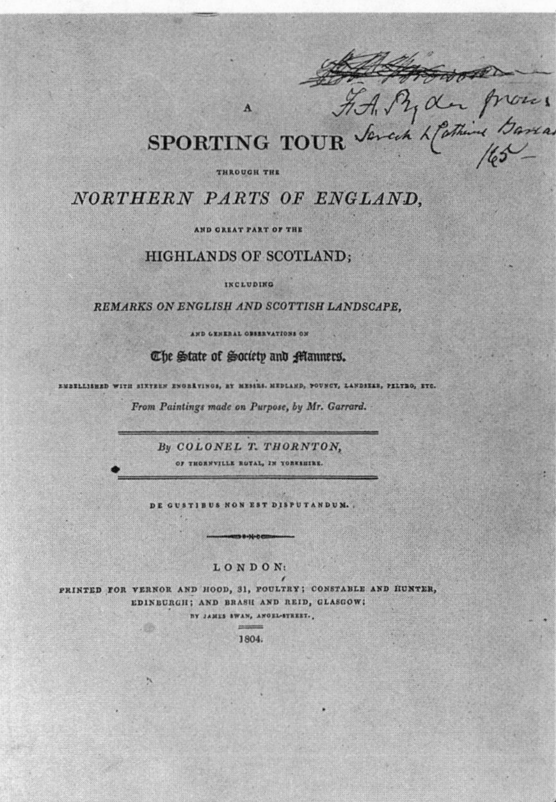

A

SPORTING TOUR

THROUGH THE

NORTHERN PARTS OF ENGLAND,

AND GREAT PART OF THE

HIGHLANDS OF SCOTLAND;

INCLUDING

REMARKS ON ENGLISH AND SCOTTISH LANDSCAPE,

AND GENERAL OBSERVATIONS ON

The State of Society and Manners.

EMBELLISHED WITH SIXTEEN ENGRAVINGS, BY MESSRS. MEDLAND, POUNCY, LANDSEER, PELTRO, ETC.

From Paintings made on Purpose, by Mr. Garrard.

By COLONEL T. THORNTON,

OF THORNVILLE ROYAL, IN YORKSHIRE.

DE GUSTIBUS NON EST DISPUTANDUM.

LONDON:

PRINTED FOR VERNOR AND HOOD, 31, POULTRY; CONSTABLE AND HUNTER, EDINBURGH; AND BRASH AND REID, GLASGOW;

BY JAMES SWAN, ANGEL-STREET.

1804.

56.1 270 x 210 mm.

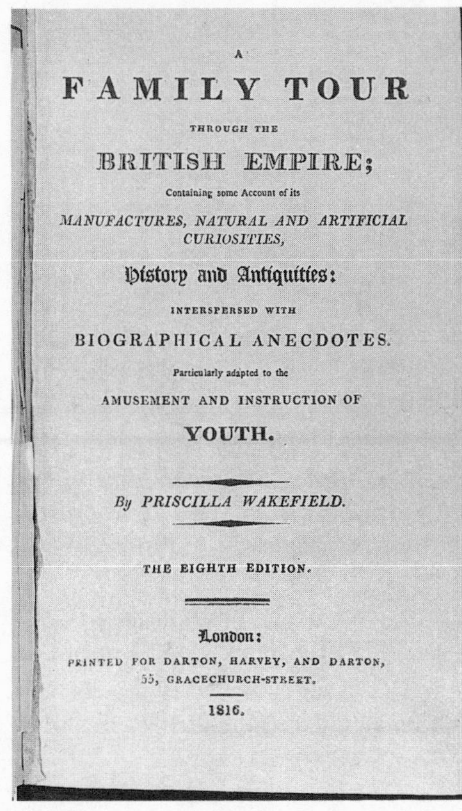

A

FAMILY TOUR

THROUGH THE

BRITISH EMPIRE;

Containing some Account of its

MANUFACTURES, NATURAL AND ARTIFICIAL CURIOSITIES,

History and Antiquities:

INTERSPERSED WITH

BIOGRAPHICAL ANECDOTES.

Particularly adapted to the

AMUSEMENT AND INSTRUCTION OF

YOUTH.

By PRISCILLA WAKEFIELD.

THE EIGHTH EDITION.

London:

PRINTED FOR DARTON, HARVEY, AND DARTON, 55, GRACECHURCH-STREET.

1816.

57.8 170 x 100 mm.

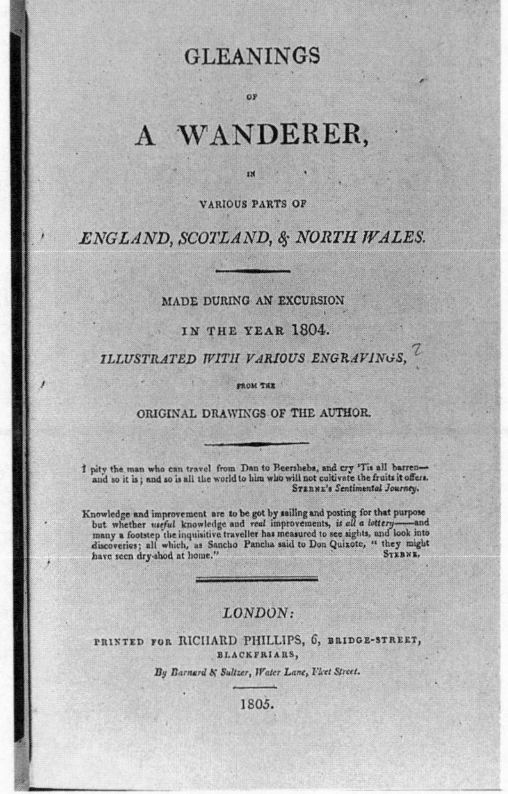

GLEANINGS

OF

A WANDERER,

IN

VARIOUS PARTS OF

ENGLAND, SCOTLAND, & NORTH WALES.

MADE DURING AN EXCURSION

IN THE YEAR 1804.

ILLUSTRATED WITH VARIOUS ENGRAVINGS,

FROM THE

ORIGINAL DRAWINGS OF THE AUTHOR.

I pity the man who can travel from Dan to Beersheba, and cry 'Tis all barren—and so it is; and so is all the world to him who will not cultivate the fruits it offers.
STERNE's *Sentimental Journey.*

Knowledge and improvement are to be got by sailing and posting for that purpose but whether *useful* knowledge and *real* improvements, *is all a lottery*——and many a footstep the inquisitive traveller has measured to see sights, and look into discoveries; all which, as Sancho Pancha said to Don Quixote, " they might have seen dry-shod at home."
STERNE.

LONDON:

PRINTED FOR RICHARD PHILLIPS, 6, BRIDGE-STREET, BLACKFRIARS,

By Barnard & Sultzer, Water Lane, Fleet Street.

1805.

58 210 x 137 mm.

Keswick, ascent of Skiddaw; Penrith. He was primarily interested in collecting geological specimens, which he compared with minerals from the Alps, Sweden and other lands. He included, somewhat irrelevantly, a chapter on Jade, and chapters on Crosthwaite's and Hutton's museums at Keswick, and Mr Todhunter's museum at Kendal. He paid a shilling to see Green's exhibition at Ambleside. He also recorded botanical and ornithological specimens.

Copies: K; Armitt; BL; Jackson

Ref: Upcott, p. 1284

JAMES DENHOLM 1772-1818

James Denholm was a drawing teacher in Glasgow, and President of the Glasgow Philosophical Society.

55 ***A tour to the principal Scotch and English Lakes***. Glasgow: Printed by R. Chapman, for A. Macgoun, Bookseller. 1804. Octavo.†

Text: Title, verso blank; Preface one page, verso blank; Contents [v], vi, Text [9]-306; Imprint on verso p. 306, *Printed by R. Chapman, Trongate, Glasgow*

Plate: Engraved frontispiece

Map: Folding map of Loch Lomond and Loch Long

Lakes: pp. 243-306

Itinerary: Penrith, Ullswater, Haweswater, Derwentwater, Watendlath, Borrowdale, Bassenthwaite, Buttermere, Thirlmere, Grasmere, Windermere, Esthwaite and Coniston (only Ennerdale and Wastdale not included)

King's copy: Rebound, bookplate: 'C' and coronet

Note: The *Tour* is reprinted from *The History of the City of Glasgow and suburbs . . . to which is added, a sketch of a tour to the principal Scotch and English lakes*. Glasgow: 1798.

Copies: K; Armitt; Jackson; Cornell

THOMAS THORNTON 1757-1823

Colonel Thomas Thornton of Thornville Royal in Yorkshire and the West Yorkshire Militia, and MP for York, lived in Yorks., Beds., Wilts., London and France. He was a sportsman , a falconer and a 'character'. On one occasion he hired the Château de Chambord, describing himself as 'Prince of Chambord and Marquis le Pont'. His tour of 1786 was made partly by sea and was largely devoted to 'hunting, shooting, angling and hawking'.

56.1 ***A sporting tour through the Northern Parts of England, and great part of the Highlands of Scotland . . .*** London: printed for Vernor and Hood, 31, Poultry; Constable and Hunter, Edinburgh; and Brash and Reid, Glasgow; by James Swan, Angel Street. 1804. Quarto.†

Text: Half-title, verso blank; Title, verso blank; Advertisement 2 pp; List of plates 1 p., verso blank; Table of contents 18 pp.; Errata 1 p., verso blank; Text [1]-312; Index 4 pp.; Imprint on verso p. 312, *J. Swan, Printer. Angel Street, London.*

Plates: 16 engraved and etched plates by Messrs. Medland, Pouncy, Landseer, Peltro, etc. 'from paintings made on purpose, by Mr. Garrard'. No Lake District views.

Lakes: pp. 281-6.

Itinerary: Keswick, Derwentwater, Thirlmere, Grasmere, Rydal, Ambleside, Eskdale, Ponsonby House, Muncaster, Coniston, Rydal, Windermere and Kendal

King's copy: In contemporary half-calf, marbled boards, leather labels. Inscribed on title-page 'F.A. Ryder from Sarah & Catherine Barras /65-'.

Notes: Colonel Thornton was accompanied by Mr Garrard, a pupil of William Gilpin. He met Peter Crosthwaite at Keswick. At Rydal he visited Sir Michael Fleming, with whom he made his way over Red Bank, Wrynose and Hard Knott passes to stay with Mr Stanley at Ponsonby House near Calder Bridge. Between active periods of shooting and coursing they rode back to Rydal Hall.

Walter Scott reviewed the *Sporting Tour* in the *Edinburgh Review*, 1805 and found it 'somewhat tedious'.

Copy: K; BL; Jackson

56.2 ——— A new edition, with coloured plates by C.E. Lodge, portraits and selections from the original illustrations: Sir Herbert Maxwell's Sporting Library (London, 1896) Quarto.

Copy: Barrow-in-Furness

'PRISCILLA WAKEFIELD' 1751-1832

Mrs Bell, pseudonym 'Priscilla Wakefield', Quaker, philanthropist, was the author of books for children.

57.1 ***A family tour through the British Empire . . . Particularly adapted to the amusement and instruction of youth.*** London: Darton and Harvey. 1804. Duodecimo. Map.

Lakes: Chapters 6 and 7

Copies: BL; and University of Chicago

57.1a ——— [American edition] Philadelphia: Sold by Jacob Johnson & Co., A. Bartrum, printer. 1804. Duodecimo. Map.

Copies: BL; and National Union Catalogue (14 libraries)

57.2-15 ——— Other editions:
2nd 1805 Harvard
4th 1808 BL
5th 1810 BL; University of California, LA
6th 1812 BL; University of California, LA
8th 1816 See below, no. 57.8
9th 1818 BL
11th 1823 Jackson; BL
14th 1835 BL; Boston Public Library
15th 1840 Duke University, North Carolina
3rd, 7th, 10th, 13th editions, no information

All editions: London: Darton and Harvey: Darton, Harvey & Darton; or similar. Duodecimo.

57.8 ——— The eighth edition. London: Printed for Darton, Harvey and Darton, 55, Gracechurch Street. 1816. Duodecimo.†

Text: Title, verso blank; Preface [iii], iv; A Family Tour 1-454; Notes 8 pp.; Itinerary 7 pp., Imprint on last page, *Printed by Darton, Harvey, and Co. Gracechurch Street, London.* blank; adverts. 6 pp.

Map: A map of the British Empire [British Isles] engraved for Priscilla Wakefield's Family Tour. Coloured, folding. Size 450 × 360 mm.

Itinerary: Kendal, Windermere, Coniston, Rydal, Grasmere, Thirlmere, Keswick, ascent of Skiddaw, Borrowdale, Ullswater. The tour through the British Empire was in fact limited to the British Isles.

King's copy: Rebound. Inscribed on paste-down endpaper 'Elizabeth Vicars the Gift of Miss Tinney on her birthday – April 22nd. 1817. aged 9 years.' Label on paste-down endpaper 'Sold by Duffield, Bookseller, Stationer and Binder 11 Milsom Street, Bath.'

Copies: K; Jackson; New York Public Library

1805

RICHARD PHILLIPS (publisher)

58 ***Gleanings of a wanderer . . . made during an excursion in the year 1804 . . .*** [Anonymous] London: printed for Richard Phillips, 6 Bridge-Street, Blackfriars, By Barnard & Sulzer, Water Lane, Fleet Street. 1805. Quarto.†

Text: Title, verso blank; Text [3]-168; Index 4 pp. [179-182]

Plate: One tinted aquatint of Loch Leven. No Lake District views. Although the title includes 'Illustrated with various engravings, from the original drawings of the author', all copies examined have only one plate.

Lake District: pp. 134-42

Itinerary: Carlisle, Bassenthwaite, Keswick, Derwentwater, Thirlmere, Grasmere, Rydal, Windermere, Kendal

King's copy: Rebound

Copies: K; BL

JOSEPH MAWMAN (publisher)

59 ***An excursion to the Highlands of Scotland and the English Lakes . . .*** London: printed for J. Mawman, Poultry. By T. Gillet, Salisbury-square. 1805. Octavo.†

Text: Half-title, verso blank; Title, verso blank; Letter (J. Mawman, Poultry, 4th April, 1805) [v], verso blank; To the Reader [vii], verso blank; Contents ix-xv; Directions & Errata [xvi]; Text [5]-291. Imprint p.291 *J. Gillet, Printer, Salisbury.*

Plates: 3 engravings. Only one Lake District view: Plate 3 Patterdale. Signed: *Drawn by J.M.W. Turner R.A. Engraved by J. Heath.* Imprint: *London, Published May 1, 1805, by J. Mawman, Poultry.*

Map: Folding map of the route from London to Inverary

Lakes: Chapters 15, 16, 17, 18, pp. 187-243

Itinerary: Penrith, Keswick, Ullswater, Borrowdale, Watendlath, Honister to Buttermere, Crummock, Grasmere, Rydal, Windermere

King's copy: In contemporary mottled calf, gilt, rebacked, original leather label remounted on spine. Inscribed on free endpaper, 'With the author's respectful Compts.' Armorial bookplate.

Copies: K; Armitt; BL; Wordsworth

1806

BENJAMIN TRAVERS

60 ***A descriptive tour to the Lakes of Cumberland and Westmoreland, in the autumn of 1804.*** [Anonymous] London: printed for T. Ostell, Ave-Maria-Lane, By W. Pople, Old Boswell Court, Strand. 1806. Duodecimo.†

Text: Title, verso blank; Author's note (London, July 1 1806) 1 p., verso blank; Dedication [v]-viii; Text [1]-158; Addenda [159]-164; Imprint p. 164, *Printed by W. Pople, Old Boswell Court, Strand.*

Notes: Upcott gives the author as Benjamin Travers, but Hodgson (p. 280) gives Benjamin Train Jnr. Inscribed in the Armitt copy is 'The Author Benj. Travers, see Jollie's Cumberland Guide and Directory 8vo. 1811'.

The *Descriptive tour* was previously printed in 'The numbers of a respectable Magazine, June 1805-March 1806'.

Itinerary: Travers visited Rydal, Coniston and Grasmere from Windermere; from Keswick to Buttermere and Crummock over Honister; ascent of Skiddaw; return to Windermere and up Langdale, not often visited by tourists at that time. The Tour was made in August 1804.

King's copy: In original grey paper boards, rebacked, uncut, inscribed on the title-page 'James Lidderdale'

Copies: K; Cornell; Jackson

1807

THOMAS SANDERSON 1759-1829

Thomas Sanderson, Cumbrian poet and schoolmaster, contributed 'Ode to the Genius of Cumberland' to Hutchinson's *History of Cumberland* (28), and published *Original Poems* (Carlisle, 1800).

61.1 ***A companion to the Lakes in Lancashire, Westmoreland, and Cumberland.*** Carlisle: printed by B. Scott, in the Market-Place. 1807. Duodecimo.†

Text: Title, verso blank; Letter of Dedication (Kirklington, June 8th 1807) [iii]-v; To the Reader [vi]; Distances of Places [vii], viii; Contents [ix], x; Text [1]-136; Appendix [137]-139; Specimen 139-143; Glossary [144].

King's copy: In printed grey paper boards as issued, rebacked, uncut. Upper cover as title-page except quotation is replaced by 'Lovely indeed the mimic works of ART, / But NATURE'S works far lovelier COWPER'. 'Price 4*s*.' added. On lower cover, quotation from Mr Cumberland.

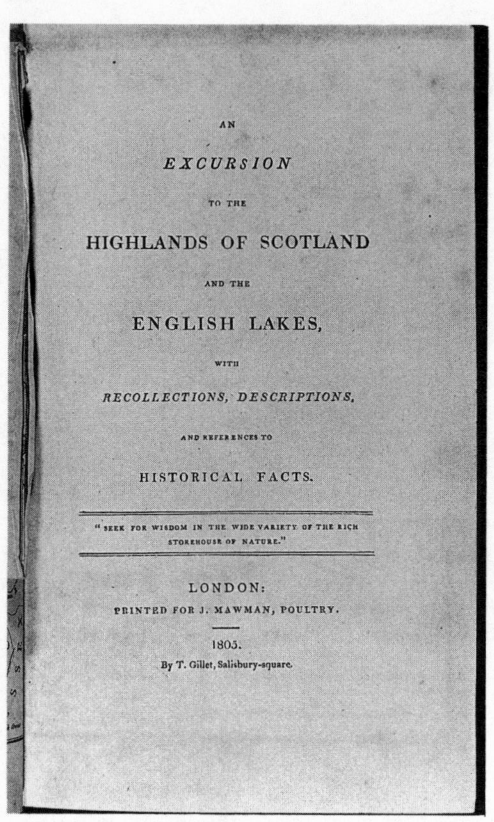

AN
EXCURSION
TO THE
HIGHLANDS OF SCOTLAND
AND THE
ENGLISH LAKES,
WITH
RECOLLECTIONS, DESCRIPTIONS,
AND REFERENCES TO
HISTORICAL FACTS.

"SEEK FOR WISDOM IN THE WIDE VARIETY OF THE RICH STOREHOUSE OF NATURE."

LONDON:
PRINTED FOR J. MAWMAN, POULTRY.
1805.
By T. Gillet, Salisbury-square.

59 205 x 125 mm.

James Lidderdale

A
DESCRIPTIVE TOUR
TO THE
LAKES
OF
Cumberland and Westmoreland,
IN THE
AUTUMN OF 1804.

Hic secura quies, et nescia fallere vita,
Dives opum variarum; *hic* latis otia fundis,
Speluncæ, vivique lacus; *hic* frigida Tempe,
Mugitusque boum, mollesque sub arbore somni.
Georg. Lib. 2.

LONDON:
PRINTED FOR T. OSTELL, AVE-MARIA-LANE,
By W. Pople, Old Boswell Court, Strand.
1806.

60 170 x 108 mm.

A
COMPANION
TO
THE LAKES
IN
LANCASHIRE, WESTMORELAND,
AND
Cumberland.

By Thomas Sanderson.

The earth was made so various that the mind
Of desultory man, studious of change,
And pleas'd with novelty, might be indulg'd.
COWPER.

Carlisle:
Printed by B. Scott, in the Market-Place.
1807.

61.1 170 x 98 mm.

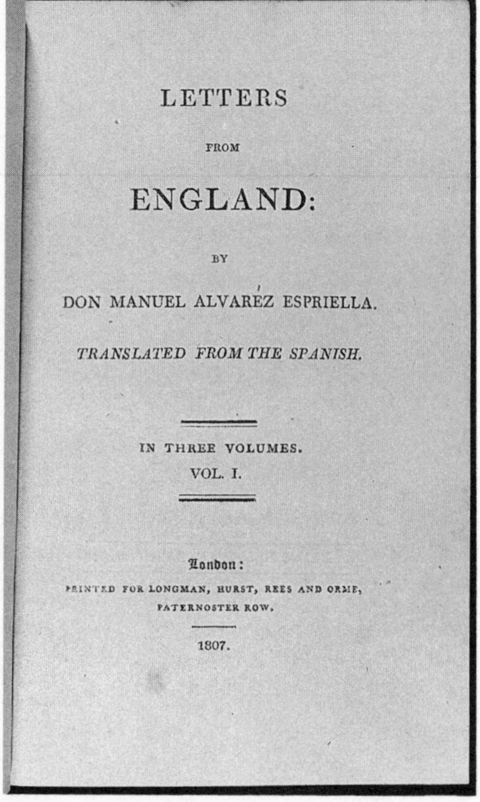

LETTERS
FROM
ENGLAND:
BY
DON MANUEL ALVARÉZ ESPRIELLA.
TRANSLATED FROM THE SPANISH.

IN THREE VOLUMES.
VOL. I.

London:
PRINTED FOR LONGMAN, HURST, REES AND ORME, PATERNOSTER ROW.
1807.

62.1 168 x 98 mm.

Note: The book covers all the principal lakes except Wastwater. 'With my own observations I have incorporated those of our most popular writers . . . It requires great powers to supply anything better than the masterly delineations of PENNANT, GILPIN, and YOUNG' (To the Reader). The *Companion* is largely a compilation of extracts from the works of these and other writers.

Copies: K; Armitt; BL; Jackson; Wordsworth

61.2 ——— Second edition. 1808.

Copy: Armitt

ROBERT SOUTHEY 1774-1843

In 1803 Robert Southey and his wife moved into Greta Hall, Keswick, already occupied by the Coleridges and their landlord, William Jackson. Here Southey lived until his death in 1843. He was buried at Crosthwaite. He constantly met the Wordsworths, was a friend of Joseph Wilkinson (see 73), and William Westall, for whom he wrote the descriptions for *Views of the Lake and of the Vale of Keswick* (92). Westall also provided the illustrations for Southey's *Colloquies* (107). Southey was keenly interested in Lake District topography. See (92) and (107).

62.1 ***Letters from England: by Don Manuel Alvarez Espriella. Translated from the Spanish.*** 3 vols. London: printed for Longman, Hurst, Rees and Orme, Paternoster Row. 1807. Duodecimo.†

Text: Vol. 1 Title, imprint on verso, *Richard Taylor and Co., Shoe Lane;* Preface by the Translator [iii], iv; Preface [v]-viii; Contents [ix]-xv; blank; Text [1]-308. Imprint repeated on p. 308.
Vol. 2 Title, Contents [v]-xii; Text [1]-398.
Vol. 3 Title, imprint on verso, *Richard Taylor and Co. Shoe-Lane;* Contents [iii]-vi; Text [1]-394.

Lakes: Letters 41, 42, 43, 44, Vol. 2, pp. 186-244

Itinerary: Windermere, Coniston, Ullswater and Penrith, then from Keswick, Skiddaw, Borrowdale, Wastdale, Ennerdale, Crummock and Buttermere. This is one of the earlier descriptions of Wastdale and Ennerdale.

Note: The letters purported to be translations of those of a Spanish visitor, in order to leave Southey freer to criticise the English, their prejudices and their hypocrisy

King's copy: In contemporary dark red morocco, printed label on the paste-down endpaper, gilt. *Bound by T. Sowler, 22 St. Ann's Square, Manchester.* Bookplate, Jonathan Hargreaves

Copies: K; Armitt; BL; Cornell

62.2 ——— Second edition. 1808

King's copy: In contemporary half dyed calf, marbled boards, gilt. Given to the College by Sheila Munby. Bookplate A.N.L. Munby.

Copies: K; BL; Wordsworth

62.3 ——— Third edition. 1816

Ref: Upcott, p. xxxviii.

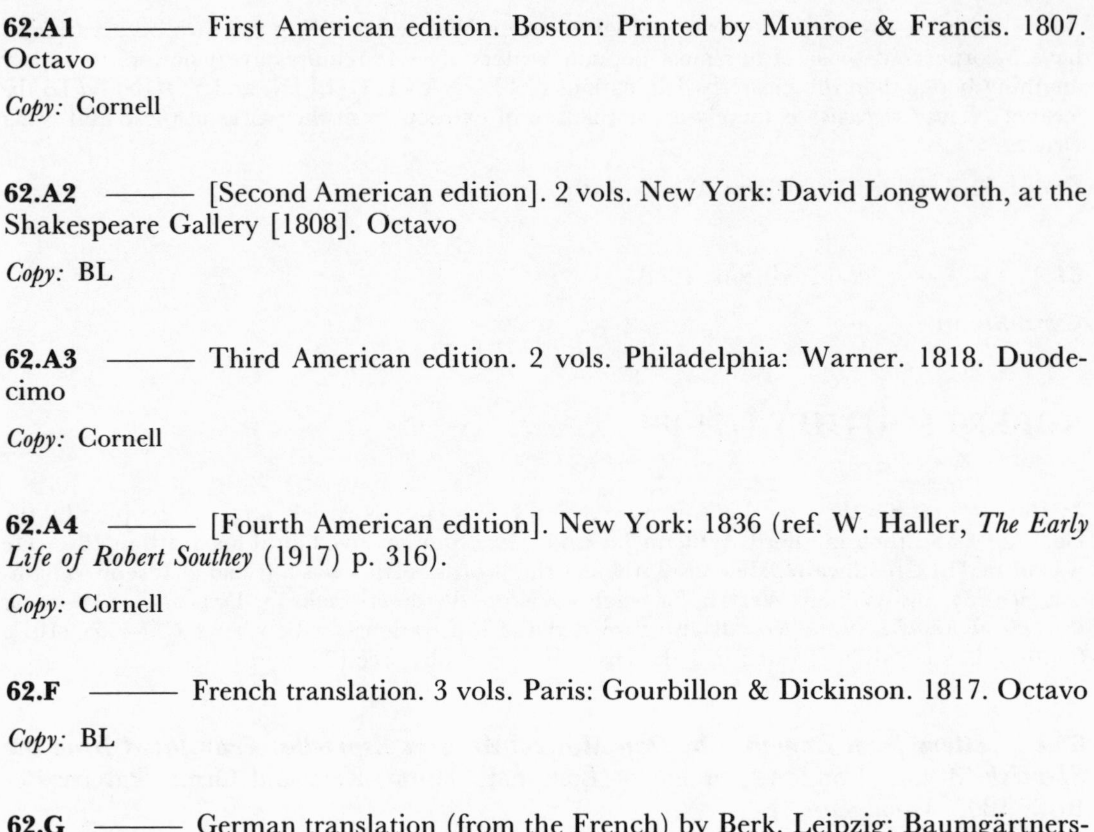

62.A1 ——— First American edition. Boston: Printed by Munroe & Francis. 1807. Octavo

Copy: Cornell

62.A2 ——— [Second American edition]. 2 vols. New York: David Longworth, at the Shakespeare Gallery [1808]. Octavo

Copy: BL

62.A3 ——— Third American edition. 2 vols. Philadelphia: Warner. 1818. Duodecimo

Copy: Cornell

62.A4 ——— [Fourth American edition]. New York: 1836 (ref. W. Haller, *The Early Life of Robert Southey* (1917) p. 316).

Copy: Cornell

62.F ——— French translation. 3 vols. Paris: Gourbillon & Dickinson. 1817. Octavo

Copy: BL

62.G ——— German translation (from the French) by Berk. Leipzig: Baumgärtnerschen. 1818. Octavo

Copy: BL

The National Union Catalogue records a London, 1821 edition, in Cornell University Library.

1809

WILLIAM GREEN 1760-1823

William Green was born in Manchester, where he studied surveying. He moved to London where he studied engraving, particularly aquatint. In 1778 he was involved in a survey of Lancashire – north of the Sands. At Ulverston he met Thomas West (9, 13, 14) who encouraged him to become an artist. He visited the Lakes several times between 1791 and 1800, when he settled at Ambleside and devoted his energies to recording the scenery and buildings of the Lakes. Forty-eight views of the Lake District (large coloured aquatints) were published in Manchester in 1795, and were described in a pamphlet, *A description of a series of picturesque views in the North of England*, printed at G. Nicholson and Co's office, 4 Palace Street, 1798 (copies: Armitt; Manchester Reference Library). Green was responsible for engraving his own plates, being assisted in the colouring by his daughters. He opened exhibition and sales rooms in Ambleside and Keswick. Dr Spiker, visiting Keswick in 1806, saw Mr Green's exhibition (87 vol.1, p.269). See Charles Roeder, *William Green the Lake Artist . . . A Biographical sketch* (reprinted from the *Transactions of Lancashire and Cheshire Antiquarian Society* (R. Gill, Manchester, 1897) vol. XIV, which includes a chronological list of works published by Green; and M.E. Burkett and J.D.G. Sloss, *William Green of Ambleside . . .* (Kendal, 1984).

William Green published an enormous number of prints in a variety of sizes, forms of engraving and colouring. These are only included in this list if they were normally sold bound or gathered in wrappers. In a long footnote in the *New Guide,* vol 1, pp. 66-8 (69), Green gives particulars and prices of many of the prints, and there are also advertisements for several prints on the covers of the *New Guide.*

63 ***Seventy eight studies from nature***. London: Longman, Hurst, Rees, and Orme; and W. Green, Ambleside. 1809. Oblong folio. Title; text; 78 soft-ground etchings (380 × 550 mm).

For titles of plates see Abbey, *Life* 134. The plates were intended to be used as exemplars for students of landscape studies, and showed details of rocks and trees, with a few landscape views, from drawings made in the neighbourhood of Ambleside, Rydal, Grasmere, Langdale, Patterdale, Keswick, Borrowdale and Wastdale.

Copies: Armitt; Jackson; Wordsworth

Ref: Abbey *Life*, 134 (coloured); Upcott, pp. 132-3

64 ***Sixty studies from nature.*** Ambleside: William Green. Issued unbound. No title; no text. Imprints 1808-1810. 60 soft-ground etchings, plate size 467 × 667 mm., numbered top right corner, imprints: *Drawn and engraved by William Green and published at Ambleside* (date).

1 Coniston Water***
2 Buildings at Coniston Water Head***
3 Yewdale near Coniston***
4 Rothay Bridge near Ambleside*
5 Ambleside from the Gale*
6 Windermere*
7 Cottage in Ambleside*
8 Bark Mill, Ambleside***
9 Mills at Ambleside*
10 Stock Gill near the Salutation Inn***
11 Stock Gill*
12 Cherry Tree, Stock Gill*
13 Stock Gill, Ambleside*
14 Study in Stock gill*
15 Stock Gill Force***
16 Pelter Bridge. Rydal*
17 Cottage at Rydal***
18 Lower Fall at Rydal***
19 Rydal Beck above the lower Water-fall***
20 Windermere from Rydal Park*
21 Rydal Water from Rydal Park***
22 Oak in Rydal Park*
23 Scene in Rydal Park***
24 Rocks on Loughrigg Side*
25 Goody Bridge in Grasmere*
26 Bramrigg Gill*
27 St. John's Vale*
28 Helvellyn from the foot of Leathes Water**
29 Mill, Legberthwaite**
30 Derwent Water from Castlerigg**
31 Islands on Derwent Water from Castlerigg***
32 Derwent Water from Crow Park***
33 Derwent Water from Isthmus**
34 Falcon Crag on Derwent Water***
35 Skiddaw taken near Lowdore***
36 Barrow Cascade*
37 Stonycroft Bridge**
38 Low Snab in Newlands**
39 Grange in Borrowdale*
40 Road between Grange Bridge and Bowder Stone***
41 Borrowdale near Bowder Stone**
42 Bowder Stone*
43 Folly Bridge in Borrowdale***
44 Birch Tree in Coom Gill*
45 Stockley Bridge*
46 Overbeck Bridge in Wasdale*
47 Wast Water*
48 Stanley Gill*
49 Godrell Crag on the River Duddon*
50 Vale of Langdale from Base Brown***
51 Langdale Pike from Oak How**
52 Row Head in Langdale**
53 Langdale Head**
54 Gimmer Crag in Langdale**
55 Dove Crag Hartshope*
56 The Vale of Patterdale*
57 Patterdale Church**
58 Yew Tree in Patterdale Church Yard*
59 Farm House at Glen Coin*
60 Glen Coin*

*June 4 1808 **Augt. 1 1809 ***June 24 1810

King's copy: Bound in half-russia, marbled boards, with the plates folded in half.

Copies: K; Armitt; BL; Wordsworth (incomplete)

Ref: Upcott, p. 134

65 ***A description of sixty Studies from Nature; etched in the soft ground, by William Green, of Ambleside; after drawings made by himself in Cumberland, Westmorland, and Lancashire. Comprising a general guide to the beauties of the North of England. . . .*** London: Printed for the Author by J. Barfield, 91, Wardour Street, and published by Messrs. Longman, Hurst, Rees, and Orme, Paternoster-row; Mr. Mann, 114 New Bond-street; and W. Green, Ambleside, Westmorland. 1810. Duodecimo.†

Text: Title, verso blank; Introduction [iii]-x; Text [1]-122; Imprint, *Printed by J. Barfield, Wardour-Street, Soho.*

Notes: This is a description of the 60 prints published separately (64) 'Proposals were made in 1807 for publishing sixty prints . . . In 1808 thirty of the sixty were laid before the public, in 1809 twelve more; and the remaining eighteen are now published.' Introduction.

'The Price of the Prints, unbound, including the Description, is Ten Guineas; the Description may be had separately for Two Shillings and Sixpence' (in title).

King's copy: Bound in the original grey paper boards with green printed paper label on upper cover. Inscribed on paste down endpaper 'A Surtees July 22nd 1813 Ambleside'.

Copies: K; Armitt; BL; Cornell; Jackson

Ref: Upcott, p. 134

66 ***Exhibition and sale rooms of drawings and prints, of the lakes, mountains, river scenes and buildings in Cumberland, Westmoreland.*** Soulby: Ulverston. 1812. Pamphlet

Catalogue, including 'Address by the artist explaining his entries for publication' which contains interesting information about Green's methods of working

Copy: Jackson

67 ***A description of a series of sixty small prints, etched by William Green, of Ambleside, from drawings made by himself.*** London: printed for the author by John Tyler, Rathbone Place, and published by William Green, Ambleside. 1814. Oblong Quarto. †

Text: Title, author's note on verso, *72, Newman Street, London. August 15, 1814;* Text [3]-34; Imprint on verso p.34, *J. Tyler, Printer, Rathbone Place*

Plates: 60 soft-ground etchings, plate size 186 × 240 mm. Imprints: *Published at Ambleside, Augst. 1, 1814.* Watermarks: *J. Whatman 1813.*

1 Coniston Water
2 Coniston Water Head
3 Scene near Coniston Water Head
4 Shepherds Bridge in Yewdale
5 Estwaite Water
6 Head of Windermere from Low Wood
7 Islands on Windermere from Skelgill
8 Windermere, from Belman Ground
9 Windermere from the Ferry
10 Kentmere Hall
11 Skelwith Force
12 Little Langdale Tarn
13 Blea Tarn
14 Langdale Pikes from Oak How

15 Row Head
16 Scene near Langdale Chapel
17 Loughrigg Tarn
18 Elter Water
19 Rydal Water
20 Grasmere, from Loughrigg Fell
21 Grasmere from Town End
22 Grasmere from Tail End
23 Goody Bridge
24 Easedale from Butterlip How
25 Leaths Water from Armbath
26 Foot of Leaths Water
27 Soskeld Bridge
28 Cottage in St. Johns Vale
29 Derwent Water from Castlerigg
30 Head of Derwent Water
31 Derwent Water and Bassenthwaite
32 Derwent Water from Lowdore
33 Lowdore Water-Fall
34 Bowder Stone
35 Eagle Crag near Stonethwaite
36 Langthwaite Bridge
37 Stockley Bridge §
38 Honister Crag
39 Crummock Water and Buttermere
40 Crummock Water
41 Lows Water
42 Ennerdale Water
43 Wast Water
44 Wast Water from the Road
45 Schofell on Wast Water
46 Goldrill Crag
47 Wallowbarrow Crag
48 Brother Water
49 Wooden Bridge in Hartshope
50 Grizedale Bridge
51 Glen Coin
52 Ulls Water from Gowbarrow
53 Ulls Water Head
54 Ulls Water Looking into Glenridden
55 Purse Bay on Ulls Water
56 Ulls Water looking towards Grizedale
57 Brougham Castle
58 Askham Church
59 Haws Water
60 Haws Water from Fordlingdale Beck

Note: Each plate is accompanied by descriptive text. They were issued in two forms: (a) uncoloured and untinted; (b) heightened with monochrome washes and white body colour. In the tinted plates skies were added, considerable liberties were taken in altering and adding foliage, highlights were scratched out, and shadows added. This work was probably done by Green's daughters. Charles Roeder in a note in his Chronological List (see introductory note to Green above) says that these prints 'appeared also aquatinted, same size'. This probably refers to the tinted issue as no aquatinted plates are known, and it is improbable that aquatint was ever added to them.

King's copies: (a) in half calf, marbled boards, gilt (b) half olive morocco, red paper boards, gilt

Copies: K; Armitt; Cornell; Jackson; Kendal

68 ***Lake scenery*** [1815] Oblong folio (title on cover)

No title, no text

Plates: 60 coloured aquatints. Plate size 157 × 210 mm. Numbered top right corner. Imprints: *Published at Ambleside, June 1, 1815, by Wm. Green.* Watermarks: *J. Whatman 1811.*

1 Coniston Water
2 Coniston Water
3 Man Mountain on Coniston Water
4 Coniston Water Head
5 Esthwaite Water
6 Stock Gill
7 Scandale Beck
8 Windermere taken near Low Wood
9 North End of Curwen's Island on Windermere
10 Curwen's Island on Windermere from the Station
11 Foot of Windermere from the Station
12 Windermere from Low Wray
13 Blea Tarn
14 Langdale Head from Wall End
15 Elter Water and Windermere
16 Elter Water
17 Loughrigg Tarn
18 Brother Water
19 Ulls Water from Glencoin
20 Ulls Water taken from Lyulph's Tower
21 Ulls Water from Low Field
22 Ulls Water
23 Ulls Water from the Purse Bay
24 Scene on the River Lowther

A
DESCRIPTION
OF SIXTY
Studies from Nature;
ETCHED IN THE SOFT GROUND,
BY
WILLIAM GREEN,
OF
AMBLESIDE;
AFTER DRAWINGS MADE BY HIMSELF IN
CUMBERLAND, WESTMORLAND,
AND LANCASHIRE.
COMPRISING,
A GENERAL GUIDE
TO THE
BEAUTIES OF THE NORTH OF ENGLAND.

The Price of the Prints, unbound, including the Description, is Ten Guineas; the Description may be had separately for Two Shillings and Sixpence.

LONDON:
Printed for the Author, by J. BARFIELD, 91, Wardour Street.
AND PUBLISHED BY
Messrs. LONGMAN, HURST, REES, and ORME, Paternoster-row; Mr. MANN, 114, New Bond-street; and W. GREEN, Ambleside, Westmorland.
1810.

65 190 x 112 mm.

THE
Tourist's New Guide,
CONTAINING
A DESCRIPTION
OF THE
LAKES, MOUNTAINS,
AND
Scenery,
IN
Cumberland, Westmorland, and Lancashire,
With some Account of their
BORDERING TOWNS AND VILLAGES.

BEING THE RESULT OF
OBSERVATIONS MADE DURING A RESIDENCE OF EIGHTEEN YEARS IN
AMBLESIDE AND KESWICK.

BY *WILLIAM GREEN.*

IN TWO VOLUMES.

VOL. I.

KENDAL:
Printed and Published, by R. Lough and Co. and Sold by them at the Chronicle Office, Finkle Street: also by J. Richardson, 91, Royal Exchange, London; Constable, Edinburgh; Smith, Liverpool; Messrs. I. Clark, and Co. Manchester; Wilcockson, Preston; Dewhurst, Lancaster; Foster, Kirby Lonsdale; Ashburner, Ulverstone; Gaythorpe, Whitehaven; Jollie, Scott, and Thurnam, Booksellers, Carlisle; Shaw, Penrith; Bateman, Appleby; M. and R. Branthwaite, Dowson, Gritton, Todhunter, and Messrs. Bellingham and Airey, Kendal, and by the Author, at Ambleside.
1819.

69a 225 x 140 mm.

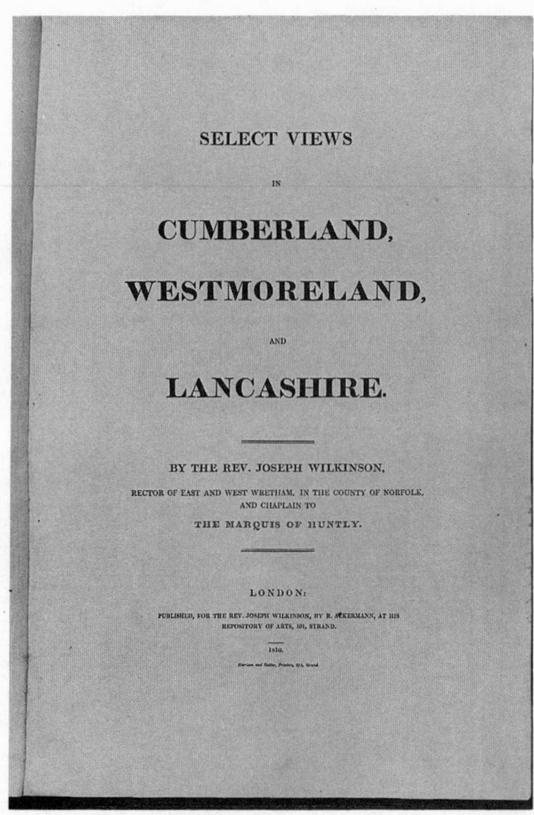

SELECT VIEWS
IN
CUMBERLAND,
WESTMORELAND,
AND
LANCASHIRE.

BY THE REV. JOSEPH WILKINSON,
RECTOR OF EAST AND WEST WRETHAM, IN THE COUNTY OF NORFOLK,
AND CHAPLAIN TO
THE MARQUIS OF HUNTLY.

LONDON:
PUBLISHED, FOR THE REV. JOSEPH WILKINSON, BY R. ACKERMANN, AT HIS REPOSITORY OF ARTS, 101, STRAND.
1810.

73.1 490 x 330 mm.

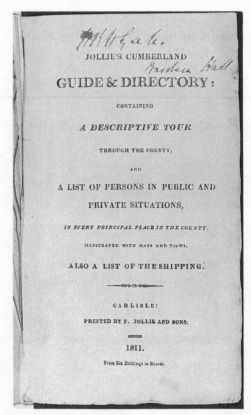

JOLLIE'S CUMBERLAND
GUIDE & DIRECTORY:
CONTAINING
A DESCRIPTIVE TOUR
THROUGH THE COUNTY,
AND
A LIST OF PERSONS IN PUBLIC AND
PRIVATE SITUATIONS,
IN EVERY PRINCIPAL PLACE IN THE COUNTY.
ILLUSTRATED WITH MAPS AND VIEWS.
ALSO A LIST OF THE SHIPPING.

CARLISLE:
PRINTED BY F. JOLLIE AND SONS.
1811.
Price Six Shillings in Boards.

74 206 x 127 mm.

25 Haws Water
26 View down Haws Water from Mardale
27 Head of Haws Water
28 Rydal Water
29 Outlet to Grasmere Lake
30 Grasmere
31 Easdale Tarn
32 St. Johns Vale
33 Leaths Water
34 Raven Crag on Leaths Water
35 Helvellyn from Leaths Water
36 Derwent Water from Castle Rigg
37 Derwent Water from Isthmus
38 Derwent Water from Barrow Common
39 Saddleback from Derwent Water
40 Derwent Water from Castle Cragg
41 Derwent Water taken from near Sprinkling Tarn
42 Crosthwaite Church near Keswick
43 Bassenthwaite Water
44 Bowder Stone
45 Stonethwaite Bridge
46 Eagle Crag
47 Borrowdale from Greenup Vale
48 Sty Head Tarn
49 Sprinkling Tarn
50 Buttermere from Gatesgarth Dale
51 Buttermere from Crummock Water
52 Crummock Water and Buttermere
53 Head of Crummock Water
54 Lows Water
55 Ennerdale Water
56 Head of Wast Water from Crook
57 Screes on Wast Water
58 Scofell on Wast Water
59 Yewbarrow from Bowderdale
60 Wallowbarrow Crag

Notes: These are the 60 aquatints, referred to by number and described in *The Tourist's New Guide* (69), and advertised on the cover: 'Printed on super-royal quarto drawing-paper – Price Five Guineas, Single Prints, Two Shillings and Sixpence each. The above sixty Plates are all new subjects, and like the small etchings, have been reduced from large drawings, or from sketches made on super-royal paper and attempt to display in miniature the grandeur and vastness of the most stupendous English scenery. The above sixty Aquatints in printers' colours, price three guineas. The same Aquatints (proof impressions) in printers' colours, quarto imperial, price Four Guineas.'

Charles Roeder's Chronological List records:
Same set in India ink, £3.3*s*., 13½ in. × 9½ in. and 7 in. × 4½ in.
Same set in printers' colours. £4.4*s*. on 9to. imperial.
Same set etched. £1.1*s*. on 8vo. paper.
Same set etched. £1.5*s*. upon larger paper.

King's copy: In contemporary half green morocco, marbled boards, gilt, leather label on upper cover lettered 'Lake Scenery', endpapers watermarks: *J. Whatman 1818.*

Copies: K; Armitt; Cornell; Wordsworth (incomplete)

69a ***The Tourist's New Guide, containing a description of the lakes, mountains, and scenery, in Cumberland, Westmorland, and Lancashire, . . . being the result of observations made during a residence of eighteen years in Ambleside and Keswick*** Kendal: Printed and Published, by R. Lough & Co. and Sold by them at the Chronicle Office, Finkle Street: also by J. Richardson, 91, Royal Exchange, London; Constable, Edinburgh; Smith, Liverpool; Messrs. I. Clark, and Co. Manchester; Wilcockson, Preston; Dewhurst, Lancaster; Foster, Kirby Lonsdale; Ashburner, Ulverstone; Gaythorpe, Whitehaven; Jollie, Scott, and Thurnam, Booksellers, Carlisle; Shaw, Penrith; Bateman, Appleby; M. and R. Branthwaite, Dowson, Gritton, Todhunter, and Messrs. Bellingham and Airey, Kendal, and by the author, at Ambleside. 2 vols. 1819. Octavo.†

Text: Vol. 1 Half-title, verso blank; Title, verso blank; Preface [v]-xi; [xii] blank; Index [iii]-viii; blank leaf; Text [1]-461; [462] blank; Errata 1 p., verso blank.
Vol. 2 Half-title, verso blank; Title, verso blank; Index [iii]-[ix]; [x] blank; Text [1]-507; [508] blank; List of Excursions [i]-lv imprint: *Kendal Printed by R. Lough and Co. Finkle Street;* [lvi] blank; Errata 1 p., verso blank.

Plates: 24 aquatints in printers' colours. Vol., page and line reference in lower right corner. Plate size: 135 × 225 mm. Imprints: *Published at Ambleside, Augt. 1819 by Wm. Green.*

Vol. 1

1 Coniston Water Head*
2 Windermere from Belle Grange
3 Windermere from Low Wood*
4 Islands on Windermere
5 Grasmere*
6 Lough Rigg Tarn
7 Lower Fall at Rydal
8 Ulls Water
9 Ulls Water from House Holm*
10 Haws Water
11 Haws Water*
12 Rydal Water
13 Leaths Water
14 Leaths Water from Bucks Holm*

Vol. 2

15 Derwent Water near Barrow Beck
16 Derwent Water distance Skiddaw*
17 Derwent Water from Crow Park*
18 Bassenthwaite Water
19 Bowder Stone*
20 Derwent Water from Strands Hagg*
21 Crummock Water*
22 Crummock and Buttermere Waters
23 Ennerdale Water*
24 Over Beck Bridge on Wast Water

* the twelve plates included in the One Guinea issue. See next item.

Map: 'The District of the Lakes. By J.Otley Keswick 1818', Folding. Plate size: 330 × 270 mm. Scale: 4 in. = 1 mile. *Engraved by J. & G. Menzies, Edinr.* Watermark 1817.

Notes: This is the first edition of Otley's New Map of the Lakes. See 88.1.

The 60 prints described but not included in the *Guide* are those published in 1815, see 68.

King's copy: Bound in the original grey printed paper boards, with advert. on upper and lower covers. Both volumes inscribed, 'William Fleming his book', altered from 'Mary Fleming her book' on paste-down endpapers. The *Guide* is advertised as:
(a) 'on a superior paper, with a map and twenty four prints, two guineas'
(b) 'with a map and twelve prints, one guinea' – see next item

69b ——— Exactly as previous item except not on a superior paper and only twelve prints.

King's copy: Bound in the original printed paper boards (as previous item), rebacked red cloth. Both volumes inscribed 'Eliza Arabella Barry The Cottage Malvern Wells', on the paste-down endpapers; and vol. 1 'Herbert New from Sidney P. Ryland', on free endpaper.

69c ——— As 69a except 12 soft-ground etchings added. Imprint: *Published at Ambleside by Wm. Green 1820.* Volume, page and line references on plates. The subjects are buildings and antiquities, not landscape. Issued 1820 or later.

King's copy: Bound in contemporary moiré cloth, red leather labels. A slip at the end of vol. 2 draws attention to Mr. Todhunter's Museum omitted from the account of Kendal. Both volumes inscribed 'S. Mashiter [?], Heysham'.

Notes: Referring to a list of the 12 etchings Sanderson says, 'this list may be no guide to the collation of another copy as I believe Green stuck in any dozen of plates belonging to his various publications which he happened to have most of'.

The book was also issued with 12 etchings and no aquatints, and 12 etchings and 12 aquatints.

Green's *Guide* is a far more complete and detailed description of the whole of the Lake District than any previous work. Wordsworth, who was on good terms with Green, described it as 'a complete Magazine of minute and accurate information'. As the book consisted of two heavy octavo volumes, tourists cannot have been intended to treat it as a pocket guide.

Copies: K; Armitt; Cornell; Jackson; Kendal; Wordsworth

Ref: Abbey, 190.

70 ***Views of Ambleside*** Ambleside: William Green. 1821

36 soft-ground etchings; plate sizes: 325 × 450 mm and 250 × 330 mm. Imprint: *Etched from Nature by William Green, and Published at Ambleside, May 1, 1821.* No title. No text. Numbered upper left

1 Ambleside from Red Bottom
[2] Scene in Stock Gill
[3] Kelsick Buildings Ambleside
4 Ambleside Market Place
5 Old Buildings in Ambleside
6 Old Homes in Ambleside
7 Ambleside from the Gale
8 The Oaks, from the Salutation Coach House
9 The Oaks and How Head, Ambleside
10 The Old Ladies and Salutation Inn
11 Buildings near Stock Bridge
12 Bridge House, Ambleside
13 Corn and Bark Mills, Ambleside
14 Ambleside Corn Mill
15 Ambleside from the Butts
16 Salutation Inn
17 Stock Bridge, Ambleside
18 Rydal Mount
19 Ivy Cottage, Rydal
20 Ivy Cottage from the Road
[21] Rattle-Gill*
22 Ambleside from Coat Row
[23] Ambleside Church and How Head*
24 Buildings in Ambleside*
25 Salutation Inn, Ambleside*
[26] Market Place, Ambleside*
[27] Ambleside, from Coat How*
[28] Ambleside*
[29] How Hill, Ambleside*
[30] Kelsick Buildings*
[31] Ambleside Church*
[32] Rattle-Gill, Ambleside*
[33] Ambleside, from the Mill Lands
[34] Gale Firs, Ambleside
35 Bridge House, Ambleside*
36 Rydal Mount

* smaller sized plate

16 of these plates were issued in printed grey paper wrappers, lettered, 'Sixteen etchings from nature by William Green. Price one guinea. Published at Ambleside by W. Green, 1821' (copy Armitt)

King's copy: Bound in contemporary half dark green morocco, marbled boards, repaired, new leather label on upper cover. Watermarks: 1819, 1820, 1821. Watercolour drawings of a street scene and of a Norman church are mounted on the paste-down endpapers.

Note: Roeder's Chronological List records 'Forty Views of Ambleside and Keswick etched from nature from Wm. Green, 21 in × 15 in.'

Copies: K; Armitt; Cornell

71 ***Forty etchings from nature***. Ambleside: William Green. 1822. Title printed on upper cover.†

No title, no text; Prospectus 1 p., verso blank

40 etchings (6 'hard' and 34 soft-ground); plate size: 150 × 210 mm; Imprint, *Etched from Nature by William Green: Published at Ambleside, Feby. 1, 1822.* Numbered upper right.

1 Entrance from the South into Ambleside
2 Buildings in Ambleside
3 The Cross House and Bedlam in Ambleside*
4 Ambleside Cross House as altered in 1819*
5 Cumpston Lodge*
6 Ambleside Church
7 Ambleside from Stony Lane
8 Clappersgate
9 Skelwith Fold
10 Inn at Skelwith Bridge
11 Loughrigg Fell
12 Ellers in Loughrigg
13 Coat How near Rydal
14 South Entrance into Rydal
15 Buildings in Rydal*
16 Cottage in Rydal
17 Hartshead in Rydal
18 Ivy Cottage Rydal
19 Town Hall, Keswick*
20 Keswick Work House
21 Crosthwaite Church
22 Long Bridge near Keswick
23 Portinscale
24 Portinscale*

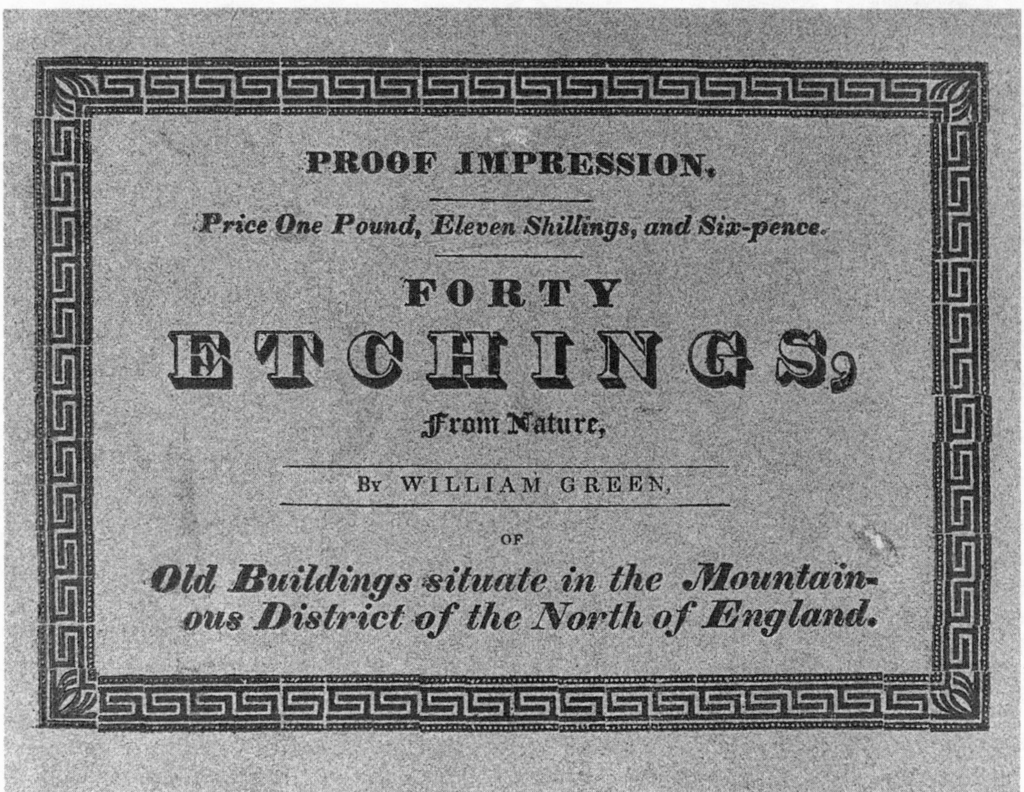
PROOF IMPRESSION.

Price One Pound, Eleven Shillings, and Six-pence.

FORTY

ETCHINGS,

From Nature,

By WILLIAM GREEN,

OF

Old Buildings situate in the Mountainous District of the North of England.

71 238 x 335 mm.

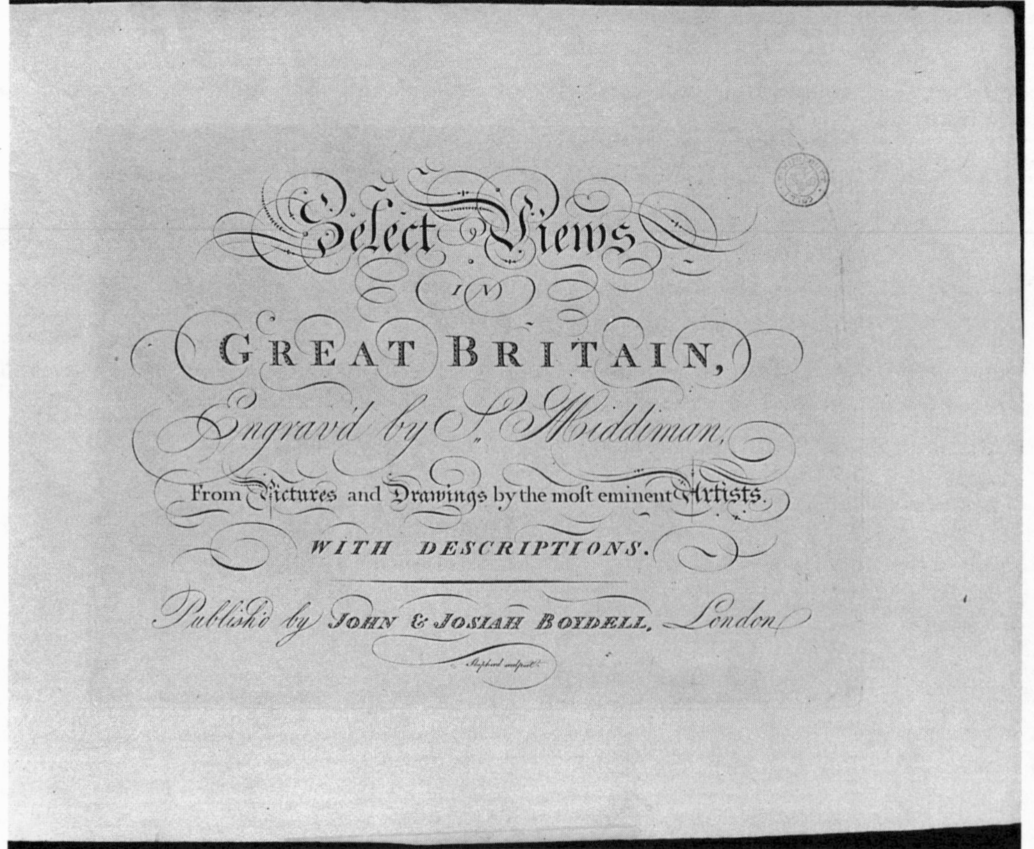
Select Views

IN

GREAT BRITAIN,

Engrav'd by S. Middiman,

From Pictures and Drawings by the most eminent Artists.

WITH DESCRIPTIONS.

Publish'd by JOHN & JOSIAH BOYDELL, London

77 215 x 275 mm.

25 Village of Portinscale
26 Portinscale
27 The How near Portinscale
28 Monk Hall near Keswick
29 Ormanthwaite Green
30 The Gill in Applethwaite
31 Baxters in Applethwaite
32 Applethwaite
33 Applethwaite
34 Applethwaite
35 Applethwaite
36 Village of Applethwaite
37 Applethwaite
38 Mill Beck
39 Little Crosthwaite
40 Mire House

* 'hard ground or needle etchings'

Notes: The Prospectus is for 'Two Hundred Scenes of Farm Houses, Cottages, Abbies [sic], Churches, Castles, Old Halls, and Bridges.'

'Letter Press, describing the relative situation of the buildings and their histories, where important, will be given to the whole two hundred subjects, when complete; or to the present or any future part, when it shall be ascertained that work will not be continued.' The work was never continued, and only these 40 prints were published.

Green explains that 'to save from the wreck of time and the busy hand of man the best specimens of this mountain architecture, is one of the principal objects of the present publication'.

Forty etchings from nature is not included in Roeder's Chronological List.

King's copy: In the original blue-grey printed paper wrappers: 'Proof Impression. Price One Pound, Eleven Shillings, and Six-pence. Forty Etchings from Nature, by William Green, of Old Buildings situate in the Mountainous District of the North of England'. The proof impressions bear numbers and titles but no imprints. Watermarks: J. Whatman 1818, 1819, 1820, 1821.

Copies: K; Cornell; Wordsworth

1810

JOHN MARSHALL (of Newcastle)

72.1 ***The village paedagogue, a poem . . . with a walk from Newcastle to Keswick.*** Newcastle: for the Author. 1810. Small Quarto.

Copy: Jackson

72.2 ——— Second edition. 1817.

Copies: Armitt; BL; Cornell; Jackson

72.3 ——— Third edition. 1819.

Copy: Jackson

JOSEPH WILKINSON (artist) 1764-1831

The Revd Joseph Wilkinson, amateur artist and parish priest, was born at Carlisle. Until 1804 he made his home largely at Ormathwaite under Skiddaw with his wife's relatives, Dr and Mrs William Brownrigg (see 2). In 1803 he became vicar of East Wretham in Norfolk and in 1804 left the north for good.

73.1 ***Select Views in Cumberland, Westmoreland, and Lancashire.*** London: published, for the Rev. Joseph Wilkinson, by R. Ackermann, at his Repository of Arts, 101, Strand. 1810. Harrison and Rutter, Printers, 373 Strand. Folio.†

Text: Title, verso blank; Contents 1 p, verso blank; Letter of dedication 2 pp; Introduction [i]-xxxiv; Section I [35], 36; Section II [37]-46; imprint on p. 46, *Harrison and Rutter, Printers, 373, Strand.*

Plates: 48 soft-ground etchings; Signed: *Rev. Jos. Wilkinson delt.* and *W.F. Wells sc.* [or *sculpt.*]: imprint: *Published* [date] *by R. Ackermann, 101 Strand, London.* Plate size: 492 × 330 mm.

Part I
1 View near Brothers water. *Jan 1 1810.*
2 Ennerdale Broad-water. *Jan 1 1810.*
3 Derwent-water, from Applethwaite. *Jan 1 1810.*
4 Cottages at Brathwaite. *Jan 1 1810.*

Part 2
5 View in the Vale of Newlands. *Feb 1 1810.*
6 Cottages in Applethwaite, looking from Skiddaw. *Feb 1 1810.*
7 Cottages in the Vale of Newlands, with Robinsons crag. *Feb 1 1810.*
8 Therl-mere, or Leath-water [should be 'Thirl-mere or Leathes-water'] *Feb 1 1810.*

Part 3
9 View on the Grange-river, Borrowdale. *March 1 1810.*
10 View on the Grange-river, Borrowdale, looking towards Derwent-water. *March 1 1810*
11 View in St. John's Vale, with Green crag, &c. *March 1 1810.*
12 Cottage in the Vale of Newlands, near Stare-bridge. *March 1 1810.*

Part 4
13 Stye-head Tarn, with Aron, or Great End, above Borrowdale. *April 1 1810.*
14 Cottages at Brathwaite. *April 1 1810.*
15 View on the Banks of Wast-water.*April 1 1810*
16 View in St. John's Vale, near Wanthwaite. *April 1 1810*

Part 5
17 Langdale Chapel, Vale of Langdale. *May 1 1810.*
18 Scale, or Skell-gill Farm House, above Portinscale. *May 1 1810.*
19 View near Seatoller, Borrowdale. *May 1 1810.*
20 Legbethwaite Mill, St. John's Vale, taken after much rain. *May 1 1810*

Part 6
21 Wast-water, looking up to Wast-dale Head. *June 1 1810.*
22 View on the Ambleside road near Bridge foot, with part of St. John's Vale. *June 1 1810.*
23 Part of Skiddaw, from Applethwaite Gill. *June 1 1810.*
24 Stony-croft Bridge, Vale of Newlands. *June 1 1810.*

Part 7
25 Bassenthwaite Lake, from Embleton Vale. *July 1 1810.*
26 Vale of the Lune, Lonsdale looking towards Ingleborough Hill & Hornby Castle. *July 1 1810.*
27 Estwaite water, from below Bellemount. *July 1 1810.*
28 Smelting Mill, near Thornthwaite. *July 1 1810.*

Part 8
29 Lanercost Priory, Cumberland. *August 1 1810.*
30 Hawes water. *August 1 1810.*
31 View on Coniston-water. *August 1 1810.*

Part 9
32 South View of Furness Abbey, Lancashire. *Sept 1 1810.* This is the plate carried over from Part 8.
33 Penny bridge between Ulverstone & Coniston, with the tide in. *Sept 1 1810.*
34 Coniston Water-head. *Sept 1 1810.*
35 Newby bridge, foot of Winandermere. *Sept 1 1810.*
36 View on Winandermere. *Sept 1 1810.*

Part 10
37 View on the banks of Coniston-water. *Oct 1 1810.*
38 Dulmail-raise, on the Ambleside Road. The heap of Stones in the foreground perpetuate the name and fall of the last King of Cumberland. *Oct 1 1810.*
39 Cottages in the Vale of Lorton. *Oct 1 1810.*
40 Syulph's [should be 'Lyulph's] Tower, Ullswater. *Oct 1 1810.*

Part 11
41 View above Seatoller. *Novr 1 1810.*
42 Cottage at Nebthit, with Blackbarrow-crag. *Novr 1 1810.*
43 Cottage near Rydal. *Novr 1 1810.*
44 Cottages at Ambleside. *Novr 1 1810.*

Part 12
45 View on Kirkstone, between Ambleside and Patterdale. *Decr 1 1810.*
46 Brathay-bridge, near Ambleside. *Decr 1 1810.*
47 Cottage in the vale of Newlands, between Keswick and Buttermere. *Decr 1 1810.*
48 Elter Water. *Decr 1 1810.*

Notes: Select views was published in 12 monthly parts (as list of plates above) in printed paper wrappers.§ Upper wrapper reads: *No. 1* [12] *Select Views* . . . Published for the Rev. Joseph Wilkinson, by R. Ackermann at his Repository of Arts, 101 Strand, where subscriptions are received and specimens of work may be seen. N.B. Subscriptions are likewise received at all the principal book and print sellers in the United Kingdom. Price 10*s*. 6*d*. [each part]. William Savage, printer, Bedford Bury, London [not Harrison and Rutter, printers of letterpress]. Prospectus of the series and imprint of Savage on lower wrapper.

The plates appear to have been issued coloured and uncoloured and loose.

King's copy: In one volume, in stiff marbled paper wrappers. Watermarks: Text: *Edmunds & Pine 1804;* Plates: *J. Whatman 1811.* Two errors in the titles of the plates have been corrected: plate 8 'Thirl-mere or Leathes-water' replaces 'Therl-mere or Leath-water', and plate 40 'Lyulph's Tower' replaces 'Syulph's Tower'. The Abbey copy has 1804 watermarks, the King's copy is evidently a late issue. The sequence of the plates differs from some other copies.

In the King's collection there is also a copy of Part 1 as issued,§ consisting of Dedication, one leaf; Introduction one gathering, pp. [i]-iv; Plates 1, 2, 3 4; inscribed on upper cover 'Geo. Beauchamp Esqr. Received 10/6 H Y Sturley'. No watermarks.

Copies: K; Armitt (in original parts); BL; Cornell; Jackson; Kendal; and Wordsworth (unbound sheets, some watermarks 1824).

Ref: Abbey, 188 (in parts), Upcott, p. 131

73.1a ——— Issued with new title-page. London: Ackermann. 1817. S. Mills, printers Thetford (imprint on title-page). Text not reprinted; imprint on last page, *Harrison and Rutter*. Plates unchanged.

Copies: Alpine Club, London (plates tinted yellow); Library of Congress; Ohio State University

73.2 ——— [Second edition]. 1821. Same as previous issues, but reprinted by C. Lloyd, Thetford.

Note: This can be considered to be the true third edition of Wordsworth's *Guide*, the *Duddon sonnets*, 1820 (95.2), being the second.

Copies: Cornell; Wordsworth (coloured), watermarks 1825

Notes: The plates were large soft-ground etchings (492 × 330 mm) prepared by William Frederick Wells, an accomplished London engraver and landscape artist who faithfully reproduced Wilkinson's somewhat amateurish drawings. In the Wordsworth Library at Dove Cottage there is an album containing the pencil drawings made by Wilkinson as models for the plates. In the margins of these drawings there are pencil sketches of groups of people and animals, drawn by an artist more skilful than Wilkinson. These groups are incorporated in the etchings in preference to Wilkinson's less accomplished groups. The views cover all the principal lakes, including Ennerdale and Wastdale, excluding only Haweswater.

The introduction and descriptive notes were supplied by William Wordsworth, an acquaintance of Wilkinson; but Wordsworth stipulated that he should remain anonymous as he did not wish his name to be associated with Wilkinson's poor drawings. The text which was to become Wordsworth's *Guide to the Lakes* bears little relation to Wilkinson's plates.

The origins and preparation of the manuscript, and the development and bibliography of the *Guide,* are fully discussed in *The prose works of William Wordsworth,* W.J.B. Owen and J.W. Smyser, eds (Oxford, 1974).

For Wordsworth, see 95.2 and 122

1811

FRANCIS JOLLIE (printer and publisher) 1755-1820

Francis Jollie, printer, publisher and bookseller, came to Carlisle from the Montrose area. With his sons he published the *Carlisle Journal,* starting on 27 October 1798; Hutchinson's *History of the county of Cumberland* (28); Housman's *Topographical Description of Cumberland* and *Descriptive Tour* (41).

See 'The Jollies, father and sons, printers of Carlisle', by C.F. Barnes, (Cumbria Archives, Carlisle Library and Museum, Oct. 1976).

74 ***Jollie's Cumberland Guide & Directory: containing a descriptive tour through the County*** . . . Carlisle: Printed by F. Jollie and Sons. 1811. Price Six Shillings in Boards. Octavo.†

Text: Title, verso blank; Divisional Title, 'Part 1', verso blank; Dedication (F. Jollie, Carlisle Dec. 24, 1810), verso blank; Table of Contents etc. [v]-viii; Carlisle Directory [1]-84; Directories [i]-xxxix; Advert. [xl]; Divisional Title, 'Part II', verso blank; Cumberland Guide etc. [1]-129; Index, 1 p.; Errata, 2 pp; Imprint on last p., *F. Jollie & Sons, Printers, Carlisle.*

Illustrations: 4 engravings (one folding). No Lake District views.

Maps: Map of Cumberland and 3 folding maps. Size: 205 × 115 mm. Scale 6½ miles = 1 inch

Lakes: Tour through the Lakes, etc., chapter 9, pp. 40-53

King's copy: In mottled calf, gilt, leather label; F.W.G. (F.W. Garnett of Windermere; see 94.2), uncut.

Book plate of James Losh, Lambert St. Inscribed on free endpaper, 'To Margaret & Jemima North, from their affectionate aunt Margaret Baldwin 30th July 1824', on title page, 'F.R.H. [?] Gale, Bardsea [?] Hall'.

Copies: K; Armitt; Cornell (Directory only); Jackson; Wordsworth

Ref: Upcott, pp. 115-16

1812

SHAW (publisher)

75.1 ***A companion by the way; or, a guide to the Lakes, in Cumberland, Westmorland and Lancashire. From a late survey.*** Penrith: printed by M. Harrison, for Longman, Hurst, Rees, Orme and Browne, Paternoster Row, London. 1812. Duodecimo.

Folding map of the Lakes

Copies: BL; Cornell; Jackson

75.2 ***A guide to the Lakes in Cumberland, Westmorland and Lancashire; or a pocket companion in which every lake is separately described, together with many other remarkable curiosities. From a late survey.*** Second edition [of *A companion by the way,* 75.1], with additions. Penrith: printed by J. Shaw, for Crosby & Co. J. Richardson, and Gale, & Co. London; M. & R. Branthwaite, Kendal. &c. &c. 1814. Duodecimo.†

Text: Title, verso blank; Advertisement 1 p.; Introduction 1 p.; Guide to the Lakes [1]-96; Specimen of the Cumberland dialect 97-104; Tables 105-114; Contents 115, 116. Imprint on last page, *M. Harrison, Printer.*

Map: Folding map of the lakes, plate size, 165 × 210 mm. Scale, 1in. = 7½ miles

King's copy: In original blue printed paper wrappers, uncut. Title on upper cover differs from title page. 'and the different curiosities respectively pointed out.' replaces 'together with many other remarkable curiosities.'
'Third Edition, considerably improved' replaces 'Second Edition with additions.'
'for Baldwin, Craddock, and Joy, Paternoster Row, London; Oliver and Boyd, Edinburgh; and most other booksellers. 1816.' replaces 'for Crosby & Co. . . . Kendal, &c. &c. 1814.'

Inscribed in pencil on paste-down endpaper 'This book belongs to William Green, at Mr Slee's Terril near Penrith.'

Advertised on lower cover:
Just published
1 Crosthwaite's plans of the different Lakes . . . price 10*s.* 6*d.* half bound
2 Green's 60 Etchings of the Lakes, after nature, particularly adapted to such as are desirous of studying the art, price £1. 5*s.* 6*d.*
3 Green's 26 Views of the Lakes in Cumberland, Westmorland and Lancashire, price £1. 6*s.* 0*d.*
4 Cary's Map of the Lakes, in case, price 10*s.* 6*d.*
5 A small Map of the Lakes, adapted for the Pocket, price 1*s.*
6 Cary's Book of the Roads . . . half bound, 15*s.*
7 Wallis's new pocket Edition of the English Counties, or Travellers Companion . . . with a general Map of England and Wales, price 15*s.*

Copies: K; Jackson

75.3 ***A portable guide to the Lakes, in Cumberland, Westmorland, and Lancashire; wherein the various lakes are described, more immediately in the neighbourhood: from a late survey.*** Third edition [of 75.1], with additions. Penrith: printed by and for J. Shaw and sold by Baldwin, Craddock and Joy, London; Oliver and Boyd, Edinburgh; Wilson and Sons, York; Mozley, Derby; M. and R. Branthwaite, Kendal; Crosthwaite, Keswick; Rook, Wigton; Bailey, Cockermouth; Foster, Workington; and by the Booksellers in general. 1818. Octavo.

Folding map of the Lakes.

Issued in printed boards. 1820 on cover of Jackson copy. Entry in Sanderson: '*Shaw's portable guide to the Lakes,* 1829.'

Copies: Armitt; Jackson

75.4 ***The tourist's guide to the Lakes, in Cumberland, Westmorland, and Lancashire: wherein the lakes and scenery are described from a late survey.*** Third edition [fourth edition of 75.1], with additions.

Penrith: printed by and for J. Shaw, and sold by Baldwin, Craddock, and Joy, London; Oliver and Boyd, Edinburgh; Wilson and Son, York; Mozley, Derby; M. and R. Branthwaite, Kendal; Rook, Wigton; Thurnam, Carlisle; &c. &c. 1825 (and 1826, 1830) Octavo.

Imprint on title-page differs in 1826 issue: 'printed for J. Shaw, sold by W. Joy and T. Tegg, London: Oliver and Boyd, Edinburgh; Wilson and Sons, York; Mozley, Derby; M. & R. Branthwaite, Kendal; Thurnam and Snowden, Carlisle; &c. &c.'

Folding map of the Lakes

Issued in printed boards

Copies: Armitt (1830); B.L (1826); Jackson (1830); Wordsworth (1825)

These four books, published in Penrith, with different titles and imprints, are all editions of the same guide. It is the first complete guide to the Lakes which is of a suitable size for the pocket (1812). The fifth edition is *Allison's northern tourist's guide,* 1834 (114.5).

WILLIAM COMBE 1741-1823 and **THOMAS ROWLANDSON** (artist) 1756-1827

Neither Combe nor Rowlandson visited the Lakes, though Rowlandson made a picturesque tour of North Wales with Henry Wigstead in 1797.

76 ***The tour of Doctor Syntax in search of the picturesque. A poem.*** Published 1st May 1812 at Ackermann's Repository of Arts, 101 Strand, London. 1812. Octavo.

Text: Title (engraved), verso blank; Advertisement [i]-iii, imprint on verso, *Diggens, Printer, St. Ann's Lane, London;* Text (Poem) [1]-275; blank [276]; Directions to Binder 1 p., verso blank.

Plates: Title-page and 30 coloured aquatints drawn and etched by Rowlandson. Only Lake District plate no. 16, Doctor Syntax sketching the lake. *Published May 1 1812.*

Notes: First published in *The poetical magazine* as 'The schoolmaster's tour', 1809-11. Issued canto by canto. Rowlandson depicted an incident and sent the drawing to Ackermann who passed it on to Combe who in turn wrote the accompanying verses. The work is a direct satire of the late William Gilpin and his theories of the picturesque. The page heading is 'Doctor Syntax's tour to the Lakes'; and the climax of the tour is when Syntax reaches the Lake of Keswick.

Enormously popular from the outset Doctor Syntax went into many editions, starting with two in 1812, three in 1813, others in 1815, 1817, and two in 1819. A French edition, *Le Don Quichotte romantique, ou voyage du Docteur Syntaxe, à la recherche du pittoresque . . .* , translated by M. Gandais, was published in Paris in 1821, with lithographs by Malapeau; a German edition, *Die Reise des Doktor Syntax um das Malerische aufzusuchen* with lithographs by F.E. Rademacher in Berlin in 1822; a Danish edition, *Doktor Syntaxes Reise aster det Maleriske,* translated by K.L. Rahbet, Copenhagen, 1820, printed title page and no illustrations; and several American editions.

King's copy: Second edition 1812 in mottled calf, leather label, gilt.

Note: For a full note see R.V. Tooley, *English books with coloured plates* (1954) no. 427, pp. 345-6

Ref: Abbey, *Life,* 215, 269

Copies: K; Armitt; BL; Wordsworth (1812)

1813

SAMUEL MIDDIMAN (engraver) 1750-1831

Samuel Middiman exhibited landscape drawings at the Incorporated Society and the Royal Academy from 1772. He studied engraving under Byrne (see 85) and Boydell.

77 ***Select views in Great Britain, engraved by S. Middiman, from pictures and drawings by the most eminent artists. With descriptions.*** London: Published by S. Middiman, No. 3 Grafton Street, Tottenham Court Road. [1784-1792], Oblong quarto.

Issued in parts in printed grey paper wrappers. Each part containing four plates with four leaves of description in English and French. Part I included a sheet of Proposals, dated October 1, 1783, announcing 'A Collection of Select Views' to be published in 25 numbers, one to be published every three months, Price five shillings.

Numbers I-VI On covers: 'Published by S. Middiman'. . . [as title]. And sold by W. Watts, Kemp's Row, Ranelagh Walk, Chelsea.

Numbers VII, VIII On covers, 'Sold also by W. Faden, Geographer to His Majesty, Charing Cross.' replaces 'And sold by W. Watts . . . '.

Numbers IX, X On cover, 'Published . . . by John and Josiah Boydell, No. 90 Cheapside. And sold by G. Nicol, Bookseller to His Majesty, Pall Mall Where may be had the preceding numbers.' replaces 'Published . . . S. Middiman . . .'.

Number XI On cover, 'And at the Shakespeare Gallery, Pall Mall' replaces 'And sold by C. Nicol . . . Pall Mall'.

Number XII On cover, 'This Publication will be comprised in Twenty Five Numbers' is omitted.

Plates: Lake District views only listed

Number I
1 Winandermere-Lake. *Painted by G. Barrett R.A. July 1 1784*
2 Keswick Lake. *Drawn by J. Smith.*

Number II
5 View at Grange Bridge (Keswick-Lake on plate) *Drawn by J. Smith. July 30th 1784.*
6 Ulleswater. *Painted by G. Barrett. July 30th 1784.*

Number III
10 Coniston Lake. *Drawn by F. Wheatly. Jany. 21st 1785.*
11 Skelwith Cascade. *Drawn by J. Smith. Jany. 21st 1785.*

Number IV
14 Coniston Lake. *Painted by F.Wheatly. Jany. 21st 1785.*

Number V
17 View near Ambleside. *Drawn by F. Wheatly. Decr. 12 1785.*
18 View of a Water-fall near Ambleside. *Painted by J. Barret. Decr. 12 1785.*

Number VI
21 Winandermere Lake. *Drawn by F. Wheatly. May 25 1786.*
22 View at Ambleside. *Painted by C. Powel. May 25 1786.*

Number VII
25 View near Keswick. *Drawn by F. Wheatly. Jany. 25 1787.*

Number VIII
29 Winandermere Lake. *Drawn by F. Wheatly. July 2 1787.*
30 View near Lancaster Sands. *Drawn by F. Wheatly. July 2 1787.*

Numbers IX, X, XI, XII, no Lake District views

All 48 plates signed: *Engraved by S. Middiman.* Imprints on plates 1-32: *Published . . . by S. Middiman, London.* 33-36: *John & Josiah Boydell, London.* 37-41: *John & Josiah Boydell, Cheapside, London.* 42-48: *John & Josiah Boydell, Cheapside & at the Shakespeare Gallery, Pall Mall* London [or similar]. Plate sizes: 160 × 210 mm.

Notes: The 25 numbers were never completed, and no more prints were issued until five additional plates with imprints, *Pubd. Jany. 1 1813 by Boydell & Co. 90 Cheapside, London,* were published.

The 53 plates were then issued as a book, with a printed half-title, the engraved title-page altered to show 'Published by John & Josiah Boydell'†. Advertisement in English and French, one leaf, plates unaltered, descriptive letterpress unaltered, one page. Index of Names, one page, List of Subjects, where situated, and by whom painted, &c. Advertisement dated London, December, 1812.

King's copy: In contemporary quarter red roan, marbled boards, no letters. It is the 1813 edition as published by Boydell, with the 5 additional plates (none of which is a Lake District view).

Copies: K; Armitt (Parts I-XII); BL; Jackson; and PB (Parts I-XII).

Ref: Upcott, p. xxxiv

Reissued 1830. Library of Congress; Boston Public Library

DUKE OF RUTLAND 1778-1857

78 ***Journal of a tour to the northern parts of Great Britain (1796).*** London: printed for J. Triphook, no. 38, St. James's-Street. 1813 [Anonymous]

Text: Half-title, verso blank; Title, imprint on verso, *J. Brettell, Rupert Street, Haymarket, London;* Text [1]-297; imprint, *J. Brettell, Rupert Street, London;* Table [299], 300.

Plates: 10 sepia aquatints from drawings by C. Rutland, and engraved plan and table. No Lake District views.

Lakes: pp. 250-53

Itinerary: Returning from Scotland; Penrith, Ullswater, Keswick, Grasmere, Windermere, Kendal. 13-16 October 1796

King's copy: In contemporary mottled calf, gilt, ducal crest and coronet, 1813, on spine, rebacked spine remounted, gilt. Bookplate, Thomas Cholmondeley of Vale Royall in Cheshire Esqr.

Note: John Henry Manners, 5th Duke of Rutland, accompanied by the Revd Mr King and Mr Culling Smith, made an extensive tour from London to Scotland returning by the Lake District, where they visited Lord and Lady Gordon near Keswick, the Bishop of Llandaff at Calgarth and Mr Curwen on Belle Isle.

Copies: K; BL

1814

ANONYMOUS

79 ***Letters from Albion to a friend on the continent, written in the years 1810, 1811, 1812, 1813.*** 2 vols. London: printed for Gale, Curtis, and Fenner, Pater-Noster Row; By S. Hamilton, Weybridge, Surrey. 1814. Octavo. Translated from German.

Lakes: Letters 28, 29, 30

Copy: Armitt

1815

ROBERT FREEBAIRN (artist) 1765-1808

Robert Freebairn was a pupil of Richard Wilson. He studied and worked in Italy. Though chiefly an oil painter he was elected to the Old Water-Colour Society in December 1805. His son Alfred Robert Freebairn, 1794-1846, was primarily an engraver.

80 ***Outlines of Lancashire scenery, from an unpublished sketch book of the late R. Freebairn, designed as studies for the use of schools and beginners, and etched by the younger Freebairn.*** London: published by Messrs. Colnaghi and Co., Cockspur Street. 1815. G. Smeeton, Printer, St. Martin's Lane. Oblong folio.†

No text.

OUTLINES

OF

LANCASHIRE SCENERY,

FROM AN UNPUBLISHED SKETCH BOOK

OF THE LATE

R. FREEBAIRN,

DESIGNED AS STUDIES FOR THE USE OF SCHOOLS AND BEGINNERS,

AND

ETCHED BY THE YOUNGER FREEBAIRN.

LONDON:

PUBLISHED BY MESSRS. COLNAGHI AND CO. COCKSPUR STREET.

1815.

G. Smeeton, Printer, St. Martin's Lane.

80 253 x 330 mm.

BRITANNIA DEPICTA;

A SERIES OF VIEWS

(With brief Descriptions)

OF THE MOST INTERESTING AND PICTURESQUE OBJECTS

IN GREAT BRITAIN.

THE COUNTIES ALPHABETICALLY ARRANGED.

PART V.

CONTAINING TWENTY-EIGHT VIEWS IN CUMBERLAND.

ENGRAVED FROM DRAWINGS MADE

By J. FARINGTON, Esq. R. A.

LONDON:

Printed for T. CADELL and W. DAVIES, Strand, Booksellers to the Royal Academy;

By G. Sidney, Northumberland Street.

1816.

85 277 x 387 mm.

Plates: 23 etchings. Numbered upper right corner. No signatures; no imprints. Plate sizes: 1-19, 200 × 285 mm; 20-25, 285 × 440 mm.

1 [Thirlmere Water]
2 [Near Ulverstone Lancashire]
3 [Furness Abbey Lancashire]
4 [Near Lancaster]
5 [Near Ambleside]
6 [Windermere Lake Ambleside]
7 [Near Lancaster]
8 [Windermere Lake Lancashire]
9 [Near Lancaster]
10 [Lake of Windermere]
11 [Druid's Temple near Keswick]
12 [St. John's Vale near Keswick]
13 [Ulswater]
14 [Dacre Castle near Ulswater]
15 [Ulswater]
16 [Dacre Castle near Ulswater]
17 [Ulswater]
18 [Lancaster Bridge]
19 [Ulswater from the lodge of the Duke of Norfolk Gowbarrow]*
20 [Lancaster Castle]
21 [Ulswater from Patterdale]*
22 [Lancaster Castle]*
23 [Lancaster Castle]*
24 [Lancaster Castle]*
25 [Lancaster Castle]*
*Folding

King's copies: Two copies, neither of which is complete. Both in brown paper wrappers; on upper cover of one printed title, 'Outlines of Lancashire Scenery. Price [blank]', in oval border, to which 'and the Lakes of Cumberland and Westmoreland [price] 15/-' has been added in MS. Both uncut.

Copies: No other copies located

REV. D.C.P.

81 ***A compendious tour through parts of Cumberland, Westmoreland and Lancashire written for rural festivity . . . in shorthand at Crackenthorpe Mill near Appleby.*** Carlisle. [1815]

Note: Advertised in a catalogue of Arnold Varty, Bookseller, Ambleside, 1973. This is the only record of this book. The identity of the Revd D.C.P. is not known.

LOUIS SIMOND

Louis Simond was born in France. He resided for more than thirty years in the USA and spent nearly two years in Great Britain, 1810-11. The dates of his birth and death are not known. His wife was English.

82.1 ***Journal of a tour and residence in Great Britain, during the years 1810 and 1811, by a French Traveller*** . . . 2 vols. Edinburgh: printed by George Ramsay and Company, for Archibald Constable and Company, Edinburgh; and Longman, Hurst, Rees, Orme and Brown, London. 1815. Octavo.†

Text: Vol. 1 Half-title, verso blank; Title, verso blank; Notice [v]-vii: blank; Preface [ix]-xiii; blank; Divisional title, 'Journal of a tour and residence in Great Britain', verso blank; Directions to the Binder [1]; Advert. for the works of Jonathan Swift [2]-5; Publisher's advert. 6-8; Text [1]-382. Imprint, *Printed by George Ramsay & Co. Edinburgh, 1815.*

Vol. 2 Half-title, verso blank; Title, verso blank; Text [1]-340; Index [341]-360; imprint as vol. 1.

Plates: 21 aquatints, 15 in vol. 1, 6 in vol. 2. Signed: *L.S.* [the author] *del. J. Clark direx.* Imprint: *Edinburgh. Published by A. Constable & Co. Jany. 1815.*

Issued coloured and uncoloured

Only Lake District plate, no. 11, Eagles Crag near Ulswater

Cut in the text: vol. 1, p. 346, The Bowder Stone; Folding table, vol. 1, p. 170.

Lakes: vol. 1, 259-60

Itinerary: Kendal, Ambleside, Ulswater, Penrith; vol. 2 Ulswater, Windermere, Langdale, Coniston, Grasmere, Derwentwater, Borrowdale, Crummock, Buttermere, Leatheswater, Windermere

King's copy: In the original brown-paper boards, repaired, with printed paper labels remounted on spine, lettered 'Travels in Great Britain by a Frenchman.' vol. 1 [or vol. 2] Price £2. 2*s*., uncut. Plates uncoloured. Watermarks: text, J. Whatman 1812; plates, J. Whatman 1814. Inscribed 'Ex Libris J.A. Lloyd', free endpapers both vols. Lacks 'Directions to Binder' and adverts.

Notes: In August 1810 Simond spent five days at Ambleside, and 'invited by friendship, as well as the attractions of the scenery', he returned to the Lake District in September after a Scottish tour. He was shown the beauties of Grasmere by Wordsworth, visited Dungeon Gill, stayed three weeks in Keswick and Buttermere, and finally left on 17 November.

The journal begins 24 December 1809. It was written in English.

Copies: K; and PB (coloured)

82.2 ——— Second edition, corrected and enlarged. 2 vols. 1817.

Copies: Armitt; BL

82A ——— American edition. 2 vols. New York: Published for the Author; and for sale by Eastburn Kirk and Co., and the principal booksellers throughout the United States. T. & W. Mercein, Printers. 1815. No plates. Octavo.

Copy: Cornell

82F.1 ——— *Voyage d'un Français en Angleterre, pendant les Années 1810 et 1811;* . . . 2 vols. A Paris chez Treuttel et Würtz, Libraires, rue de Bourbon, no. 17. Et à Strasbourg, même Maison de commerce. 1816. Orné de 15 Planches et de 13 Vignettes. 13 sepia aquatints engraved by Tiraiger, 2 engravings. Octavo.

Copies: Cornell; and PB

82F.2 ——— *Voyage en Angleterre, pendant les années 1810 et 1811 . . . Par Ls. Simond.* Seconde édition, revue corrigée et augmentée. 2 vols. A Paris . . . A Strasbourg et à Londres, même Maison de commerce. 1817. Octavo. 13 sepia aquatints, 2 engravings as 1816, but new plates not signed.

Copy: PB

Ref: Abbey, 18. In Abbey copy the plates are signed as in the 1816 edition (82 F.1) bound with text and title of 1817.

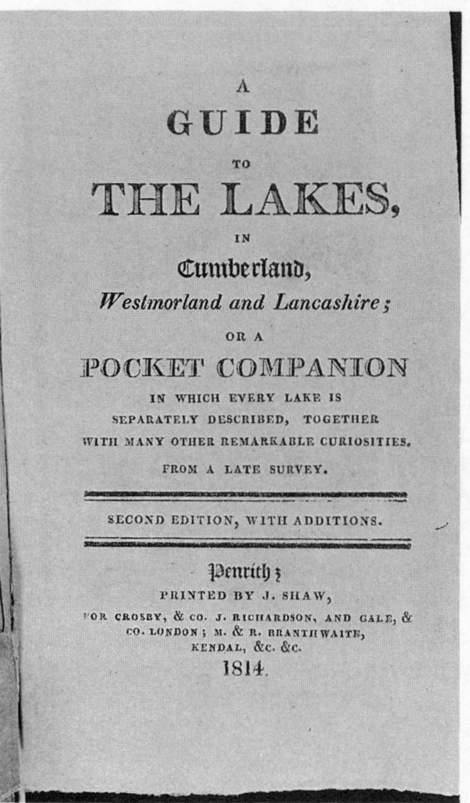

A GUIDE TO THE LAKES, IN Cumberland, Westmorland and Lancashire; OR A POCKET COMPANION IN WHICH EVERY LAKE IS SEPARATELY DESCRIBED, TOGETHER WITH MANY OTHER REMARKABLE CURIOSITIES. FROM A LATE SURVEY.

SECOND EDITION, WITH ADDITIONS.

Penrith; PRINTED BY J. SHAW, FOR CROSBY, & CO. J. RICHARDSON, AND GALE, & CO. LONDON; M. & R. BRANTHWAITE, KENDAL, &c. &c. 1814.

75.2 165 x 95 mm.

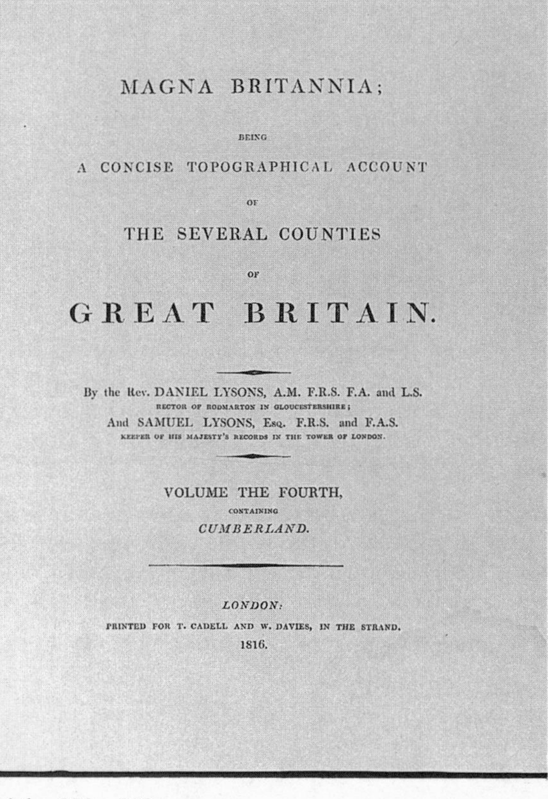

MAGNA BRITANNIA; BEING A CONCISE TOPOGRAPHICAL ACCOUNT OF THE SEVERAL COUNTIES OF GREAT BRITAIN.

By the Rev. DANIEL LYSONS, A.M. F.R.S. F.A. and L.S. RECTOR OF RODMARTON IN GLOUCESTERSHIRE; And SAMUEL LYSONS, Esq. F.R.S. and F.A.S. KEEPER OF HIS MAJESTY'S RECORDS IN THE TOWER OF LONDON.

VOLUME THE FOURTH, CONTAINING CUMBERLAND.

LONDON: PRINTED FOR T. CADELL AND W. DAVIES, IN THE STRAND. 1816.

84.1 273 x 218 mm.

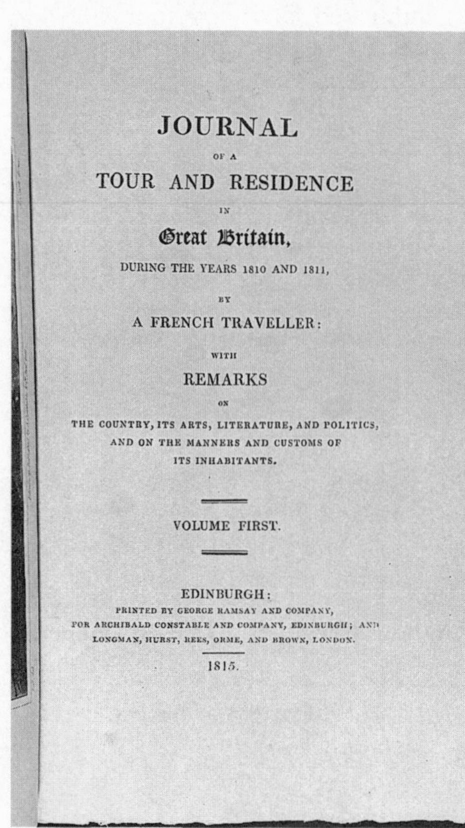

JOURNAL OF A TOUR AND RESIDENCE IN Great Britain, DURING THE YEARS 1810 AND 1811, BY A FRENCH TRAVELLER: WITH REMARKS ON THE COUNTRY, ITS ARTS, LITERATURE, AND POLITICS, AND ON THE MANNERS AND CUSTOMS OF ITS INHABITANTS.

VOLUME FIRST.

EDINBURGH: PRINTED BY GEORGE RAMSAY AND COMPANY, FOR ARCHIBALD CONSTABLE AND COMPANY, EDINBURGH; AND LONGMAN, HURST, REES, ORME, AND BROWN, LONDON. 1815.

82.1 230 x 145 mm.

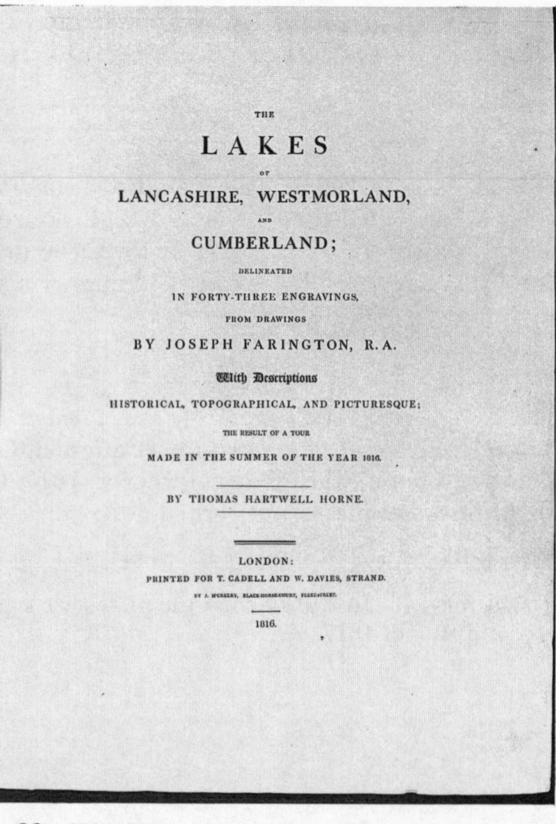

THE LAKES OF LANCASHIRE, WESTMORLAND, AND CUMBERLAND; DELINEATED IN FORTY-THREE ENGRAVINGS, FROM DRAWINGS BY JOSEPH FARINGTON, R.A. With Descriptions HISTORICAL, TOPOGRAPHICAL, AND PICTURESQUE; THE RESULT OF A TOUR MADE IN THE SUMMER OF THE YEAR 1816.

BY THOMAS HARTWELL HORNE.

LONDON: PRINTED FOR T. CADELL AND W. DAVIES, STRAND. 1816.

86 390 x 285 mm.

CHARLES PARISH 1766-1824

Charles Parish, Fellow of Queens' College, Cambridge, and later Lecturer at St Cuthbert's, Carlisle, was a friend and schoolfellow of Wordsworth at Hawkshead.

83 ***The minstrels of Windermere. A poem.*** London: for the author. Duodecimo.

A collection of poems, several of which are of Lake District topographical interest.

Copies: BL; Wordsworth

1816

DANIEL LYSONS 1762-1834 and SAMUEL LYSONS 1763-1819

Daniel Lysons was born at Rudworth, Gloucestershire. Divine and topographer. Curate Mortlake and Putney. Chaplain to Horace Walpole. Worked on Survey of London. F.S.A., F.R.S., F.L.S. His brother, Samuel Lysons, artist and antiquary. Called to the Bar, 1808. Vice-president and Treasurer, Royal Society 1810. Antiquary and professor R.A. 1818, F.S.A., F.R.S.

84.1 ***Magna Britannia; being a concise topographical account of the several counties of Great Britain. Volume the fourth containing Cumberland.*** London: printed for T. Cadell and W. Davies, in the Strand. 1816. Quarto (only 6 vols. published)†

Text: Half-title, verso blank; Title, verso blank; Contents 2 pp.; List of plates 2 pp.; Divisional title, 'Cumberland vol. IV', verso blank; General History [iii-ccx]; Parochial History [1]-177; blank; Index [189]-198; Errata 198

Plates: Only one Lake District view, The Bowder Stone and Borrowdale. Signed: *Drawn by Joseph Farington R.A. Etched by Letitia Byrne.* Imprint: *Published Sept. 20 1815 by T. Cadell and W. Davies, Strand.*

Map: Cumberland, coloured, 460 × 275 mm, folding. Scale: 1 mile = 7 inches. Signed: *Matlow Sc. Russel Court.* Imprint: *Published Decr. 1, 1815 by T. Cadell & W. Davies, Strand, London*

King's copy: In contemporary diced calf, leather labels, gilt repaired. Binder's label on pastedown endpaper. 'Bound by R. Bailey & Co. Wooton'.

Notes: Large paper copies of this volume were issued (Upcott).

The Lysons brothers collaborated in producing *Magna Britannia* which was to have been an account of all the counties of Great Britain in alphabetical order. However only six volumes were published, ending with Devon. After the death of Samuel in 1819 the enterprise was abandoned.

Copies: K; Armitt; BL; Cornell; Jackson; Wordsworth

Ref; Upcott, p. xxiii and Supplement, p. 600

84.2 ——— Another issue. London: Cadell and Greenland. n.d. (later than 1822).

Copy: Armitt

WILLIAM BYRNE (engraver) 1743-1805

85 ***Britannia Depicta; a series of views (with brief descriptions) of the most interesting and picturesque objects in Great Britain . . . Part V Containing twenty-eight views in Cumberland.*** Engraved from drawings made by J. Farington, Esq., R.A. London: for T. Cadell and W. Davies, Strand, Booksellers to the Royal Academy; by G. Sidney, Northumberland Street. 1816. Oblong Quarto.

Title printed on wrapper.†

Text: List of plates 1 p.; l p. of text on verso of each plate.

Plates: 28 engravings. 26 are impressions from the same plates as nos. 17-42, Horne *The Lakes* (86)

'. . . also some sets struck off, proof impressions, to accompany the Large Paper copies of Lysons' *Magna Britannia'* (Upcott).

Additional plates:

Naworth Castle. *March 7, 1816 Signed T. Hearne F.S.A. delt. J. Landseer engraver to the King sculp.*
Carlisle from Stanmore, *Drawn by J. Powell Engraved by J. Landseer A.R.A.*

King's copy: In original printed grey paper wrappers uncut, bound at top. Repaired.

Notes: Britannia Depicta was published as an illustrated companion to *Magna Britannia.* It was considered that the plates would be 'valuable for artists and connoisseurs'. Like *Magna Britannia,* it never got beyond the sixth part.

Copies: K; Armitt; BL; Wordsworth

Ref: Upcott, supplement pp. 602-3.

Note: For Farington, see also 22 and 86

THOMAS HARTWELL HORNE 1780-1862

Divine, biblical scholar, bibliographer and writer on controversial subjects. F.S.A., B.D., Cambridge.

86 ***The lakes of Lancashire, Westmorland, and Cumberland; . . . from drawings by Joseph Farington, R.A. . . . the result of a tour made in the summer of the year 1816*** London: printed for T. Cadell and W. Davies, Strand, by J. M'Creery, Black Horse-Court, Fleet-Street. 1816. Quarto.†

Text: Title, lines from Pope and Beattie on verso; Preface [iii], iv; Contents v-vii; Directions [viii]; Text 1-96; Imprint on p. 96, *J. M'Creery, printer, Black-Horse-Court, Fleet Street, London*

Plates: 43 engravings: Signed, *Drawn by J. Farington R.A.,* except pl. 21 and 30, signed *Jos. Farington R.A. delt.* Engraver noted after title. Imprints: *London: published* [date] *by Cadell & W. Davies, Strand.* Plate sizes vary from 300 × 230 mm to 274 × 225 mm.

1 South View of Lancaster. *W. Woolnoth. May 1 1816.*
2 East View of Lancaster. *S. Middiman. May 1 1816.*
3 Bowness and the Lake Windermere. *J. Scott. May 1 1816.*
4 Windermere from below Bowness looking to the North. *J. Scott. May 1 1816.*

5 Windermere from Calgarth Park looking to the South. *F.R. Hay. May 1 1816.*
6 Windermere from Low Wood. *J. Byrne. May 1 1816.*
7 Head of Windermere. *J. Scott. May 1 1816.*
8 Ambleside. *J. Pye. May 1 1816.*
9 Waterfall at Ambleside. *S. Middiman. May 1 1816.*
10 Culleth Force. *S. Middiman. May 1 1816.*
11 Coniston Lake. *F.R. Hay. May 1 1816.*
12 Hawkshead and Esthwaite Water. *F.R. Hay. May 1 1816.*
13 Waterfall at Rydal. *S. Middiman. May 1 1816.*
14 Rydal Mere. *W. Woolnoth. May 1 1816.*
15 Grasmere. *J. Pye. May 1 1816.*
16 Thirlmere. *F.R. Hay. Septr. 15 1815.*
17 Derwentwater from Brough-top. *F.R. Hay. Septr. 15 1815.*
18 Keswick and Skiddaw. *J. Byrne. Septr. 15 1815.*
19 View from the Road from Keswick to Borrowdale. *F.R. Hay. Septr. 15 1815.*
20 East side of Derwentwater, looking towards Lowdore Waterfall. *F.R. Hay. Septr. 15 1815.*
21 Lowdore Waterfall. *J. Landseer F.S.A. Sculp. May 7 1816.*
22 Skiddaw and Derwentwater from Lowdore Waterfall. *J. Scott. Septr. 15 1815.*
23 The Grange in Borrowdale. *J. Scott. Septr. 15 1815.*
24 Castle Crag and Bowder Stone. *J. Byrne. Septr. 15 1815.*
25 Wastdale Village. *J. Landseer A.R.A. Septr. 15 1815.*
26 Muncaster Castle and Eskdale. *John Pye. Septr. 15 1815.*
27 Honister Crag. *S. Middiman. Septr. 15 1815.*
28 Buttermere and Crommack Water. *F.R. Hay. Septr. 15 1815.*
29 The Village of Lowswater. *J. Scott. Septr. 15 1815.*
30 Cockermouth. *J. Landseer F.S.A. sculp. March 7 1816.*
31 Maryport. *F.R. Hay. Septr. 15 1815.*
32 Bassenthwaite Lake from the Hill above Armathwaite. *F.R. Hay. Septr. 15 1815.*
33 Saddleback and the River Rothway. *W. Woolnoth. Septr. 15 1815.*
34 Scene at Nunnery. *S. Middiman & John Pye. Septr. 15 1815.*
35 Ulswater from Pooley Bridge. *S. Middiman. Septr. 15 1815.*
36 Water Millock and the lower end of Ulswater. *J. Scott. Septr. 15 1815.*
37 Ulswater and Liulph's Tower. *John Pye. Septr. 15 1815.*
38 The Head of Ulswater from Gowbarrow Park. *F.R. Hay. Septr. 15 1815.*
39 The Head of Ulswater, Patterdale, and the Mountain Helvellyn. *S. Middiman. Septr. 15 1815.*
40 North East View of Carlisle. *W. Woolnoth. Septr. 15 1815.*
41 View of Gilsland Spa. *S. Middiman. Septr. 15 1815.*
42 Brougham Castle. *S. Middiman. May 1 1816.*
43 Hawswater. *S. Middiman. May 1 1816.*

Map: Folding map of the Lakes in the Counties of Lancashire, Westmoreland and Cumberland. Signed: *Herbert delt. H. Mutlow Sculp.* Imprint: *London. Published Augst. 10th. 1816 by Cadell & W. Davies, Strand.* Size: 618 × 420 mm. No scale indicated.

Note: Copies were issued with proof impressions of the plates (Upcott, p. 603). Although some of the views are similar, the plates are different from those in Farington's *Views of the Lakes,* 1789, (22). (Martin Hardie in *Water colour painting in England* (1966) and Iolo A. Williams in *Early English water-colours* (1952) are both wrong in describing this book as a revised edition of the 1789 *Views of the Lakes.* The letterpress as well as the plates are completely different.)

King's copy: In original brown-paper boards, printed paper label, uncut

Copies: K; Armitt; BL; Cornell; Jackson; Kendal; Wordsworth; and Alpine Club, coloured.

Ref: Upcott, supplement pp. 603-5

Note: For Farington, see also 22 and 86

R.H. SPIKER

Librarian to the King of Prussia. Member of the Philosophical Society and of the Society for the encouragement of Arts, Manufacturers and Commerce of London.

87G ***Reise durch England, Wales, Schottland in Jahre 1816***

Leipzig: Göschen. 1816. Engravings. Octavo.

Copy: BL

87.1 ——— ***Travels through England, Wales, & Scotland in the year 1816*** 2 vols. London: Printed for Lackington, Hughes, Harding, Mavor and Jones, Finsbury Square. 1820. Duodecimo. Dedicated to the friends of England. Translated from the German.†

Text: Vol. 1 Title, imprint on verso *Printed for J.D. Dewick, 46 Barbican, London:* Dedication [1]-4; Adverts. [ix]-xii; Contents [13]-20; Text [1]-325; Adverts. 1 p.
Vol. 2 Title, imprint on verso as vol. 1; Text [1]-283

Lakes: Chapters XIII and XIV, pp. 244-81

Itinerary: Penrith, Ullswater, Keswick, Derwentwater, Grasmere, Rydal, Windermere, Coniston, Esthwaitewater, Bowness, Kendal.

King's copy: In contemporary half russia, marbled boards, gilt, leather labels. In Vol. 1 pages 97-120 wrongly numbered as 73-96. Chapters wrongly numbered as follows – 8 as 7, 10 as 9, 12 as 11, 13 as 11, 14 as 12, 15 as 13, 16 as 14.

Copies: K; BL

87.2 ——— (Second edition) 2 vols. London: Harding. 1828. Duodecimo.

Copy: Armitt

1818

JONATHAN OTLEY 1766-1856

Jonathan Otley was born at Scroggs, near Loughrigg Tarn in Langdale, son of a wood-sieve and basket maker. Self-educated. Settled in Keswick about 1797. Combined his callings of watch-maker and surveyor with acting as guide. Became an authority on local fact and fable, and a keen amateur of geology and the physical sciences. Accompanied John Dalton (of the Atomic Theory) and Adam Sedgwick. Anticipated Sedgwick's work on the geology of the Lakes. Friend of Peter Crosthwaite (see 17). See 'Jonathan Otley, the geologist and guide' by J. Clifton Ward, *Transactions of the Cumberland Association*, pt 2 (1876/7), which includes a list of Otley's writings. See also 102.

88.1 ***A new map of the district of the Lakes, by J. Otley, Keswick.*** 1818.

Signed: Engraved by J & G Menzies Edinr. Size: 325 × 265 mm. Scale: 1 in. = 4 miles

Issued coloured and uncoloured.

Note: 'In 1817 I constructed a map of the district which I had engraved and published in 1818. It was chiefly sold folded for the pocket'. Otley in reply to a letter from Mr. Thos Sanderson of London, 1840.

88.2 ——— Second edition. 1823.

Map exactly as 1818, except *2nd Edit. 1823* has been added. Price 3*s.* 6*d.*

King's copy: Folded, coloured, dissected and mounted on linen, in marbled paper slip-case with scarlet printed paper label.† 9 sheets of tabulated information mounted on verso

1	Title	6 & 7	The Keswick Guide
2	Explanation	8	The Laker's Guide
3	Description	9	The Tourist's Guide
4 & 5	Mountain Guide		

88.3-8 ——— Other editions: [3rd] 1827
[4th] 1833
[5th] 1837
[6th and 7th] no information
[8th] 1850

King's copy: The 1837 edition is the same as 1823 except imprint *Keswick Published by Jona. Otley, 21st June 1827. And with additions 20th July 1833 and 1837.* In brown cloth slip-case. Blue printed paper label on upper cover. *'Otley's Map of the Lake District Price 3s. 6d'.* The information sheets mounted on verso are similar to 1823 but revised. One more is added inside upper cover. Title mounted on verso: 'A correct map of the Lake District; with the height of the principal hills, their bearings and distances; the stages and interesting excursions.'

1819

JOHN ROBINSON 1774-1840

John Robinson, author and divine, was born at Temple Sowerby, and educated at Penrith Grammar School. Headmaster and perpetual curate of Ravenstonedale, 1813-33. Rector of Clifton, 1818, and of Cliburn, 1833 (all in Westmorland). See 113.

89.1 ***A guide to the Lakes, in Cumberland, Westmorland, and Lancashire, illustrated with twenty views of local scenery, and A travelling Map of the adjacent Country.*** London: printed for Lackington, Hughes, Harding, Mavor, and Jones, Finsbury-Square. 1819. Octavo.†

Text: Title, imprint on verso, *London: printed by Thomas Davison, Whitefriars;* Preface [iii]-v; blank; Contents [vii], viii; Directions & Errata one leaf; Text [1]-322; Table and Itinerary 323-328, Imprint repeated p. 328,

Plates: 22 uncoloured aquatints; no signatures; imprints; *London. Published June 1, 1819, by Lucking-ton & Co.*

1	Hawes Water	12	Wythburn or Leathes Water
2	Ullswater, from Stybarrow Crag	13	Grasmere
3	Goldrill Bridge in Patterdale	14	Rydal Water
4	Brother Water, near Patterdale	15	Brathay Bridge, Near Ambleside
5	Keswick Lake, Derwentwater	16	Windandermere, from the ferry, near the station
6	Lowdore	17	Coniston Lake, from Nibthwaite Forge
7	Bowder Stone	18	Furness Abbey
8	Borrowdale, from Bowder Stone	19	Furness Abbey
9	Buttermere Water	20	Newby Bridge, at the foot of Windandermere
10	Cromack Water		
11	Smallthwaite Bridge		

Map: Coloured folding Map of the Country in the Vicinity of the Lakes. Signed: *Neele & Son sc. 352 Strand.* Imprint, *London, Published July 1 1819 by Lackington & Co. Finsbury Square.*

Note: The guide describes a series of tours, covering all of the main valleys of the Lake District except Ennerdale, Eskdale and Dunnerdale. The tabulated itinerary is of a route from London to Penrith by Hatfield, Worksop, and Borough Bridge; and from Kendal to London by Lancaster and End Moor. 'The author has incorporated' observations of the scenery of the Lakes 'of our most celebrated tour writers . . . indeed, a work of this kind would be very defective, if it should not contain the masterly delineations of Pennant, Gilpin, Young and Budworth.'

King's copy: In contemporary tree-calf, leather label, gilt.

Copies: K; Armitt; BL; Cornell; Jackson; Kendal; Wordsworth

89.2 ——— 'A new edition'.
Title as 1819 except imprint altered to 'London: Whittaker, Treacher & Co. Ave-Maria Lane. 1831.'

Note: Except for the title-page with the altered imprint this is a reissue of the first edition. The letterpress including the errata has not been reset, and the plates and map are identical. Advertised as 'In post 8vo., a New Edition, with Twelve Aquatint Views of the most beautiful Scenery, and a Map, price 12*s.* cloth, lettered'.

King's copy: In publisher's dark blue cloth, printed paper label. Inscribed, 'J. Gifford'. and label of 'Richard H. Kelly' on paste-down endpaper.

Copies: K; no other copies located

CATHERINE HUTTON 1766-1845

The novelist Catherine Hutton was the daughter of William Hutton, Birmingham topographer, bookseller, author and poet. She published a life of her father in 1816, and revised his history of Birmingham. Visited Keswick probably in 1801.

90 ***Oakwood Hall, a novel, including a description of the Lakes of Cumberland and Westmoreland***. 3 vols. London: Longman, Hurst, Rees, Orme and Brown. 1819. Duodecimo. Enlarged and corrected from *La Belle Assemblée.*

Letters 19 from Ambleside; 20 and 21 from Keswick; 22 from Milnthorp.

Note: Miss Hutton's heroine, Jane Oakwood, makes a standard tour of the Lakes. She visits Windermere, Ullswater, and Keswick, where one of the party ascends Skiddaw, and she describes the mock naval battle in the Derwentwater Regatta. She returns to Windermere by Grasmere and Rydal. The four chapters are a conventional tour description, and do not in any way advance the plot of the novel.

Copies: BL and Cambridge University Library.

WILLIAM WESTALL 1781-1850

William Westall was the brother of Richard Westall (1765-1836), the brother-in-law of William Daniell (1769-1837) and a friend of Robert Southey. He first went to the Lakes in 1811; and until 1820 he spent some time every winter near Keswick. He married Ann Sedgwick of Dent, sister of Professor Adam Sedgwick, geologist of the Lake District. Westall was primarily a topographical artist and a highly skilled engraver. He was generally responsible for preparing his own plates. See 107.

91 ***A series of views of the lakes of Cumberland and Westmorland***. Demy Quarto. Issued in four parts, plates coloured or uncoloured

Part 1 Title on upper wrapper† Imprint: *London: Published by Hurst, Robinson, and Co. (late Boydell) 90 Cheapside. 1819. W. Wilson, Printer, 4 Greville Street, Hatton-Garden, London.*

Plates: 4 aquatints, signed *Drawn & Engraved by W. Westall A.R.A.;* Imprint: *Published July 1, 1819, by Hurst, Robinson, & Co. 90 Cheapside*

1 Keswick Lake, from the North Side of Castelet
2 Portinscale Bridge, near Keswick
3 Lowdore Waterfall
4 Keswick Lake, seen from above Lowdore.

Part 2 Upper wrapper as Part 1 except:
'No. II' replaces 'No. I'
'Views of Keswick' replaces 'Views in the Vale of Keswick'
'late Boydell' omitted from publisher's imprint
Printer's imprint omitted
'1820' replaces '1819'

Plates: 4 aquatints as Part I except dated *April 1, 1820*

5 Keswick Lake, from Barrow Common
6 Keswick Bridge
7 Keswick & Grisedale Pike
8 Keswick Lake from Saddleback

Part 3 Upper wrapper as Part 2 except:
'No. III' replaces 'No. II'
'Price 11*s* 6*d*' replaces 'Price 10*s*'
No titles of views
'Each of the principal Lakes' replaces 'Each of the Lakes'
'A descriptive Account, with references to the Plates, will accompany the Views of each Lake' is added
'A descriptive account of Keswick Lake . . . will be given in the Third Number, which will complete the first portion of the work.'

New imprint: *London: Published by Rodwell and Martin, New Bond Street; J.M. Richardson, Cornhill; and W. Westall, 20 Euston Crescent. 1820.* Printer's imprint as Part 1.

Plates: 4 aquatints as Part 1 except imprint altered to *Published June 1 1820 by Rodwell & Martin, New Bond Street* (plates 7, 8, 10 dated *July 1, 1820*)

9 Keswick Lake, near Waterend
10 Keswick Lake, from the East side §
11 Keswick Lake, From Applethwaite
12 Skiddaw

Part 3 contains title-page and text as advertised on wrapper

Text: Title, imprint on verso, *W. Wilson, Printer 4 Greville-Street, Hatton Garden, London;* Text [1]-8; imprint repeated on last page.

Part 4 Upper wrapper as Part 3 except:
'No. 4 (numeral inscribed) replaces 'No. III' (numeral printed)
'Price 11*s* 6*d*' replaces 'Price 10*s*'
Publisher's imprint omitted
Printer's imprint as Parts 1 and 3

Plates: 4 aquatints as previous parts except dated *May 1 1821*

13 Lake Windermere. From above Stors
14 Stock-gill Force
15 On Lake Windermere. Between Bowness & Ambleside
16 Lake Windermere. From above Rayrigg

King's copy: As issued in original printed wrappers. Plates uncoloured; watermarks Part 3, 1818.

Note: It was intended that each of the Lakes would form a distinct work, not exceeding three numbers containing four plates each, but Windermere was abandoned after the first four plates (Part 4) had been published. The first three parts were published separately as *Views of the Lake and Vale of Keswick* (see 92 below)

Copy: K

92 ***Views of the Lake and of the Vale of Keswick***. London: Published by Rodwell and Martin, New Bond Street. 1820. Demy Quarto. Issued in boards; uncoloured plates Price £1 13*s*., coloured plates Price £3 3*s*.

Text: As issued in Part 3 of previous item (91). Different title.

Plates: 12 aquatints as Parts 1, 2 and 3 of previous item, but bound in different order – 3, 2, 12, 4, 9, 10, 7, 6, 1, 11, 8, 5.

King's copy: As issued in the original brown-paper boards, uncut, with printed paper label on upper cover: *Twelve Views of the Lake and of the Vale of Keswick. Drawn and engraved by W. Westall, A.R.A. Price £1 : 13s. Bds.* The plates are coloured. Watermarks 1818. The Abbey copy is the same except the plates are bound in a different order, and the label on the cover reads *'Coloured Plates. Price £3:3s. Bds.'* and not '*Price £1 : 13s. Bds.*', which indicates that the King's copy was coloured after issue.

Note: The anonymous text was written by Robert Southey. Southey wrote to Westall on 8 Dec. 1820: 'I am glad to hear you are employed upon your views of Winandermere . . . when you want your letter-press, if you cannot persuade Wordsworth to write it (who would in all respects be the best person) I will do for you the best I can' *(Southey: Life and Correspondence*, ed. C.C. Southey, 6 vols. [London, 1850]. Vol. 5, pp. 50, 51). The authorship is confirmed by a letter from Sara Hutchinson to John Monkhouse, 15 October 1820, when she sent him parts 2 and 3, saying 'the extra 18d upon the 3rd. is occasioned by the Letter press . . . Southey furnished the matter gratis . . . Keswick Lake is now finished – Winandermere will be out this Winter we expect [but it was not]' (*The Letters of Sara Hutchinson*, ed. K Coburn, (1954) p. 213).

A copy has been examined consisting of title, text, 10 uncoloured plates and one additional plate, in paper wrappers with a printed label, 'Price [ ], Southey's description of Keswick Lake with Views by W. Westall, A.R.A. London.'

Copies: K; Armitt; Wordsworth

Ref: Abbey, 191

93 ***Views of the Lakes of Cumberland and Westmorland*** Drawn on zinc by W. Westall, A.R.A. Printed by Chapman, Patenties, 18 Change Alley. London: Ackermann, and Co., 96 Strand. n.d. [*c*. 1830]. Price 2*s*. 6*d*. No text, title on wrapper.

Plates: 6 engravings:

1 Skiddaw & Keswick Lake
2 Keswick Lake
3 On Rydal Lake
4 Rydal Lake
5 Rydal Hall
6 Lake Windermere

Signed: W.W. Printed from Zink by Chapman & Co. 27 Cornhill

Copy: Jackson

---

17 aquatint views of the Lakes by Westall were published by Ackermann, 1831-9 (bound set, Armitt). These are panoramas varying in length from 490 to 800 mm. They record the landscape with great faithfulness. The names of the prominent features in the views are engraved on the plates.

At the time when Westall was working on these panoramas, he was a regular visitor at Rydal Mount and was preparing a series of illustrations for Wordsworth's poems. The work was never completed, but some of the engravings were published in paper wrappers without letterpress as *Views of the Lake Country to illustrate the poems of W. Wordsworth Esq.* Drawn from nature and engraved by W. Westall A.R.A. To be completed in six parts. London: Published by Edward Moxon, Dover Street. 1812.

Various other collections of Westall's Lake District prints were published by Ackermann and others.

JAMES DUGDALE

94 ***The new British traveller; or, modern panorama of England and Wales; . . . Illustrated by a complete set of correct maps, views of public buildings, antiquities, etc. etc.*** 4 vols. London: Vols. 1, 3, 4, printed by and for J. and J. Cundee, Ivy Lane, Paternoster-Row; Vol. 2, Published by J. Robins & Co., Albion Press, Ivy Lane, Paternoster-Row. 1819. Engravings and maps.

Lakes: Cumberland, vol. 1, pp. 523-628; Lancashire, vol. 2, pp. 274-342; Westmorland, vol. 4, pp. 424-44.

Copies: BL; Kendal

1820

WILLIAM WORDSWORTH 1770-1850

William Wordsworth was born at Cockermouth on 7 April 1770. The principal dates relevant to his life in the Lake District are: 1776-7 attends infant school in Penrith; 1779 goes to Hawkshead Grammar School; 1789 long vacation at Penrith; 1794 visits Lakes; 1799 walking tour in the Lakes with his brother John and Coleridge; 20 December 1799 settles at Dove Cottage, Grasmere; 1805 *The Prelude* finished; 1808 moves to Allan Bank; 1811 moves to Grasmere Rectory; 1813 settles at Rydal Mount for life; 23 April 1850 dies; buried Grasmere church yard.

95.2 ***The River Duddon, a series of Sonnets: Vaudracour and Julia: and other poems. To which is annexed, a topographical description of the Country of the Lakes, in the North of England.*** London: Printed for Longman, Hurst, Rees, Orme, and Brown, Paternoster-Row. 1820. Octavo.† Vol. 3 of *Poems by William Wordsworth*

Second edition of Wordsworth's *Guide*. For first edition see Wilkinson (73).

Text: Sub-title, Vol. III, imprint on verso, *Printed by A. & R. Spottiswoode, Printers Street, London;* Title, imprint repeated on verso; Dedication, verso blank; Advertisement, verso blank; Contents [vii], viii; Divisional Title, 'The River Duddon', note on verso; Text [3]-68; Divisional Title, 'Vaudracour and Julia', note on verso; Text [71]-212; Divisional Title, 'Topographical Description of the country of the Lakes in the North of England' note on verso; Text [215]-321; Errata; imprint repeated.

Notes: 'This essay, which was published several years ago as an introduction to some Views of the Lakes, by the Rev. Joseph Wilkinson . . . is now, with emendations and additions attached to these volumes' (note to the Topographical Description, p. [214]).

The 'Introduction' and 'Section 1' of *Select Views* are reproduced as one essay, adapted and with many additions and omissions. All references to Wilkinson's plates are removed.

The text is based on 'An unpublished tour', MS. reproduced as Appendix II, pp. [288]-348, *The prose works of William Wordsworth*, eds W.J.B. Owen and J.W. Smyser, (1974)

It was written 'in the same spirit which dictated several of the poems, and from a belief that it will tend naturally to illustrate them.'

King's copy: Rebound. F.W.G. (F.W. Gale) stamped on spine (see 74).

Copies: K; Armitt; BL; Cornell; Wordsworth

95.3 ——— ***A description of the scenery of the Lakes in the North of England. Third edition, (now first published separately) with additions, and illustrative remarks upon the Scenery of the Alps.*** Imprint as 1820. Duodecimo.† 500 copies printed.

Text: Title, imprint on verso, *London: Printed by A. & R. Spottiswoode, New-Street-Square;* Contents [iii], iv; Description [1]-101; Miscellaneous observations 102-136; Directions and information for the tourist; imprint repeated.

Map: Engraved folding map of the Lakes. Signed: *Drawn and engraved by Sidy. Hall, Bury Strt. Bloomsby.* Imprint *London, Published by Longman, Hurst, Rees, Orme & Brown, Paternoster Row,* 1822 Size: 254 × 203 mm. Scale: 1¾ in. = 10 miles.

Notes: The book was now divided into three main parts: 'Description of the Scenery of the Lakes', 'Miscellaneous Observations' and 'Directions and Information for the Tourist'. The third part was based on Section 2 of the previous edition, and from the second paragraph, p. 114 to the end the material is all new. The additions include the Excursion to the top of Scawfell (pp. 130-136), transcribed with some alterations from Dorothy Wordsworth's 'Excursion up Scawfell Pike, October 7, 1818', which is an extract from a letter, now lost, written by D.W. to the Revd William Johnson, 21 October 1818, see *Journals of Dorothy Wordsworth*, ed. E. de Selincourt (London, 1941) Appendix, vol. 1, pp 425-30. Dorothy had been responsible for some of the descriptions which form Section II of the original *Select Views* (see also Owen and Smyser, vol. 2, pp. 361-78).

King's copy: In publisher's flowered green cloth, leather label on spine. Book plate, Hugh Walpole.

Copies: K; BL; Cornell; Jackson; Kendal; Wordsworth

95.4 ——— Fourth edition. 1823. 1,000 copies printed.

Title as third edition except: 'Fourth edition' replaces 'Third edition'

Note: The text was revised and considerably enlarged. The additions included descriptions of waterfowl and of night scenes, and a new Division, 'Excursions to the Top of Scawfell and on the Banks of Ullswater' in which Dorothy's account of the excursion of November 1805 is added to her Scawfell account (see Owen and Smyser, vol. 2, pp. 368-78).

King's copy: Interleaved and bound in diced calf, rebacked. Some MS notes and sketches added *c.* 1835

Copies: BL; Cornell; Jackson; Wordsworth

95.5 ——— ***A guide through the district of the Lakes in the North of England, with a description of the scenery, &c. for the use of tourists and residents.*** Fifth edition, with considerable additions. Kendal: Published by Hudson and Nicholson, and in London by Longman & Co., Moxon, and Whittaker & Co. 1835. Small Octavo.†

1,500 copies printed.

Note: In this, the last edition to be published under the editorship of Wordsworth, the book was rearranged with 'Directions and information for the Tourist' (in three Sections), 'Miscellaneous

TRAVELS
THROUGH
ENGLAND, WALES, & SCOTLAND,
IN THE YEAR 1816.

BY DR. S. H. SPIKER,
LIBRARIAN TO HIS MAJESTY THE KING OF PRUSSIA.

DEDICATED TO THE FRIENDS OF ENGLAND.

Translated from the German.

IN TWO VOLUMES.

VOL II.

LONDON:
PRINTED FOR LACKINGTON, HUGHES, HARDING, MAVOR, AND JONES, FINSBURY SQUARE.
1820.

87.1 175 x 100 mm.

THE
RIVER DUDDON,
A SERIES OF
Sonnets:
VAUDRACOUR AND JULIA:
AND
OTHER POEMS.
TO WHICH IS ANNEXED,
A TOPOGRAPHICAL DESCRIPTION
OF THE
Country of the Lakes,
IN THE NORTH OF ENGLAND.

By WILLIAM WORDSWORTH.

LONDON:
PRINTED FOR LONGMAN, HURST, REES, ORME, AND BROWN,
PATERNOSTER-ROW.
1820.

95.2 220 x 140 mm.

A
DESCRIPTION
OF THE
SCENERY OF THE LAKES
IN
THE NORTH OF ENGLAND.

THIRD EDITION,
(NOW FIRST PUBLISHED SEPARATELY)
WITH ADDITIONS,
AND ILLUSTRATIVE REMARKS UPON THE
Scenery of the Alps.

By WILLIAM WORDSWORTH.

LONDON:
PRINTED FOR
LONGMAN, HURST, REES, ORME, AND BROWN,
PATERNOSTER-ROW.
1822.

95.3 157 x 95 mm.

A
GUIDE
THROUGH THE
DISTRICT OF THE LAKES
IN
The North of England,
WITH
A DESCRIPTION OF THE SCENERY, &c.
FOR THE USE OF
TOURISTS AND RESIDENTS.

FIFTH EDITION,
WITH CONSIDERABLE ADDITIONS.

By WILLIAM WORDSWORTH.

KENDAL:
PUBLISHED BY HUDSON AND NICHOLSON,
AND IN LONDON BY
LONGMAN & CO., MOXON, AND WHITTAKER & CO.
1835.

95.5 170 x 107 mm.

Observations', 'Excursions', 'Ode: The Pass of Kirkstone', and, added by the publisher, with permission of the Author, 'Itinerary of the Lakes'.

King's copy: In publisher's patterned brown cloth, printed paper label on spine, 'Wordsworth's Guide through the Lake District'. 4*s*.'

Copies: K; Armitt; BL; Cornell; Jackson; Wordsworth

The differences between the five original editions of the *Guide* are dealt with in detail in Owen and Smyser, *The prose works of William Wordsworth*, vol. 2.

The *Guide* was taken over by the publisher of the fifth edition and incorporated in Hudson's *Complete guide* (1842), see 122.

Wordsworth's *Guide* has been reprinted several times. It appeared in two Victorian collections of Wordsworth's prose writings, one edited by Alexander B. Grosart in 1876, and the other by William Knight in 1896. It was published separately as *Wordsworth's Guide to the Lakes. Fifth edition (1835)*, with a scholarly introduction, appendices and notes by Ernest de Selincourt, and 8 illustrations, London, 1906 (republished in paperback, with 10 illustrations, Oxford, 1977). A facsimile of the fifth edition with a short introduction by J.W. Lucas, was published by the Tantivy Press, Malvern (1948). Another separate reprint of the fifth edition, with a critical introduction by W. Merchant and some illustrations by John Piper was published in London (1951), and Bloomington, Indiana (1952). W.J.B. Owen and Jane Worthington Smyser in their authoritative *The prose works of William Wordsworth* (Oxford, 1974) not only reprint the fifth edition but collate the various versions of the *Guide*, and publish much relevant, previously unpublished, writing. *The illustrated Wordsworth's guide to the Lakes* (Webb & Bower, Exeter, 1987) with an introduction, notes and captions by Peter Bicknell, includes 198 illustrations.

JOHN BRIGGS 1788-1824

John Briggs, writer of prose and poetry, was born in Cartmel, Lancashire. A 'Sketch' of his life is included in *The remains* . . . (97).

96 ***The Lonsdale magazine, or Provincial Repository, for the year*** [date]. ***Comprising topographical and biographical sketches*** . . . Edited by J. Briggs. In 3 vols. Price one shilling [each part]

Vol. 1 Kirkby Lonsdale: Printed and published by A. Foster. 1820.†
Vol. 2 Kirkby Lonsdale: Printed and published by J. Foster. Sold also by Mr. Richardson, Royal Exchange, London. 1821.
Vol. 3 Kendal: Printed and published by J. Briggs, Gazette Office, sold also by Mr. Richardson, Royal Exchange, London. 1822.

Text: Vol. 1 Title, verso blank; Preface [iii], iv; Text (12 monthly parts) [1] – 556; imprint at the end of each month: *Printed by A. Foster, Repository Office, Kirkby Stephen.*
Vol. 2 Title, verso blank; Preface [iii], iv; Text [1]-476; Imprints as vol. 1.
Vol. 3 Title, verso blank; Preface [iii], iv; Text [1]-475; Directions to the binder [476]; imprints at the end of each month except December: *Printed by J. Briggs, Gazette Office, Kendal.*

Plates: Vol. 1 1 coloured aquatint, 1 coloured etching, 2 aquatints, 1 engraving, 1 folding table. Watermarks 1818.
Vol. 2 12 aquatints (one per month).
Vol. 3 12 aquatints (one per month).
No Lake District views.

Issued in monthly parts in printed paper wrappers

Articles on matters related to the scenery of the Lake District:

Vol. 1 Evening upon the Banks of Coniston Lake, p. 78
Excursion to the Lake of Windermere, pp. 427-31
The Floating Island, by Mr J. Otley, From Mr. Green's New Guide, pp. 15, 16
The Bottom Wind on Derwent Lake, by J. Otley, p. 297
Remarks on the Succession of Rocks in the District of the Lakes. Letter from J. Otley, pp. 433-5
Green's Guide. Library review pp. 24, 27, 35, 170
Windermere: a Poem, pp. 34-5
The Pass of Kirkstone. A poem by Mr. Wordsworth, from the Duddon Sonnets, pp. 321-2

Vol. 2 Belle Isle on Windermere; a Description, p. 81, with plate
Letters from the Lakes by 'Leonard Atkins' [J. Briggs], pp. 6, 47, 86, 123, 164, 206, 243, 289, 347, 365

Vol. 3 Tales of the Lakes by 'Leonard Atkins', pp. 11, 45, 85, 129, 162, 212, 255, 292, 328, 385, 404, 444
Westmorland as it was, from the Rev. Mr. Hodgson's topographical and historical Description of this County, pp. 258, 288, 324, 378, 409
Wordsworth's Excursion to the Top of Scawfell. Extracted from Wordsworth's *Guide*, p. 429

Note: Owing to financial instability and his failure to procure support for volume 2, John Briggs could not find a publisher for volume 3, which he had to publish himself from the offices of the *Kendal Gazette*, of which he was at that time editor.

King's copy: In three volumes, rebound. Also in King's Collection No. XIX. July, 1821, in original printed paper wrappers as issued. 'For the accommodation of more distant Subscribers, it is likewise published in London, by Mr. Richardson, 91 Royal Exchange: By which arrangement it may be procured through the medium of the booksellers in any part of the United Kingdom'.

Copies: K; Armitt; BL; Cornell; Jackson; Wordsworth

(*The North Lonsdale magazine and Lake District miscellany*, conducted by J.P. Morris, F.A.S.I., began publication in July 1866, from the *Advertiser* Office, Ulverston)

97 ***The Remains of John Briggs: late editor of "The Lonsdale Magazine[*"*], and of "The Westmorland Gazette": Containing Letter from the Lakes; Westmorland as it was; theological essays; . . . To which is added, a sketch of his life. Published for the benefit of his Widow and Children.*** Kirkby Lonsdale: printed and sold by Arthur Foster. 1825. Duodecimo.†

Text: Half-title, verso blank; title, verso blank; blank, note on verso; Contents [v], vi; Text [7]-395; Note [396]; Subscribers 397-408; Imprint, *Printed by A. Foster, Kirkby Lonsdale.*

Contents: Letters from the Lakes
Excursion over Harter Fell to Longsleddale
Westmorland as it was
Light
Tales
Theological Essays
Fugitive pieces
A sketch of the life of John Briggs

King's copy In contemporary olive half-calf, marbled boards

Copies: K; Armitt; BL; Cornell; Jackson; Kendal; Wordsworth

Note: 'A few supernumerary copies of "Letters from the Lakes", "Westmorland as it was", and the "Sketch of the Life of John Briggs", are printed, and may be had separately.' (advert. in *Remains*).

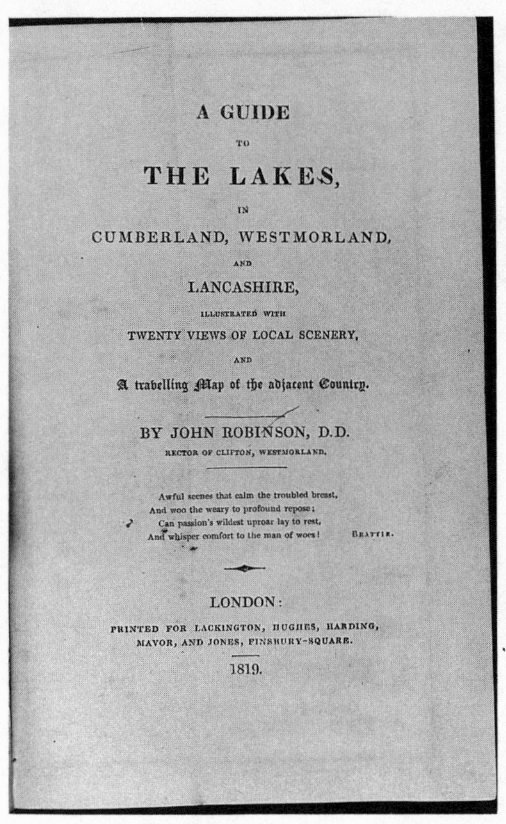

A GUIDE
TO
THE LAKES,
IN
CUMBERLAND, WESTMORLAND,
AND
LANCASHIRE,
ILLUSTRATED WITH
TWENTY VIEWS OF LOCAL SCENERY,
AND
A travelling Map of the adjacent Country.

BY JOHN ROBINSON, D.D.
RECTOR OF CLIFTON, WESTMORLAND.

Awful scenes that calm the troubled breast,
And woo the weary to profound repose;
Can passion's wildest uproar lay to rest,
And whisper comfort to the man of woes! BEATTIE.

LONDON:
PRINTED FOR LACKINGTON, HUGHES, HARDING,
MAVOR, AND JONES, FINSBURY-SQUARE.
1819.

89.1 186 x 123 mm.

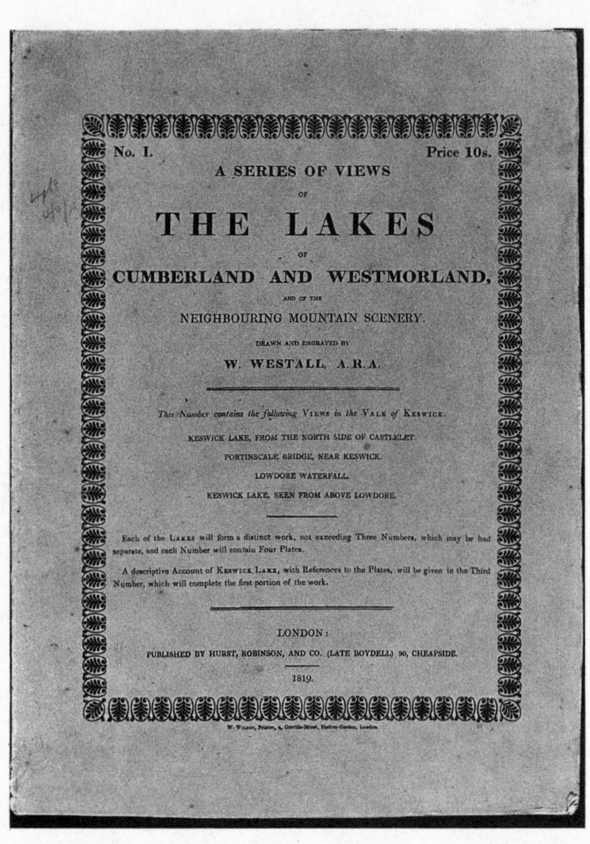

No. I. Price 10s.
A SERIES OF VIEWS
OF
THE LAKES
OF
CUMBERLAND AND WESTMORLAND,
AND OF THE
NEIGHBOURING MOUNTAIN SCENERY.
DRAWN AND ENGRAVED BY
W. WESTALL, A.R.A.

This Number contains the following VIEWS *in the* VALE *of* KESWICK.
KESWICK LAKE, FROM THE NORTH SIDE OF CASTLELET.
PORTINSCALE BRIDGE, NEAR KESWICK.
LOWDORE WATERFALL.
KESWICK LAKE, SEEN FROM ABOVE LOWDORE.

Each of the LAKES will form a distinct work, not exceeding Three Numbers, which may be had separate, and each Number will contain Four Plates.

A descriptive Account of KESWICK LAKE, with References to the Plates, will be given in the Third Number, which will complete the first portion of the work.

LONDON:
PUBLISHED BY HURST, ROBINSON, AND CO. (LATE BOYDELL) 90, CHEAPSIDE.
1819.

W. Wilson, Printer, 4, Greville-Street, Hatton-Garden, London.

91 385 x 280 mm.

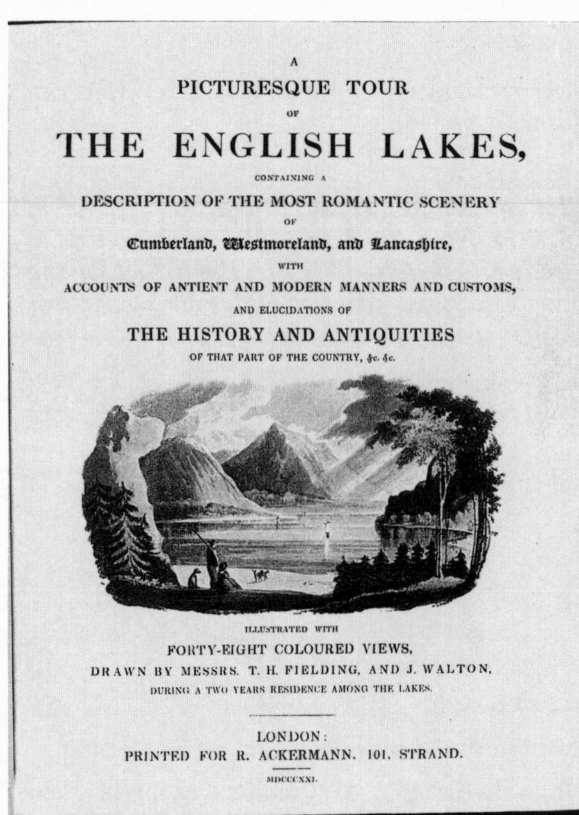

A
PICTURESQUE TOUR
OF
THE ENGLISH LAKES,
CONTAINING A
DESCRIPTION OF THE MOST ROMANTIC SCENERY
OF
Cumberland, Westmoreland, and Lancashire,
WITH
ACCOUNTS OF ANTIENT AND MODERN MANNERS AND CUSTOMS,
AND ELUCIDATIONS OF
THE HISTORY AND ANTIQUITIES
OF THAT PART OF THE COUNTRY, &c. &c.

ILLUSTRATED WITH
FORTY-EIGHT COLOURED VIEWS,
DRAWN BY MESSRS. T. H. FIELDING, AND J. WALTON,
DURING A TWO YEARS RESIDENCE AMONG THE LAKES.

LONDON:
PRINTED FOR R. ACKERMANN, 101, STRAND.
MDCCCXXI.

100 266 x 210 mm.

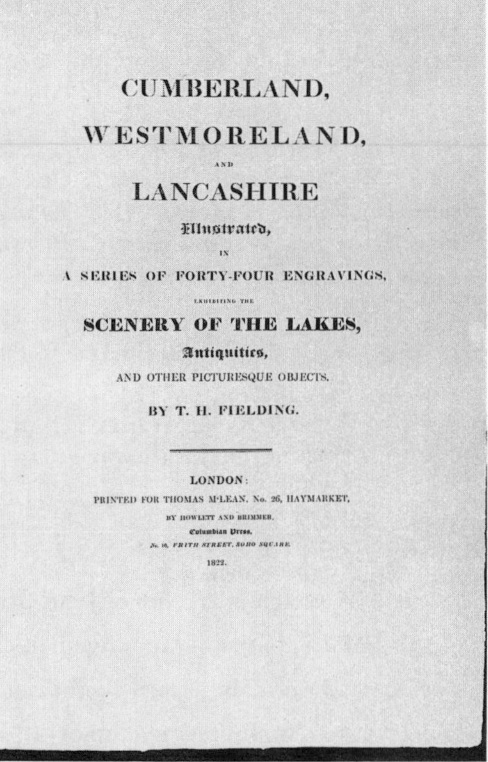

CUMBERLAND,
WESTMORELAND,
AND
LANCASHIRE
Illustrated,
IN
A SERIES OF FORTY-FOUR ENGRAVINGS,
EXHIBITING THE
SCENERY OF THE LAKES,
Antiquities,
AND OTHER PICTURESQUE OBJECTS.
BY T. H. FIELDING.

LONDON:
PRINTED FOR THOMAS M'LEAN, No. 26, HAYMARKET,
BY HOWLETT AND BRIMMER,
Columbian Press,
No. 10, FRITH STREET, SOHO SQUARE.
1822.

101 430 x 283 mm.

98 ***Letters from the Lakes: to which are added, an excursion over Harter-Fell to Longsleddale; and the Farewell to the Lakes.*** Kirkby Lonsdale: printed and sold by Arthur Foster. 1825. Duodecimo.†

Off-print from *Remains*, with new title-page, and altered pagination

King's copy: In half maroon morocco, original marbled boards. Printed white paper label lettered 'Letters from the Lakes 1825' tipped in at end of volume

Copies: K; Cornell; Jackson

99 ***A sketch of the life of John Briggs.*** Kirkby Lonsdale: printed and sold by Arthur Foster. 1825. Duodecimo.†

Off-print of pages [355]-396 of *Remains*, with new title-page, and altered pagination.

King's copy: In brown paper wrappers

Copies: K; Wordsworth

No copies of the supernumerary issue of 'Westmorland as it was' have been located.

1821

THEODORE HENRY ADOLPHUS FIELDING (artist) 1781-1851 and JOHN WALTON (artist)

T.H.A. Fielding, eldest brother of Copley Fielding, was a landscape painter and engraver who exhibited at the Royal Academy and elsewhere from 1799. He wrote an important series of books on painting in oil and watercolours, practical perspective and the art of engraving.

100 ***A picturesque tour of the English Lakes, containing a description of the most romantic scenery of Cumberland, Westmoreland, and Lancashire. . . . Illustrated with forty-eight coloured views, drawn by Messrs. T.H. Fielding, and J. Walton, during a two years residence among the lakes.*** London: Printed for R. Ackermann, 101, Strand. 1821. Quarto.†

Text: Title, verso blank, imprint on verso: *London: Printed by William Clowes, Northumberland Court*; Preface pp. [iii]-vi; Contents and List of Plates, 1 leaf; Text pp. [1]-288; imprint repeated on last page.

Plates: 49 coloured aquatints, each with imprint: *Published* [date] *at R. Ackermann's, 101, Strand.* Artist as given.

1 Saddleback & St. John's Vale. *T.H. Fielding: Jan 1 1821.*
2 (Vignette on title-page.) Unsigned: undated
3 Purple Tarn, top of Saddleback. *T.H. Fielding: Feb 1 1821.*
4 North West View of Furness Abbey. *T.H. Fielding. May 1 1820.*
5 Coniston Water. *J. Walton. May 1 1820.*
6 Copper Mill, Coniston Fell. *J. Fielding. May 1 1820.*
7 Yewdale Crags. *J. Fielding. May 1 1820.*
8 Esthwaite Water. *T.H. Fielding. June 1 1820.*
9 Ferry on Windermere. *J. Walton. June 1 1820.*

10 Station on Windermere. *J. Walton. June 1 1820.*
11 Windermere. *J. Walton. July 1 1820.*
12 Low Wood Inn. *T.H. Fielding. June 1 1820.*
13 Windermere. From Trout-beck Lane, with Langdale Pikes. *T.H. Fielding. July 1 1820.*
14 Windermere Head. *T.H.Fielding. July 1 1820.*
15 Ambleside. *T.H. Fielding. Aug 1 1820.*
16 Stockgill Force. *J. Walton. Aug 1 1820.*
17 Skelwith Force. *T.H. Fielding. Aug 1 1820.*
18 Stickle Tarn, near the top of Langdale Pikes. *T.H. Fielding. July 1 1820.*
19 Rydal Water. *J. Walton. Aug 1 1820.*
20 Rydal Water, from White Moss. *J. Walton. Sept 1 1820.*
21 Grasmere Church & Helm Crag *J. Walton. Sept 1 1820.*
22 Grasmere. *T.H. Fielding. Sept 1 1820.*
23 Wyburn Water & Helvellyn. *T.H. Fielding. Sept 1 1820.*
24 Keswick Lake. *T.H. Fielding. Oct 1 1820.*
25 Lowdore Fall. *T.H. Fielding. Oct 1 1820.*
26 Keswick. *W. Westall. Jan 1 1821.*
27 Sty Head Tarn, top of Sty Head. *T.H. Fielding: Jan 1 1821.*
28 Sty Head. *T.H. Fielding: Jan 1 1821.*
29 Wast Water. *T.H. Fielding: Dec 1 1820.*
30 Calder Abbey. *T.H. Fielding: Dec 1 1820.*
31 Ennerdale Water. *T.H. Fielding: Dec 1 1820.*
32 Lowes Water. *T.H. Fielding: Nov 1 1820.*
33 Cromack Water. *T.H. Fielding: Nov 1 1820.*
34 Scale Force. *T.H. Fielding: Dec 1 1820.*
35 Buttermere. *J. Walton: Oct 1 1820.*
36 Cockermouth Castle. *T.H. Fielding: Nov 1 1820.*
37 Bassenthwaite Lake. *T.H. Fielding: Nov 1 1820.*
38 Skiddaw, from the head of Lowdore Fall *J. Walton: Oct 1 1820.*
39 Cottages in St. John's Vale. *T.H.Fielding: Feb 1 1821.*
40 Penrith Castle. *T.H. Fielding: Feb 1 1821.*
41 Brougham Castle. *T.H. Fielding: Feb 1 1821.*
42 Haws Water. *T.H. Fielding: March 1 1821.*
43 Ullswater, from Stybarrow Crag. *T.H. Fielding: March 1 1821.*
44 Grisedale Pike. *T.H. Fielding: March 1 1821.*
45 Patterdale Church, Ullswater Head. *J. Walton: March 1 1821.*
46 Deepdale. *T.H. Fielding: April 1 1821.*
47 Broader Water. *J. Walton. April 1 1821.*
48 Kirkstone Spring. *T.H. Fielding: April 1 1821.*
49 Kirkstone Pass. *T.H. Fielding: April 1 1821.*§

Issued in 12 monthly parts in printed paper wrappers, and on completion in boards, 750 at £3. 13*s*. 6*d*, and 100 on large or elephant paper at £6. 6*s*.

It is not known who wrote the text, though it was probably Fielding, who was also responsible for preparing all the plates.

King's copy: Rebound.

Copies: K; Armitt; BL; Cornell; Kendal; Wordsworth

Ref: Abbey, 192; Tooley, 219

Barnes lists a second edition (1821) which was in the Barrow-in-Furness Public Library, but the title-page and all the plates have been removed from this copy.

Sanderson from 'Natalie's Advertisement of about 1843' – 'The Lake Scenery of England. Pictorial Tour of the English Lakes, illustrated with forty-eight coloured plates.'

1822

THEODORE HENRY ADOLPHUS FIELDING

101 ***Cumberland, Westmoreland, and Lancashire illustrated, in a series of forty-four engravings, exhibiting the scenery of the Lakes, antiquities, and other picturesque objects.*** London: printed for Thomas M'Lean, No. 26, Haymarket, by Howlett and Brimmer, Columbian Press, No. 10, Frith Street, Soho Square. 1822. Folio.†

Text: Half-title, verso blank; Title, verso blank; Address, verso blank; 1 p. List of Plates, verso blank; Text, 88 pp. (unnumbered).

Plates: 44 aquatints. Each plate signed: *T. Fielding delt.* Imprints: *London: Published by Thomas McLean, Haymarket, 1822.*

1 Naworth Castle.
2 Cromack Water.
3 Green Crag.
4 Penrith.
5 Skiddaw over Derwent Water.
6 Stockgill Force.
7 Brougham Castle.
8 Rydal Water.
9 Kendal Castle.
10 Dungeon Force.
11 Waste Water. 'Wast Water' in text.
12 View at Ambleside.
13 Ulls Water.
14 Egremont Castle. 1821.
15 Ambleside.
16 Lanercost Priory.
17 Nook End Bridge.
18 Blea Tarn.
19 Lowther Castle.
20 The Lakes of Cromack and Buttermere.
21 St. Herbert's Island. 'St. Hubert's' in text.
22 Blencowe Hall.
23 Red Tarn.
24 Mill at Ambleside.
25 Part of Furness Abbey.
26 Saddleback.
27 Yew Tree at Blelham Tarn.
28 Cockermouth.
29 Rydal Heads. 1821.
30 Mayburgh.
31 Carlisle Cathedral.
32 Wyburn Water.
33 Coniston Tell. 'Coniston Fell' in text.
34 Monuments in Calder Abbey.
35 Coniston Old Hall.
36 Bowder Stone.
37 Derwent Water.
38 Workington.
39 Elter Water.
40 Dalton.
41 Little Langdale Water.
42 Borrowdale.
43 Loughrigg Tarn.
44 Eagle Crag.

Notes: For the second issue, date unknown, more figures were added in the foreground to most of the plates.

Unlike *A picturesque tour* (100), which is a tour illustrated with plates, this is a book of plates with descriptive letterpress.

Issued in three forms:
(a) Uncoloured proofs before letters (copies: K; Armitt; ref. Abbey, 195)
(b) Coloured (copies: Cornell; Wordsworth)
(c) Second issue, plates altered (ref. Tooley, 216).

In 1840 W.H. Clark, stationer to the King, 59 Charing Cross, advertised 'To admirers of the Fine Arts! Fielding's Lake and Mountain Scenery, in Cumberland, Westmoreland and Lancashire. A series of elegant Aquâ Tintâ Engravings, beautifully coloured from the original Drawings, by Fielding, illustrative of the Lakes and Scenes most remarkable for picturesque beauty, or grandeur and sublimity; forming a complete Panorama of the above Romantic Counties. They are, also, particularly adapted for the *Young Artist, Copyist, Tourist, and Portfolio* and are complete in the following 45 numbers, mounted on Tinted Drawing Boards, and may be had *separately*, Price Sixpence Each; or, *The Set (45 in number) may be had in various bindings.*'

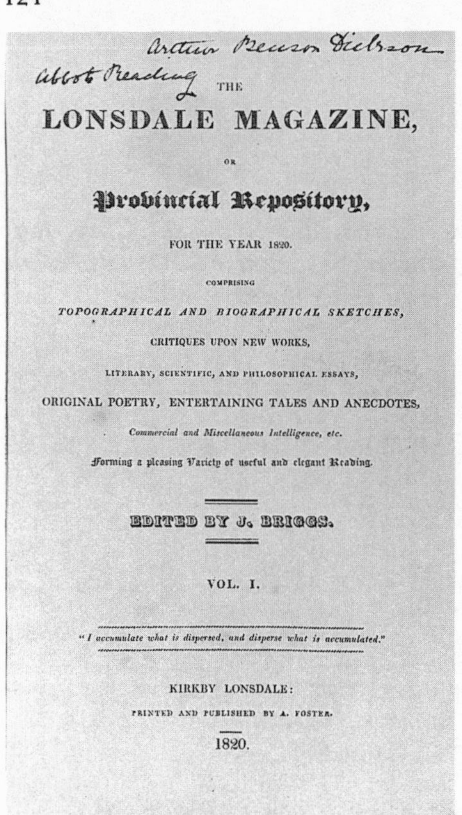
Arthur Benson Dickson
Abbot Reading

THE

LONSDALE MAGAZINE,

OR

Provincial Repository,

FOR THE YEAR 1820.

COMPRISING

TOPOGRAPHICAL AND BIOGRAPHICAL SKETCHES,

CRITIQUES UPON NEW WORKS,

LITERARY, SCIENTIFIC, AND PHILOSOPHICAL ESSAYS,

ORIGINAL POETRY, ENTERTAINING TALES AND ANECDOTES,

Commercial and Miscellaneous Intelligence, etc.

Forming a pleasing Variety of useful and elegant Reading.

EDITED BY J. BRIGGS.

VOL. I.

"I accumulate what is dispersed, and disperse what is accumulated."

KIRKBY LONSDALE:

PRINTED AND PUBLISHED BY A. FOSTER.

1820.

96 210 x 130 mm.

THE

Remains

OF

JOHN BRIGGS:

LATE EDITOR OF

"The Lonsdale Magazine, and of "The Westmorland Gazette:"

CONTAINING

Letters from the Lakes;

WESTMORLAND AS IT WAS;

THEOLOGICAL ESSAYS;

TALES;

REMARKS ON THE NEWTONIAN THEORY OF LIGHT;

AND

FUGITIVE PIECES.

TO WHICH IS ADDED,

A SKETCH OF HIS LIFE.

Published for the benefit of his Widow and Children.

KIRKBY LONSDALE:

PRINTED AND SOLD BY ARTHUR FOSTER.

MDCCCXXV.

97 175 x 98 mm.

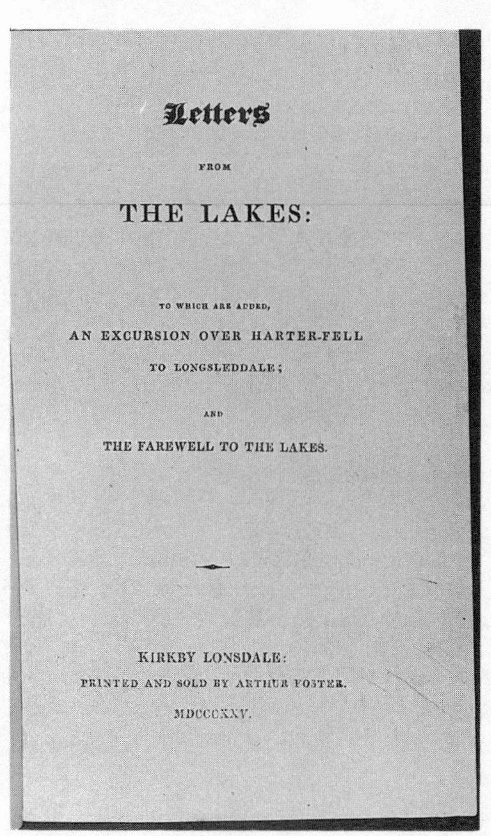
Letters

FROM

THE LAKES:

TO WHICH ARE ADDED,

AN EXCURSION OVER HARTER-FELL

TO LONGSLEDDALE;

AND

THE FAREWELL TO THE LAKES.

KIRKBY LONSDALE:

PRINTED AND SOLD BY ARTHUR FOSTER.

MDCCCXXV.

98 172 x 106 mm.

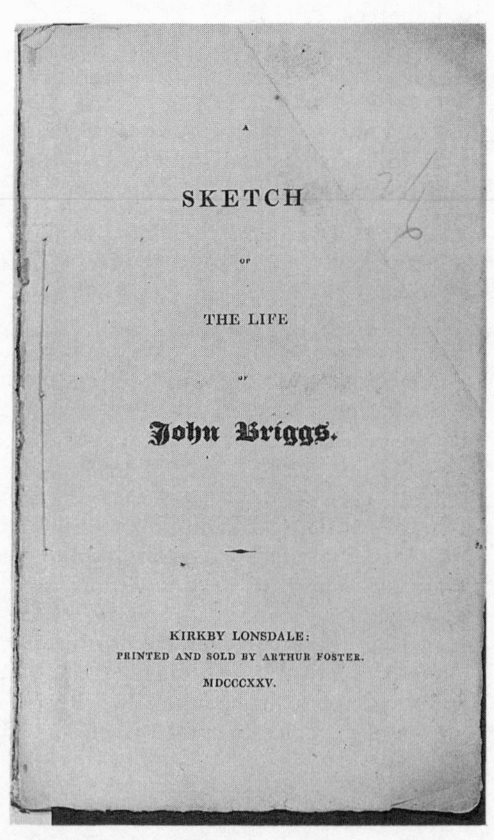
A

SKETCH

OF

THE LIFE

OF

John Briggs.

KIRKBY LONSDALE:

PRINTED AND SOLD BY ARTHUR FOSTER.

MDCCCXXV.

99 172 x 106 mm.

King's copy: In contemporary half red roan, marbled boards, Fielding's Lakes on spine, and 'Fielding's Lakes' inscribed in brown ink on the upper cover. The plates are uncoloured proofs before letters on India paper, with no titles, signatures, or imprints. Copies in this state are not rare. The Abbey copy appears to be identical with this one; and there are two similar copies in the Armitt Library. Coloured prints of four of the plates, altered for the second issue, have been added.

1823

JONATHAN OTLEY

See 88

102.1 ***A concise description of the English Lakes, the mountains in their vicinity, and the roads by which they may be visited; with remarks on the mineralogy and geology of the district.*** Keswick; published by the author. By J. Richardson, Royal Exchange, London; and A. Foster, Kirkby Lonsdale. 1823. Duodecimo.

'In 1823 I arranged a description of the lakes and mountains, with the stages and other requisites for a Guide, to which were added some essays which I had wrote for the Lit. and Phil. Soc. of Manchester, making together a book of 136 pages; sold at 4*s.* 6*d.* in printed covers. 600 copies.' (particulars given by Otley in 1840, in reply to a letter by Mr Thos. Sanderson of London). Otley explains that 'before this little manual made its appearance the public had been supplied with Guides to the Lakes in various forms; but wholly devoted to the picturesque appearance of the country in exclusion to other important considerations.' He therefore supplied a purely factual guide, with clearly arranged information for the tourist, including sections on mineralogy and geology.

Copies: Armitt; Jackson

102.2 ——— *A concise description of the English Lakes, and Adjacent Mountains, with general directions to tourists; and observations on the mineralogy and geology of the district; on meteorology; the floating island in Derwent Lake; and the black-lead mine in Borrowdale.* Second edition. Keswick: published by the author. By John Richardson, Royal Exchange, London; and Arthur Foster, Kirkby Lonsdale. 1825. Duodecimo.

Text: Half-title, on verso quotation and imprint, *Printed by Arthur Foster, Kirkby Lonsdale;* Title, verso blank; Preface 1 p., verso blank; Contents [v]; Text [7]-141; imprint verso 141.

Map: Folding map of the District of the Lakes as 88

Note: 1,000 copies printed. Issued in printed paper boards. 'A second edition is now offered to the public, with such improvements as have been judged likely to render it a more useful companion without making it more cumbrous or more expensive' (Preface).

King's copy: In contemporary calf, rebacked. Inscribed on half-title, 'Isabella Banks 1891'. Label on paste-down endpaper, 'Jas. Clegg, Bookseller, Rochdale. Books purchased.'

Copies: K; Armitt; Cornell; BL; Jackson; Kendal

102.3 ——— Third edition. [printed cover]†

Title as second edition except:

'and a map of the district' is added after ' . . . directions to tourists,'
'and an account of an excursion to the top of Skiddaw' is added after ' . . . black-lead mine in Borrowdale'
'Third edition' replaces 'Second edition'
'1827' replaces '1825'

Text: Similar to second edition except: 'An account of an excursion to the top of Skiddaw' and, after 'The floating island in Derwentwater lake', a note by Mr. Dalton on a paper by Mr. Otley published in the *Memoirs of the Literary and Philosophical Society of Manchester* (vol. 3, new series) are added.

Map: 'A new map on a somewhat enlarged scale has been engraven expressly for the third edition . . . with . . . improvements' (Preface).

Note: 150 pages. 1200 copies printed. Issued in printed paper boards, Price 4*s*. 6*d*., and publisher's cloth, printed paper labels.

King's copy: In original printed paper boards, uncut, upper cover as title-page except 'Price Four Shillings and sixpence' and ornamental border are added. On lower cover advert for the Map of the Lakes. 'It is sold separately, as usual, neatly coloured and folded into a case for the pocket; with Tables showing the height and position of remarkable mountains, distances of places, &c. – price 3/6. Keswick, May, 1827.' Inscribed on title page, 'J.B. Tercy [?]'.

Copies: K; Armitt; BL; Cornell; Jackson; Kendal; Wordsworth

102.4 ——— Fourth edition.

Title as third edition except:

'notices of the botany, mineralogy, and geology of the district; observations on meteorology; the floating island in Derwent Lake; and the black-lead mine in Borrowdale' replaces 'Observations on the mineralogy . . . top of Skiddaw'

'1830' replaces '1827'

'Fourth edition' replaces 'Third edition'

Text: Similar to third edition except: text revised; Preface rewritten; 8 p. of botanical notices added; 'An excursion to Skiddaw' omitted.

Plates: 9 sketches of the outlines of mountains on numbered pages, designed and engraved by Otley:

1 Outline of Skiddaw and Saddleback (formerly Blencathra). As seen on approaching Keswick from the South: with names prior to the inclosure of the Commons in 1810. p. 47
2 Some of the Western Mountains, as seen from Helvellyn. p.57
3 The Mountains of Coniston, Langdale, etc. as they appear from the road between Troutbeck Bridge and Bowness. p. 97
4 The Mountains of Ulswater: as seen from Pooley Bridge. p. 109
5 The Mountains South West of Derwentwater; as seen from Keswick. p.115
6 The Mountains of Crummock and Buttermere: as seen from the Road between Scale-Hill and Loweswater. p.125
7 The Mountains round Wastwater: as seen from the Strands in Nether Wasdale. p.129
8 The Mountains of Ennerdale: as seen from Kirkland. p.131
9 The Mountains of Patterdale: as seen from the Slate Quarry on Place Fell. p. 137

Map: As third edition

Note: 180 pages. 1000 copies printed. Preface rewritten

King's copy: In publisher's red cloth, printed paper label. Inscribed on title-page 'Fanny Fletcher Nov 9th.'

Copies: K; Armitt; BL; Kendal; Wordsworth

102.5 ——— Fifth edition.

Title as fourth edition except:

'Fifth edition' replaces 'Fourth edition'

'By Simpkin and Marshall, Stationer's Court' replaces 'By John Richardson, Royal Exchange'

'1834' replaces '1830'

Text: Similar to fourth edition except: Preface and text revised; 10 pages of Botanical notes and Index added

Plates: 11 sketches. 9 as previous edition, re-engraved; 2 additional

1 As 3 above. p.7
2 As 9. p.11
3 Mountains of Grasmere and Rydal, as seen from Red Bank Head. p. 15
4 As 5. p.2
5 As 6. p.25
6 As 8. p.27
7 As 7. Title altered: Mountains of Wast-Water: as seen from Nether Wasdale. p.31
8 As 1. Title altered: Skiddaw and Saddleback (formerly Blencathra): As seen on entering Keswick from the South: With ancient names. p.49
9 As 2. Title altered: A Group of Mountains, Seen from Helvellyn, looking to the South-West. p. 63
10 Mountains North-East of Windermere, as seen from Bowness. p.99
11 As 4. Title altered: 'Mountains of Ulswater.' p.113

Map: As third edition, 'and with additions 20th. July 1833'.

Note: 184 pages and Index. 1200 copies printed. Price in cloth five shillings.

King's copy: In publisher's dark green cloth, printed paper label. Inscribed on paste-down endpaper 'Wm. Bromley Keswick'. Pencil list of place-names on endpapers.

Copies: K; Armitt; BL; Cornell; Jackson; Wordsworth

102.6 ——— Sixth edition.

Title as fifth edition except:
'Sixth edition' replaces 'Fifth edition'.
'Stationer's Hall Court' replaces 'Stationer's Court'.
'1837' replaces '1834'.

Text: Similar to fifth edition; one-page Explanation of the map added; 12 pp. of Botanical notes.

Plates: 11 outlines of mountains in the text, all as in fifth edition, but different order and pagination. Otley in the note in Sanderson gives 'twelve woodcuts and copper of my own drawing and engraving'.

Map: As third edition, 'and with additions 20th. July 1833: and 1837'

Note: 1200 copies printed. Text revised. Preface unaltered, paragraphs 5 and 6 reversed.

King's copy: In publisher's patterned brown cloth, printed paper label. Inscribed on paste-down endpaper, 'Alfred Haviland, London 22nd. August 1891' on free endpaper 'T.E.G. Viret', added in pencil, 'The Revd. B. Pope's nephew, vicar of Nether Stowey, Somerset, with whose brothers I went to school.' Extensive pencil annotations.

Copies: K; BL; Cornell; Jackson; Kendal

Note: The sixth edition was also issued dated 1838 (copies: BL; Cornell; Jackson) and 1842 (copy: Jackson)

102.7 ——— *A descriptive guide to the English Lakes, and adjacent mountains: with notices of the botany, mineralogy, and geology of the district.* Seventh edition. To which is added, an excursion through Lonsdale to the caves. [Imprint as previous edition] 1843.† Vignette on title-page of The Scroggs (birthplace of the author). Issued 1845.

Text: Similar to sixth edition. 'Lonsdale and the Caves', 33 pp. added

Plates: 13 outlines of mountains and 33 cuts in text. The outlines are now true plates and not paginated and incorporated in the text. They are all re-drawn and re-engraved. 'Most of the illustrations are from accurate drawings by Mr. T. Binns, Portrait Painter, Halifax, and are all engraven by Mr. O. Jewitt, of Headington, Oxford.'

Outlines of mountains:

1 Windermere from Bowness
2 Windermere from the road between Troutbeck and Bowness
3 Grasmere
4 Coniston Water
5 Derwent Water
6 Ulswater
7 The Mountains of Patterdale
8 Hawes Water
9 Crummock and Buttermere
10 Ennerdale
11 Mountains of Wastwater
12 Skiddaw and Saddleback
13 A Group of Mountains seen from Helvellyn

Map: Coloured folding map re-engraved. *Published by Jona. Otley 2d. Augt. 1841. Engd. by J. Menzies & Son Edinr.* Size: 366 × 264 mm. Scale: 1 in. = 4 miles

Note: At the end of the Preface there is a note to celebrate Otley's Guide having been read for Twenty Years. Keswick March 28th. 1845.

King's copy: In publisher's blind-stamped maroon cloth. Inscribed on paste-down endpaper 'J. Jones Kelsale Keswick 21st. May 1845'. Bookseller's label 'R. Rothschild-Davidson (Booksellers) Ltd., 1 Monmouth Street, London WC1.

Copies: K; Armitt; Cornell

Note: The seventh edition was also issued dated 1842 (copy, Cornell) and 1844 (copy, Armitt)

102.8 ——— Eighth edition.

Title as seventh edition except:
'Eighth edition' replaces 'Seventh edition',
'1849' replaces '1843'

Text: Similar to seventh edition; four pages of adverts. added

Plates: As seventh edition; 46 illustrations, additional cuts

Map: As seventh edition except imprint dated 2d. May 1849, and railways added

Note: 216 pages. 1250 copies printed. Preface unaltered; text amended

King's copy: In publisher's blind-stamped maroon cloth, similar to the previous edition. 1849.

Copies: K; Armitt, 1849; Cornell, 1849; Jackson, 1850; Kendal, 1849, 1850; Wordsworth, 1850

A *memoir of Jonathan Otley the old original guide to the English Lakes* by Dr Lietch of Derwent Bank was published as a pamphlet in memory of David Lietch, MD in March 1882. The Memoir was originally written by David Lietch in 1857 as a Preface to the Guide Book (Otley's). It therefore appears that there was an edition of Otley's Guide *c.* 1857. Adverts. on the endpapers of the pamphlet consist of three extracts from reviews by Prof. Sedgwick, G.B. Airy (Astronomer Royal) and Derwent Coleridge of *Otley's Old Original Guide to the English Lakes*, all three dated 1857.

See also: 'Jonathan Otley, the geologist and guide' by J. Clifton Ward, *Transactions of the Cumberland Association*, Part II (1876-7). This includes a list of Otley's writings.

1824

THOMAS WILKINSON 1751-1836

Thomas Wilkinson, Quaker, writer, pacifist and poet, farmed forty acres at Yanwath, near Penrith. He was a friend of the Wordsworths and of Thomas Clarkson, and a supporter of William Wilberforce. Wordsworth's poem which begins 'Spade with which Wilkinson hath tilled his lands' refers to him.

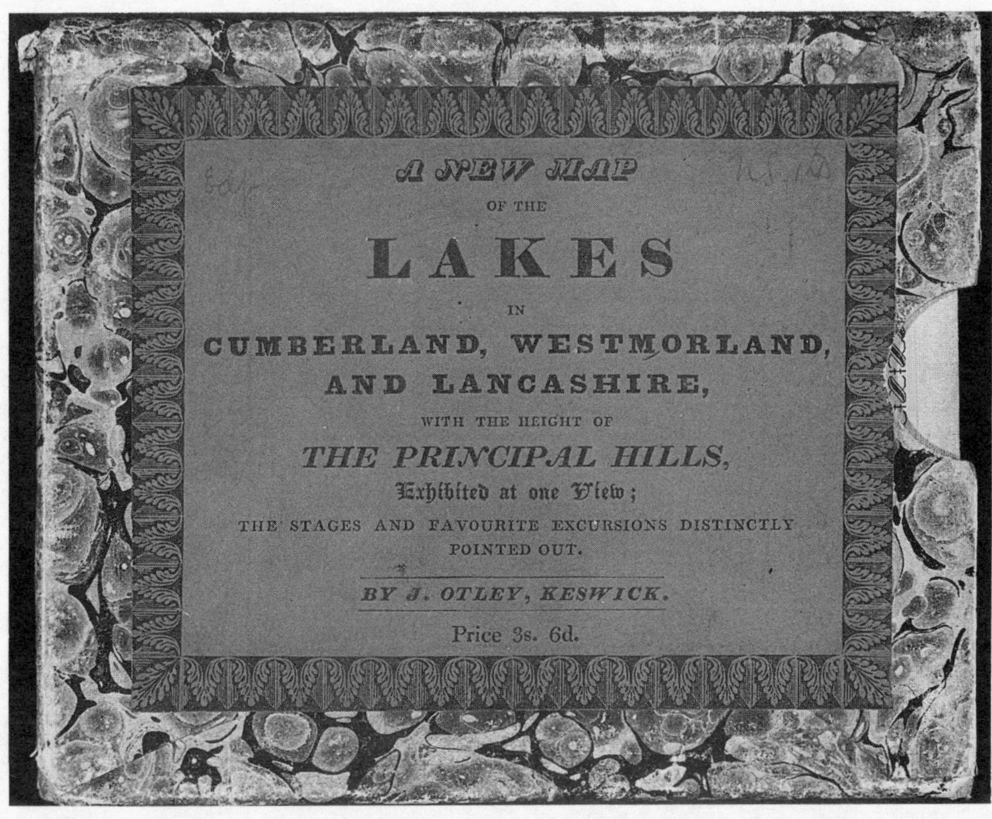
A NEW MAP
OF THE
LAKES
IN
CUMBERLAND, WESTMORLAND,
AND LANCASHIRE,
WITH THE HEIGHT OF
THE PRINCIPAL HILLS,
Exhibited at one View;
THE STAGES AND FAVOURITE EXCURSIONS DISTINCTLY POINTED OUT.

BY J. OTLEY, KESWICK.

Price 3s. 6d.

88 92 x 111 mm.

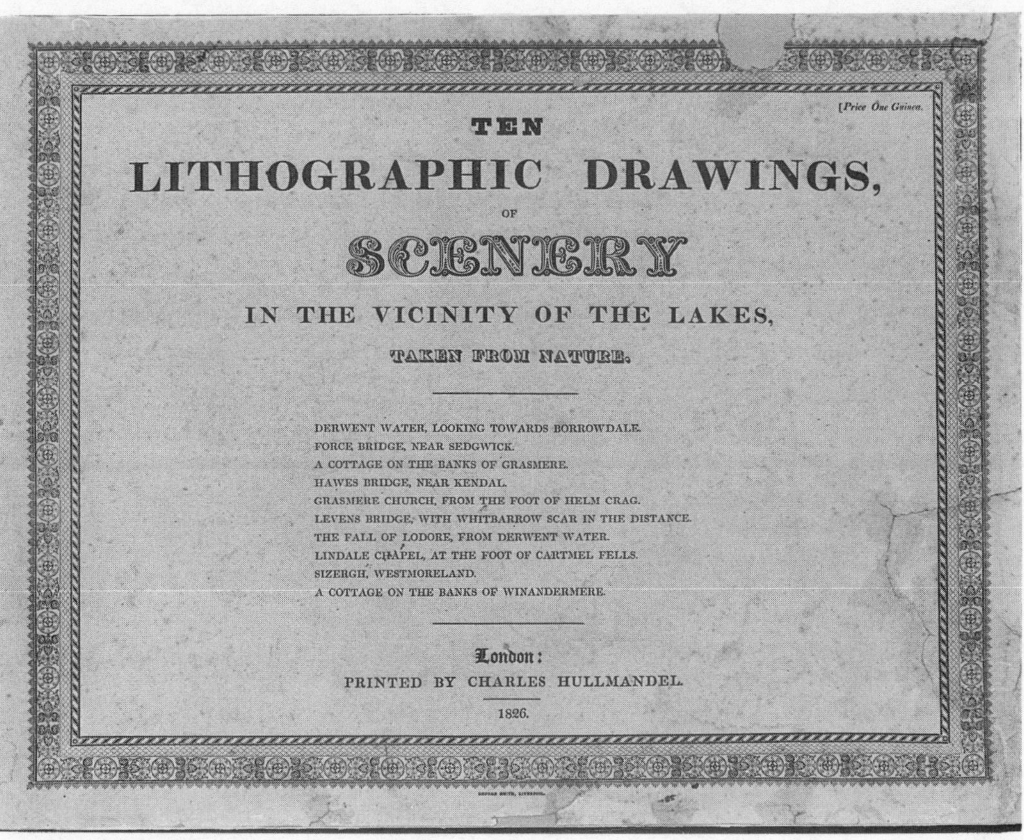
[Price One Guinea.

TEN
LITHOGRAPHIC DRAWINGS,
OF
SCENERY
IN THE VICINITY OF THE LAKES,
TAKEN FROM NATURE.

DERWENT WATER, LOOKING TOWARDS BORROWDALE.
FORCE BRIDGE, NEAR SEDGWICK.
A COTTAGE ON THE BANKS OF GRASMERE.
HAWES BRIDGE, NEAR KENDAL.
GRASMERE CHURCH, FROM THE FOOT OF HELM CRAG.
LEVENS BRIDGE, WITH WHITBARROW SCAR IN THE DISTANCE.
THE FALL OF LODORE, FROM DERWENT WATER.
LINDALE CHAPEL, AT THE FOOT OF CARTMEL FELLS.
SIZERGH, WESTMORELAND.
A COTTAGE ON THE BANKS OF WINANDERMERE.

London:
PRINTED BY CHARLES HULLMANDEL.
1826.

104 366 x 433 mm.

103 ***Tours to the British Mountains, with the descriptive poems of Lowther, and Emont Vale.*** London: Printed for Taylor and Hessey, 93, Fleet Street, and 13, Waterloo Place, Pall Mall. 1824. Octavo†

Text: Title, imprint on verso, London: *printed by S. and R. Bentley, Dorset Street*; Advertisement (dated London, 18th May 1824), verso blank; Preface [v]-vii; blank; Text [1]-320, imprint repeated on p. 320; 8pp. publisher's advert.

'Lowther', a poem 'addressed with true esteem to the Earl of Lonsdale', pp. [275]-289

Lakes: pp. 160-236

Armitt copy contains 'Letter and life of T.W.', by Mary Carr, bound in.

Notes: The book is based on 'memorandums' of his excursions in Scotland and the North of England, made twenty or more years before its publication. It is divided into short chapters or sections, under separate heads. Wilkinson explored the mountains of the Lake District and climbed their summits, with energy and devotion, rare among other tourists who were still primarily interested only in the lakes and valleys. Wilkinson considered mountains 'the productions of a Divine Hand: they impress us with awe, as the works of Almighty Power'.

King's copy: In original grey paper boards, repaired, printed paper label remounted on spine, oval black leather label lettered 'Lowther', on upper cover. 'Lonsdale' inscribed in ink on upper cover.

Copies: K; Armitt; BL; Cornell; Jackson; Kendal; Wordsworth

1826

CHARLES HULLMANDEL (publisher and lithographer) 1789-1850

Charles Hullmandel, the son of a German musician, was the pioneer of lithography in England. He was born and died in London. His publications included the important *The art of drawing on stone* (1824).

104 ***Ten lithographic drawings, of scenery in the vicinity of the Lakes, taken from nature.*** London: printed by Charles Hullmandel. 1826. Drawn on stone by I.C. and S.A. (Misses Cropper and Atkins). Oblong folio. Issued in printed paper wrappers. Price one guinea. No text; 1 p. dedication, verso blank

The dedication is to William Wilberforce (see 164); imprint, *George Smith Lithog. Liverpool.*

No title-page, title printed on cover† George Smith, Liverpool. Price one guinea

Plates: 10 lithographs, signed: *Drawn on stone by I.C. & S.A.*. Imprint: *Printed by C. Hullmandel*

1 Derwent Water looking towards Borrowdale
2 Force Bridge, near Sedgwick
3 A cottage on the banks of Grasmere
4 Hawes Bridge, near Kendal
5 Grasmere Church, from the foot of Helm Crag
6 Levens Bridge, with Whitbarrow Scar in the distance
7 The Fall of Lodore, from Derwent Water
8 Lindale Chapel, at the foot of Cartmel Fells
9 Sizergh, Westmoreland
10 A cottage on the banks of Winandermere

King's copy: In original printed grey paper wrappers. Inscribed on dedication page 'Elizth. Wheeler' 'Alexandrina Peckover'.

Note: This is probably the first Lake District book to be illustrated with lithographs. (Lithographs of drawings by Francis Nicholson of Lake District scenes, also published by Hullmandel, are dated 1821, but they were not issued as a book.)

Copies: K; Armitt

1827

CHARLES COOKE

105 ***The tourist's and traveller's companion to the Lakes of Cumberland, Westmoreland, and Lancashire; including a description of the surrounding scenery, the vales, mountains, adjacent towns and villages, local peculiarities, &c.*** [anonymous]. London: printed for Sherwood, Jones, and Co. Paternoster-Row. And sold by all booksellers. n.d. (1827 or earlier)

Copies: Armitt; and Alpine Club

NATHANIEL HAZELTINE CARTER 1787-1830

Poet and writer, native of New Hampshire, USA.

106.1 ***Letters from Europe comprising the journal of a tour . . . in the years 1825, '26, '27.*** 2 vols. New York: Carvill. 1827. Octavo.

Lakes: Letters xviii, xix, xx,

Copies: BL; Cornell

106.2 ——— Second edition. 1829.

Copy: Library of Congress

1829

ROBERT SOUTHEY 1774-1843

See 62 and 92

107.1 ***Sir Thomas More; or colloquies on the progress and prospects of society***. 2 vols. London: John Murray, Albemarle-Street. Printed by William Clowes. 1829. Octavo.

Plates: 6 steel engravings after William Westall, engraver's name after title:

Vol. 1
1 The Druidical Stones, *Robert Wallis*
2 Derwentwater, Bassenthwaite, and Skiddaw, from Walla Crag. *Robert Wallis*
3 Derwentwater from Strandshagg. *E. Goodill*

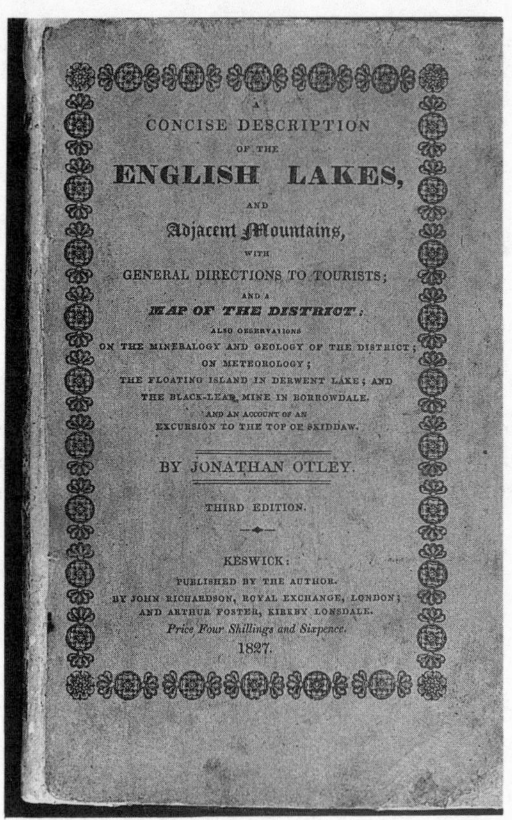

A
CONCISE DESCRIPTION
OF THE
ENGLISH LAKES,
AND
Adjacent Mountains,
WITH
GENERAL DIRECTIONS TO TOURISTS;
AND A
MAP OF THE DISTRICT:
ALSO OBSERVATIONS
ON THE MINERALOGY AND GEOLOGY OF THE DISTRICT;
ON METEOROLOGY;
THE FLOATING ISLAND IN DERWENT LAKE; AND
THE BLACK-LEAD MINE IN BORROWDALE.
AND AN ACCOUNT OF AN
EXCURSION TO THE TOP OF SKIDDAW.

BY JONATHAN OTLEY.

THIRD EDITION.

KESWICK:
PUBLISHED BY THE AUTHOR.
BY JOHN RICHARDSON, ROYAL EXCHANGE, LONDON;
AND ARTHUR FOSTER, KIRKBY LONSDALE.
Price Four Shillings and Sixpence.
1827.

102.3 185 x 115 mm.

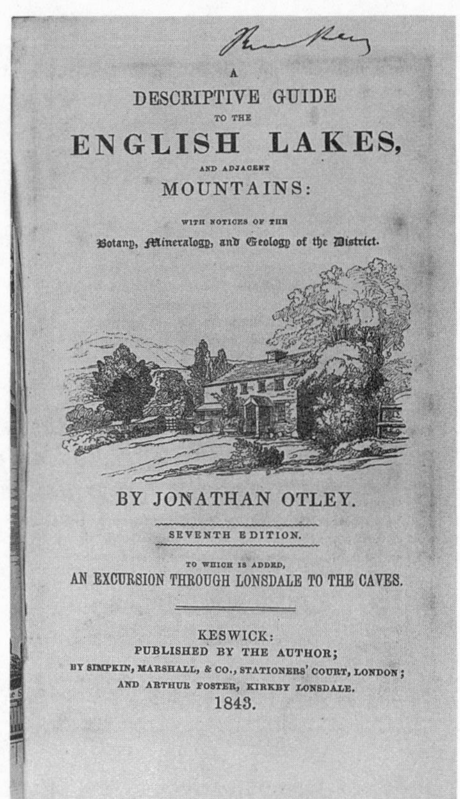

A
DESCRIPTIVE GUIDE
TO THE
ENGLISH LAKES,
AND ADJACENT
MOUNTAINS:
WITH NOTICES OF THE
Botany, Mineralogy, and Geology of the District.

BY JONATHAN OTLEY.

SEVENTH EDITION.

TO WHICH IS ADDED,
AN EXCURSION THROUGH LONSDALE TO THE CAVES.

KESWICK:
PUBLISHED BY THE AUTHOR;
BY SIMPKIN, MARSHALL, & CO., STATIONERS' COURT, LONDON;
AND ARTHUR FOSTER, KIRKBY LONSDALE.
1843.

102.7 182 x 105 mm.

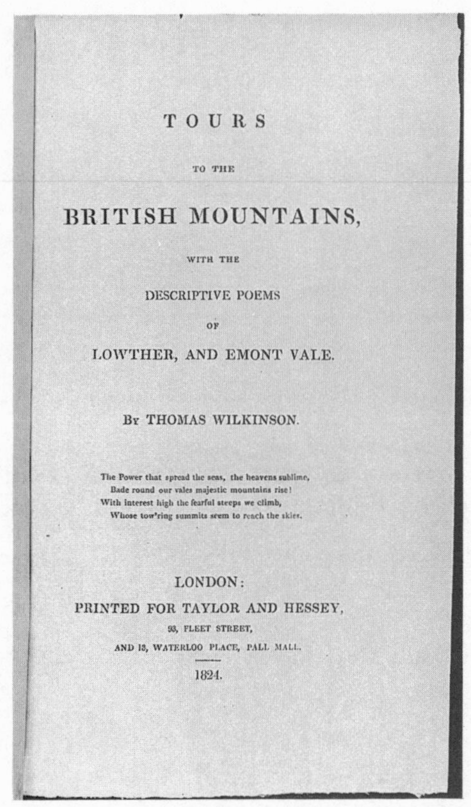

TOURS
TO THE
BRITISH MOUNTAINS,
WITH THE
DESCRIPTIVE POEMS
OF
LOWTHER, AND EMONT VALE.

BY THOMAS WILKINSON.

The Power that spread the seas, the heavens sublime,
Bade round our vales majestic mountains rise!
With interest high the fearful steeps we climb,
Whose tow'ring summits seem to reach the skies.

LONDON:
PRINTED FOR TAYLOR AND HESSEY,
93, FLEET STREET,
AND 13, WATERLOO PLACE, PALL MALL.
1824.

103 195 x 120 mm.

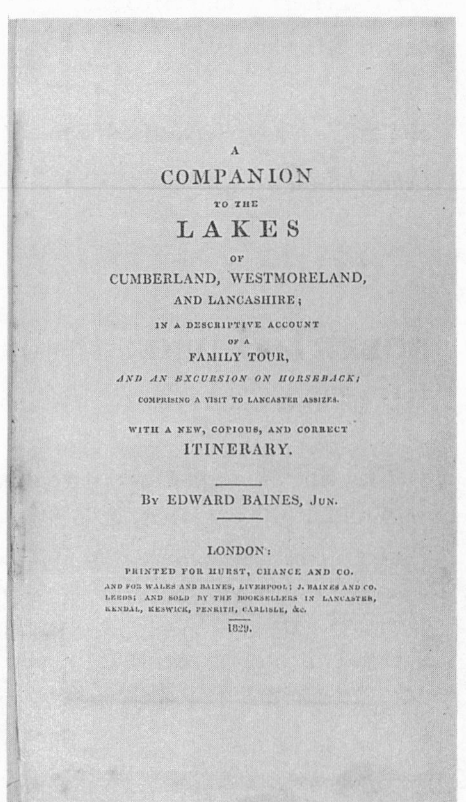

A
COMPANION
TO THE
LAKES
OF
CUMBERLAND, WESTMORELAND,
AND LANCASHIRE;
IN A DESCRIPTIVE ACCOUNT
OF A
FAMILY TOUR,
AND AN EXCURSION ON HORSEBACK:
COMPRISING A VISIT TO LANCASTER ASSIZES.
WITH A NEW, COPIOUS, AND CORRECT
ITINERARY.

BY EDWARD BAINES, JUN.

LONDON:
PRINTED FOR HURST, CHANCE AND CO.
AND FOR WALES AND BAINES, LIVERPOOL; J. BAINES AND CO.
LEEDS; AND SOLD BY THE BOOKSELLERS IN LANCASTER,
KENDAL, KESWICK, PENRITH, CARLISLE, &c.
1829.

108.1 190 x 110 mm.

Vol. 2
4 Crosthwaite Church and Skiddaw. *W.R. Smith*
5 Thralkeld Tarn. *Robert Wallis*
6 Greta Hall, Derwentwater and Newlands *W.R. Smith*

Note: The *Colloquies* are a series of imaginary conversations with Sir Thomas More, interspersed with descriptions of the district of Keswick.

Copies: Armitt; BL; Jackson;. Wordsworth

107.2 ——— 'Second edition in two volumes' 1831. All as 1829

'cloth, lettered £1.10*s*. for two vols.' (on printed label)

Copies: BL; Wordsworth

Reprinted in Cassel's National Library, New York, 1887 and 1894.

EDWARD BAINES 1800-1890

Sir Edward Baines, (1774-1848), journalist, printer and MP for Leeds, was a journalist, economist and writer on political and social subjects, son of Edward Baines.

108.1 ***A companion to the Lakes of Cumberland, Westmoreland, and Lancashire; in a descriptive account of a family tour, and an excursion on horseback . . with a new, copious, and correct itinerary***. London: Printed for Hurst, Chance and Co. and for Wales and Baines, Liverpool; J. Baines and Co. Leeds; and sold by the booksellers in Lancaster, Kendal, Keswick, Penrith, Carlisle, &c. 1829. Duodecimo.†

Text: Title, verso blank; Preface [iii]-vii; blank, (errata slip); Contents [ix]-xii; Text [1]-271; imprint on 271 verso, *Liverpool: Printed by W. Wales and Co. Castle-Street*; A new itinerary of the Lakes [1]-42; Index [43]-48.

Map: Folding coloured Map of the Lakes of Westmoreland, Cumberland, and Lancashire. Chas. Fowler, Surveyor, Leeds, 1829. Size: 328 × 260 mm. Scale: 1 in. = 3 miles. Signed: *W.H. Lizars Sculpt. Edinr.* Imprint: *Published by W. Wales & Co. For Baines's "Companion to the Lakes"*.

Note: The *Companion* is intended to serve as a Guide, but it is also an account of a tour made by the author with a family party of two ladies and two gentlemen. The 'Excursion on horseback' is intended to cover those parts of the Lake District which were not visited by the party, e.g., Furness and Coniston; Langdale and an ascent of Bowfell and Scawfell Pikes; Hawkshead, Rydal, Keswick, Honister Crag, Watendlath and Carlisle. 'The Itinerary is a feature of this work entirely original, nothing of the kind being contained in any existing Guide to the Lakes. It is designed to communicate in a few pages, and arranged in the most convenient order all the information which a traveller can need with regard to the objects to be seen, the methods of seeing them, and the accommodations to be met with' (Preface).

King's copy: In publisher's green cloth, printed paper label, uncut.

Copies: K; Armitt; Cornell; Jackson

108.2 ——— Second edition. 1830

Title as first edition except:

'and on foot' added to 'on horseback'

'comprising a visit to the Lancaster Assizes' omitted

'Second Edition' added

Imprint altered to: 'London: Simpkin and Marshall; John Baines and Co. Leeds; Wales and Baines, Liverpool; M. and R. Branthwaite, Kendal, and all booksellers at Kendal, Carlisle, Penrith, Keswick, Ulverston, Lancaster, &c. &c.'

'1830' replaces '1829'

Notes: The Preface is completely rewritten. The main text is expanded, revised and corrected, with important additions. The division into chapters and the chapter headings are altered, 18 chapters taking the place of 22. 'Excursion on horseback' remains in 3 chapters, and apart from a few minor alterations and the addition of a few new paragraphs is unaltered. 'Excursion on foot (made in 1829)' is added, 15 pp.; it covers Kendal to Bowness and Hawes Water, ascent of Hill Bell and High Street – Ullswater – Derwentwater – Grasmere. The 'Itinerary' is revised – 'Made from actual Survey' [in June, 1828] and corrected to 1830. Baines of Leeds supersedes Wales of Liverpool as the printer – imprint on last page: *Leeds: Printed by Edward Baines and Son.*

The map is as the first edition except that, 'Chas, Fowler, Surveyor, Leeds' has been removed; '1830' replaces '1829'; and the imprint is altered to *Published by Hurst, Chance & Co. London; John Baines & Co. Leeds; & Wales & Baines, Liverpool.*

'This volume is intended to combine the accuracy of a *Guide-Book* with the liveliness and the interest of a *Personal Narrative*'.

King's copy: In publisher's maroon flowered cloth, printed paper label. Uncut. Price 7*s*. One leaf of 'Critical notices of Baines's Companion to the Lakes', from periodicals dated Sept. 5 1829 to July 25 1830, of different paper and type-face from the rest of the letterpress appears between the title-page and the Preface.

Copies: K; Armitt; Cornell; Jackson

108.3 ——— Third edition

Title as second edition except:

'Third edition' replaces 'Second edition'

In imprint 'Baines and Newsome, Leeds' replaces 'John Baines and Co. Leeds'

'1834' replaces '1830'

Notes: The preface is revised, dated Leeds, June 9, 1834. The main text is revised and corrected, with added notes, but much of it is not reset. A 'Second excursion on foot', made in the autumn of 1833, 26 pages, is added; it covers Ambleside to Wythburn – across the fells to Watendlath, Lowdore, Keswick, Borrowdale, Seatoller, the Wad Mines, ascent of Great Gravel, Langstrath and the Stake to Langdale Pikes, Great Langdale, Ambleside. The 'Itinerary' is corrected to 1834. Baines remains the printer: imprint on last page, *Edward Baines and Son, Printers, Leeds.*

'The volume is sold both with and without the Map (corrected down to the year 1834) and Frontispiece – of course at different prices' (note to Preface). The map was 'sold separately on canvas, in case, with an Itinerary of the Lakes' consisting of 7 pp. duodecimo.

The two excursions on foot were examples of unusually enterprising early fell-walking. Baines made the second unaccompanied, at a time when few tourists ventured beyond the valleys without local guides.

The map is as the second edition except that '1834' replaces '1830'; and the imprint is altered to *Published by Simpkin & Marshall, London, Baines & Newsome, Leeds, & Wales & Baines, Liverpool.*

Plate: One steel engraving, frontispiece, Derwentwater and the Borrowdale Mountains. Signed: *Drawn by T. Allom. 1834 Engraved by R. Sands.*

King's copy: In publisher's stamped green cloth, printed paper label. Uncut. Price 7*s.* 6*d.* Two leaves 'Critical notices' of first, second, and third editions bound in before frontispiece.

Copies: K; Armitt; Jackson; Kendal; Wordsworth

Barnes gives a fourth edition, 1836

1830

SAMUEL LEIGH (publisher)

109.1 ***Leigh's guide to the Lakes and mountains of Cumberland, Westmoreland, and Lancashire. Illustrated with a map of the country, and maps of Windermere, Derwent Water, Borrowdale, Ullswater, Grasmere, Rydal Water, and Langdale.*** London: printed for Samuel Leigh, 18, Strand. 1830 (on cover). Duodecimo.†

Text: Title, imprint on verso, *London: Printed by William Clowes, Stamford Street*; Quotations, 1 p., verso blank; Contents [v]-viii; Text [1]-[129]; Glossary [130]; Index [131]-136, imprint repeated on p. 136.

Plates: 4 coloured maps of lakes, Signature, *Josiah Neele Sc. 352, Strand*
1 Windermere Scale: 1 in. = 3 miles
2 Grasmere, Rydal & Langdale 1 in. = 1½ miles
3 Derwent Water & Borrowdale 1 in. = 1½ miles
4 Ulles Water 1 in. = 1½ miles

Map: A New Map of the Lakes in Westmoreland, Cumberland &c. Folding, coloured. Size: 518 × 384 mm. Scale: 1 in. = 3½ miles, Similar to map in *Ford's Guide* (118).

King's copy: In publisher's green cloth, rebacked with engraved and aquatint view mounted on upper cover and engraved title mounted on free endpaper. Label mounted on free endpaper, 'Price 7/-, Thos. Hodgson, Stationers &c. St. John Street, Liverpool'.

Note: The inclusion of detailed maps of special areas in a pocket guide is an innovation

Copies: K; Armitt; BL; Cornell

109.2 ——— Second edition. 1832

Title as first edition except:
'Second edition, enlarged and improved' is added
Imprint altered to 'London: Printed for M.A. Leigh, 421, Strand (removed from 18, Strand).' 1832.

King's copy: In publisher's green cloth, with engraving on upper cover and title on free endpaper, as first edition. 'London. 1835. 7/-', on cover. Plates: watermarks 1833. Label mounted on paste-down endpaper, 'Sold by J. Gardner. No. 163, Regent Stt. London'. 4 pp. publisher's adverts. for Travellers Guides bound in at end.

Copies: K; Armitt; BL; Jackson; Wordsworth

109.3 ——— Third edition. 1835

Title as second edition except:
'Westmorland' replaces 'Westmoreland'
'Third edition, carefully revised and corrected' replaces 'Second edition, enlarged, and improved'
'Leigh & Son' replaces 'M.A. Leigh'
'1835. Price seven shillings' replaces '1832'

'Printed by William Clowes and Sons, Duke Street, Lambeth' replaces 'Printed by William Clowes, Stamford Street'

Note: Text largely not reset

King's copy: In publisher's cloth with engraved titles, all as second edition. 1835 on cover. Bookplate on paste-down endpaper, *Ex Libris Henry Longman.* Inscribed on free endpaper, 'Mrs Stocks Heaton Mersey'

Copies: K; BL; Cornell; Jackson; Kendal; Wordsworth

109.4 ——— Fourth edition. 1840. Leigh & Co.

Copies: K; BL; Cornell; Jackson; Kendal

1831

GIDEON MICHAEL ANGELO MAUDE

110 ***A tour into Westmoreland, and to the moors, with remarks on grouse shooting, and a description of the country in the north of England*** 1831. No imprint. Duodecimo.†

Text: Title, verso blank; quotation from Chaucer, 1 p., verso blank; Preface [v]-vii; blank; Text [9]-115

Plates: 4 etchings
1 The landlady horror struck – rushed down stairs Signed: *Drawn and designed by G.M.A. Maude.*
2 Grouse shooting, Don and Flora Signed: *Drawn and designed by Michael Angelo Maude.*
3 "We were wonderful astonished to find ourselves suddenly enveloped in a thick cloud of soot" Signed: *Drawn and designed by G.M.A. Maude.*
4 Scene in Westmoreland. Signed: *Drawn by Michael Angelo Maude 1831.*

Map: Folding etched map of the Lakes of Cumberland, Westmoreland and Lancashire, Signed: *Drawn by G.M.A. Maude.* Imprint: *Leeds published by Thomas Inchbold.* Scale: 1 in. = 3 miles. Size: 197 × 120 mm

Note: This is an unusual and somewhat facetious account of a sporting tour, illustrated with a map and four plates drawn by the author. His tour only took him as far into the Lakes as Windermere and Belle Isle, but the map covers the whole of the Lake District.

King's copy: Rebound, uncut

Copies: K; Armitt; and Emmanuel College, Cambridge

1832

JOHN BREE

111 ***Saint Herbert's Isle: a legendary poem; in five cantos. With some smaller pieces. By the late John Bree, Esq. of Emerald, near Keswick.*** London: Printed for Longman, Rees, Orme, Brown, Green, and Longman. 1832. Octavo.†

Text: Title, Imprint on verso, *Manning and Smithson, Printers, 4, London House Yard, St. Paul's, London;* blank; Dedication 1 p., verso blank; Prefatory Sonnet, 1 p., verso blank; Contents 1 p., verso blank; Errata slip; Subscribers [ix]-xv; blank, Text 1-175; Imprint on verso last page, *Manning & Co. Printers, 4 London House Yard, St. Paul's.*

King's copy: In grey boards, leather labels

Copies: K; Armitt; BL; Cornell

LEIGH'S GUIDE

TO THE

LAKES AND MOUNTAINS

OF

CUMBERLAND, WESTMORELAND,

AND

LANCASHIRE.

ILLUSTRATED WITH

A MAP OF THE COUNTRY, AND MAPS OF WINDERMERE,
DERWENT WATER, BORROWDALE, ULLSWATER,
GRASMERE, RYDAL WATER,
AND LANGDALE.

LONDON:
PRINTED FOR SAMUEL LEIGH,
18, STRAND.

109.1 175 x 106 mm.

A TOUR

INTO

WESTMORELAND,

AND TO THE MOORS,

WITH

REMARKS ON GROUSE SHOOTING,

AND

A DESCRIPTION OF THE COUNTRY IN THE NORTH
OF ENGLAND.

BY GIDEON MICHAEL ANGELO MAUDE.

MDCCCXXXI.

110 186 x 110 mm.

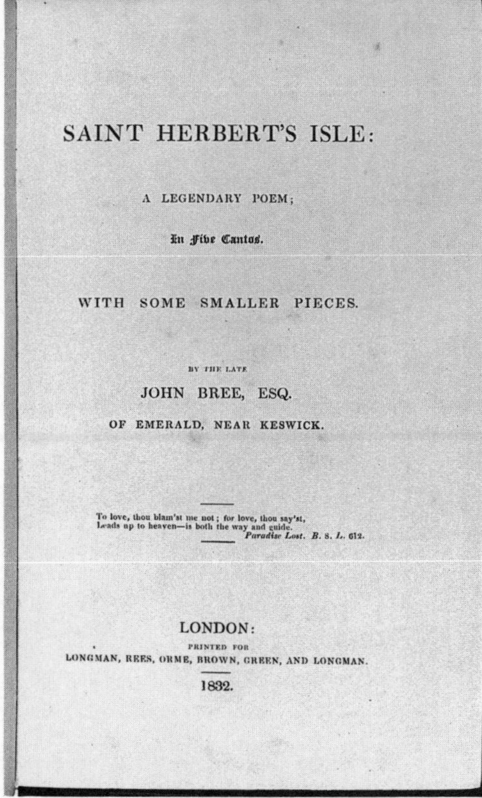

SAINT HERBERT'S ISLE:

A LEGENDARY POEM;

In Five Cantos.

WITH SOME SMALLER PIECES.

BY THE LATE

JOHN BREE, ESQ.

OF EMERALD, NEAR KESWICK.

To love, thou blam'st me not; for love, thou say'st,
Leads up to heaven—is both the way and guide.
Paradise Lost. B. 8. L. 612.

LONDON:

PRINTED FOR

LONGMAN, REES, ORME, BROWN, GREEN, AND LONGMAN.

1832.

111 196 x 122 mm.

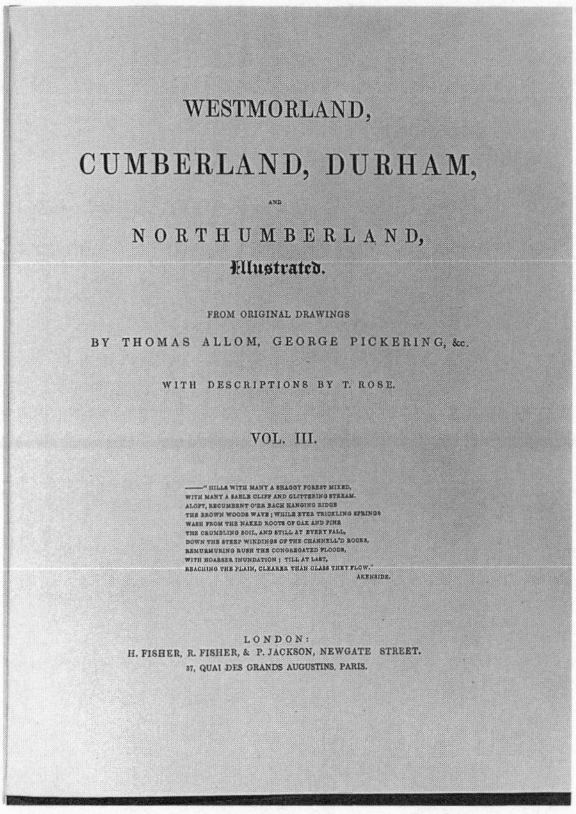

WESTMORLAND,

CUMBERLAND, DURHAM,

AND

NORTHUMBERLAND,

Illustrated.

FROM ORIGINAL DRAWINGS

BY THOMAS ALLOM, GEORGE PICKERING, &c.

WITH DESCRIPTIONS BY T. ROSE.

VOL. III.

——"HILLS WITH MANY A SHAGGY FOREST MIXED,
WITH MANY A SABLE CLIFF AND GLITTERING STREAM.
ALOFT, RECUMBENT O'ER EACH HANGING RIDGE
THE BROWN WOODS WAVE; WHILE EVER TRICKLING SPRINGS
WASH FROM THE NAKED ROOTS OF OAK AND PINE
THE CRUMBLING SOIL, AND STILL AT EVERY FALL,
DOWN THE STEEP WINDINGS OF THE CHANNELL'D ROCKS,
REMURMURING RUSH THE CONGREGATED FLOODS,
WITH HOARSER INUNDATION; TILL AT LAST,
REACHING THE PLAIN, CLEARER THAN GLASS THEY FLOW."
AKENSIDE.

LONDON:
H. FISHER, R. FISHER, & P. JACKSON, NEWGATE STREET.
37, QUAI DES GRANDS AUGUSTINS, PARIS.

112 275 x 212 mm.

THOMAS ROSE

112 ***Westmorland, Cumberland, Durham, and Northumberland, illustrated. From original drawings by Thomas Allom, George Pickering, &c. with descriptions by T. Rose.*** London: H. Fisher, R. Fisher, & P. Jackson, Newgate Street. 37 Quai des Grands Augustins, Paris. 3 vols. 1832 (on engraved title), n.d. (on title), imprints on plates 1832-35. Quarto.†

Text: Vol. 1 Engraved title, verso blank; title, verso blank; Address one page; list of plates 1 p.; Text [1]-76
Vol. 2 Title, verso blank; note on frontispiece, 1 p.; list of plates, 1 p.; Text [77]-148
Vol. 3 Title, verso blank; note on frontispiece, 1 p.; list of plates, 1 p.; Text [149]-220

Plates: Vol. 1 Engraved title with vignette and 72 steel engravings on 36 plates
Vol. 2 Frontispiece and 72 engravings on 36 plates
Vol. 3 Frontispiece and 69 engravings on 36 plates

2 views on 1 plate except where noted as 'full page'.
Plate size: 285 × 225 mm

Only plates of Lake District views listed. C= Cumberland W= Westmorland

Artists:	A = T. Allom	G = H. Gastineau	P = G. Pickering
Engravers:	Ad = H. Adlard	B = J.C. Bentley	Bo = H. Bond
	Br = S. Bradshaw	Bu = D. Buckley	C = E. Challis
	Co = W.J. Cooke	E = J. Engleheart	F = W. Floyd
	Gr = A.W. Graham	J = T. Jeevons	K = W. Kelsall
	L = S. Lacey	Mo = C. Mottram	Lo = J.W. Lowry
	M = W. Miller	P = le Petit	Ph = J. Phelp
	Re = J. Redway	Sa = R. Sands	Sh = T.H. Shepherd
	St = J. Starling	Ta = W. Taylor	T = W. Tombleson
	V = J. Varral	W = H. Waller	

Vol. 1
Title. Vignette. Langdale Pikes, W 1832 A J [full page]

7 Colwith Force, W 1832 A T
8 Dungeon Gill 1832 A T

10 Windermere Lake from the Ferry House 1832 A Ta

13 View of Ulleswater looking towards Patterdale 1832 A L
14 Derwent Water from Castle Head, C 1832 A L

18 Upper Reach, Ulleswater 1832 A L

21 Bowness & Windermere Lake, W 1832 A le P

25 Blea Tarn, W 1832 A G
26 Windermere Lake from Low Wood Inn 1833 A G

31 The Lower Fall at Rydal, W 1833 P le P
32 Stock-Gill Force, W 1833 A le P

35 Derwent Water & Lowdore, C 1833 G le P
36 Thirlmere, or Wythburn Water, C 1833 G le P

37 Skiddaw from Applethwaite 1833 G le P
38 Airey Force, C 1833 A B

39 Ullswater from Pooly Bridge 1833 A M

43 Derwentwater from Applethwaite 1833 G le P
44 Keswick, from Greta Bridge 1833 G le P

47 The Mill on Stock-Gill, near Ambleside 1833 G J
48 The Upper Fall at Rydal, W 1833 G J

51 Woodhall near Cockermouth 1833 A le P
52 Crummock Water, C 1833 A le P

55 Mardale Head, W 1833 A C
56 Grassmere Lake & Village, W 1833 P Mo

59 Lowdore Cataract, C 1833 A B
60 Scale Force, C 1833 A B

61 Valley of Troutbeck, W 1833 A le P
62 Stickle Tarn, Langdale Pikes, from Pavey Arc, W 1833 A le P

63 Buttermere, C 1833 A Sa
64 Rosthwaite, Borrowdale from the Road to Watenlath 1833 A Sa

70 Hawes-water, from Thwaite Force, W 1833 A le P

71 Castle Crag, Borrowdale from the Village of Grange, C 1833 A B
72 Scawfell Pikes from Sty Head, C 1833 A B

Vol. 2
Frontispiece. Windermere Lake, looking down 1835 P le P [full page]

1 Elterwater, Great Langdale, W 1833 A le P
2 Thrang Crag Slate Quarry, Great Langdale, W 1833 A le P

3 Ennerdale Water, from How Hall, C 1833 A
4 Watenlath, & the Stream of Lowdore 1833 A Sa

5 Grassmere from Butler Crags, W 1833 A La

8 Derwentwater, & the Village of Grange, from the Entrance to Borrowdale 1833 A le P

9 Bridge House, Ambleside, W 1833 A J
10 Approach to Ambleside, W 1833 A J

11 Dallam Tower, Near Milnthorp 1833 A le P

13 Loweswater, from Water End, C 1833 A F
14 Honister Crag, C 1833 A F §

29 Second Reach of Ulswater 1834 A Sa
30 Rydal Water, near Ivy Cottage, W 1834 A Sa

33 Brother's Water from Kirkstone Foot, W 1834 A Sa
34 Patterdale Bridge, W 1834 A Sa

39 Ferry House, Regatta, Windermere Lake 1834 A St
40 Storrs Hall, Windermere Lake, W 1834 A St

41 Thirlmere Bridge, looking North, C 1834 A le P
42 Thirlmere & Helvellyn, from Raven Crag 1834 A le P

47 Birker Force, C 1834 A Bo
48 Barrow Fall, near Derwentwater 1834 A Bo

51 Eamont Bridge, from the Westmorland Side 1834 A T
52 Patterdale, going towards Ambleside, W 1834 A Ta

58 Wastdale Head, Scawfell Pikes, C 1834 A Lo

63 Kentmere Head, and Slate Quarries W 1834 A Br
64 Kendal, from Green Bank 1834 A Br

65 Waterfall, near Sty Head, C 1834 A La

67 Mardale Green, W 1834 A Sa
68 Small-water Tarn, from Nanfield, looking into Mardale 1834 A Sa

71 Sty Head Tarn, C 1834 A le P
72 Eskdale Mill, Wilton Beck, C 1834 A le P

Vol. 3
Frontispiece. Eskdale, looking towards Scawfell, C 1835 P V [full page]

3 Helvellyn, from the North West, C 1834 A Sa

7 Borrowdale, C 1834 A le P

13 Grassmere from Loughrigg Fell 1835 P le P
14 Rydal Hall from Fox How, W 1835 P le P

21 Bowness from Belle Isle, Windermere 1835 A Re
22 The Rushbearing at Ambleside, W 1835 A Re

23 Mill Beck, & Buttermere Chapel, C 1835 A St
24 The Vale of St. John, Saddleback in the distance 1835 A St

25 Whitehaven, C 1835 P J
26 Muncaster Castle 1835 P J

29 Derwent & Bassenthwaite Lakes, – Keswick & Skiddaw in the distance, C 1835 P le P [full page]

30 Mill Beck, Great Langdale 1835 A Br

31 Stybarrow Crag, W 1835 A Br

32 Eagle Crag from Rosthwaite, Borrowdale 1835 A Sa
33 Castle Rock, Vale of St. John, looking South, C 1835 A Sa

36 The Druids' Stones, near Keswick 1835 A Ad
37 Holme Hall, near Ravenglass, C 1835 A Ad

42 Rydal Water & Grassmere, from Rydal Park, W 1835 P Co [full page]

43 Wasdale Hall, C 1835 A W
44 Wastwater, C 1835 A W

47 Long Sleddale Slate Quarries, W 1835 A Lo
48 Bley-water Tarn from the top of High Street Mountain 1835 A Lo

49 Windermere, Esthwaite Water & Ambleside from Rydal Park 1835 P E
50 Ambleside, W 1835 P E

53 Windermere, Esthwaite and Coniston Lakes 1835 P le P [full page]

54 Hayswater from the Top of High-Street Mountain 1835 A Ad
55 Grisedale, near Ulleswater 1835 A Ad

60 Bassenthwaite Lake, looking South, C 1835 A Ph
61 Keswick, Derwent, &c. from the Road to Kendal 1835 A Ph

62 Clare Moss, from Little Langdale Head 1835 A W

64 View from Langdale Pikes, looking South East, W 1835 A K
65 View from Langdale Pikes, looking towards Bowfell, W 1835 A K

66 Goldrill Beck & Ullswater, C 1835 P Bu
67 Buttermere Lake & Village, C 1835 P Bu

68 Skelwith Bridge, W 1835 A Sh
69 Scout Scar, Near Kendal, W 1835 A Sh

Imprint: Fisher Son & Co. [date]

King's copy: 3 vols in half leather, green leather labels

Notes: Published in 26 parts as Pts. 10-35 of the Fourth Series of *Fisher's picturesque illustrations of Great Britain and Ireland.* 'The fourth series comprising the splendid lake scenery, seats, &c. of Westmorland, Cumberland, Durham, & Northumberland: from original drawings by Thomas Allom; with historical and topographical descriptions, by Thomas Rose. London. Fisher, Son & Co., Newgate Street. Simpkin and Marshall; C. Tilt; and all booksellers.'

Part 1 Seventeen engravings, price four shillings
Part 2 Eight engravings, price two shillings. 'The proprietors of this Work beg to state, that, at the request of various Subscribers, they have divided the Four Shilling Part into two portions . . . at Two Shillings each; . . . and thus to continue afterwards in each alternate month'.

Part 26 included a printed title (to supplement the engraved title issued in Pt. 1), a Preface and Index, for binding the work in one volume. A supplementary number was prepared, containing three titles, Prefaces, Indices and Cancels, and two engravings as Frontispieces for the Second and Third Volumes.

Three annual volumes were advertised in the parts as follows:

In Part 10 the publishers advertised: 'Subscribers to this work are respectfully informed, that a portion of it is bound up into a Volume, and will be published on the 6th of December, under the following Title, forming an elegant CHRISTMAS AND NEW YEAR GAGE D'AMITIÉ. December 12th, in quarto, handsomely bound, gilt edges, Price One Guinea, The northern Tourist; containing seventy three Views of Lake and Mountain Scenery, etc. in Westmorland, [etc]. Two other editions – one with Descriptions in French, and one in German, will be published at the same time.' (1832).

In Part 16 a new edition of the *Northern Tourist* or *Gage d'Amitié* (as before), handsomely bound, price 21*s*. to be published on 21st October (1834), together with Volume Two which 'will be ready in December'.

In Part 17 a third volume, to be published on 1st December 1835, with a note that *The Northern Tourist* for 1834 (vol. 2) had lately been reprinted.

As well as in the three annual volumes of the *Northern Tourist* or *Gage d'Armitié,* the plates were republished in a variety of forms and editions with differing titles, and differing selection and grouping of the plates, such as *The British Switzerland or picturesque rambles in the English Lake District.* 2 vols. London & New York: The London Printing and Publishing Co. Ltd. [1856-60]. Quarto. 143 engravings of Lake District views.

Almost every aspect of Lake District scenery was covered, including views from fairly remote spots high in the fells. Allom in particular, 'fearless of danger, patient of fatigue', was indefatigable in collecting views. The plates were used as illustrations in various other publications, sold separately as albums of views, and used as letter-headings for writing paper.

Copies: K; Armitt; BL; Cornell; Jackson; Kendal; Wordsworth (parts)

1833

JOHN ROBINSON 1774-1840

See 89

113 ***Views of the Lakes in the north of England, from original paintings by the most eminent artists: with historical and descriptive illustrations.*** London: C. Tilt, Fleet Street; Longman & Co. Paternoster Row; Whittaker and Co. Ave Maria Lane; J. Brown, Penrith; and J. Cockburn, Carlisle. 1833 [Part 1], 1834 [Part 2]. Quarto

Issued in two parts in printed paper wrappers, with wording similar to title; part number, price, printer's imprint and ornamental border added. Ordinary copies, price 4*s*. India proofs, price 6*s*. 6*d*. Imprint on cover, *Rickerby, Printer, Sherbourn Lane* (cover, part 1†)

Text: Title, imprint on verso, *London: J. Rickerby, Printer, Sherbourn Lane;* Advertisement, verso blank; Text 1-20,

Plates: 6 steel engravings

Part 1

Ullswater (from Yew Crag). From a painting by Glover in the collection of John Marshall Esq. Hallsteads.

Signed: *Drawn by J. Nutter. Engraved by W.J. Cooke. 1832*

Derwent Water, from the Foot of Castle Hill.

Signed: *Drawn by M.E. Nutter. Engraved by W.J. Cooke. 1832*

Derwent Water, from the Foot of Barrow.

Signed: *Painted by T.C. Hofland. Engraved by W.R. Smith. 1833.*

Part 2

Ullswater from the Matterdale Road. From a painting in the possession of H. Howard Esqr. Greystoke Castle.

Signed: *Drawn by T.C. Hofland. Engraved by J.W. Cooke 1834.*

Head of Buttermere, from a painting by R. Wilson.

Signed: *Engraved by W.R. Smith. 1834.*

Hawes Water, from a picture in the possession of S. Simpson Esqr.

Signed: *Painted by R. Wilson. Engraved by W.J. Cooke. 1834.*

All plates: *Printed by E. Brain. Published by James Brown, Penrith, and John Cockburn, Carlisle* [date].

King's copies: As issued in printed buff paper wrappers. Part 1 (India paper) 1833. Prospectus on lower wrapper. Part 2 (India proofs) 1834. Adverts. for part 1 on lower wrapper.

Also 'ordinary copy' of Part 2.

Notes: The 'eminent artists' are of some interest. John Glover (1767-1849), born in Leicestershire; worked as a writing master at Appleby Grammar School 1786-94; visited the Lakes on several occasions and did many paintings of the district; owned a house at Patterdale. Matthew Ellis Nutter (1795-1862), born Carlisle, where he worked as a drawing master; portrait, landscape and architectural painter and print-maker. Thomas Christopher Hofland (1777-1843), born Worksop; pupil of J. Rathbone (see 30); drawing master, Derby and London. The engraver J. Nutter was probably a member of M.E. Nutter's family working in his engraving business. R. Wilson is probably Captain R. Wilson, of Carlisle; died 1838, an amateur painter in watercolour who did many drawings of the Lake District in the early nineteenth century. None of these artists was represented by illustrations in other Lake District books.

Robinson's book does not seem to have been a success, as it was not continued after the publication of the first two parts.

Copies: K; BL; Jackson; Kendal

1834

J. ALLISON (editor and publisher)

Allison took over and continued the publication of 'Shaw's Guide' (see 75).

114.5 ***Allison's northern tourist's guide to the Lakes, of Cumberland, Westmorland, and Lancashire; wherein the mountains, lakes, and scenery are correctly described; and the stages and favourite excursions distinctly pointed out.*** Fifth edition [of 'Shaw's Guide']. With considerable additions. . . . (lines from 'Lake of Windermere', by T. Blake). Penrith: printed by J. Allison; sold by Whittaker and Co. Ave-Maria Lane, London; Mozley, and Son, Derby; H. Scott, Carlisle; Hudson and Nicholson, Kendal; G. Ewbank, Durham; Messrs. Cowper, mineralogists, Keswick; Jefferson, Cockermouth; and Gibson, Whitehaven. 1834. Octavo. Folding map of the Lakes.

Copies: Armitt; Jackson

114.6 ——— Sixth edition.† 1835. Title as 1834 except lines from Blake omitted and imprint differs. Octavo.

Imprint: Sold also by J.F. Mason, 444 West Strand, London; Mozley and Son, Derby; Bancks and Co., St. Anne's Square, Manchester; W. Davison, Alnwick; H. Scott, Carlisle; Messrs. Cowper, Mineralogists, Keswick; and G. Bennett, Cockermouth. [Whittaker; Ewbank; and Jefferson, omitted]

Text: Title, verso blank; advertisement [iii]; Introduction [iv], v; Table [vi]; Altitudes [vii], viii; Waterfalls [ix]; Distances [x]-xii; Text [13]-126; Traveller's Guide [127]-128; Lists [129]-[131]; Contents [132]-[136]; adverts. 136.

Map: A New and Correct Map of the Lakes . . . Published by J. Allison, Penrith 1840. Engraved by J. Roy, 97 near the Coffee House, Carlisle. Folding. 317 × 260 mm. Scale 1 in. = 4 miles (in King's copy).

King's copy: In printed paper boards with vignette view on upper cover, repaired. No date on cover. Imprint differs from title; 'S. Jefferson, Carlisle' and 'T. Wilson, York' added, 'H. Scott, Carlisle' and 'G. Bennett, Cockermouth' omitted.

Copies: K; BL; Cornell

114.7 ——— Seventh edition. 1837

Copies: Armitt; BL; Kendal; Wordsworth

114.8 ——— Eighth edition. 1835.

Title as sixth edition, except:
'eighth edition' replaces 'sixth edition'
'very' is added to 'considerable additions'
'1839' replaces '1835'

Imprint: Penrith: Printed by J. Allison; Sold also by Ackermann and Co., 96, Strand, London; Oliver and Boyd, Edinburgh; Mozley and Sons, Derby; Banks and Co., St. Anne's Square, Manchester; Wilson and Sons, York; Jefferson, Carlisle; J. and E. Cowper, Mineralogists, Keswick; Gibson, Whitehaven; Dawson, Kendal; and Jackson, Ulverston, added. [Mason; Davison; Scott; and Bennett, omitted.]

Text altered and enlarged. Dedication to Wordsworth (J. Allison, Penrith, August 1st 1839) and a Glossary are added.

King's copy: In publisher's green cloth, lettered and decorated in gilt on upper cover. Map, dated 1840, similar to 1835, except 324 × 270 mm.

Copies: K; Armitt

1835

JOHN CHARLES BRISTOW

His *Poetical Works* were published, London, 1850.

115 ***Ullsmere, a poem.*** London: Samuel Hodgson, Wimpole Street. 1835. Octavo. Engraving by Westall.

Copies: Cornell; Jackson

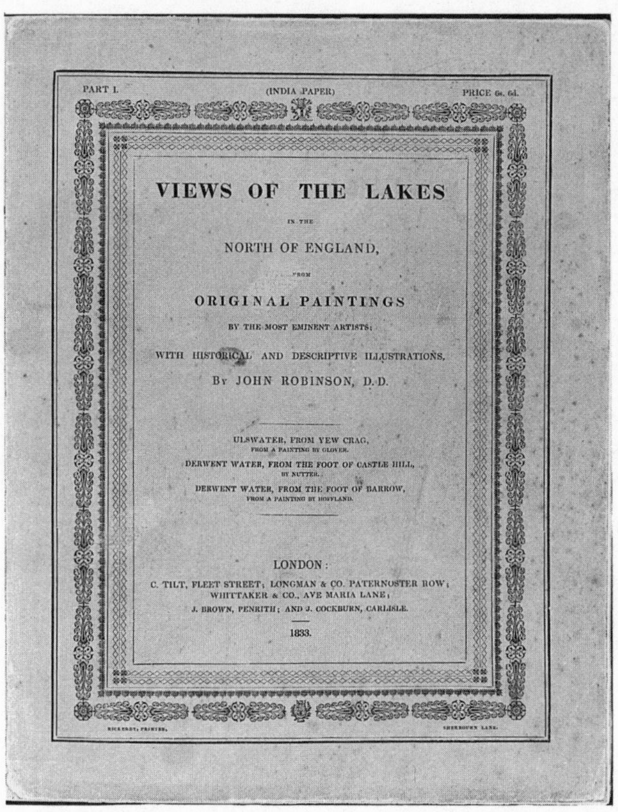

PART I. (INDIA PAPER) PRICE 6s. 6d.

VIEWS OF THE LAKES

IN THE

NORTH OF ENGLAND,

FROM

ORIGINAL PAINTINGS

BY THE MOST EMINENT ARTISTS;

WITH HISTORICAL AND DESCRIPTIVE ILLUSTRATIONS,

BY JOHN ROBINSON, D.D.

ULSWATER, FROM YEW CRAG,
FROM A PAINTING BY GLOVER.
DERWENT WATER, FROM THE FOOT OF CASTLE HILL,
BY NUTTER.
DERWENT WATER, FROM THE FOOT OF BARROW,
FROM A PAINTING BY HOFFLAND.

LONDON:
C. TILT, FLEET STREET; LONGMAN & CO. PATERNOSTER ROW;
WHITTAKER & CO., AVE MARIA LANE;
J. BROWN, PENRITH; AND J. COCKBURN, CARLISLE.

1833.

113 285 x 223 mm.

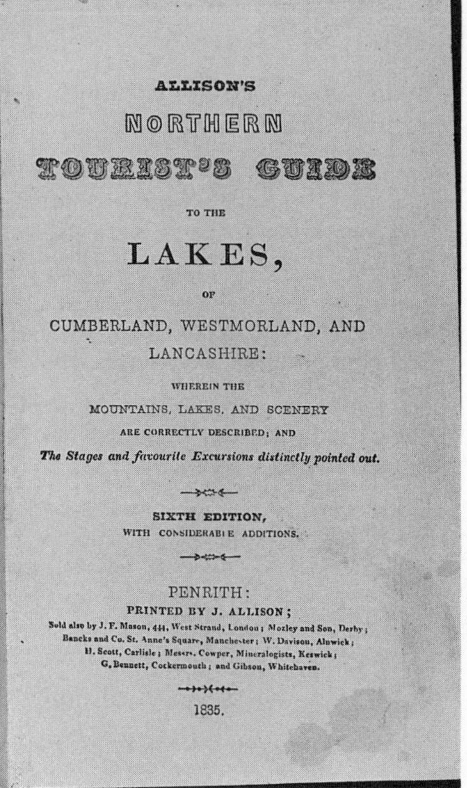

ALLISON'S

NORTHERN

TOURIST'S GUIDE

TO THE

LAKES,

OF

CUMBERLAND, WESTMORLAND, AND LANCASHIRE:

WHEREIN THE
MOUNTAINS, LAKES, AND SCENERY
ARE CORRECTLY DESCRIBED; AND
The Stages and favourite Excursions distinctly pointed out.

SIXTH EDITION,
WITH CONSIDERABLE ADDITIONS.

PENRITH:
PRINTED BY J. ALLISON;
Sold also by J. F. Mason, 444, West Strand, London; Mozley and Son, Derby; Bancks and Co. St. Anne's Square, Manchester; W. Davison, Alnwick; H. Scott, Carlisle; Messrs. Cowper, Mineralogists, Keswick; G. Bennett, Cockermouth; and Gibson, Whitehaven.

1835.

114.6 166 x 102 mm.

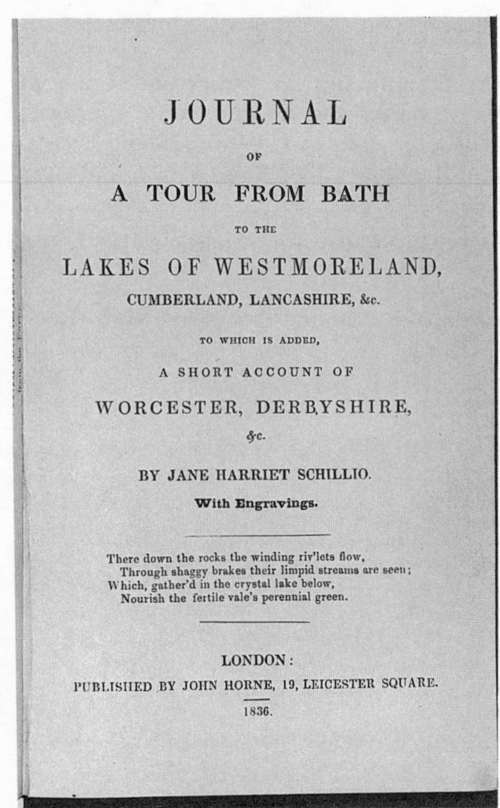

JOURNAL

OF

A TOUR FROM BATH

TO THE

LAKES OF WESTMORELAND,

CUMBERLAND, LANCASHIRE, &c.

TO WHICH IS ADDED,

A SHORT ACCOUNT OF

WORCESTER, DERBYSHIRE,

&c.

BY JANE HARRIET SCHILLIO.

With Engravings.

There down the rocks the winding riv'lets flow,
Through shaggy brakes their limpid streams are seen;
Which, gather'd in the crystal lake below,
Nourish the fertile vale's perennial green.

LONDON:
PUBLISHED BY JOHN HORNE, 19, LEICESTER SQUARE.

1836.

117 162 x 100 mm.

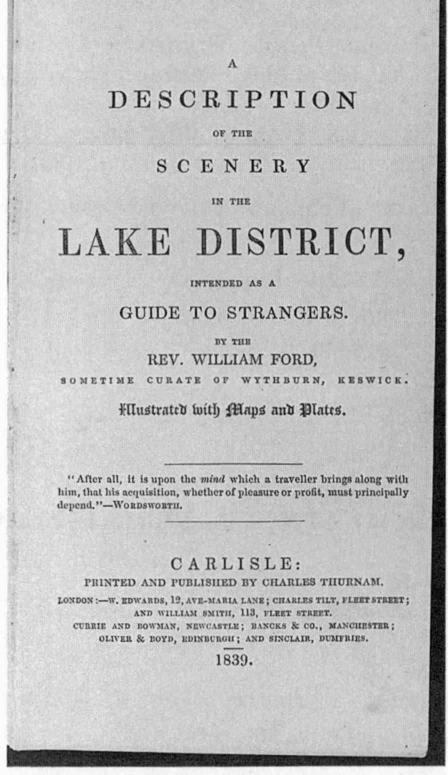

A

DESCRIPTION

OF THE

SCENERY

IN THE

LAKE DISTRICT,

INTENDED AS A

GUIDE TO STRANGERS.

BY THE

REV. WILLIAM FORD,

SOMETIME CURATE OF WYTHBURN, KESWICK.

Illustrated with Maps and Plates.

"After all, it is upon the *mind* which a traveller brings along with him, that his acquisition, whether of pleasure or profit, must principally depend."—WORDSWORTH.

CARLISLE:
PRINTED AND PUBLISHED BY CHARLES THURNAM.
LONDON:—W. EDWARDS, 12, AVE-MARIA LANE; CHARLES TILT, FLEET STREET;
AND WILLIAM SMITH, 113, FLEET STREET.
CURRIE AND BOWMAN, NEWCASTLE; BANCKS & CO., MANCHESTER;
OLIVER & BOYD, EDINBURGH; AND SINCLAIR, DUMFRIES.

1839.

118.1 175 x 100 mm.

1836

GEORGE TATTERSALL 1817-1849

George Tattersall, the grandson of Richard Tattersall, the founder of 'Tattersall's' (bloodstock auction house founded 1766), was an artist and illustrator of sporting books, using the pseudonym 'Wildrake'.

116 ***The lakes of England.*** London. Published by Sherwood & Co. Paternoster Row, and Hudson & Nicholson, Kendal. (1836) Octavo.§

Text: Half-title, Tablets of an Itinerant, imprint on verso *Wilson & Son, Printers, 57, Skinner-Street, London;* engraved Title, verso blank; Dedication (signed George Tattersall), verso blank; Preface (London, April 15, 1836) [v]-vii; List of Plates [viii]; Contents [ix]-xii; Text [1]-125; blank; Divisional title, 'An Itinerary'; Contents 1 p.; Text 129-156; Index [157]161; blank; Subscribers [163]-165; Imprint (as on title page) [166]; Errata 1 p., verso blank; adverts. [1]-24.

Plates: 41 plates 'etched on steel by W.F. Topham from original drawings by the Author' and engraved title-page. Imprint: *London, Pubd. April 15th, 1836, by Sherwood & Co.*

Vignette on title-page: [Horse in Lake District scene]

1 Upper Reach Windermere
2 Lower Reach Windermere
3 Windermere from Rayrigg Bank
4 Coniston Water from Waterhead
5 Upper Reach, Coniston
6 Little Langdale
7 Blea Tarn
8 The Valley of the Stake
9 Grasmere from Loughrigg Fell
10 Rydal Water
11 Great Langdale

Views from the Summit of the Langdale Pikes

12 Looking North
13 Looking East
14 Looking South
15 Looking West

16 Thirlmere from Rays Gap
17 Thirlmere from the North
18 The Vale of St. John
19 Derwent Water and the entrance to Borrowdale

Views from the Summit of Helvellyn

20 Looking North
21 Looking East
22 Looking South
23 Looking West

24 Borrowdale from the Road near Rosthwaite
25 Honister Crag
26 Buttermere Lake
27 Crummock Lake from the East
28 Newlands Vale from Robinson Fell
29 Derwent Water and Bassenthwaite Lake from the road to Watendlath
30 Stye Head Tarn
31 Wastwater, Scawfell and Scawfell Pikes from the road to Calder Bridge
32 Ennerdale Lake
33 Loweswater from the North-West

Views from the Summit of Skiddaw

34 Looking North
35 Looking East
36 Looking South
37 Looking West

38 Haweswater from above Thwaite Force
39 Ullswater, from Pooley Bridge
40 Second Reach, Ullswater from Place Fell
41 Upper Reach Ullswater

Map: Folding coloured map of the Lakes of England by George Tattersall, 1836. *London. Published by Sherwood & Co. 23 Paternoster Row, April 15, 1836. J. Netherclift Lithog: 23 King William Street, West Strand.* 345 × 270 mm. Scale 1 in. = 4 miles

King's copy: In publisher's maroon blind-stamped cloth. Inscribed on free endpaper 'J.W. Gilbert The Close Sept. 25th 1874'.

Copies: K; Armitt; BL; Cornell; Jackson; Kendal

JANE HARRIET SCHILLIO

117 ***Journal of a tour from Bath to the lakes of Westmoreland, Cumberland, Lancashire, &c . . . .*** London: published by John Horne, 19, Leicester Square. 1836. Octavo†

Text: Half-title, verso blank; Title, imprint on verso, *J. Eames, Printer, 7 Tavistock Street, Covent Garden;* Subscribers [v], vi; Preface [vii], viii; Text [1]-79. Imprint repeated on p.79.

Plates: 4 lithographs, signed *C. Warren delt.*
1 Winandermere from the Ferry (frontispiece)
2 Winandermere
3 Derwentwater
4 Borrowdale

Lakes: pp. 38-74

Itinerary: Left Kendal 4 August 1819; based on Bowness and Ambleside, visiting Coniston and Furness, until 3 September; at Keswick, making excursions to Borrowdale and Buttermere, and up Skiddaw, until 12 October; returning to Kendal.

Note: The author includes several of her own poems

King's copy: In contemporary dark blue diced cloth.

Copies: Armitt; BL

1839

WILLIAM FORD

The Revd William Ford was for a time curate of Wythburn, Thirlmere.

118.1 ***A description of the scenery in the Lake District, intended as a guide to strangers.*** Carlisle: printed and published by Charles Thurnam. London:W. Edwards, 12, Ave-Maria Lane; Charles Tilt, Fleet Street; and William Smith, 113, Fleet Street; Currie and Bowman, Newcastle; Bancks & Co., Manchester; Oliver & Boyd, Edinburgh; and Sinclair, Dumfries. 1839. Duodecimo.†

Text: Title, verso blank; Advertisement 1 p., verso blank; Contents 2 pp.; Itinerary 1 p.; blank; Introduction [i]-ix; blank [x]; Text [1]-162, Tables 163, 167; blank [168]; Index [169]-175; Imprint on p. 175, *Charles Thurnam, Printer, Carlisle.*

Plates: 3 double-page engravings, each a panoramic view over a coloured map. Signed, *Engd, by W.H. Lizars,*

1 Windermere
2 Derwent Water and the Vale of Keswick
3 Ulles Water

Folding table of distances.

Map: A Map of the Lake District of Cumberland, Westmoreland and Lancashire, with a slip added to show the Hexham, Newcastle and Carlisle railway. Coloured, folding. 448 × 350 mm. Scale, 1 in. = 3½ miles.

King's copy: In publisher's purple stamped cloth, engraved title with engraved view of waterfall mounted on upper cover.§ Map mounted on linen.

Notes: This is the earliest use of the term 'Lake District' in the title of a book.

Quotation from Wordsworth on title-page. Ford states his obligation to Mr. Wordsworth for his 'admirably descriptive sketch', and to William Green for his 'elaborate Guide Books'. But he adds that it has been his own object 'to combine the advantages of both by avoiding the minute detail of the artist and amplifying the slight poetical touches of the author of *The Excursion.'*

Copies: K; BL; Kendal

118.2 ——— Second edition 1840

Title as 1839 except:

'sometime curate of Wythburn, Keswick' omitted.
'carefully revised throughout' added.
Imprint altered to 'Carlisle: published by Charles Thurnam: London, C. Tilt 86 Fleet Street; R. Groombridge, Panyer Alley, and all other booksellers. 1840'.

Text similar, minor additions and alterations only. Introduction unaltered.

King's copy: Binding similar to 1st edition (1839). Lacks map.

Copies: K; Armitt; Kendal; Jackson

118.3 ——— Third edition 1843

Copies: BL; and Alpine Club

118.4 ——— Fourth edition 1845

Title as 1840 except:

'carefully revised and illustrated with maps and plates' replaces 'carefully revised throughout'
'Wordsworth' omitted after quotation
Imprint altered, 'London: R. Groombridge & Sons, 5, Paternoster Row. Carlisle: Charles Thurnam, 5 English Street. 1845'
'Price Four Shillings Plain, or Five Shillings with the Maps Coloured' added.
'Lake District' printed in red. Ornamental border.

No significant alterations to text

King's copy: In publisher's blind-stamped dark green cloth. Map uncoloured, mounted on linen, paper slip added. Inscribed on free endpapers 'Wm. Bromley, Keswick'.

Copies: K; Armitt; Wordsworth; and Alpine Club (1844)

118.5 ——— Fifth edition, 1847. Reissue of 4th edition, not reset.

Note: 'Price Four Shillings Plain, or Five Shillings with the Maps coloured'.

King's copies: In dark green striped cloth, engravings mounted on covers as 1839. Map with slip, not mounted on linen, coloured. 1850 title-page differs, printed in black and red.

Copies: K (1847 and 1850); BL (1847); Kendal (1849)

118.6 ——— Sixth edition. No information

118.7 ——— Seventh edition. 1852

Copies: Jackson; and Barrow-in-Furness

5th, 6th and 7th editions, imprint: *London: Groombridge; Carlisle: Thurnam*, or similar, duodecimo.

119 ***Ford's handbook to the Lakes.*** Carlisle: Charles Thurnam. 1852. Duodecimo.

An abbreviated version of Ford's *Description* (118).

Copy: Barrow-in-Furness

1841

JOSEPH ONWHYN (publisher)

Joseph Onwhyn specialised in the publication of guide books.

120 ***Onwhyn's pocket guide to the Lakes; or, tourist's companion to the beauties of Cumberland, Westmoreland, and Lancashire: affording all necessary information on the subject of routes, distances, inns, travelling expenses, conveyances, &c.*** Illustrated with a map. London: J. Onwhyn, 4 Catherine Street, Strand. 1841. Duodecimo.

Copies: Armitt; BL

JOHN HUDSON (editor, printer and publisher)

121.1 ***A hand-book for lake visitors, with a new map of the Lake District; to which is appended an account of Furness Abbey . . .*** Kendal: published by Hudson and Nicholson; and in London by Whittaker and Co., Ave-Maria Lane. 1841. Duodecimo.

Engraving, map.

The *Hand-book* is a shorter and condensed version of the *Complete guide* (122).

Copies: Armitt; Kendal

121.2 ——— Second edition, 1843

Copies: BL; Cornell; Kendal

121.3 ——— Third edition, 1847

Text: Title, verso blank; Preface one page; Text [5]-42. Imprint on p. 42, *Kendal, printed by John Hudson.*

Plate: Frontispiece oval engraving Kendal, *Lizars* etc [engravers] One plan in text.

Map: Folding Map of the Lakes of Cumberland, Westmorland, & Lancashire. Signed, *Engraved by A.B. Johnson, Birmingham.* Size 350 × 305 mm. Scale: 1 in. = 4 miles

King's copy: In printed paper boards

Copy: K

121.4 ——— Fourth edition. No information.

121.5 ——— Fifth edition, 1856

121.6-9 ——— Sixth to ninth editions. No information.

All editions, imprint: *Kendal: Hudson,* or similar

121.10 Tenth edition n.d. (*c.* 1873) Kendal: Titus Wilson

Copies: Armitt; Jackson; Wordsworth

122.1 ***A complete guide to the Lakes, comprising minute directions for the tourist, with Mr. Wordsworth's description of the country, &c. and three letters upon the geology of the Lake District, by the Rev. Professor Sedgwick.*** Edited by the publisher. Kendal: published by Hudson and Nicholson. London: Longman and Co., and Whittaker and Co. Liverpool; Webb, Castle St. Manchester; Simms and Co. 1842. Duodecimo. Engravings, map and 4 diagrams.

This is the sixth edition of Wordsworth's *Guide* (95).

Copies: Armitt; Cornell; Kendal; Wordsworth

122.2 ——— Second edition†, 1843

Text: Title, imprint on verso. *Kendal printed by J. Hudson;* Advertisement [iii], iv; Advertisement to the second edition [v], vi; Contents [iii]-ix; Stages [x]; Introduction [i]-vii; blank; Directions and information [1]-114; divisional title, 'Description of the scenery of the Lakes', verso blank; text [117]-179; blank; divisional title, 'Geology of the Lake District in three letters', (A. Sedgwick, Cambridge, May 30, 1842), verso blank; text [185]-245; blank; Appendix [247-250]; A glossary [251]-259, imprint on verso of p. 259, *Kendal: printed by J. Hudson.*

Plates: Engraved frontispiece, *Head of Windermere from Lowood.* Signed, *Willm. Banks. W.H. Lizars.* Imprint, *Published by Hudson & Nicholson; Kendal.*
4 engraved outlines of mountains
Plan in text, p. 11
Diagram p. [184]

Map: Folding Map of the Lakes. Size: 345 × 290. Scale: 1 in. = 4 miles

King's copy: In publisher's brown cloth, lettered on upper cover, *Complete Guide. Wordsworth's scenery of the lakes of England with directions for the tourist. Edited by J. Hudson.* Inscribed on free endpaper 'J. Musgrave Edenhall'. Lacks map.

Note: 'The whole of the 'Description of the Scenery of the Lakes' and a considerable portion of the 'Directions and Information for the Tourist' are adapted from Wordsworth's Guide' (advertisement p. [iii]).

Copies: K; Armitt; BL; Cornell; Kendal

122.3 ——— Third edition, 1846 'Four letters on the geology of the Lake District' replaces 'Three letters . . . '

King's copy: Bound as second edition (1843) except green not brown cloth. Map mounted on linen.

Copies: K; Armitt; Cornell; Jackson; Kendal

122.4 ——— Fourth edition, 1853 'Five letters on the geology of the Lake District' replaces 'Four letters . . .'

Text: Title, verso blank; Advertisement (Kendal July 1853) [iii], iv (dated July 1953); Contents [v]-vii; Stages [viii]; Glossary [ix]-xii; Introduction [i]-viii; Directions and information [1]-166; Divisional title, 'Geology of the Lake District', verso blank; text [169]-258; Appendix [259]-262; List of fossils [263], 264; Botanical notes [265]-268; List of shells [269], 270. Imprint on p. 270 *Kendal: printed by John Hudson.*

Plates: As previous editions, and two circular maps:
1 Eight miles round Grasmere
2 The vicinity of Keswick
Scale: 1 in. = 5½ miles.

Map: Folding map of the Lakes, Pub. John Hudson, engraved Wm. Banks. Size 395 × 310mm. Scale: 1 in. = 3½ miles.

King's copy: Contemporary half black dyed leather, marbled boards. Map coloured.

Copies K; BL; Cornell; Jackson

122.5 ——— Fifth edition, 1859

Copies: Cornell 1864; Kendal; Wordsworth 1859; BL

ADAM BLACK (publisher) 1794-1874

Adam Black, politician, publisher and bookseller, carried on a business in Edinburgh, at first alone and later with his nephew Charles Black. The firm held the copyright of the *Encyclopaedia Britannica*, and of Walter Scott's Works. Black's series of Picturesque Guides, which presented a wealth of well-written and clearly arranged up-to-date information for tourists, were popular and were constantly revised and reprinted.

123.1 ***Black's picturesque guide to the English Lakes with a copious itinerary; a map, and four charts of the Lake District; and engraved views of the scenery.*** Edinburgh: Adam and Charles Black, North Bridge, booksellers and publishers to the Queen. 1841. Octavo.†

Text Half-title, imprint on verso, *T. Constable, 11 Thistle Street, Printer to Her Majesty*; Preface (Edinburgh 15th June 1841) [v], vi; Contents [vii], viii; Abstract of Tours [ix]-xi; Description of Engravings [xii]; Text [1]-154; one leaf adverts.

Plates: Two steel engravings
1 Ullswater, from Gowbarrow Park. Signed, *T.M. Richardson Junr. William Frost* (frontispiece)
2 Derwentwater. Signed, *Montague Stanley A.R.S.A. W. Miller.*

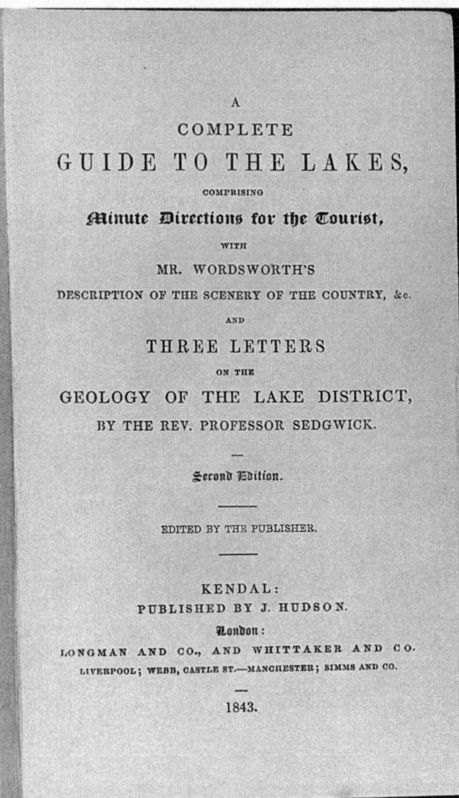

A
COMPLETE
GUIDE TO THE LAKES,
COMPRISING
Minute Directions for the Tourist,
WITH
MR. WORDSWORTH'S
DESCRIPTION OF THE SCENERY OF THE COUNTRY, &c.
AND
THREE LETTERS
ON THE
GEOLOGY OF THE LAKE DISTRICT,
BY THE REV. PROFESSOR SEDGWICK.

Second Edition.

EDITED BY THE PUBLISHER.

KENDAL:
PUBLISHED BY J. HUDSON.
London:
LONGMAN AND CO., AND WHITTAKER AND CO.
LIVERPOOL; WEBB, CASTLE ST.—MANCHESTER; SIMMS AND CO.

1843.

122.2 180 x 110 mm.

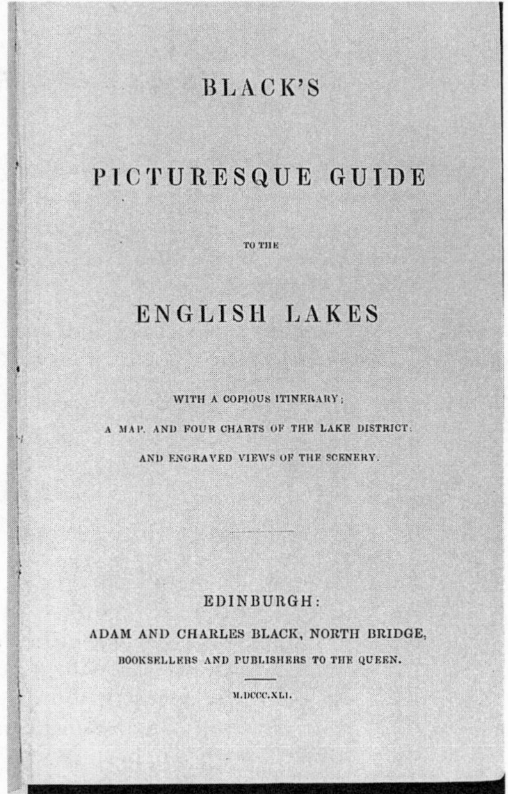

BLACK'S
PICTURESQUE GUIDE
TO THE
ENGLISH LAKES

WITH A COPIOUS ITINERARY;
A MAP, AND FOUR CHARTS OF THE LAKE DISTRICT;
AND ENGRAVED VIEWS OF THE SCENERY.

EDINBURGH:
ADAM AND CHARLES BLACK, NORTH BRIDGE,
BOOKSELLERS AND PUBLISHERS TO THE QUEEN.
M.DCCC.XLI.

123.1 165 x 105 mm.

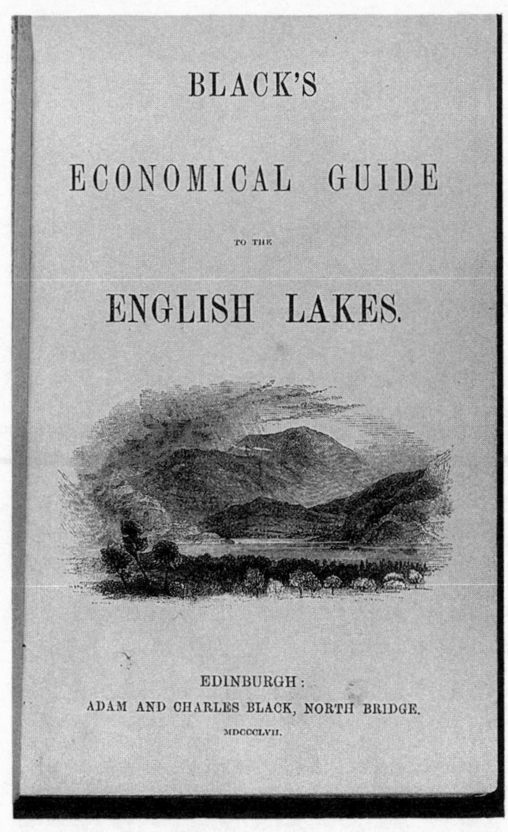

BLACK'S
ECONOMICAL GUIDE
TO THE
ENGLISH LAKES.

EDINBURGH:
ADAM AND CHARLES BLACK, NORTH BRIDGE.
MDCCCLVII.

124.2 170 x 110 mm.

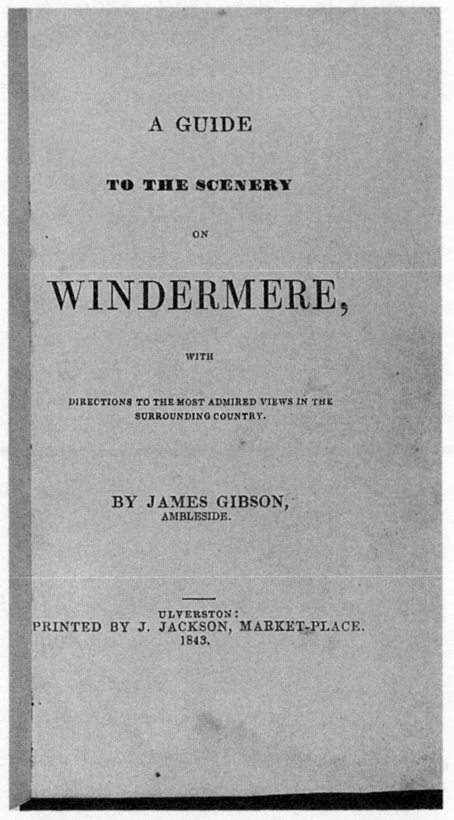

A GUIDE
TO THE SCENERY
ON
WINDERMERE,
WITH
DIRECTIONS TO THE MOST ADMIRED VIEWS IN THE SURROUNDING COUNTRY.

BY JAMES GIBSON,
AMBLESIDE.

ULVERSTON:
PRINTED BY J. JACKSON, MARKET-PLACE.
1843.

133 160 x 100 mm.

Two woodcuts
1 Rydal Lake. Signed, *G.F. Sargent delt. E. Evans sc.*
2 Buttermere. Signed, *Mont. Stanley del. E. Evans sc.*

Three cuts in text

Maps: Four maps, ('charts') *Drawn by Sidney Hall. Engd. by J. Bartholomew, Edinr.*
1 Derwentwater & Bassenthwaite
2 Buttermere, Crummock and Loweswater
3 Ulleswater
4 Winandermere

Folding map: The Lake District of Cumberland, Westmorland & Lancashire. *Engraved by S. Hall, Bury Strt., Bloomsbury.* Size: 162 × 195 mm. Scale: 1 in. = 1 mile.

King's copy: In publisher's dark green cloth, gilt letters on upper cover. Price 5*s*.

Copies: K; BL

123.2-21 ——— Other editions:

2nd	1844	K; Wordsworth;
3rd	1845	BL; Armitt (1846); K (1849); Barrow-in-Furness;
4th	1850	Jackson; Barrow-in-Furness
5th	1850	K; Armitt; Cornell; Jackson (1851); Wordsworth
6th	1853	K; BL; Kendal; Wordsworth; Barrow-in-Furness (1854)
7th	1856	Jackson; Barrow-in-Furness
8th	1857	Cornell
[9th]	1858	K; Armitt; BL
10th	1859	Jackson
11th	1861	Armitt
12th	1863	Barrow-in-Furness
13th	1865	Jackson
14th	1866	BL; Jackson
15th	1868	Barrow-in-Furness
16th	1870	Kendal
17th	1870	BL; Alpine Club; Boston Public Library (1873)
18th	1874	Jackson; Kendal
19th	1877	Barrow-in-Furness (1879)
20th	1881	University of Virginia; BL (1882); Kendal; University of Yale (1886)
21st	1886	Abbot Hall, Kendal (1888)

and later editions

All editions imprint: *Edinburgh: Black*, with engravings and maps. Quarto.

Black's Guide was constantly amended and augmented from edition to edition. An essay on 'The geology of the district, by John Phillips F.R.S., G.L., Professor of Geology in King's, London', and 12 outline views of Mountain Groups (2 views to a page) were added in the 2nd edition, in 1844. In 1853 an additional map of the Lancaster and Carlisle Railway: and in 1857 25 woodcuts, engraved by Edmund Evans from drawings by Birket Foster, were added (also published separately, see 125). The [9th] 1858, edition, was larger in format and contained 66 more pages of letterpress than the first edition.

124.1 ***Black's guide to the English Lakes. With map, charts, and illustrations.*** Edinburgh: Adam and Charles Black, North Bridge. 1856. Octavo.

Text: Title, verso blank; Index [iii], iv; Abstract of tours 1 p., verso blank; Text [3]-75; Synoptical views 3 pp.; Black's guide book advertiser [1]-64

Plates: 2 woodcuts of Rydal and Buttermere, as *Black's picturesque guide.* 1841 (123.1)

Maps: 2 (only) engraved maps, 2 and 4, and folding map of The Lake District, as 1841, except imprint, *Printed by Schenck Edinr. Edinburgh, published by A. & C. Black*, added to folding map.

Note: This is an abbreviated version of *Black's picturesque guide*. The Itineraries are the same as those in the 6th, 1853, edition, except Itinerary XII, London to Lancaster and Carlisle, by Railway, has been added. Geology of the Lakes and Memoranda for botanists are not included. It was usually issued with 6 or more pages of 'Black's guidebook advertiser'.

King's copies: There are two copies of this edition in the King's collection. Both are bound in green cloth with gilt letters and decoration on the upper cover and spine. But the stamped pattern differs. One is in limp boards and the other in stiff boards with a binder's label on the paste-down endpaper, *Bound by John Gray, Edinburgh*. Additional advertisements on the endpapers differ. The 7th edition of *Black's picturesque guide* is advertised in both.

Copies: K; Armitt; Jackson; Kendal

124.2 ——— *Black's economical guide to the English Lakes* Engraved vignette. 1857†

Note: This is a reissue of the previous item. Main text not reset. List of Best Hotels added.

King's copy: In green cloth similar to 124.1

Copies: K; Cornell; Wordsworth

124.3-18 ——— Other editions:

1866 and 1868 both Jackson
No edition specified on title editions of 1871, 1872, 1873 in National Union Catalogue
13th 1876
14th no information
15th Barrow-in-Furness 1876; University of Yale 1880
16th, 17th no information
18th Kendal 1878

All editions imprint *Edinburgh: Black*. Octavo.

124.21 ——— *Black's shilling guide to the English Lake District*. 21st edition. 1897

Copy: Kendal

124.22-23 ——— Other editions:

22nd 1897, 1899; 23rd 1900, and later.

MYLES BIRKET FOSTER 1825-1899 (artist)

Myles Birket Foster, R.W.S., was born in North Shields, where his parents were friends of Thomas Bewick. He was apprenticed to the wood-engraver, Peter Landells. Birket Foster produced an enormous number of wood-blocks for books and periodicals. In about 1859 he began to concentrate on watercolour painting.

125 ***Views of the English Lakes.*** Edinburgh: Adam and Charles Black, North Bridge. n.d. [*c* 1857]. Small oblong folio.†

Plates: 25 woodcuts, signed *B. Foster E. Evans*[engraver]:
Vignette on title page
1 Derwentwater from Friar's Crag
2 Bowness
3 Windermere from the Ferry
4 Windermere from near Bowness
5 At Low-wood Hotel
6 The Ferry Hotel, Windermere
7 Mills at Ambleside
8 Rydal Lake
9 Lower Fall Rydal
10 Rydal Mount
11 Grasmere
12 The Langdales
13 Lake Coniston
14 Furness Abbey
15 Greta Bridge, Keswick
16 Friars Crag, Keswick
17 Lowdore Waterfall
18 Honister Crag
19 Yew trees, Borrowdale
20 Buttermere
21 Skiddaw
22 Ullswater
23 Airey Force
24 Patterdale Church
25 Kirkstone Pass

These are the illustrations used in *Black's picturesque guide* in 1857 and later editions, and advertised in 'Black's guide book advertiser'.

King's copy: In publisher's stamped yellow cloth

Copies: K; Cornell

1842

FRANCIS EDWARDS (of Ulverston)

126 ***Furness and Furness Abbey: or a companion through the Lancashire part of the Lake District***. Ulverston: Atkinson; London: Whittaker. 1842. Octavo.

Copies: Armitt; BL; Jackson; Wordsworth

JOHN and **FREDERICK HARWOOD** (publishers)

127 ***Views of the Lakes.*** London: J. and F. Harwood. 1842. Small oblong folio (title on cover)
No title; no text.

Plates: 25 steel engravings, Signed *London, J. & F. Harwood, 26 Fenchurch Street.* Number and date: (details from a King's copy).
1 Esthwaite Water and Village of Sorey, Westmoreland. *No. 470* [No date]
2 Windermere Lake, Westmoreland. [No number] June 10. 1842
3 Saddleback from the Vale of St. John *No. 471 Augt. 18, 1842.*
4 Ambleside, Westmoreland *No. 433 Augt. 27, 1842.*
5 Windermere from Bowness [No number] *July 11, 1842.*
6 Great Rydal Lake, Westmoreland [No number] *Sept. 16th. 1842.*
7 Bowder Stone, Borrowdale [No number] *Sept. 27, 1842.*
8 Derwentwater & Keswick from Skiddaw *London J. & F. Harwood.* [No number or date]
9 Dunmail Raise, Cumberland [No number or date]
10 Loweswater and Buttermere [actually Crummock and Buttermere] [No number]*August 17 1842.*
11 Ulleswater, Cumberland [No number] *Sepr. 15, 1842*
12 Lodore, Cumberland [No number] *Sepr. 27, 1842.*

Notes: These steel engravings were produced by the Harwoods in large numbers for many years.

In the 'Handbook to the English Lakes Advertiser' in *Black's Guide*, 1853, the following advertisement is included:

Harwood's Splendid Views in the Lake District. [titles of 26 views]. Prices, per Quire, on Cream Letter Paper, 3s. 6d each. The same may be had Coloured after the Original Drawings, and mounted on Crayon Boards, at 1s. each.

Sold by Atkinson, Hudson, Dawson, Branthwaite, and Hargreaves, Kendal; Garnett, Post Office, Windermere; Allen, Stringer, Atkinson, and Belcher, Bowness; Nicholson and Troughton, Ambleside; Ivison, Keswick; and all respectable Stationers and Booksellers.

Harwood's Views of the Lake District may also be had in Books, very neatly done up in Illuminated Covers.

Books, with Six Views, price 1*s.*
Ditto, with Nine, 1*s.* 6*d.*
Ditto, with Twelve, 2*s.*
Ditto, with Fifteen, 2*s.* 6*d.*
Ditto, with Eighteen, 3*s.*
Ditto, with Twenty-one, 3*s.* 6*d.*
Ditto, with Twenty-four, 4*s.*
Ditto, with Twenty-seven, 4*s.* 6*d.*
Ditto, with Thirty, 5*s.*

Illustrated Sketch Books, Plain and Metallic
Memorandums, &c.
John Harwood, Fenchurch Street, London.

The list of booksellers, several of whom appear in the imprints on the title-pages of Lake District books as publishers, is an interesting record of where the books were sold.

King's copies: As issued in decorated papers boards, title on yellow printed label, *Views of the Lakes*, mounted on cover. Also two sets of 30 prints 'neatly done up in Illuminated Covers'. Publisher's cloth (one red, one blue), gilt title, *Harwood's Illustrations of the Lakes*, and decorated surround, stamped and gilt. One copy: latest dated print, Low Wood Hotel Windermere; signed, *John Harwood, 26 Fenchurch St. London. Decr. 6th. 1852 No. 809.* Other copy: latest dated print, Array Force, Gowbarrow Park. Near Ullswater; signed, *London J. Harwood, 26 Fenchurch Street. No. 772 1849.* 27 plates signed, *John Harwood* [or similar]. Other 3 plates: A Glimpse through the Trees, Rydal Water, near the Residence of the late W. Wordsworth Esqr. Signed *W.P. George. No. 804. London J. Harwood, 26, Fenchurch St.*; Greta Hall and Keswick Bridge, *Drawn by W. Westall, A.R.A. Engraved by Edwd. Finden. No. 326* [no date].

1843

DARTON and **CLARK** (publishers)

128 ***The pocket guide to the English Lakes: being a companion to Darton and Clark's map of the Lake District***. London: Darton and Clark, Holborn Hill. 1843 (on upper cover) Duodecimo.

Copies: Jackson; and Alpine Club

129 ***The circuit of Lakes in Cumberland, Westmoreland and Lancashire***. [A map] London: Darton and Clark, Holborn Hill. 1843.

Copies: Jackson; and Alpine Club

Note: The Guide and the Map were sold together neatly bound in cloth boards for the pocket

SKETCH

OF

FURNESS AND CARTMEL,

COMPRISING THE HUNDRED OF

LONSDALE NORTH OF THE SANDS.

BY

CHARLES M. JOPLING.

LONDON, WHITTAKER & Co., AVE-MARIA LANE:
ULVERSTON, STEPHEN SOULBY,
MDCCCXLIII.

131 167 x 107 mm.

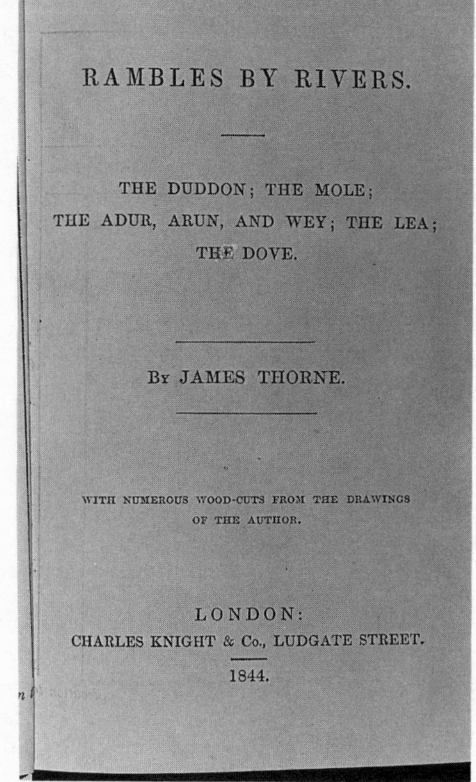

RAMBLES BY RIVERS.

THE DUDDON; THE MOLE;
THE ADUR, ARUN, AND WEY; THE LEA;
THE DOVE.

By JAMES THORNE.

WITH NUMEROUS WOOD-CUTS FROM THE DRAWINGS
OF THE AUTHOR.

LONDON:
CHARLES KNIGHT & Co., LUDGATE STREET.
1844.

134 150 x 92 mm.

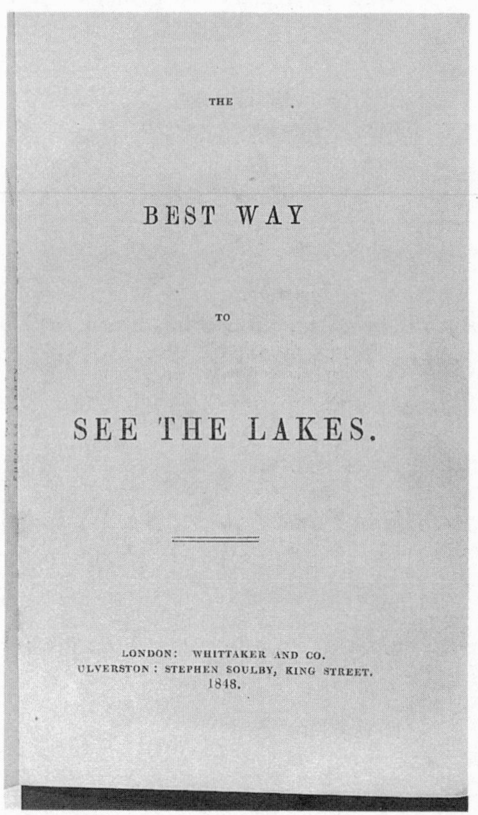

THE

BEST WAY

TO

SEE THE LAKES.

LONDON: WHITTAKER AND CO.
ULVERSTON: STEPHEN SOULBY, KING STREET.
1848.

132.1 175 x 114 mm.

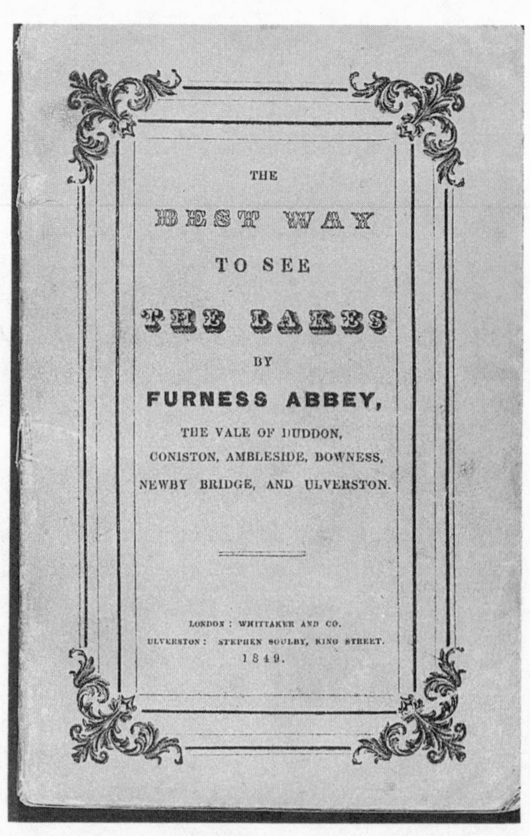

THE
BEST WAY
TO SEE
THE LAKES
BY
FURNESS ABBEY,
THE VALE OF DUDDON,
CONISTON, AMBLESIDE, BOWNESS,
NEWBY BRIDGE, AND ULVERSTON.

LONDON: WHITTAKER AND CO.
ULVERSTON: STEPHEN SOULBY, KING STREET.
1849.

132.1 175 x 114 mm.

J. and C. WALKER (publishers and mapmakers)

130 ***Cumberland*** By J. & C. Walker

Folding map, dissected, mounted on linen and coloured. Size: 418 × 340 mm. Scale: approx. 1 in = 5 miles. Imprint: *Published by Longman, Rees, Orme, Brown & Co. Paternoster Row, London. 1843*

Mounted inside cover, title, *Walker's County Maps*, and tables of population, distances, etc

King's copy: In brown cloth binder, with blue printed paper label on upper cover, *Walker's Cumberland*. Price 2.6. Paper label on spine, *Cumberland*

'This County possesses some of the most picturesque and beautiful scenery in the kingdom'

CHARLES M. JOPLING

131 ***Sketch of Furness and Cartmel, comprising the hundred of Lonsdale north of the Sands***. London: Whittaker & Co., Ave-Maria Lane; Ulverston: Stephen Soulby. 1843. Octavo.†

Text: Title, imprint on verso *Ulverston; Printed by Stephen Soulby, King Street;* Preface (Furness Abbey, May 1843) [v], vi; Contents [vii], viii; Text [1]-256; Appendix [257]-272; Index & Postscript [273]-275, imprint repeated on verso p. 275

Plates: (King's copy) 5 steel engravings, 7 woodcuts
1 North East View of Furness Abbey (frontispiece)
2 Ambleside, Westmorland. *London: J. & F. Harwood, 26 Fenchurch Street.* No. 433 Augt. 27 1842
3 Bowness Church
4 Bowness (engraving imprint cut)
5 Ulverston Church
6 Windermere (engraving imprint cut)
7 Conistone Water. *London J. Harwood, 26 Fenchurch Street.* No. 598 Sep. 4 1845
8 Derwent Water. Imprint as 2. No. 470. no date
9 The Guests' Chapel, Furness Abbey
10 South and East Fronts of Conishead Priory
11 Pele Castle
12 Holker Hall

Woodcuts in the text

Maps: 1 Folding coloured Map of Furness and Cartmel. *Maclure Macdonald and Macgregor, Lithographers Liverpool*
2 Folding coloured A Geographical Map of Furness and Cartmel. Imprint as 1.

King's copy: In half red morocco, marbled boards. Plate 7 in this copy is dated Sep 4 1845 (publication date of the book 1843). It is probable that it was not issued with the five Harwood engravings, nos. 2, 4, 6, 7, 8, and that they were added when the copy was bound.

Copies: K; BL; Wordsworth

132.1 ***The best way to see the Lakes***. London: Whittaker and Co.; Ulverston: Stephen Soulby, King Street. 1848. Duodecimo.†

Text: Title, verso publisher's note and imprint, *S. Soulby; Printer, King Street, Ulverston;* Text [3]-64

Plates 1 engraving, 8 woodcuts, nine cuts and a plan of Furness Abbey in the text
1 Furness Abbey. Signed *Morrison Brown Pinxt. Ackermann & Co. Exect.*
2 The North Front, Conishead Priory

3, 4, 5, 6, 7, 8, same as plates 11, 1, 9, 3, 5, 10, previous item (131).

Map: Map of the Lake District, coloured, 1848

Note: 'This little book is principally a selection from the *Sketch of Furness and Cartmel* [no. 131], published a short time ago by Mr. Soulby.'

King's copy: In original printed grey paper boards, lettered, 'The best way to see the Lakes by Furness Abbey, the Vale of Duddon, Coniston, Ambleside, Newby Bridge, and Ulverston.' 1849† (not 1848 as title)

Copies: K; Armitt; Jackson

132.2 ——— [Second edition] *Furness Abbey and the best way to see the Lakes.* 1853

King's copy: In original printed green paper boards. Ornamental borders differ from no. 132.1. Adverts. on lower cover.

Copies: K; Cornell

These guides published by Soulby of Ulverston are typical of the many inexpensive volumes which were being published locally to meet the growing demand from the tourists. Atkinson of Kendal, Garnett of Windermere, Thurnam of Carlisle, and Jackson of Ulverston were some of those busily engaged in this field.

JAMES GIBSON (of Ambleside)

See 146.3

133 ***A guide to the scenery on Windermere, with directions to the most admired views in the surrounding country***. Ulverston: printed by J. Jackson, Market-Place. 1843. Quarto.†

Text: Title, verso blank; Title repeated, verso blank; Text [3]-43; Sonnet [44]; imprint, *J. Jackson, printer, Market Place, Ulverston*

Note: Sonnet on p. 44, 'The Laker and the resident. A sonnet by H. Coleridge Esq. Written for this book.'

King's copy: Rebound, green cloth. Inscribed on free endpaper 'Walmesley, Prospect Cottage'

Copies: K; BL

1844

JAMES THORNE 1815-1881

James Thorne contributed articles on antiquarian and topographical subjects to various periodicals.

134 ***Rambles by rivers*** . . . London: Charles Knight & Co., Ludgate Street. 1844. Duodecimo.†

The Duddon only Lake District river.

Text: Title, imprint on verso, *London: Printed by Clowes and Sons, Stamford Street;* Contents vii, verso blank; Text [9]-244. Imprint repeated on p. 244.
Section on The Duddon pp. [9]-37

Plates: 'Numerous wood-cuts from the drawings of the author'
Lake District views: Cuts in the text:
[The source of the Duddon]
[Cockley Brig]
[The Stepping-Stones]
[Seathwaite Chapel]
[On the Duddon at Seathwaite]
[Duddon Sands]

King's copy: In publisher's cloth, stamped 'Knight's Weekly Volume for all Readers'. Includes 8 pp. 'Book-Clubs for all readers' and circulation form. Label on paste-down endpaper 'Appletreewick and Skyholme Sunday School [in Wharfdale]', inscribed 'no. 35 2 weeks reading'.

Copies: K; Armitt

1845

JOHN HENRY MICHELL 1760-1844

The Revd J.H. Michell, educated at Eton and King's College, Cambridge, held several livings in East Anglia.

135 ***The tour of the Duke of Somerset, and the Rev. J.H. Michell, through parts of England, Wales, and Scotland, in the year 1795***. London: printed by R. Clay, Bread Street Hill. 1845. Octavo.†

Text: Title, verso blank; Preface [iii], iv; Contents [v]-viii; Text [1]-221; blank; Table of distances [228]-227, imprint on verso of p. 227, *London: R. Clay, Printer, Bread Street Hill*

Notes: The author's companion was Edward Adolphus Seymour (afterwards St Maur) 11th Duke of Somerset (1775-1853).
'The narration was composed for the private use of the writer who occasionally referred to it with much pleasure, and finally bequeathed it to his travelling companion. He now commits it to the press [fifty years after the tour] that it may be perused by those friends who have some recollection of the persons, or of the scenes which it describes' (Preface). 'In the course of the journey the Duke availed himself of his talent for drawing in sketching several views' [p.221].

Lakes: Chapters 3 and 4

Itinerary: Tour of the Lakes 25 June to 3 July 1795. Kendal, Windermere, Coniston, Rydal, Grasmere, Thirlmere, Derwentwater, Loweswater, Crummock, Buttermere, Ullswater, ascended Skiddaw

King's copy: In contemporary dark brown morocco, gilt. Bookplate, Abel E Shaw Stewart.

Copies: K; BL

JOHN JACKSON (publisher)

136 ***The tourist's manual: or pocket guide to the Lakes of Lancashire, Westmorland, & Cumberland.*** ['Jackson's Guide'] Ulverston: published by John Jackson. London: Whittaker & Co., Ave Maria Lane. 1845. Small quarto. Engravings, map, plan.

Copy: Barrow-in-Furness

137.2 ***A complete and descriptive guide to the Lakes . . .*** Ulverston: published by John Jackson. London: Whittaker & Co. 1847 Quarto. Second edition of 136.†

Text: Title, verso blank; Preface 1 p.; Routes and Excursions 2 pp.; blank; Text [1]-88; Table 89. Imprint on verso p. 89 *Ulverston: printed by J. Jackson, Market-Place*

Plates: 4 engravings. 1 and 3 signed: *Nicholls Sc.* 2 and 4 unsigned.
1 Windermere (frontispiece)
2 The Castle or Pile of Foundrey. From the Sea.
3 Pile pier, Rampside, with Barrow in the distance. From the Sea.
4 Furness Abbey

Whole-page ground plan of Furness Abbey on p. 19

Map: Folding map of the Lakes. Signed: *Drawn & Engd. by W. Izars, Edinr.* Imprint: *Published by J. Jackson, Bookseller, Ulverston.* Size 390 × 280 mm. Scale approx. 1 in. = 5 miles.

King's copy: In green printed paper boards, rebacked. Upper cover as title with vignette view added, signed: *Nichols Sc.*

Copies: K; Armitt; BL

For third edition see 146.3

1846

CHARLES MACKAY 1814-1889

138.1 ***The scenery and poetry of the English Lakes. A summer ramble.*** With illustrations from original sketches; drawn on wood by W. Harvey, J. Gilbert, D.H. M'Kewan, D. Cox, Jun., W.C. Smith, G. Fennel, W. Dickes, W.P. Smith, and E. Gilks, engraved by Thomas Gilks. London: Longman, Brown, Green, and Longmans, Paternoster Row. 1846. Octavo.†

Text: Half-title (woodcut), verso blank; Title, printer's device on verso, *London S. & I. Bentley. Wilson & Fley, Printers;* Preface [iii], iv; Contents [v]-vii; blank; List of illustrations [ix]-xi, blank; Table of Distances [xiii]-xvi; Text 1-229; Tables 231-234, device and imprint similar to verso of title; advert. 4 pp.

Plates: 10 wood engravings. Signed (various) *Del. T. Gilks. Sculp*
1 Scale Force *D.H. M'Kewan* (on buff ground)
2 (Half-title) *W. Harvey.* View of Windermere and portraits of Wordsworth, Southey and Coleridge (on buff ground)
3 Coniston, Old Man *D. Cox, Jun.*
4 Colwith Force *W. Dickes*
5 Ullswater from Gowbarrow Park *D.H. M'Kewan*
6 Airey Force *D.H.M'Kewan*
7 Furness Abbey *E. Gilks*
8 Lodore Fall *E. Gilks*
9 Stanley Gill Eskdale *D.H. M'Kewan*
10 Returning from a successful Border Incursion *J. Gilbert*

52 cuts, illustrative headings and initials in the text, drawn in wood by the artists noted above. All engraved by Thomas Gilks.

King's copy: In dark green stamped cloth.

Copies: K; Armitt; BL; Cornell; Jackson; Kendal; Wordsworth

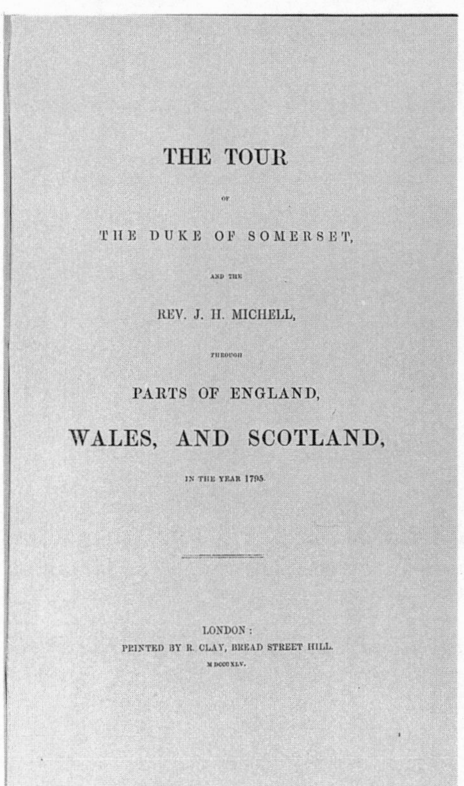

THE TOUR

OF

THE DUKE OF SOMERSET,

AND THE

REV. J. H. MICHELL,

THROUGH

PARTS OF ENGLAND,

WALES, AND SCOTLAND,

IN THE YEAR 1795.

LONDON:
PRINTED BY R. CLAY, BREAD STREET HILL.
M DCCC XLV.

135 240 x 150 mm.

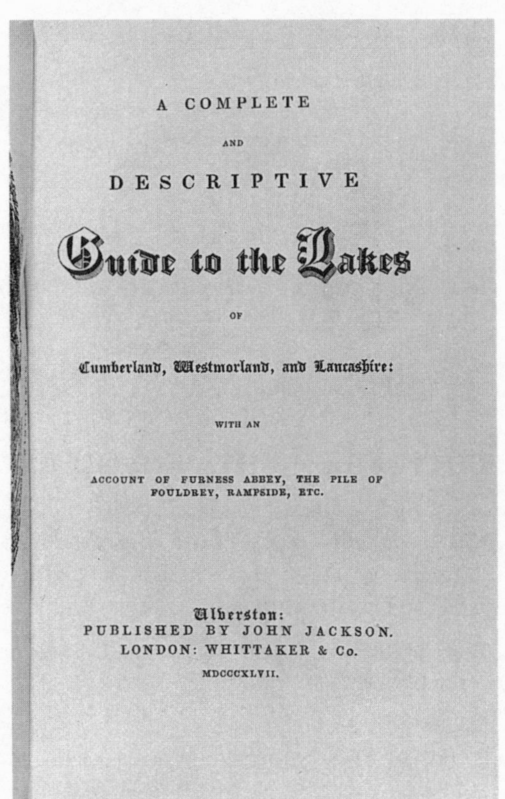

A COMPLETE

AND

DESCRIPTIVE

Guide to the Lakes

OF

Cumberland, Westmorland, and Lancashire:

WITH AN

ACCOUNT OF FURNESS ABBEY, THE PILE OF FOULDREY, RAMPSIDE, ETC.

Ulverston:
PUBLISHED BY JOHN JACKSON.
LONDON: WHITTAKER & Co.
MDCCCXLVII.

137.2 166 x 108 mm.

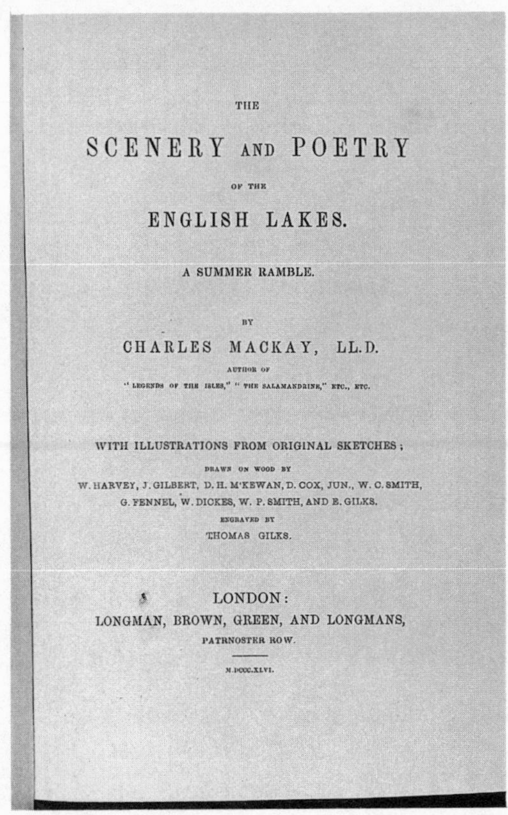

THE

SCENERY AND POETRY

OF THE

ENGLISH LAKES.

A SUMMER RAMBLE.

BY

CHARLES MACKAY, LL.D.

AUTHOR OF
"LEGENDS OF THE ISLES," "THE SALAMANDRINE," ETC., ETC.

WITH ILLUSTRATIONS FROM ORIGINAL SKETCHES;
DRAWN ON WOOD BY
W. HARVEY, J. GILBERT, D. H. M'KEWAN, D. COX, JUN., W. C. SMITH,
G. FENNEL, W. DICKES, W. P. SMITH, AND E. GILKS.
ENGRAVED BY
THOMAS GILKS.

LONDON:
LONGMAN, BROWN, GREEN, AND LONGMANS,
PATERNOSTER ROW.

M.DCCC.XLVI.

138.1 196 x 127 mm.

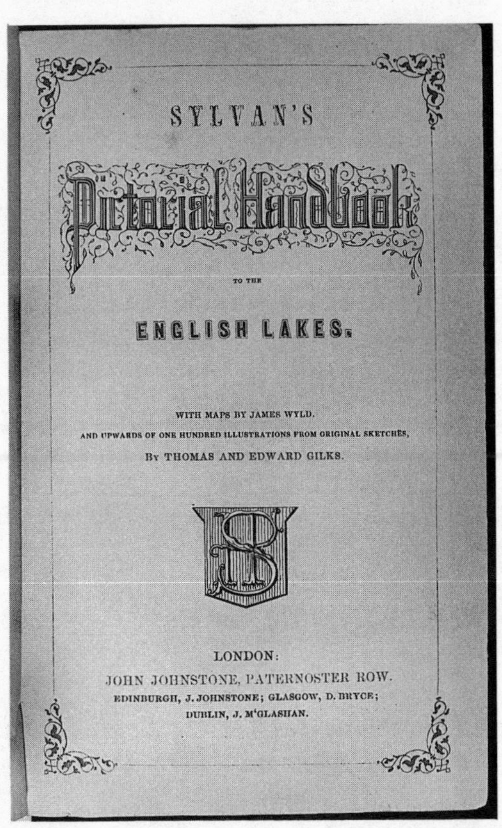

SYLVAN'S

Pictorial Handbook

TO THE

ENGLISH LAKES.

WITH MAPS BY JAMES WYLD.
AND UPWARDS OF ONE HUNDRED ILLUSTRATIONS FROM ORIGINAL SKETCHES,
By THOMAS AND EDWARD GILKS.

LONDON:
JOHN JOHNSTONE, PATERNOSTER ROW.
EDINBURGH, J. JOHNSTONE; GLASGOW, D. BRYCE;
DUBLIN, J. M'GLASHAN.

139.1 166 x 103 mm.

138.2 ——— Second edition, 1852

Title as 1846 except:

'With numerous illustrations from original sketches' replaces 'with illustrations from original sketches etc.'
'Second edition' is added
'1852' replaces '1846'

Copies: BL; Jackson; Kendal

Note: The plates and the cuts are similar to those in *Sylvan's pictorial handbook* (139).

1847

THOMAS and EDWARD GILKS (artists)

139.1 ***Sylvan's pictorial handbook to the English Lakes.*** London: John Johnstone, Paternoster Row. Edinburgh, J. Johnstone; Glasgow, D. Bryce; Dublin, J. M'Glashan. [1847]. Duodecimo.†

Text: Half-title, imprint on verso *London: printed by John Wertheimer and Co., Finsbury Circus*; Title, verso blank; Contents 2 pp.; Text [1]-[242]; Tables 243, 244; Index [245]-248; 28 pp., adverts.

Plates: 9 wood engravings:
1 Barrow Fall, Signed *T. Gilks* (on buff ground)
2-9 as 4, 3, 7, 9, 8, 1, 5, 6 in Mackay's *Scenery and Poetry*, 138.
118 cuts in text similar to 138.

Maps: 4 engraved maps by James Wyld. Scale approx. 1 in = 3½ (miles).

Folding, A Map of the English Lake District, engraved expressly for *Sylvan's Pictorial Handbook* by James Wyld. Size: 540 × 400 mm. Scale: 1 in. = 3 miles.

King's copy: In publisher's maroon stamped cloth

Notes: Sylvan's Pictorial Handbooks were a series of guides to such places as the Clyde, Loch Lomond, Arran and the Caledonian Canal. The title emphasises the importance which was placed on illustration. Mackay's *Scenery and Poetry* with its similar illustrations was advertised in *Sylvan's Pictorial Handbook.*

Copies: K; Armitt; BL; Jackson; Kendal; Wordsworth

——— Facsimile edition. Evans and Long Associates, Dewsbury, Yorks. (1974)

139.2 ——— Second edition. Liverpool: Geo. Phillips. 1847

Copy: Jackson

Note: Hodgson, p. 273, records '2nd ed. 1852. front., illus., maps. Liverpool, Philip.'

T. ATKINSON (publisher and printer)

140.1 ***Hand-book to the English Lakes.*** Kendal: published by T. Atkinson. London: Hamilton, Adams, and Co. 1847. Octavo.†

Text: Title, verso blank; Preface [iii], iv; Text [1]-60. Imprint on p.60 *Kendal: printed by T. Atkinson Stricklandgate.*

Plates: 6 woodcuts:

1 The Hotel at Birthwaite
2 Viaduct on the Kendal and Windermere Railway
3 Wray Castle
4 Coniston Hall
5 Rydal Mount
6 View of Keswick

Woodcuts in the text

Map: Folding map of the Lake District. Signed: *Thomas Hill delt. W.H. Lizars Sculpt.* Imprint: *Published by Thos. Atkinson. Kendal.* Size 300 × 187.5 mm. Scale: 1 in. = 4 miles.

King's copy: In printed green paper boards, with title and decorative border on upper cover, price one shilling.

Note: 'The recent construction of railways to the lake district has afforded great facilities to the tourist'. The Windermere railway was opened in 1847. The *Hand-book*, published in the same year, includes a print (no. 2) of a viaduct on the railway, and the map shows the Kendal-Windermere and the Furness-Kirkby-Irelith railways.

Copies: K; Armitt; BL; Jackson; Kendal; Wordsworth

140.2 ——— Second edition, 1847 – No plates. Frontispiece and 5 woodcuts in the text are from the same blocks as the plates in the first edition.

King's copy: In dark green publisher's cloth, lettered in gilt on upper cover. Price 1*s*.6*d*. Map coloured.

Note: 'The rapid and extensive sale of the first impression of this Hand Book has enabled the Publisher to produce, in a few weeks from its first appearance, a Second Edition, with considerable alterations and amendments' (Preface, p.iv).

Copies: K; Armitt

140.3-8 ——— Other editions:

'four thousand' Kendal (1849)
3rd, 4th no information
5th 1850 Armitt
6th 1851 Barrow
7th 1852 Jackson; Kendal
8th 1853 Jackson; Wordsworth; Jackson (1856); Jackson (1857)

All editions imprint except 8th: *Kendal: Atkinson. London: Hamilton Adams and Co.* Octavo. 8th edition imprint: *Kendal: published by T. Atkinson; London: Longmans & Co.; Hamilton & Co., Menzies, Edinburgh.*

1848

GEORGE BRADSHAW 1801-1853 (publisher)

George Bradshaw was the originator of railway guides. He first produced *Railway Time Tables* in 1839; this developed into *Bradshaw's Monthly Railway Guide* in 1841.

141 ***The Lakes . . . with a map of the Lakes' District, time tables of the railways, steamers, and coaches, and list of excursions that may be made in one week . . .*** Bradshaw and Blacklock, printers, Brown Street, Manchester, and Fleet Street, London. 1848. Pamphlet†

Text: Title, verso blank; Text [3]-7; List of hotels [8]

Map: Folding map of the Lake District. 1848. Size: 153 × 115 mm. Scale: approx. 1 in. = 6½ miles

Note: The map shows the Furness Railway from Peel Harbour to Broughton; and the Kendal and Windermere Railway (opened 1847). Steamers connected Liverpool, Fleetwood and Southport with Peel pier. The *Helvellyn* plied from Fleetwood to Peel in 1½ hours, and Herr Schmidt and his band performed on board. Coaches connected Broughton with Ambleside, and Furness with Newby Bridge. The Windermere steam yachts connected Newby Bridge with Bowness and Ambleside 'July, 1848 – For the Departures on this route after 1st August, see *Bradshaw's Guide*'.

King's copy: As issued in stiff brown paper covers, lettered 'The tourists' guide to the lakes.' No other copy seen or recorded.

HENRY TUDOR

Author of *Narrative of a tour in North America &c.*

142.1 ***Domestic memoirs of a Christian family resident in the County of Cumberland. With descriptive sketches of the scenery of the British Lakes.*** London: J. Hatchard and Son, Piccadilly; booksellers to the Royal Family. 1848. Octavo.†

Text: Title, imprint on verso, *printed by J.G. Palmer, Savoy Street, Strand:* Dedication 1 p., verso blank; Preface [v]-vii; Illustrations [viii]; Text 1-416.

Plates: 5 steel engravings from drawings by Allom, Pickering and Gastineau. These are the same as plates in Vol. 1, 13, 14, 26, 39; Vol. 2, 67, of Thomas Rose's *Westmorland, Cumberland* etc. (112).

Note: The book was written for the edification of children. 'Train up a child in the way he should go: and when he is old, he will not depart from it. Prov. [erbs] xxii. 6' [title-page]. The profits of the book were devoted to the cause, and in aid of the funds, of the Church Missionary Society.

King's copy: In publisher's stamped brown cloth

Copies: K; Armitt; BL; Cornell; Jackson

142.2 ——— Second edition, 1854

Copy: BL

1849

ALEXANDER CRAIG GIBSON 1813-1874

Alexander Craig Gibson, doctor and antiquary, was born at Harrington, Cumberland. He practised at Branthwaite and Ullock, Cumberland, moved to Coniston in 1843, to Hawkshead in 1849, and settled in Cheshire in 1857. He wrote *The folk speech of Cumberland* (Carlisle, 1869) and 'The geology of the Lake District' in Harriet Martineau's *Complete guide* (155). He contributed widely to antiquarian and medical periodicals.

HAND-BOOK

TO

THE ENGLISH LAKES.

WITH MAP AND ENGRAVINGS.

KENDAL:
PUBLISHED BY T. ATKINSON.
LONDON: HAMILTON, ADAMS, AND CO.

1847.

140.1 161 x 98 mm.

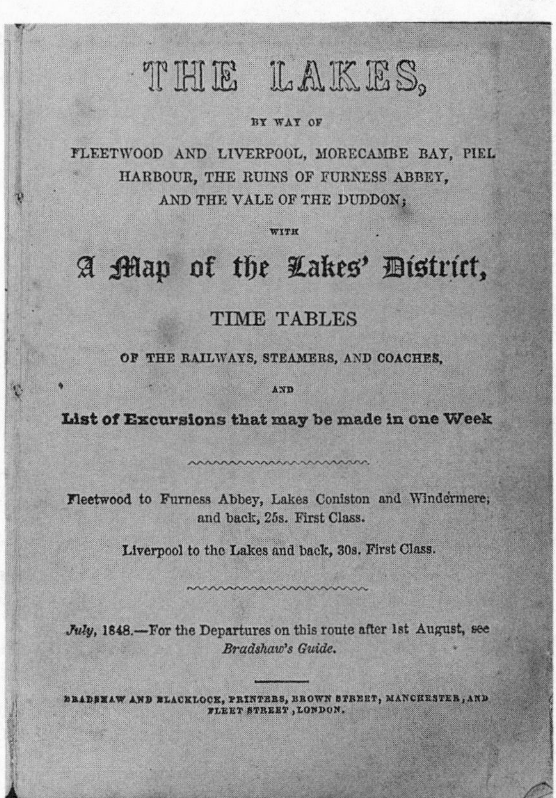

THE LAKES,

BY WAY OF

FLEETWOOD AND LIVERPOOL, MORECAMBE BAY, PIEL HARBOUR, THE RUINS OF FURNESS ABBEY, AND THE VALE OF THE DUDDON;

WITH

A Map of the Lakes' District,

TIME TABLES

OF THE RAILWAYS, STEAMERS, AND COACHES,

AND

List of Excursions that may be made in one Week

Fleetwood to Furness Abbey, Lakes Coniston and Windermere; and back, 25s. First Class.

Liverpool to the Lakes and back, 30s. First Class.

July, 1848.—For the Departures on this route after 1st August, see *Bradshaw's Guide.*

BRADSHAW AND BLACKLOCK, PRINTERS, BROWN STREET, MANCHESTER, AND FLEET STREET, LONDON.

141 119 x 82 mm.

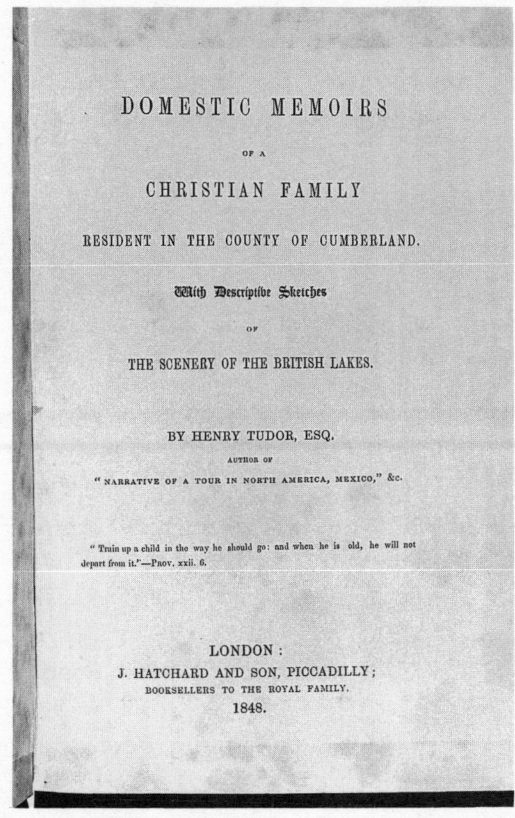

DOMESTIC MEMOIRS

OF A

CHRISTIAN FAMILY

RESIDENT IN THE COUNTY OF CUMBERLAND.

With Descriptive Sketches

OF

THE SCENERY OF THE BRITISH LAKES.

BY HENRY TUDOR, ESQ.

AUTHOR OF

"NARRATIVE OF A TOUR IN NORTH AMERICA, MEXICO," &c.

"Train up a child in the way he should go: and when he is old, he will not depart from it."—Prov. xxii. 6.

LONDON:
J. HATCHARD AND SON, PICCADILLY;
BOOKSELLERS TO THE ROYAL FAMILY.
1848.

142.1 220 x 142 mm.

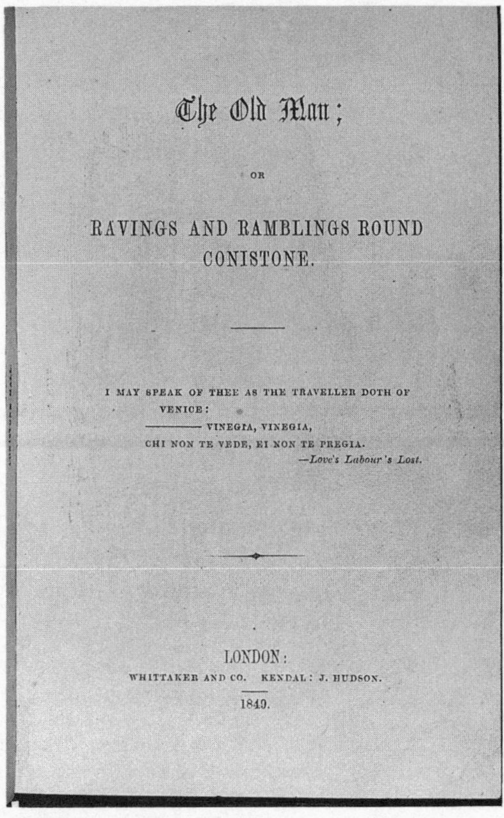

The Old Man;

OR

RAVINGS AND RAMBLINGS ROUND CONISTONE.

I MAY SPEAK OF THEE AS THE TRAVELLER DOTH OF VENICE:
——— VINEGIA, VINEGIA,
CHI NON TE VEDE, EI NON TE PREGIA.
—*Love's Labour's Lost.*

LONDON:
WHITTAKER AND CO. KENDAL: J. HUDSON.
1849.

143.1 158 x 102 mm.

143.1 ***The old man; or ravings and ramblings round Conistone.*** [Anonymous] London: Whittaker and Co. Kendal: J. Hudson. 1849. Quarto.†

Text: Title, verso blank; Index [iii]-vi; Note (signed A.C.G., Yewdale Bridge, May 21st, 1849), blank; Text [5]-146; Imprint, *George Lee, printer, Kendal* [147]: blank.

Plates: 8 woodcuts:
1 Conistone Hall
2 Source of Duddon
3 Cockley Brig
4 The stepping stones
5 Birks Bridge, River Duddon. *W. Gorway, Sc.*
6 Seathwaite Chapel
7 Gaits Water and Dhu Crags. *W. Gorway, Sc.*
8 Church Conistone. *W. Gy. Sc.*

King's copy: In publisher's stamped green cloth. Inscribed on free endpaper 'Josh. Marshall July 1849'.

Note: The old man, which had already been published in chapters in the *Kendal Mercury*, was written in response to a suggestion of 'Christopher North' made in a review of Green's *Guide*, that each locality in the Lake District should be separately described by one suitable author.

Copies: K; Armitt; BL; Cornell; Jackson; Kendal

143.1a ——— Reissue. Kendal: James Robinson, 1854

Copies: Armitt; Kendal

143.2 ——— Second edition. Revised by J. Garnett. Windermere: John Garnett and London. n.d. (1857 publisher's advert.)

Copies: BL; Jackson

143.3 ——— Third edition. Garnett's Series. Rewritten by the author Alexander Craig Gibson, FSA. Windermere: Garnett; London: Simpkin & Marshall. n.d. (1860).

Copy: Jackson

GEORGE MOGRIDGE 1787-1854

George Mogridge was a miscellaneous writer, responsible for nearly 200 tales, religious books for children, tracts and ballads, often under the pseudonym of 'Old Humphrey'.

144.1 ***Loiterings among the Lakes of Cumberland and Westmoreland. By the Author of "Wanderings in the Isle of Wight."*** London: The Religious Tract Society; instituted 1799. Sold at the Depository, 56, Paternoster Row, and 65, St. Paul's Churchyard; and by the booksellers. [*c.*] 1849† Octavo.

Text: Title, verso blank; Contents [iv], v; Introduction [vi], vii; blank; Text [1]-208; imprint, *Religious Tract Society: Instituted 1799.* p. 208

Plates: Frontispiece, coloured Baxter Print, Derwent Water Cumberland, imprint, *Baxters Patent Oil Printing, 11 Northampton Square.*

LOITERINGS

AMONG THE LAKES

OF

CUMBERLAND AND WESTMORELAND.

BY THE AUTHOR OF
"WANDERINGS IN THE ISLE OF WIGHT."

To loiter is to linger—So I stay
Where my Almighty Father's works abound;
His hand I trace while pausing on my way,
And find him near while gazing all around.

LONDON:
THE RELIGIOUS TRACT SOCIETY;
Instituted 1799.
SOLD AT THE DEPOSITORY, 56, PATERNOSTER ROW,
AND 65, ST. PAUL'S CHURCHYARD;
AND BY THE BOOKSELLERS.

144.1 133 x 105 mm.

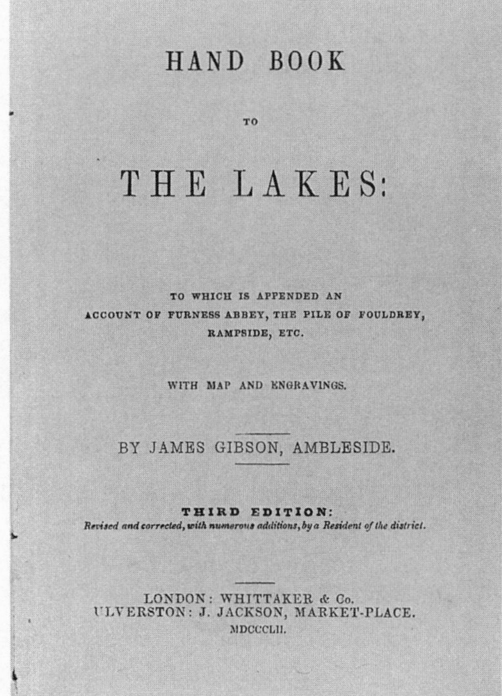

HAND BOOK

TO

THE LAKES:

TO WHICH IS APPENDED AN
ACCOUNT OF FURNESS ABBEY, THE PILE OF FOULDREY,
RAMPSIDE, ETC.

WITH MAP AND ENGRAVINGS.

BY JAMES GIBSON, AMBLESIDE.

THIRD EDITION:
Revised and corrected, with numerous additions, by a Resident of the district.

LONDON: WHITTAKER & Co.
ULVERSTON: J. JACKSON, MARKET-PLACE.
MDCCCLII.

146.3 164 x 102 mm.

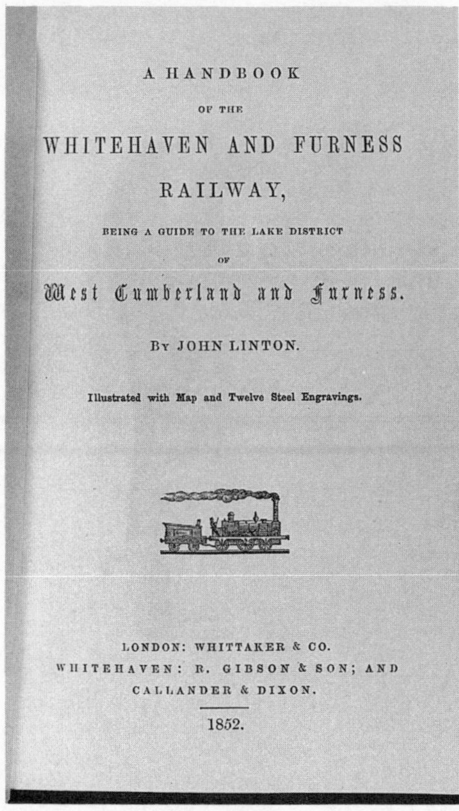

A HANDBOOK

OF THE

WHITEHAVEN AND FURNESS

RAILWAY,

BEING A GUIDE TO THE LAKE DISTRICT

OF

West Cumberland and Furness.

BY JOHN LINTON.

Illustrated with Map and Twelve Steel Engravings.

LONDON: WHITTAKER & CO.
WHITEHAVEN: R. GIBSON & SON; AND
CALLANDER & DIXON.

1852.

148 163 x 100 mm.

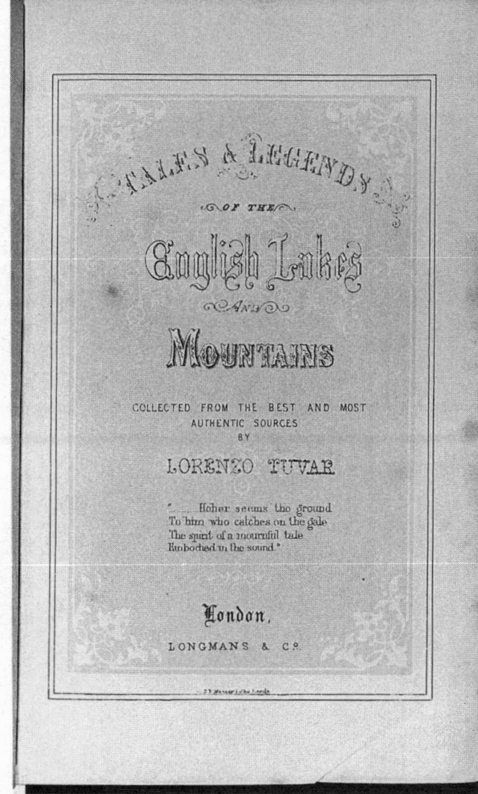

TALES & LEGENDS

OF THE

English Lakes

AND

MOUNTAINS

COLLECTED FROM THE BEST AND MOST
AUTHENTIC SOURCES
BY

LORENZO TUVAR

"......Holier seems the ground
To him who catches on the gale
The spirit of a mournful tale
Embodied in the sound."

London,

LONGMANS & C°

151.1 179 x 112 mm.

6 woodcuts, whole page in the text, versos blank

1 Windermere
2 Great Rydal Water
3 Buttermere Lake
4 Derwentwater
5 St. John's Vale
6 Ulleswater

Device. 'Finis', p. 208.

King's copy: In publisher's stamped grey cloth, gilt

Copies: K; Armitt; BL; Jackson; Wordsworth

144.2 ——— A new edition.

As first edition except:
Title: Set differently.
'A new edition' added.
Verse omitted.
Imprint altered: 'instituted 1799' omitted; 'and 164, Piccadilly' added after 'Churchyard'.

Text: As first edition except imprint on last page, London: *Printed by W. Clowes and Sons, Stamford Street;* 8 pp. advertisements.

Plates: Frontispiece similar to first edition, Baxter type print, signed *Kronheim & Co., London.* 6 woodcuts the same.

King's copy: In publisher's stamped maroon cloth, gilt.

Copies: K; Armitt

144.3 ——— Another 'New edition'. New title-page: 'By Old Humphrey' added. Text and plate as previous edition

Copies: Cornell; Kendal

1851

CHARLES GILPIN (publisher)

145 ***The ascent of Scawfell Pike; or a day in the mountains. By the author of "The Picts or Romano-British Wall".*** London: Charles Gilpin, 5, Bishopsgate Street. George Bell, 186, Fleet Street. Skeffington and Southwell, 192, Piccadilly. 1851.

Frontispiece, steel engraving of Scawfell Pike from Wast Water

Copies: Armitt; Jackson; and Barrow-in-Furness

1852

JAMES GIBSON (of Ambleside)

See 136, 'Jackson's Guide' and for Gibson, see 133

146.3 ***Hand book to the Lakes: to which is appended an account of Furness Abbey . . .*** Third edition [of 136, 137 'Jackson's Guide']. Revised and corrected, with numerous additions, by a Resident of the district. London: Whittaker & Co. Ulverston: J. Jackson, Market-Place. 1852. Small quarto.†

Text: Title, verso blank; Text [1]-93; imprint [94], *Ulverston: printed by J. Jackson, Market-Place*

Plates: 3 steel engravings:

Frontispiece, Windermere
1 Windermere (duplicate)
2 Peel Pier etc.

1 and 2 are the same as plates 1 and 3 in Jackson's *Complete . . . guide* (137)
2 woodcuts in text
Plan of Furness Abbey, p. [86]

Map: Folding map of the Lakes same as 137

King's copy: In printed green paper boards, vignette view on upper cover (same as 137). Price one shilling.

Copies: K; Armitt (1851)

146.4 ——— Fourth edition. Revised and corrected with numerous additions by a resident of the district. 1854.

Copy: Barrow-in-Furness

JOHN GARNETT (publisher)

Garnett of Windermere was in the 1850s and 1860s one of the most prolific purveyors of publications for the tourist.

147 ***Keswick and its neighbourhood: a hand-book for the use of visitors, to all the scenery, nooks, and corners of the district; with a unique map, shewing the carriage roads, usual sailing route round the lake, and the foot-paths open to the public.*** Windermere: Garnett. London: Whittaker and Co. 1852. Octavo.

Frontispiece, steel engraving of Derwent Water

Copies: Armitt; BL; Jackson

JOHN LINTON

148 ***A handbook of the Whitehaven and Furness Railway, being a guide to the Lake District of West Cumberland and Furness.*** London: Whittaker & Co. Whitehaven: R. Gibson & Son; and Callander & Dixon. 1852. Octavo.†

Text: Half-title, verso blank; Title, imprint on verso, *Printed by W.H. Lizars, Edinburgh*; Dedication (ornamental border) 1 p., verso blank; List of engravings 1 p., verso blank; Text [1]-134.

Plates: 12 steel engravings, signed: *R. Shepherd delt. W.H. Lizars Sculpt.*

1 Whitehaven from behind Corkickle
2 Ennerdale Water
3 Saint Bees
4 Egremont Castle
5 Beckermont from School Green
6 Calder Abbey
7 Seascale Hotel
8 Wastwater from Windy Knott
9 Stanley Gill. From the Moss House
10 Mountains as seen from the Esk Viaduct and the Irt Viaduct near Drigg (outlines) Signed: *W.H. Lizars, Edinr.*
11 Duddon Viaduct
12 Furness Abbey

Map: Folding Map of the Lake District and the Cumberland & West Coast Railways showing their connection with Belfast and the North as well as with Yorkshire and the South of England. Signed: *Engd. by W. Lizars, Edinr.* Size: 510 × 370 mm. Scale 4 in. = 25 miles.

King's copy: In contemporary red morocco, gilt-stamped, lettered on spine, *Whitehaven and Furness Railway guide.*

Copies: K; Armitt; Jackson; Wordsworth

WILLIAM HASWELL HILL of Manchester

149 ***A nine days ramble in the Lake District of England; by two lovers of the picturesque.*** Wakefield: Stanfield & Hepworth. 1852. Octavo.

The tour was made by Hill and his companion, referred to as 'Brown and Jones', starting in June to avoid the 'high season'. It led them up various little-visited mountains, including Helvellyn from Patterdale by Swirrel Edge, crossing from Buttermere to Wastdale by Scarf Gap and Black Sale, and from Wastdale to Grasmere in a day, over the top of Ling Mell and Scawfell Pike; all described in heavily humorous, polysyllabic, Victorian prose, which makes a curious contrast with the picturesque descriptions of their predecessors.

Copies: Jackson; and Barrow-in-Furness

JAMES FREEMAN CLARKE

Poet and editor of the *Western Messenger*, 1846, born in Boston, Mass.

150 ***Eleven weeks in Europe; and what may be seen in that time.*** Boston: Ticknor, Reed, and Fields. 1852. Octavo.

Lakes: pp. 46-51

Copies: BL; Cornell

WILSON ARMISTEAD ('Lorenzo Tuvar')

151.1 ***Tales & legends of the English Lakes and Mountains Collected from the best and most authentic sources by Lorenzo Tuvar.*** London, Longmans & Co. J.E. Masser Litho Leeds n.d. [1852] Octavo.† 28 tales and poems.

Text: Title (litho), verso blank; Preface [1]-9, verso 9, blank; Contents [11], 12; Text [13]-312. Imprint on 312, *Glasgow: W.G. Blackie and Co., printers, Villafield.*

Plates: 3 tinted lithographs:
1 Title page
2 Castle Rock in the Vale of St. John (frontispiece)
3 Charles Gough The unfortunate tourist of Helvellyn and his faithful dog

King's copy: In publisher's dark blue cloth, stamped and gilt

Copies: K; Armitt; Cornell; Kendal; Wordsworth

151.2 ——— [A new edition] by the late Wilson Armistead Author of "The Flora of Liverpool," etc. London: Simpkin, Marshall & Co. Glasgow: Thomas D. Morison. 1891. Octavo.

Text: 27 tales and poems. 'The shepherd boys of Dungeon-Ghyll' is omitted. The order and titles of the items are altered, but otherwise the text remains unaltered from the first edition.
No illustrations. Printed title-page.

King's copy: In dark green morocco, stamped, gilt

Copies: K; BL; Cornell; Jackson

——— Another edition: Manchester: Abel Heywood & Son, 56 and 58 Oldham Street, n.d., [*c.* 1880], has been reported but not examined.

EDWARD LITT LAMAN BLANCHARD 1820-1870

Sir Edward Litt Laman Blanchard, miscellaneous writer, contributed extensively to newspapers and periodicals, and produced pantomimes at Drury Lane for 37 years.

152.1 ***Adams's pocket descriptive guide to the Lake District . . . a complete companion for the tourist to the attractive scenery, picturesque antiquities, mountains, lakes, and waterfalls of this celebrated region.*** Embellished with a new and accurate map, and illustrative engravings by F.G. Delamotte. London: W.J. Adams, 59, Fleet Street, Bradshaw's Guide Office. [1852] Octavo.† Price one shilling.

Text: Title, imprint on verso, *London: printed by Petter, Duff, and Co. Playhouse Yard, Blackfriars*; Introduction [iii]-v; blank; Contents [vi], vii; Text [1]-123, device on verso 123; Index [125], 126; Advertisements 10 pp.

Plates: 5 woodcuts:
1 Brathay Bridge (frontispiece)
2 Windermere Lake, between Low-wood Inn and Ambleside
3 Keswick – Skiddaw
4 The Bowder Stone, Borrowdale
5 Crummock Water and Buttermere Lake

No signatures or imprints on plates

Map: Folding Map of the Lake District. Size 160 × 200 mm. Scale not indicated.

King's copy: In publisher's brown stamped cloth, lettered in gilt on upper cover *Adams's Guide to the English Lakes*

Copies: K; Armitt; BL

152.2 ——— *Adams's illustrated guide to the English Lakes.* London: W.J. Adams. 1853. Engravings, Map. [Second edition]

Only minor alterations from *Adams's pocket descriptive guide.*

Copies: BL; Jackson

1853

W. & K. JOHNSTON (mapmakers)

153 ***Views of the English Lakes with a new map by W. & K. Johnston, and descriptive letter-press.*** London & New York: Nelson. 1853.

12 plates. Map.

Copy: Cornell

JAMES BARKER PYNE (artist) 1800-1870

James Barker Pyne was born in Bristol and moved to London in 1835. His earliest Lake District work seems to have been 'Buttermere', exhibited at the British Institute in 1835. Subsequently he visited the Lakes regularly. In 1848 he started work on 'Grasmere from Loughrigg', the first of a series of paintings commissioned by Mr Thomas Agnew of Manchester.

154a ***The English Lake District.*** Manchester: Thos. Agnew & Sons, 1853. Large folio.

Text: Title (litho), verso blank; Introduction [iv]-vi; one page of text, verso blank, follows each of 25 plates

Plates: 25 lithographs (including title). Page size: 710 × 515 mm

1 Dungeon Gill (circular view in title)
W. Gauci, lith. Hanhart, impt.
2 Rydal Water
3 Windermere Water Head
4 Ennerdale Lake
5 Skiddaw
6 Hawes Water and Waller Gill Force
7 The Vale of Keswick, Bassenthwaite Lake and the River Greta
8 Lake Windermere. Regatta
9 Derwent Water
10 Windermere as seen from Orrest Head
J. Haghe, lith
11 Buttermere
12 Langdale Pikes
13 Druidical Circle, Keswick
14 Brothers' Water §
15 Bassenthwaite Lake, Vale & Village
16 Grasmere from Loughrigg Fell
17 Ulleswater
18 Coniston Water
19 Crummock Water
20 The Vales of Ennerdale and Buttermere
21 Lowes Water
22 Thirlmere and Wytheburn
23 The Derwent River and Borrowdale
24 Wast Water
25 Windermere Lake

All the plates, except nos. 1 and 10, are signed, *Painted by J.B. Pyne. W. Gauci, lith.* Imprint, *Manchester, published by Thomas Agnew & Sons, 1853. Printed by M. & N. Anhart.*

The plates were issued either fully coloured or tinted. Plate no. 10 in the tinted sets was issued coloured.
The plates in the King's copy, which are tinted, are marked 'Proof'.
2 wood engravings in text

Notes: The descriptive letterpress was written by the poet, songwriter and engraver, Charles Swain (1803-74). The 25 views were selected from those commissioned by Thomas Agnew.

The English Lake District was issued in parts and with the plates in two portfolios.

King's copy: One volume, rebound

Copies: K; Armitt; BL; Cornell; Jackson: Wordsworth

154b ——— Republished 'Printed in tints and coloured by hand, with descriptive letter-press Llewellyn Jewit F.S.A. etc. etc. etc.' Leeds: D. Banks, 11 Queen Street. [*c.*1870]. Folio. Chromolithographs.

154c ——— *Lake Scenery of England by J.B. Pyne. Drawn on stone by T. Picken.* Published by Day and Son. Lithographers to the Queen, London. [1859]. Small folio (Royal octavo).§

Text Half-title, verso blank; Title (chromolitho), verso blank; Introduction [i]-vii, blank; List of plates 1 p., verso blank; Text, one leaf to each plate, not numbered.

Plates: 25 chromolithographs. Page size: 285 × 210mm. The views are the same as those in *The English Lake District* (154a), but the order and the titles differ. Title-page signed *R. Dudley, Inv et Del W.P. Tymms, lith.* Other 24 signed, *J.B. Pyne, delt. T. Picken lith. Day & Son, Lithrs to the Queen.* Imprint, *London, Published June 1st 1859 by Day & Son, Gate Street, Lincoln's Inn Fields.* Size 210 × 285 mm.

2 wood engravings in text as in 154a.

Note: The letterpress descriptions are the same as in 154a. The chromolithographs are inferior to the lithographs in the larger book.

King's copy: In the publisher's green cloth, stamped and gilt

Copies: K; Armitt; BL; Cornell

Ref: Abbey, 196

National Union Catalogue records *Lake Scenery* 'Reissued 1870 by Haig Sotheran & Co., London'.

Copies: Universities of: Duke; Indiana

1855

HARRIET MARTINEAU, 1802-1876

Miss Harriet Martineau, novelist and writer on political economy and social problems, was born at Norwich. Her autobiography was published in 1877, and biographies by Mrs Fenwick Miller in 1844, and Theodora Bosanquet in 1927. In 1844 she settled in Ambleside where, with some advice from Wordsworth, she built The Knoll, her home for the rest of her life.

155.1 ***A complete guide to the English Lakes, . . . to which are added an account of the flowering plants, ferns, and mosses of the district***. Windermere: John Garnett; London: Whittaker and Co. Preface dated 1855. Quarto.† Price 7*s*.6*d*.

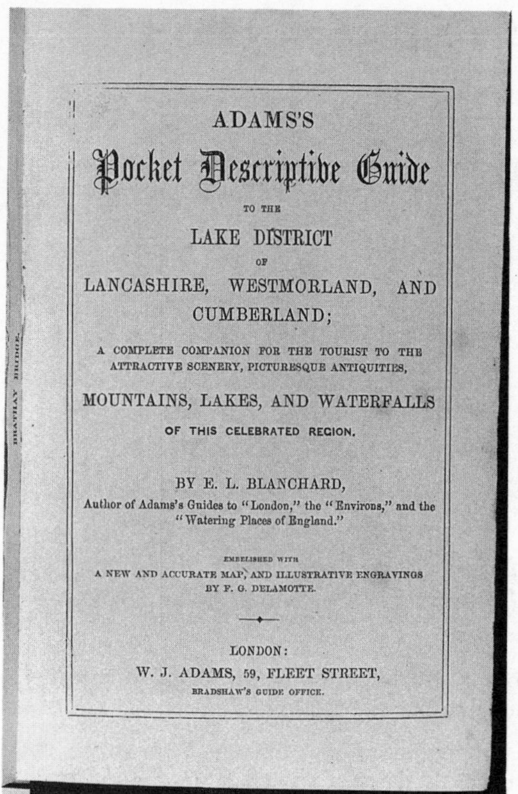

ADAMS'S
Pocket Descriptive Guide
TO THE
LAKE DISTRICT
OF
LANCASHIRE, WESTMORLAND, AND CUMBERLAND;
A COMPLETE COMPANION FOR THE TOURIST TO THE ATTRACTIVE SCENERY, PICTURESQUE ANTIQUITIES,
MOUNTAINS, LAKES, AND WATERFALLS
OF THIS CELEBRATED REGION.
BY E. L. BLANCHARD,
Author of Adams's Guides to "London," the "Environs," and the "Watering Places of England."
EMBELLISHED WITH
A NEW AND ACCURATE MAP, AND ILLUSTRATIVE ENGRAVINGS
BY F. G. DELAMOTTE.
LONDON:
W. J. ADAMS, 59, FLEET STREET,
BRADSHAW'S GUIDE OFFICE.

152.1 160 x 100 mm.

A
COMPLETE GUIDE
TO THE
ENGLISH LAKES,
BY
HARRIET MARTINEAU,
ILLUSTRATED
WITH COLOURED PRINTS, OUTLINES OF MOUNTAINS,
And a Map Coloured Geologically by John Ruthven.
TO WHICH ARE ADDED AN ACCOUNT OF THE
FLOWERING PLANTS, FERNS, AND MOSSES OF THE DISTRICT.
WINDERMERE: JOHN GARNETT.
LONDON: WHITTAKER AND CO.

155.1 280 x 220 mm.

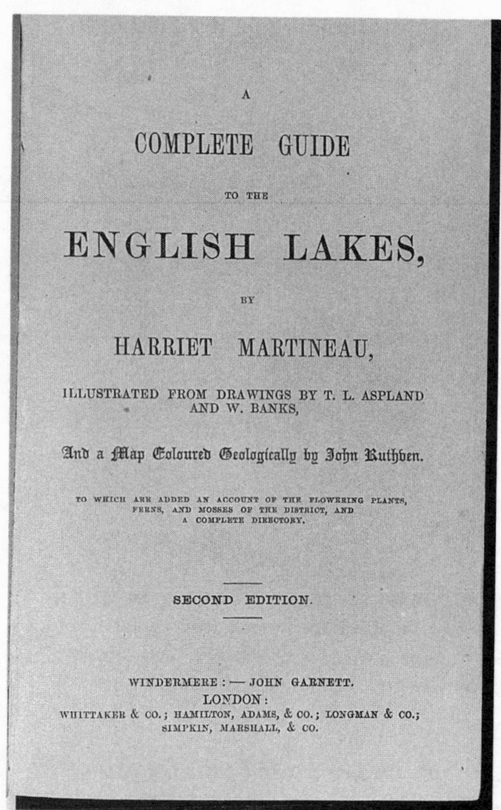

A
COMPLETE GUIDE
TO THE
ENGLISH LAKES,
BY
HARRIET MARTINEAU,
ILLUSTRATED FROM DRAWINGS BY T. L. ASPLAND AND W. BANKS,
And a Map Coloured Geologically by John Ruthven.
TO WHICH ARE ADDED AN ACCOUNT OF THE FLOWERING PLANTS, FERNS, AND MOSSES OF THE DISTRICT, AND A COMPLETE DIRECTORY.
SECOND EDITION.
WINDERMERE: — JOHN GARNETT.
LONDON:
WHITTAKER & CO.; HAMILTON, ADAMS, & CO.; LONGMAN & CO.; SIMPKIN, MARSHALL, & CO.

155.2b 159 x 105 mm.

GUIDE
TO THE
ENGLISH LAKES
BY
HARRIET MARTINEAU.
The Knoll, Ambleside,
The residence of
H. Martineau
WINDERMERE:- JOHN GARNETT.
LONDON:- LONGMAN & Co. SIMPKIN, MARSHALL & Co.
HAMILTON & Co.

155.3 160 x 106 mm.

Text: Half-title, verso blank; Title (printed in green and black), verso blank; Preface 1p. (dated March 12 1855), errata on verso; Contents 1 p., verso blank; Text [3]-71; Index [i], ii.

All pages, including blanks, except verso of title, have ornamental borders.

Plates: 4 chromolithographs, signed, *L. Aspland delt. W. Banks Sc.*
1 Dungeon Ghyll, Langdale (frontispiece)
2 Wray Castle, Windermere
3 Keswick, Cumberland, from Castlerigg
4 Rydal Water, Westmoreland.

6 outlines of mountains, signed, *L. Aspland delt. W. Banks Sc. Edinburgh*
1 Mountains seen from Lanthwaite Wood, Crummock Water
Mountains seen from the west side of Thirlmere
2 Mountains seen from Applethwaite near Keswick
Mountains on the west side of Windermere (folding)
3 Mountains seen on the Keswick Road approaching Ulswater
Mountains seen a little beyond Rydal Mount

Some copies (Barrow-in-Furness) include 6 full-page steel engravings after drawings by Aspland and Petitt

Map: Folding coloured Map of the English Lakes and adjoining country geologically coloured by John Ruthven of Kendal 1855. Signed: *Engd. by W. Banks, Edinburgh. Entered at Stationers Hall.* Imprint: *Published by John Garnett, Windermere, Ackermann & Co. London.* Size: 533 × 445 mm. Scale: 1 in. = 3½ miles.

King's copy: In dark blue publisher's cloth, gilt-stamped lettering on upper cover, lettered *Martineau's Complete Guide to the English Lakes*, gilt edges. Binder's label on paste-down endpaper: *Bound by Alexr. Banks Jr. 29 North Bridge, Edinburgh*

Notes: The *Guide* is arranged as a series of excursions and tours, first from Windermere and from Keswick (both published separately), and then as a circuit of the Lake District. It is full of practical information, such as prices of hotel rooms. It includes a section on passes and mountains, a note on the weather, tables of mountains, passes, lakes and waterfalls, a chapter on botany with tables of plants, a directory of residents with their addresses, Mr. Ruthven's map coloured geologically, and in the Pocket Edition (155.2a) copious advertisements for books, prints, hotels, lodgings, steamer services, etc.

The four coloured plates, with four additional prints, were sold separately, advertised in other editions of the *Complete Guide* as 'A Series of beautiful Chromatic Prints from Original Paintings'. 'The series, in Folio, gilt, 6*s.*; Single; Subjects handsomely mounted, 8*d.* Published by Garnett, Windermere and Ackermann, London.'

The 'Geological Map of the English Lake District, with explanatory sections and letterpress, by John Ruthven.' was sold 'mounted on cloth, and in a neat cover, 5*s.*'

Copies: K; Jackson; Kendal

155.2a ——— [True second edition] Windermere: John Garnett. London: Whittaker and Co. Preface dated 1855. Octavo. Price 5*s.*

Text: Title, imprint on verso, *Windermere: Printed by John Garnett;* Preface (The Knoll, Ambleside, March 12, 1855) [i]-iii; blank; Contents [i], ii; Index [i]-iv; List of Illustrations 1 p.; Errata 1 p.; Text [3]-233; Adverts. [i]-ix; List of illustrations and Errata repeated.

Plates: 12 steel engravings, signed *L. Aspland Delt. W. Banks Sc. Edinr.* except plates 3, 7, and 8, signed *Drawn and Engd. by W. Banks Edinr.:*
1 Ara Force (frontispiece)
2 Windermere from near Storrs
3 Windermere from Low Wood Hotel
4 Coniston from the wood above Bank ground
5 Upper Reach of Ullswater
6 Rydal Water
7 Vale of Keswick
8 Derwent Water from Castle Head
9 Wastwater
10 Honister Crag from the Quarry Road to Yew Crag
11 Borrowdale near the Bowder Stone
12 Grasmere from Red Bank

6 folding outlines of mountains as 1st edition (155.1) but on 6 separate plates.

4 engravings of hotels in adverts.: Windermere from near the hotel; Ullock's Royal Hotel, Bowness; Windermere from the Crown Hotel; Waterhead Hotel, Coniston

Map: A map coloured geologically as previous edition

King's copy: In publisher's red cloth, stamped, lettered in gilt on upper cover *Harriet Martineau's Guide to Windermere & the other English Lakes.* Binder's label. *Bound by Alexr. Banks Jr. 28 North Bridge, Edinburgh.*

Note: This is the 'Pocket edition' of the *Complete Guide.* Published in the same year as the Demy 4to, with extended and revised text, and therefore, though frequently referred to as the 'first edition', is the true second edition. A Directory of residents and adverts. are added. The chromolithographs are omitted and 12 steel engravings added. The additions include a tribute to 'Christopher North' (see 168).

Copies: K; Cornell; Jackson; Wordsworth

155.2b ——— Second edition. Windermere: John Garnett. London: Whittaker & Co.; Hamilton, Adams, & Co.; Longman & Co.; Simpkin, Marshall, & Co. (1858)†

Text: Half-title (engraved), verso blank; Title, verso blank; Preface [i], ii; Contents [i], ii; Index [i]-iv; Travelling Charges, 1 p., verso blank; Coach Fares and Routes 1 p.; Charges at Hotels and Lodgings 1 p., verso blank; Itinerary 10 pp.; Text [1]-207, blank; Mountains and Passes 209, 210; Directory [i]-xviii; Adverts. [i]-xvi; blank; xv-xvii.

Plates: 12 steel engravings:
1 Lower Fall at Rydal. *Drawn & Engd. by W. Banks Edinr.* (frontispiece)
2 Bowness from Belle Isle. *L. Aspland Delt. W. Banks Sc. Edinr.*
3 Ara Force. As 1, previous edition
4 Stockghyll Force, Ambleside. *Drawn & Engd. by W. Banks & Son Edinr.*
5 Grasmere from Red Bank. As 12, previous edition
6 Rydal Water. As 6, previous edition
7 Vale of Keswick. As 7, previous edition
8 Waterfall at Lowdore. *Drawn & Engd. by W. Banks & Son Edinr.*
9 Crummock & Buttermere. *Drawn & Engd. by W. Banks & Son Edinr.*
10 Wastwater. As 9, previous edition

Engraved half-title: vignette, The Knoll, Ambleside, the residence of H. Martineau (facsimile signature) *Engraved by W. Banks Edinr.*

6 outlines of mountains as previous edition

Map: Map of the Lakes, geologically coloured, as previous editions, folded in pocket

King's copy: In publisher's dark blue cloth, stamped, lettered in gilt on upper cover. *Martineau's Complete Guide to the English Lakes.* Some pages misnumbered.

Copies: K; BL; Kendal; Jackson; Wordsworth

155.3 ——— Third edition. Edited and enlarged by Maria Martineau (Harriet's niece]. Imprint on title as previous edition (1866).†

Notes: The format is the same as the second edition; the text is extensively revised, and set out differently; the engraved title is the same.

There are only six steel engravings, two of which differ from those in previous editions: Furness Abbey South East, *drawn and engraved by W. Banks,* and Ullswater from entrance to Grisedale. (As Garnett advertised 80 engravings in this series, it is probable that those selected for the various issues of Martineau's Guide varied. Listed here are those in the King's copy.)

Outlines of mountains as previous edition.

4 folding maps are added:

1 Windermere and Coniston Section
2 Ambleside & Ulleswater Section
3 Keswick Section
4 Wastwater Section

Imprint: *W. Banks & Son Edinr.* Size: 210 × 168 mm. Scale: 1 in. = 2 miles

King's copy: In publisher's binding uniform with previous edition. 5/- on spine. Inscribed on free endpaper 'E.M. Stack March 1887'.

Copies: K; BL; Cornell; Jackson; Wordsworth

155.4 ——— Fourth edition. With maps, plans of towns, and illustrations. Edited, with the approval of the authoress, by the printer and publisher. Windermere: J. Garnett. London: Smipkin [sic], Marshall & Co. 1871.

Notes: Text considerably altered and extended. Additional half-title.

Only one steel engraving, Windermere from near Storrs, and engraved half-title, as previous editions. 5 woodcuts in text, chapter heads added. Outlines of Mountains as previous editions.

Maps: 4 maps of Sections as previous editions, but printed in two colours, and signature *J. Bartholomew Edinr.* to which are added.

The Region of Scawfell
Map of Helvellyn 1 in. = 1 mile
Plan of Windermere & Environs
Bowness on Winander Mere
Plan of Ambleside & Environs 6 in. = 1 mile

King's copy: In publisher's green cloth, stamped and gilt title on upper cover as 2nd and 3rd editions. 5/- blind-stamped on upper cover.

Advertised as 'with Maps, Plans of Towns, and Illustrations, 3*s*.6*d*.; with additional Maps for Pedestrians, 5*s*.'

Copies: K; BL

155.5 ——— *Garnett's series of guide books. The English lake District.* With maps, plans of towns, and illustrations. Fifth edition. 1876

Generally similar to 4th edition

Copies: Armitt: BL; Cornell

The sections of the Guide on Windermere and on Keswick were published in separate volumes, see 156 and 157,

156 ***Guide to Keswick and its environs***. Windermere: John Garnett. London: Whittaker & Co. [*c*.1852] Octavo. Frontispiece: engraving, Vale of Keswick, *Drawn and Engd. by W. Banks Edinr.* Map.

This is the section on Keswick to be included in the *Complete Guide*, published three years later.

Copy: BL

GUIDE

TO

WINDERMERE,

WITH

TOURS TO THE NEIGHBOURING LAKES AND OTHER INTERESTING PLACES,

BY MISS HARRIET MARTINEAU.

With a Map,

AND ILLUSTRATIONS FROM DRAWINGS BY T. L. ASPLAND, ENGRAVED BY W. J. LINTON.

TO WHICH ARE ADDED EXCURSIONS TO AND FROM KESWICK;

ALSO AN ACCOUNT OF THE

FLOWERING PLANTS, FERNS AND MOSSES

OF THE DISTRICT,

AND A COMPLETE DIRECTORY TO WINDERMERE AND ITS NEIGHBOURHOOD.

WINDERMERE: — JOHN GARNETT.

LONDON: — WHITTAKER AND CO.

157.1 167 x 108 mm.

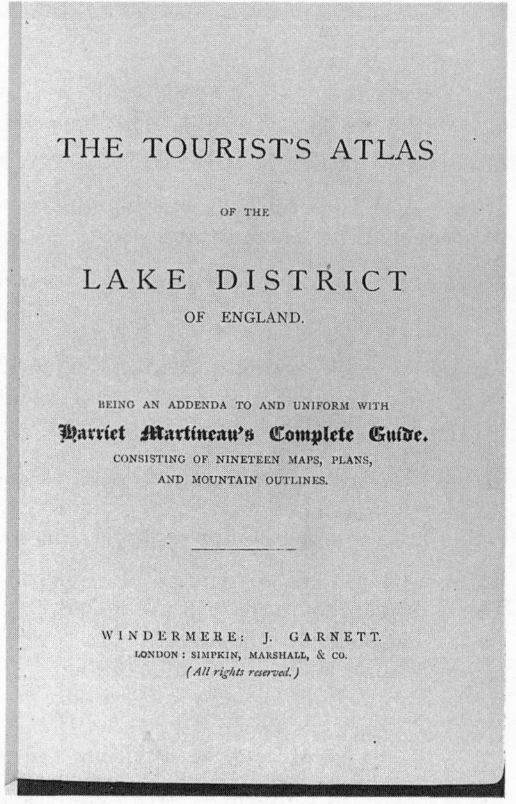

THE TOURIST'S ATLAS

OF THE

LAKE DISTRICT

OF ENGLAND.

BEING AN ADDENDA TO AND UNIFORM WITH

Harriet Martineau's Complete Guide.

CONSISTING OF NINETEEN MAPS, PLANS, AND MOUNTAIN OUTLINES.

WINDERMERE: J. GARNETT.

LONDON: SIMPKIN, MARSHALL, & CO.

(All rights reserved.)

158 175 x 115 mm.

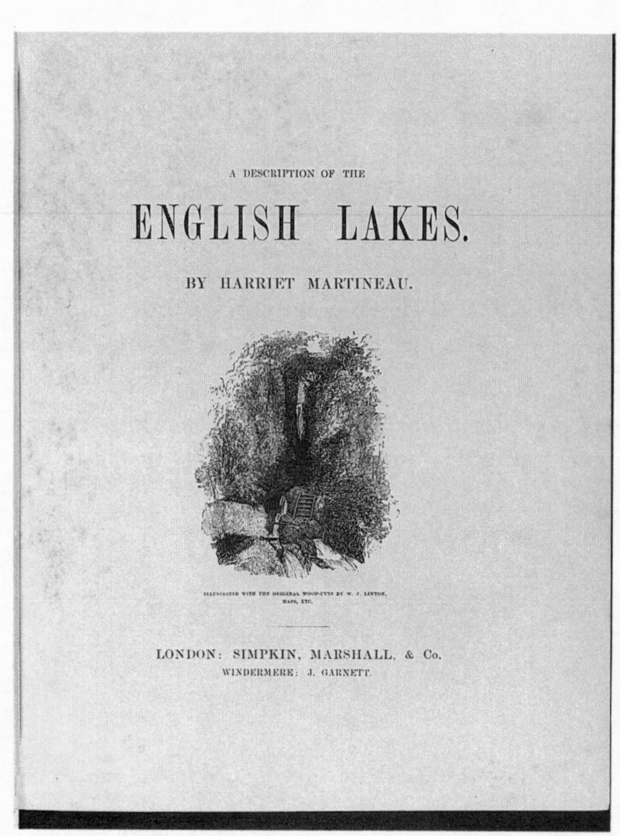

A DESCRIPTION OF THE

ENGLISH LAKES.

BY HARRIET MARTINEAU.

ILLUSTRATED WITH THE ORIGINAL WOOD-CUTS BY W. J. LINTON, MAPS, ETC.

LONDON: SIMPKIN, MARSHALL, & Co.

WINDERMERE: J. GARNETT.

159 275 x 220 mm.

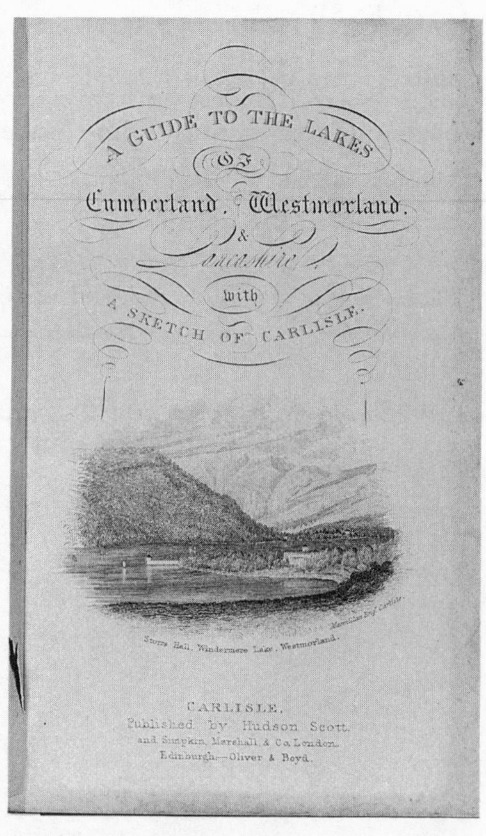

A GUIDE TO THE LAKES

OF

Cumberland, Westmorland,

&

Lancashire;

with

A SKETCH OF CARLISLE.

Storrs Hall, Windermere Lake, Westmorland.

CARLISLE,

Published by Hudson Scott,

and Simpkin, Marshall & Co. London.

Edinburgh. — Oliver & Boyd.

161 145 x 90 mm.

157.1 ***Guide to Windermere, with tours to the neighbouring lakes and other interesting places . . .*** Windermere: John Garnett. London: Whittaker and Co. [1854] Octavo† 'Foolscap Octavo. In paper cover 1*s*.; neat cloth 1*s*.6*d*.'

Text: Title, imprint on verso, *Windermere: printed by John Garnett*; Index [i], ii; Text [3]-103; adverts. [i, verso 103] - xv (imprint repeated on xv).

Plates: 6 engravings, printed on buff grounds:
1 Across the head of Stockghyll
2 Coniston from Bank Ground
3 Upper reach of Ullswater
4 Windermere from near Storrs
5 Grasmere from Red Bank
6 [Derwent Water from Castle Head]

No signature or imprint. From drawings by T.L. Aspland, engraved by W.J. Linton (title-page)

Map: Folding Map of the English Lakes. This is part of the map published by John Garnett and included in the third edition of the *Complete Guide*.

King's copy: In publisher's stamped blue cloth, lettered in gilt on upper cover, *Martineau's Guide to Windermere*

This is the section on Windermere which was included in the *Complete Guide*

Notes: The six engravings were sold separately as *Tinted outline views of the Lakes* mounted on card, in a neat portfolio.

Theophilus Lindsay Aspland (1807-90), pupil of the London aquatint engraver, George Cooke, worked chiefly in Manchester and Liverpool until 1848 when he settled at Sawrey Cottage on Esthwaite to devote himself to landscape painting and the recording of the Lake District. William James Linton (1812-98), poet, botanist and political reformer, best known as an engraver, born in London, lived for a time at Brantwood, Coniston, until 1855 when he sold it to John Ruskin. He was a skilled botanical illustrator, his *magnum opus* being *The Ferns of the Lake District* (1864). He illustrated his wife Lynn Linton's book, *The Lake Country* (1864). In 1866 he emigrated to America, where he had a profound influence on wood-engraving, and wrote *The Masters of wood engraving* (1890).

Copies: K; BL; Wordsworth

157.2 Second edition BL (1854)

157.3 Third edition K [1856]; BL; Jackson

157.4 Fourth edition BL [1860]; Price 1*s*.

All octavo.

158 ***The tourist's atlas of the Lake District of England. Being an addenda to and uniform with Harriet Martineau's Complete Guide . . .*** Windermere: J. Garnett; London: Simpkin, Marshall, & Co.†

19 maps, plans, and mountain outlines

Maps: Map of the Lakes showing the relative positions of the subjoined travelling sections

4 Maps of the sections. 1 in. = 4 miles
Region of Scafell. 1 in. = 1 mile
Map of Helvellyn. 1 in. = 1 mile

Folding map of the Lakes mounted on linen. Size: 330 × 272 mm. Scale: 1 in. = 3½ miles, in pocket
Plan of Windermere Bowness Plan of Ambleside Plan of Keswick 5 in. = 1 mile
All as the *Complete Guide*

4 Outlines of Mountains as *Complete Guide* but coloured.

King's copy: In publisher's maroon cloth, lettered on upper cover *The Tourist's Atlas of the English Lake District*, stamped and gilt.

Copies: K; BL

159 ***A description of the English Lakes. Illustrated with the original wood-cuts by W.J. Linton, maps etc.*** London: Simpkin, Marshall, & Co. Windermere: J. Garnett. (1858). 4to 'Demy 4to., gilt, 12*s*.'†

Text: Title, verso blank; Publisher's Preface (July 1858), verso blank; Contents [i], ii; Text [1]-152; Meteorology [153]-156; List of Plants etc. [157]-166

Plates: 6 engravings. Signed: *L. Aspland Delt.* (1, 5); *A. Pettitt Delt.* (2,4); *G.W. Pettitt Delt.* (3,6)
1 Stanley Ghyll, Eskdale Frontispiece
2 Head of Windermere from near Millerground Bay
3 Grasmere from Loughrigg Terrace
4 Derwentwater from behind Barrow House
5 Borrowdale from near the Bowder Stone
6 Ullswater from the entrance to Grisedale

44 woodcuts in the text, 'carefully wrought, drawn, engraved and printed under the able superintendence of Mr. W.J. Linton' (in the King's copy these are proofs on India paper mounted in the text)

Woodcut vignette on title page

The cuts are similar to those in the 4th edition of the *Complete Guide*

6 outlines of Mountains, two on each of two facing pages. Uncoloured outlines, same as those in the *Complete Guide*

Map: Ruthven's folding, Geologically Coloured Map, as *Complete Guide*

King's copy: In publisher's scarlet cloth, stamped and gilt, lettered *The English Lakes*, with *Martineau, W.J. Linton, L. Aspland, G. Petit* on border of upper cover

Notes: The *Description* is a selected version of the *Complete Guide* intended to be an attractive library, or drawing-room-table book, and not a practical guide.

Copies: K; BL; Wordsworth

——— Facsimile edition, EP Publishing Ltd, East Ardsley, Wakefield (1974)

159a ——— Another issue. *The English Lakes.* Windermere: John Garnett. London: Whittaker & Co.; Longman & Co; Hamilton Adams & Co.; and Simpkin & Co. n.d.

New title-page, otherwise reissue of text.

Copy: Barrow-in-Furness

Undated

MRS ST PAUL (artist)

160 ***Views of the lakes of Derwentwater & Windermere &c. in Cumberland and Westmoreland. Drawn by the late Mrs. St. Paul of Ewart Park Northumbd. taken from nature in 1815 and sent to the Countess of Newburgh by Charles Maximilian St. Paul with his best respects & kindest regards.*** Title inscribed and lithographed.† Folio

No text

Plates: 16 lithographs: MS titles added, no imprints.

1 Keswick near the Lake of Derwentwater
2 Lake of Derwentwater
3 Lake of Derwentwater & Barrowside
4 Lake of Windermere & the Island
5 Lake of Rydal Water
6 Lowdore Cascade
7 View from the Inn at Ambleside
8 Lake of Windermere & the Ferry & Station
9 Lake of Windermere near Bowness
10 Lake of Ullswater from Gowbarrow Park
11 Church of Patterdale from the Inn & Glenridden and Gowbarrow Fells
12 Lake of Ullswater
13 Lake of Ullswater and Parse Bay
14 Lake of Crommack water
15 Lake of Crommack water or Lower Buttermere & Wood House
16 Lake of Ulswater and Glenridden and Lyulph's Tower

MS numbers added in lower right corner. Plates, 1, 2, 6, 7, 11, 14 signed: *W. Ballantyne lithog. Edinr.* Other plates no signature.

King's copy: In maroon morocco, tooled, gilt, emblem on upper cover, *Si je Puis Slindon.* Inscribed on title-page 'Given by Anne Countess of Newburgh to Henry Howard Esq. of Greystoke April 9th. 1855.' Loose note, 'This book belongs to Henry Howard Esq of Greystoke Castle, Cumberland Slindon House Jany. 14th. 1854 Anne Newburgh'. This presentation volume, is the only copy seen or recorded.

Note: This is an early book of lithographs. The date of publication is doubtful. The earliest recorded lithographs of the Lake District are from drawings by Francis Nicholson, dated 1821, and the date of this book is probably not much later. The new process of lithography was popular for books of this sort, illustrating the work of amateurs, for limited private circulation.

Copy: K

HUDSON SCOTT (publisher)

161 ***A guide to the lakes of Cumberland, Westmorland, & Lancashire, with a sketch of Carlisle.*** Carlisle, published by Hudson Scott and Simpkin Marshall & Co. London. Edinburgh: Oliver & Boyd. n.d. [*c.* 1835]. Duodecimo.†

Text: Engraved title, verso blank; Advertisement one page, verso blank; Contents [iii]-[viii]; Tables 6 pp.; Text [1]-120.

Engraved vignette on title-page, Storrs Hall, Windermere Lake, Westmorland. Signed: *Macmillan, Engr. Carlisle.*

Map: Coloured engraved folding Map of the Lake Districts of Cumberland, Westmorland and Lancashire. Signed: *W.H. Lizards sculpt, Edinburgh.* 536 × 415 mm. Scale: 1 in. = 3 miles.

Note: A small concise pocket guide written for visitors approaching the Lakes from Carlisle

King's copy: As sold in quarter red morocco, marbled boards, with engraved title mounted on upper cover. Signed on paste-down endpaper 'H.G. Chester, May 1841', stamped with crest and 'H.G. Chester'

Copies: K; Armitt; BL; Cornell; Jackson; Kendal

THOMAS COLMAN DIBDIN (artist) 1810-1893

162 ***The lakes, waterfalls, and interesting places of Cumberland and Westmorland. From nature & on stone by T.C. Dibdin.*** London: for the proprietor by M. & N. Manhart. Quarto. *c.* 1845. Title. No text.

Plates: 12 coloured lithographs

The Market Cross Ambleside (frontispiece)
1 Keswick from Castle Rock, Cumberland
2 Grasmere, Westmorland
3 Lodore Cascade, Cumberland
4 The Bowder Stone, Borrowdale
5 Crummock Water, Cumberland
6 Ambleside, Westmorland
7 The Mill at Ambleside, Westmorland
8 Derwent Water, Cumberland
9 Buttermere from Hartley Hill
10 Rydal Water, Westmorland
11 Windermere, Westmorland. from Windermere Hotel
12 The Lower Fall at Rydal, Westmorland

Copy: Yale Center for British Art (in publisher's binding).

Written before, but published after, 1855

THOMAS COOPER

163 ***A poetical prospect of Keswick and the parts adjacent Written in the spring of the year 1752, By the late T. Cooper, curate of Loweswater. Nunc formosissimus – Virgil.*** Whitehaven: Callander and Dixon 3 Market Place 1875

Pamphlet: Title and 10 pages

Note: This poem appears to have been written a year earlier than Dr John Dalton's *Descriptive Poem* (2), and therefore to be one of the earliest descriptions of the beauties of the Lake District. Cooper's verses celebrate the bounty of nature and of agriculture in a highly Vergilian way. The 'tow'ring mountains' which 'stand, like Nature's bulwarks, to protect the land' yield 'the richest treasures' in the form of black lead and copper; they are neither beautiful nor sublime. The poet does not see the beauties of nature as a series of pictures. So Dalton's poem (2) and John Brown's description (4) remain the earliest picturesque Lake District writing.

Copy: Jackson

WILLIAM WILBERFORCE 1759-1833

William Wilberforce, born in Hull, visited the Lakes in 1776, 1777 and 1779; and in 1780 he took a seven-year lease of Rayrigg, a manor house near Windermere. His journey in 1779 was made during a long vacation from St John's College, Cambridge, in July, August and September.

164 ***Journey to the Lake District from Cambridge 1779 A diary written by William Wilberforce Undergraduate of St. John's College, Cambridge.*** Edited by his great-great-grandson C.E. Wrangham, Oriel Press, Stocksfield, Boston, Henley-on-Thames, London. 1983.

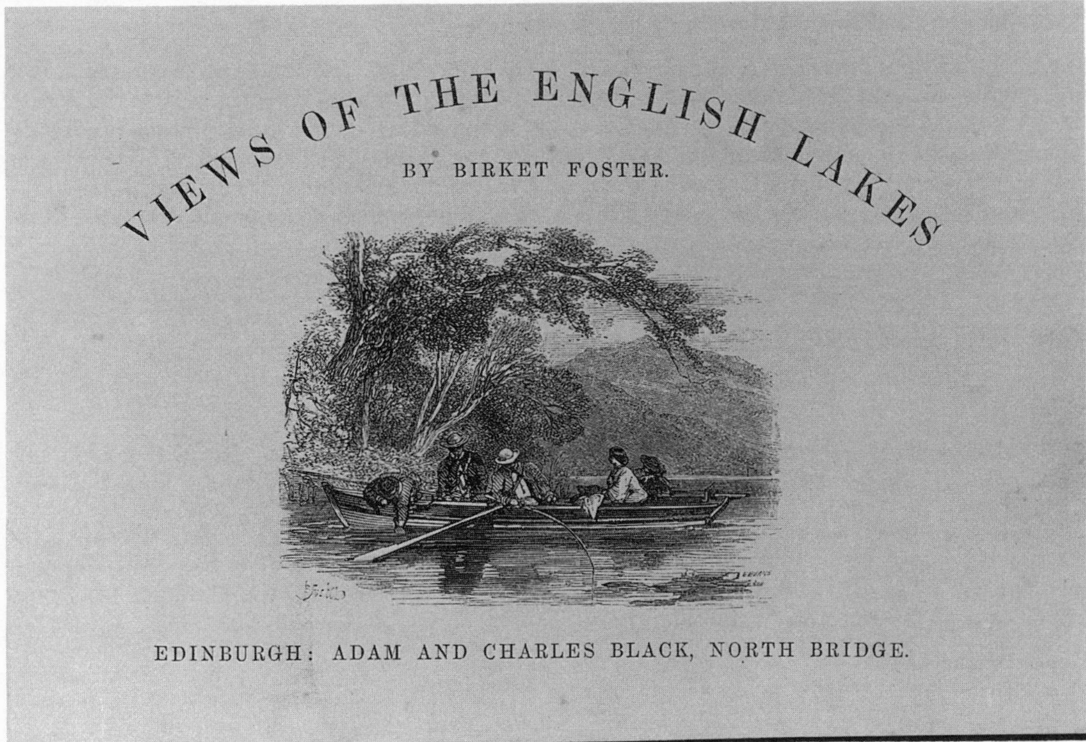

VIEWS OF THE ENGLISH LAKES

BY BIRKET FOSTER.

EDINBURGH: ADAM AND CHARLES BLACK, NORTH BRIDGE.

125 122 x 190 mm.

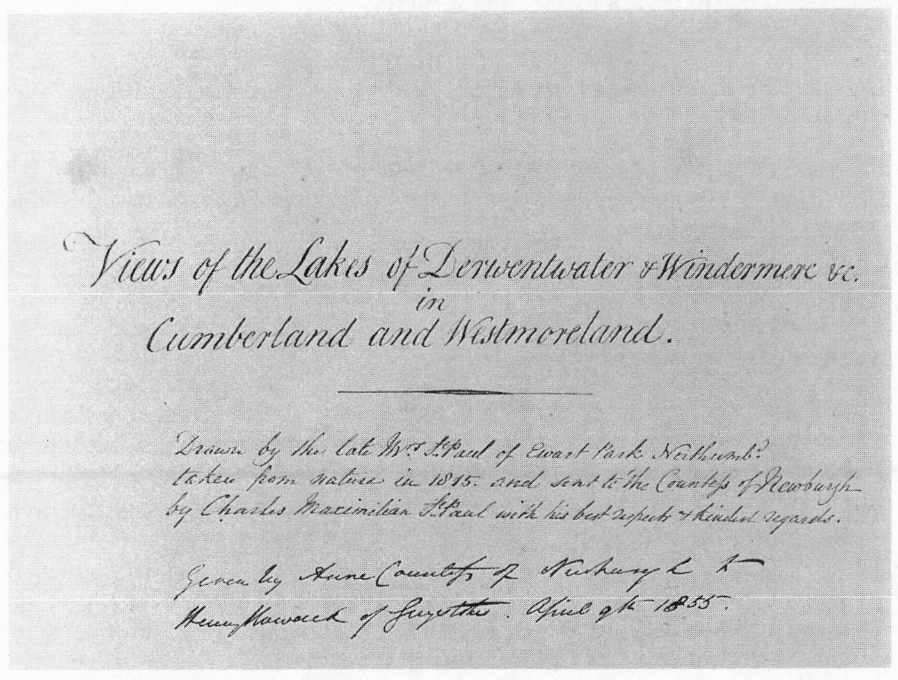

Views of the Lakes of Derwentwater & Windermere &c.
in
Cumberland and Westmoreland.

Drawn by the late Mrs St Paul of Ewart Park Northumbd
taken from nature in 1815. and sent to the Countess of Newburgh
by Charles Maximilian St Paul with his best respects & kindest regards.

Given by Anne Countess of Newburgh to
Henry Howard of Greystoke. April 9th 1855.

160 467 x 300 mm.

Reproductions of drawings and engravings, and of map.

Note: The MS has remained in the possession of the family and was published to commemorate the 150th anniversary of William Wilberforce's death and of the abolition of slavery in the British Dominions. Wilberforce spent twenty-five days in the Lakes. At Keswick he joined friends, among whom were Joseph Farington (see 22, 85, 86) and William Cookson (see 22). Wilberforce was more enterprising than most tourists of the 1770s, but he was sufficiently indoctrinated in the picturesque to carry Gray's *Journal* and West's *Guide* (first published the previous year), to visit West's stations, to employ a landscape glass, and to evoke Salvator.

GEORGE CROSSFIELD

165 ***An excursion from Warrington to the English Lakes in 1797.*** Reprinted from the *Warrington Examiner.* 1873. Pamphlet.

The excursion was made on horseback with three companions, 10-21 Sept. 1795. At Keswick the party visited Crosthwaite's Museum and Pocklington's Island, and climbed Skiddaw. The tour was limited to the usual route from Coniston to Windermere and Keswick, and back to Kendal by Penrith, Ullswater and Ambleside.

Copy: Alpine Club

WILLIAM GELL 1777-1836

Sir William Gell, Fellow of Emmanuel College, Cambridge, archaeologist, ardent hellenist and amateur artist, was among friends at Grasmere and Rydal, where he met Plumptre (see 37) and Henry Skrine (see 33). He built a house at Grasmere.

166 ***A tour to the Lakes made in 1797.*** Edited by William Rollinson. Newcastle: Frank Graham. 1968.

Notes: Gell's tour was made at a time when the tour of the Lakes had become a fashionable routine. He conformed by making pilgrimages to the Bowder Stone, the summit of Skiddaw, and Mary the Beauty of Buttermere.

The MS is in the Barrow-in-Furness Public Library.

BENJAMIN NEWTON 1761-1830

167 ***The diary of Benjamin Newton, Rector of Wath 1816-1818.*** Edited by C.P. Fendall and E.A. Crutchley. Cambridge at the University Press, 1983. Octavo.

Lakes: pp. 167-205.

Note: Newton and his wife set out on a tour from Wath, five miles north of Ripon, on 20 July 1818. They stayed at Bowness, Low Wood, Keswick, Cockermouth and Buttermere, spending a week at Allonby on the Solway coast. They returned to Wath on 11 August by way of the coast and over the sands to Lancaster. Although they carried one of William Green's books with them, and occasionally compared a prospect with the view in the book, Newton was more interested in the people he met and what he ate than in the picturesque beauties of the landscape.

King's copy: Given to the College by E.A. Crutchley.

JOHN WILSON ('Christopher North') 1785-1854

John Wilson, author, professor of moral philosophy at Edinburgh, and on the editorial staff of *Blackwood's Magazine,* bought sixty acres and a cottage at Elleray, on the slope of Orrest Head, Windermere, in 1806. He enlarged the building and made it his home until 1815 when he moved back to Edinburgh, though he still made frequent visits to the Lakes. He established himself as 'Admiral of the Lakes', kept a fleet on Windermere; and in 1825 was responsible for organising a splendid regatta to welcome Walter Scott and George Canning to the Lake District. In 1819 he invented 'Christopher North', the pseudonym under which he contributed several articles on the Lakes to *Blackwood's* and other publications.

168.1 ***Letters from the Lakes, translated from the German of Philip Kempferhausen. Written in the summer of 1818.*** Ambleside: printed and published by George Middleton. 1889. Reprinted from *Blackwood's Magazine,* 1819. Attributed to Thomas de Quincey, pamphlet. Frontispiece, portrait of Wordsworth, title, 68 pp. Printed paper covers.

Copies: K; Armitt; Kendal

168.2 ——— [Second edition] *Letters from the Lakes by Professor Wilson.* Ambleside: George Middleton. 1901

168.3 ——— *Letters from the Lakes by Professor Wilson (Christopher North).* Third edition, 1910. No frontispiece; printed card covers. 6d. net By Post 7½d.

Copy: K

168.4 ——— Fourth edition, 1930

Copy: Cornell

There is some confusion over the authorship of these letters. When they were republished in 1889 they were attributed to de Quincey, but in the 1901 edition it was established that 'Philip Kempferhausen' was the pseudonym of Prof. John Wilson; however, it was also used by J.G. Lockhart when writing for *Blackwood's Magazine.*

RICHARD COLT HOARE 1758-1838

Sir Richard Colt Hoare, Bart, F.R.S., F.S.A., of Stourhead, historian of Wiltshire, patron of the arts, antiquarian, archaeologist, and watercolour artist, travelled widely in Europe and Wales. He made many topographical drawings. In 1800 on a tour of northern England he visited the Lakes.

169 ***The journeys of Sir Richard Colt Hoare through Wales and England 1793-1810 extracted from the journals and edited with an introduction by M.W. Thompson.*** Alan Sutton [Gloucester], 1983. Octavo

Illustrated with reproductions of 38 of Hoare's drawings, but none of the Lake District

Lakes: pp. 129-39

Itinerary: Kendal, Windermere, visiting Rydal, Grasmere and Langdale, Ullswater, Haweswater, Penrith, Keswick, Buttermere by Honister, Lorton, Keswick, Penrith, visiting Haweswater and Ullswater again. 20 July-7th August, 1800

Note: Hoare had a keen eye for the picturesque. He made use of West's *Guide* and Crosthwaite's maps, he quotes Gray's *Journal* and the 'Fair Maid of Buttermere' reminded him of a 'fine Italian beauty' though her face was 'truly Grecian'. In Keswick he visited the museums of Crosthwaite and Hutton.

Appendix 1

Annotated copy of West's *Guide* (13.2)

A copy of the second edition of West's *Guide* (1780) in the King's College Collection has been annotated by two unidentified tourists: in August 1782 and September and October 1807.

The notes are of sufficient interest to be transcribed here in full.

The book has been carefully rebound to preserve the manuscript notes and to include three additional printed sheets, issued by Peter Crosthwaite in 1782. It seems probable that they were added by the first of the two tourists making his visit in that year. The three sheets are:

1 Tipped in between pp. 82 and 83:

To the Editor of the GENERAL EVENING POST

SIR,

Charmed beyond description with the unparallelled scenes I have beheld in Cumberland and Westmoreland, please to let your Paper convey my ideas from shore to shore: enchanting lakes, and stupendous mountains; verdant plains, tremendous rocks, waving woods, sweeping cataracts, natural castles, Roman camps, and the little hills, all at once conspire to raise the traveller's admiration and surprize! Here the contemplating Philosopher will meet with his heart's desire! The gay tourer with pleasures he never experienced before! The Valetudinarian may here meet with health! and the Unfortunate with calm repose! In this quarter are found almost endless scenes of matchless beauty, majestic grandeur, and delight. Brown, Pennant, Hutchinson, Gray, Young, West, and many others, have written seemingly in raptures on the various beauties of this uncommon part; and have acknowledged themselves unable to delineate, with either pen or pencil, pictures equal to half its glory! Nor is it wanting in other respects: there is scarce one necessary of life it does not produce; and all excellent in their kind; the viands are exquisite; the air salubrious in general, and fit for almost any constitution; as, in the course of one mile, we can breathe the moist, the middle state, and the pure; the warm, the temperate, and the cold. Hence it comes to pass, that this part is well adapted for the country residence of Noblemen and Gentlemen: and here they have begun to purchase, build, and settle. The many different heights, soils, and waters, afford an ample field for the noble study of botany, and of fossils; the recreations of angling, hunting, fowling, &c. The lakes and rivers, for sailing, shooting, fishing and scating; and lofty Skiddow (easy of Access) affords one of the grandest variegated prospects in nature! Hither great numbers of the Nobles and Gentry tour, (increasing yearly,) and, patriot like, spend their Money at home; where their actions demonstrate they are not disappointed in their touring expectations. The Inns are enlarging, good roads mending, singular museums, gardens, &c, furnishing; and many other inventions executing, in order to render this Northern Tour much more entertaining than the Continent. I have in my travels seen two parts of the world, but all fell far short of this magnificent place, and conclude it capable of giving the noblest and most sublime recreation, even to an Eastern Prince, or any other Potentate on earth.

I am, Sir, your very obedient servant,
[MS.] Peter Crosthwaite. Admiral of Keswick Lake
& Guide & Companion to Tourers & Lakers.
Keswick, June 24, 1782.

2 Tipped in between pp. 88 and 89:

An accurate MAP of the matchless LAKE OF DERWENT (situate in the most delightful Vale which perhaps ever human Eye beheld) near KESWICK CUMBERLAND.
a. Pocklington's Island *or* Paradise Island. *the Property of J. Pocklington Esqr. This most enchanting Spot appears like the lesser Frustrum of a large Globe, and its natural beauty is highly improved by the Ingenuity of its Owner. The Estate formerly Ld. Derwentwater's (unfortunate as the Author) extends along the winding Shore from b, to c, and half a Mile inland. d,* Lord's Island, *formerly inhabited by the Derwentwater (faded) Family, now rearing a most vigorous Plantation of various kinds of Timber Trees. e,* Sir Gilfred Lawson's Island named St. Herbert's, *it having formerly been the Hermitage of the good old Man whose name it bears, now rearing Timber like the former. f,* Rampsholm Island *in its natural state, being clad in Wood from Shore to Shore. g,* Great Waterfall. *h,* Lowdore Hotel. *i, the* Farm House *of Rowland Stephenson Esq. k,* Ld. Wm. Gordon's, *l,* Keswick Town Hall. *m, The* Silent River *entering the Lake in peace, after having been dashed in pieces Ten Thousand times and (made to murmur loudly) by the stupendous Rocks of Borrowdale. DERWENT has some times the surprising property of heaving up furious milk white Surges without one breath of Wind, abounds with delicious Fish, and in the Summer Months is Travers'd by many Noble Tourers from all Quarters. One pellucid River, and sixteen Crystal Rills have their influx into this Transparent Lake, Feed it, and the overplus makes its way down the profound Channel n, for the pathless Deep, washing in its course the Walls of Cockermouth, Workington, &c.*

P. CROSTHWAITE (Keeper of the Museum at Keswick, Guide, Pilot, Geographer and Hydrographer to TOURERS) Surveyed Derwent and constructed this MAP accordingly. Engraved by H. Ashby.

Published as the Act directs June 26th 1782 and sold by P. Crosthwaite at Keswick, and T. Hodgson Stationer No. 425 Strand LONDON

Size: trimmed to 200 × 303 mm. Scale: approx. 3 in. = 1 mile

Ms. note on map; [Lake of Derwent] 'Otherwise Keswick Lake'

Editor's note: This is the earliest version of Crosthwaite's map of the Lake of Derwent (see 17, *Notes*). It is engraved by H. Ashby and not S. Neele. It shows only the outline of the lake and of the islands, four of which, a, d, e, f are named. Otherwise, the only lettering on the map is b, c, g, h, i, k, l, m, to which the notes engraved on the plate refer. The outline of lake and islands is identical with Neele's map. It therefore appears that Neele reused Ashby's copper plate.

3 Tipped in between pp. 92 and 93, a Handbill:

Keswick, September 4, 1781.
Peter Crosthwaite, formerly a Naval Commander in the East Indies; Begs Leave to inform the *Nobility, Gentry,* and Others, that he has just now opened a MUSEUM, or Cabinet of Curiosities, at KESWICK; into which he has introduced the vast Variety of Vegetable and Fossil Productions common to the beautiful Valley of Keswick; with a great Variety of other Foreign Curiosities, the greatest Part Natural, and the Rest Artificial: with which he hopes to give pleasing Entertainment to all who choose to honour him with their Presence.

He has also procured an excellent Map of the *British Islands;* which he can lay upon *Skiddow* in a due Position with the real Islands, and direct the Sight (by the help of Instruments) in a right Line with any particular Place required; as the *British Alps, Ingleborough, Snowdon* in *North Wales,* the *Isle of Man,* (which he demonstrates to be the Centre of the British Empire in Europe) the *Nethermost Coast of Ireland, Mull of Galloway, Criffel, Carlisle, &c.*

He has also an extraordinary good *Spyglass,* and two of the best *Landscape Mirrors,* such as Mr. Gray used at the *Vicarage Garden* near *Keswick,* when he saw a Picture and said, "If I could transmit it to you, and fix it in all the Softness of its living Colours, it would fairly sell for a Thousand Pounds." *West's Guide,* page 109.

N.B. He is a *Guide, Pilot, Geographer, &c.* and would be glad to accompany *Tourers* and Others unto *Skiddow,* or elsewhere, with the above instruments at a reasonable Rate.

According to Appointment, he was head Engineer and Commander in Chief of the Fleet against *Pocklington's Island,* at KESWICK REGATTA, in *August* 1781; and it was he who planned the whole Attack, wrote the Regatta Advertisement, &c. [added in MS.]

P.S. He has besides the above Instruments others to Divert Lakers upon Derwent Water, as the Log-line & half-minute Glass; Hadley's Reflecting Quadrant for obtaining the Latitude [trimmed]

Inscribed on verso:

1817 – Oct 1st. Peter Crosthwaite has been dead some years – He is succeeded by his son Daniel a civil intelligent man whose Museum I visited. He has made large additions to it since his father's death & has a good collection of Cumberland fossils for sale, particularly the newly discovered specimens of Wolfram Tungsten Molybdena &c. &c.

Note on p. 93 refers to above:

Admiral Crosthwaite proves this by fixing one leg of his Compasses in the Center of the Isle of Man & the other in the Town of Coventry (the center of England). He then holds the Isle of Man Point fixed & turns round the Coventry Leg & it passes thro' the Center of Ireland & the Center of Scotland which demonstrates the Isle of Man to be the Center of the whole. [1782]

Notes made by tourist in 1782

Page 41, lines 19, 20: 'If in a carriage, return from the abbey by *Dalton.*'

13th Augt. 1782. In Dalton Church Yard I found the following lines engraved on the Tombstone of Miss Pearson

Spectators all as You
Pass by as You are now
So once was I as I am now
So you must be prepared
For Death & follow me

Page 54, line 6: *'Hawkshead**'

*Pretty Polly Keen the Landlord's Daughter waited on us at the Tanner's Arms where We had an excellent Dinner at 1*s*. & good Wines

Page 55, line 18: *'Ambleside'**

*A very good Inn called the Salut[atio]n. Reasonable Charges & good Accommodation. The Visitors to Keswick should return hither to sleep. Mr. Geo. Bond the Landlord gets drunk about three times a Week & tells me he dabbles a little every Day, & thinks he gets about £20 a Year by his own Drinking. He shewed us the Waterfall at the Groves, & a View from a Hill near the Village. He breeds & sells young Beagles at a guinea a couple.

Page 56, line 1: '*Windermere-water*'

16th. Augt. 1782. We did not visit Windermere till after Keswick & a deplorable visit it was. We left Ambleside this morning & got to Bowness (5 miles) about 11 o'clock. Delightful Prospect on the Lake. At Bowness We hired a Boat for the Island, and sailed to it with a fresh Breeze. After viewing the Prospects & the beautiful Mansion purchased by Miss Curwen from Mr English we prepared to sail back to Bowness for Dinner, when there suddenly arose a most violent storm that made our Attempt to cross fruitless. After a vain Endeavour to row against the Wind, we returned to Miss Curwen's house, inhabited by 17 Workmen, who should have crossed to Bowness to their Meals had not the Storm arose, which in the Afternoon & Evening increased so violently accompanied by heavy Rain & Gusts of Wind that neither Boatmen nor Workpeople dared to sail.

There was no Provision or Liquors of any kind at the Hall, and only some oaten Bread, a Cheese and a Barrel

Page 57

of small Beer at the Gardener's House, & two Cows upon the Island. These Provisions were removed to the Hall (except the Cows) about 8 o'clock in the Evening, although we had put the Garrison consisting now of 21 Souls upon short Allowance. The Storm continuing & being threatened with a Famine I recommended sleep to every body; for We had only two small Candles & never a Pack of Cards in the Hall. The Gentlemen slept on Chairs the Workmen on the floor. About 12 o'clock at night the Storm began to abait tho' it was very dark & rained hard. The Boatmen at first hesitated but afterwards recommended it to evacuate the Island, which nine of us attempted in two Boats leaving the rest behind. After a dangerous Passage in the dark & heavy Rain, we escaped the Rocks of Curlew Crags, which were invisible at that time, & arrived safe at Bowness. Thankful for our happy escape. We got a good Supper, drank Plenty of Wine & hot Negus, & tolerable Beds at the White Lion.

Editor's note: The circular classical house on Belle Isle, previously known as Long Holme, was designed in 1744 by John Plaw for Thomas English [see: John Plaw, *Rural Architecture*, London, 1794]. In 1781 it was bought by the Trustees of the young Isabella Curwen, heiress of Workington Hall and the family mines in West Cumberland. At the time of the visit in 1782 extensive additions and alterations were being made to the building. The house is still occupied by the Curwen family.

Page 84

15th. Augt. 1782. I viewed the Lake of Keswick & hired Admiral Crosthwaite to accompany Me, who gave Me the following Account of the Expedition against Pocklington's Island performed in Augt. 1781.

Joseph Pocklington Esqr. Steward & Governor of the Island.

Peter Crosthwaite, Admiral.

First. The Governor or his Deputy to hoist an English Ensign upon the Half Moon Battery Flagstaff, when he would have the Officers Seamen & Marines repair for[?]

Page 85

Gallies in Friar Crag Bay, when they will immediately embark, proceed for the Island & moor head & stern in a line a head, but somewhat curved at the Distance of two Galleys Length (120 yds) from the Half Moon Battery.

Secondly. The Commander in Chief will then send a Flag of Truce on Shore midway from each other and half a cables length between the said Battery & the Blockhouse, on the East Side of the Island, to summon the Island to surrender. The Governor will allow the Flag of Truce to depart, & probably hoist the red flag, being the Flag of Defiance, & proceed to Action, when the Gallies will return the fire keeping it up pretty constant, not in too great a haste, & taking special care of their Powder that no Person be injured by blowing up

Page 86

Pistols to represent Muskets & Muskets great Guns, to be fired low, viz resting on the Gunnels of the Gallies, that they may the better represent Cannon, five fire Arms & two Rowers to each Galley; the Arms to be worked a good Distance from each other, & no Arms but such as are good to be used which must be examined by the Admiral.

Thirdly. When the Governor would have the Fleet storm the half Moon Battery he will spread a dark large Flag against the S.E. side of Castle, high enough to be seen over people's heads; the fleet will then load weigh & land where the Truce Flag did before (being in view of the Spectators). Run slowly for the Battery, sailor like, firing into the Air when near the Works. The Garrison will retreat to the Blockhouse. Down English Colours at the Battery & up Dutch with three Chears. Then if the Blockhouse is to be stormed, let two third of the Seamen & Marines load & make an irregular & pretty quick March for the Blockhouse (the rest stay to defend the Battery) & there fire 3 Rounds, with caution, keeping the fire up as at the Gallies, which will be returned from within, or the opposite Side of the House, when the Governor

Page 87

will spread the dark Flag on the N.E. side of the Castle (as a Signal for the Besieged to retreat) & cover their retreat with a Detachment from the Castle.
Fourthly. Down English Colours at the Blockhouse and up Dutch with 3 chears as before. By this time the Tars will be pestered with Hunger & Thirst. The Governor sensible of this lays an Ambuscade of Roast Beef & Brown Ale in the Blockhouse. The Party having dined pretty smartly & drunk plentifully a Tar will put off his Jacket & spread it against the S.W. Wall of the Blockhouse as a Signal to the Governor that Bellies are full & all Hands well again. On this the Governor will bear to Arms & make a heavy fire upon the Tars with great Guns & small Arms, when they are to return it & at the same time retreat slowly towards the Gallies. In this Retreat 3 or 4 Tars must fall upon the field with whole bones but as if dangerously wounded. The Rest will escape to the Gallies except 4 who are to be taken with one of the Gallies before they have got afloat. The other 7 Gallies will fire a Low Pops [?] when under Oars as an Attempt to cover the Embarkation

Page 88

into the Galley aground, which must be taken. When the rest find she is captured they will cease firing & return to the Bay from whence they came, in order to land their wounded, stop leaks, repair their Rigging &c. Meantime the Garrison will down Dutch Colours & up English at the Battery & Blockhouse with 3 chears; carry off the wounded & finally make a general Salute for the Victory.
N.B. The Nonesuch Half Galley will repeat the Admiral's Signals at 60 Yards S.E. of the Centre of the fleet & no boats will be allowed to ply on the Lake during the Action, on Pain of all Hands being pressed & their Barks being haled high & dry on Shore, there to remain the rest of the Day.
P.S. A Surgeon & Surgeon's Mate will be wanted in the fleet.
The Galleys to fire 6 rounds at the Half Moon Battery. At storming it 2 rounds. Against the Blockhouse 3. In retreating from it 3. Total 14 rounds.

Editor's note: The first Keswick Regatta was held on 28 August 1781, an event which coincided with the opening of Crosthwaite's Museum. The Regatta included the theatrically contrived naval battle, a sham attack upon Pocklington's Island, planned, organised and advertised by Crosthwaite. 'The Account of the Expedition against Pocklington's Island performed in August 1781', which is recorded in the marginal notes, appears to be a transcript of the plan of battle issued for the instruction of the performers and probably to excite the interest of spectators. The regatta, which included the sham battle and continued till 1790, is not well documented. The events are covered by advertisements and by notices in the *Cumberland Pacquet*, but only one account received general publication. This was an article from the *Pacquet* describing the Regatta on 6 September 1782, which was included by William Cockin as an editorial note in the third edition of West's *Guide*, 1784, and has been many times reprinted. James Clarke included a general account and a 'descriptive poem' of the Regatta in his *Survey of the Lakes* (1787). Catherine Hutton, who visited Keswick, probably in 1801, describes the mock battle in her novel, *Oakwood Hall*, published in 1819, long after her visit. The source of her information is not known.

The marginal notes are unique as a recorded battle order for one of these engagements.

The artist, Robert Smirke, was present at the Keswick Regatta of 1787, where he made a sketch which was published as a coloured etching by R.M.Batty, entitled 'Regatta at Keswick in Cumberland'. This depicts events many of which correspond closely with Crosthwaite's account, notably the ambuscade of Roast Beef and Brown Ale. A copy of the print was included in the Derwentwater exhibition at Grasmere in 1986, and was reproduced in the catalogue which is full of fascinating information about the activities of Pocklington and Crosthwaite.

Page 88, line 12: 'Vicar's Isle'*

*Now called Pocklington's Island – & has an elegant House Lodge &c. built upon it.

Page 89, line 9: '*Skiddaw*'

The Mountain of Skiddaw is 1090 Yards above the Sea & 1050 above Keswick Lake. From it you may see 83 miles on a plain Surface which carries you beyond the Isle of Man. Admiral Crosthwaite's Father farmed Mount Skiddaw & the Lands 7 Miles round it under Lord Egremont at 5£. a Year. It is now raised to £15 p. Ann. & summers about 1000 sheep.

Page 93: note refers to handbill, 3 above,

Notes made by a tourist in 1817

Page 60, line 9: 'much variety of shore'

Sepr. 30th. 1817. Mr. Curwen has built an elegant house on this part of the bank – the views from which are very beautiful. J.P.

Page 60, line 19; 'the great island'

Mr Curwen's house is built on this island.

Page 67, line 6: 'Station V'

This view is from the Kendal Road & from this point I had the first view of Windermere. Sepr. 30th. 1817 J.P.

Page 68, lines 3, 4: 'which painting cannot imitate.'

Most incorrect

Page 73, line 19: 'some remains of painted glass'

Some of this glass is good but it is much broken – nearly the whole of the Crucifixion is destroyed. J.P.

There is a barrel organ in the church & the Clerk (who is self taught) has added one barrel set by himself. J.P.

Page 75: 'AMBLESIDE'

Sepr, 30 1817. Slept at Ambleside. The Inn is very ill conducted & the village scarcely commands any view of the Lake. J.P.

Page 76, line 19: 'From *Ambleside* to *Keswick*'

Oct. 1st. 1817. Went from Ambleside to Keswick.

Page 77, line 3: 'two cascades worthy of notice'

Visited the Waterfalls. The upper one is the finest fall but the lower one the most picturesque.

The house is occupied by Lady Fleming who is separated from her husband.

Page 79, line 24: 'Mr. *Gray's* description'

Saw this view from the road

Page 81, line 12: 'the stones are a heap that have the appearance of. . .'

The road passes near to this enormous cairn which is only about 30 feet long & 10 or 15 high.

Page 81, line 29: '*Catchidecam*'

This cannot be seen from the road,

Page 82, line 27: 'a good general view'

This view is very beautiful

Page 83, line 24: 'in sight of its glorious vale'

Is one of the finest views which I saw amongst [the] Lakes.

Page 148, line 6: '*Ulls-water*'

Oct 3rd. 1817. Visited Ullswater from Penrith

Page 152, line 11: 'the upper end'

The views in the higher part of this valley are superior to either Windermere or Keswick. J.P.

Page 158, line 6: 'the ascent from the lake to the top of *Kirkston*'

This road is extremely steep for a carriage. The ascent & descent are about 9 miles the whole of which I was obliged to walk.

Editor's note: In transcribing the notes some abbreviations have been expanded and some punctuation rationalised. Spelling remains unaltered.

Appendix 2

The 'Claude Glass'

In recent years the convex reflecting-glass, generally used by the early tourists and constantly referred to by them as the 'landscape glass' or 'landscape mirror', has been referred to as the 'Claude glass'. Many carried more than one optical device of this sort. Dr James Plumptre recorded that among the 'Knick Knacks' which he took to the Lakes were both a 'Claude Glass' and a 'Grays Glass'. Miss Beccabunga Veronica (see p 63), a character in Plumptre's comic opera, *The Lakers*, makes great play first with her 'Gray' alone and then combined with her 'Claude Lorrain', which appears to consist of three glasses that 'throw a Gilpin tint over these magic scenes of beauty'. The first of these is 'gorgeously glowing', the second is 'gloomily glaring' and the third blue and 'frigidly freezing'. She describes her 'Claude Lorrain' as 'an artifice which gives various tints . . . to the landscape'. It therefore seems clear that the Claude glasses were transparent tinted filters which could be used in combination with the Gray's glass. Thomas Gray had used a glass, described by Mason in a note to his publication of Gray's *Journal* as a 'plano convex mirror'. This type of glass is depicted in the well known drawing by Gainsborough generally known, it would seem erroneously, as 'A man sketching, using a Claude Glass'. West recommends the use of more than one 'landscape mirror' – 'the dark glass answers well in sunshine; but on cloudy and gloomy days the silver foil is better.' *'Gray's* Landscape Glasses [and] *Claude Lorrain's* Do.' were for sale at Crosthwaite's Museum in Keswick in 1792. The earliest reference which has come to light which actually connects the name Claude with the mirror or reflecting glass is to be found in Catalogue no. 51 of the London colourmen Charles Roberson and Co. which advertises 'Claude Mirrors in cases, from 7*s*. to 30*s*.'. The catalogue is not dated, but as it is earlier than a catalogue dated 1851 it indicates that the misnomer was in use by the middle of the century.

Index

Only authors, artists, engravers, referred to in the Chronological List are indexed, by List and not by page numbers. Names in capital letters indicate item headings, bold figures the principal entry.

PETER BICKNELL, MA, FRIBA

Fellow Emeritus of Downing College, Cambridge

He has taught and practised architecture in Cambridge for more than fifty years. Familiar with the Lake District since childhood, he has climbed extensively in the Cumbrian fells, Wales, the Highlands of Scotland, and in the Alps. He is the author of *British Hills and Mountains*.

Peter Bicknell's special interest in the art and literature of mountain regions led to his involvement in arranging and preparing catalogues for four important exhibitions at the Fitzwilliam Museum, Cambridge, and at the Grasmere and Wordsworth Museum, dealing with picturesque landscape and with the Lake District.

He is a Trustee of the Wordsworth Trust, and has recently edited the *Illustrated Wordsworth's Guide to the Lakes*.